Misfits of Avalon™

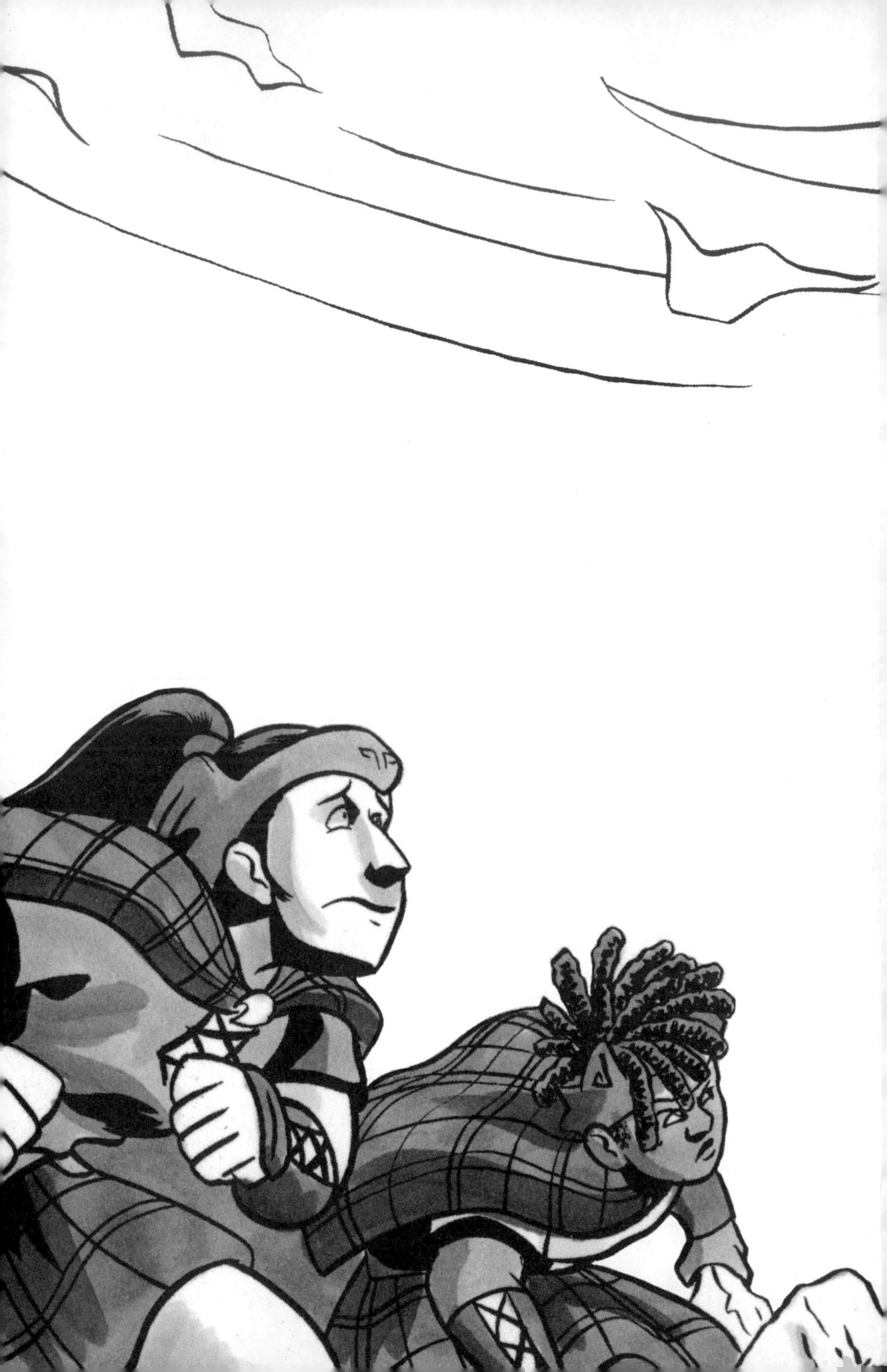

The Queen
of Air and
Delinquency

1

MISFITS of AVALON

Written & Illustrated by
Kel McDonald

DARK HORSE BOOKS

president and publisher
Mike Richardson

editor
Sierra Hahn

assistant editor
Freddye Lins

collection designer
Tina Alessi

Special thanks to Rachel Edidin and Christina McKenzie.

Neil Hankerson Executive Vice President · **Tom Weddle** Chief Financial Officer · **Randy Stradley** Vice President of Publishing · **Michael Martens** Vice President of Book Trade Sales · **Anita Nelson** Vice President of Business Affairs · **Scott Allie** Editor in Chief · **Matt Parkinson** Vice President of Marketing · **David Scroggy** Vice President of Product Development · **Dale LaFountain** Vice President of Information Technology · **Darlene Vogel** Senior Director of Print, Design, and Production · **Ken Lizzi** General Counsel · **Davey Estrada** Editorial Director · **Chris Warner** Senior Books Editor · **Diana Schutz** Executive Editor · **Cary Grazzini** Director of Print and Development · **Lia Ribacchi** Art Director · **Cara Niece** Director of Scheduling · **Mark Bernardi** · Director of Digital Publishing

MISFITS OF AVALON VOLUME 1: The Queen of Air and Delinquency

This volume collects comics originally published online at KelMcDonald.com.

Published by Dark Horse Books
A division of Dark Horse Comics, Inc.
10956 SE Main Street
Milwaukie, OR 97222

DarkHorse.com · KelMcDonald.com

International Licensing: 503-905-2377
To find a comics shop in your area, call the Comic Shop
Locator Service toll-free at 1-888-266-4226.

First edition: October 2014
ISBN 978-1-61655-538-2

1 3 5 7 9 10 8 6 4 2
Printed in the United States of America

Contents

CHAPTER 1:
Morgan the Air Raven
8

CHAPTER 2:
Elsie the Earth Cow
50

CHAPTER 3:
Kimber the Fire Wolf
90

CHAPTER 4:
Rae the Water Eel
132

CHAPTER 1:

Morgan the Air Raven

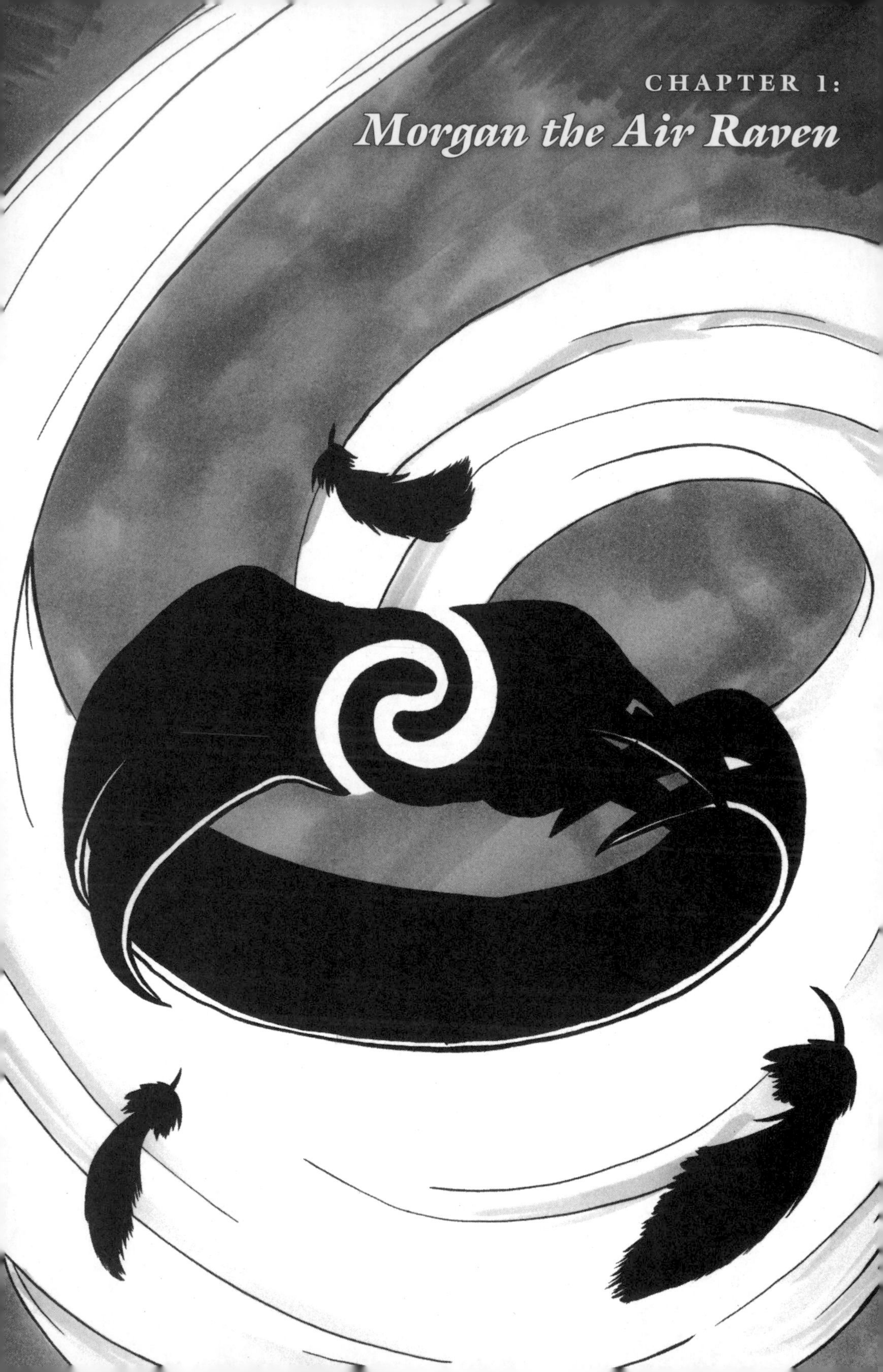

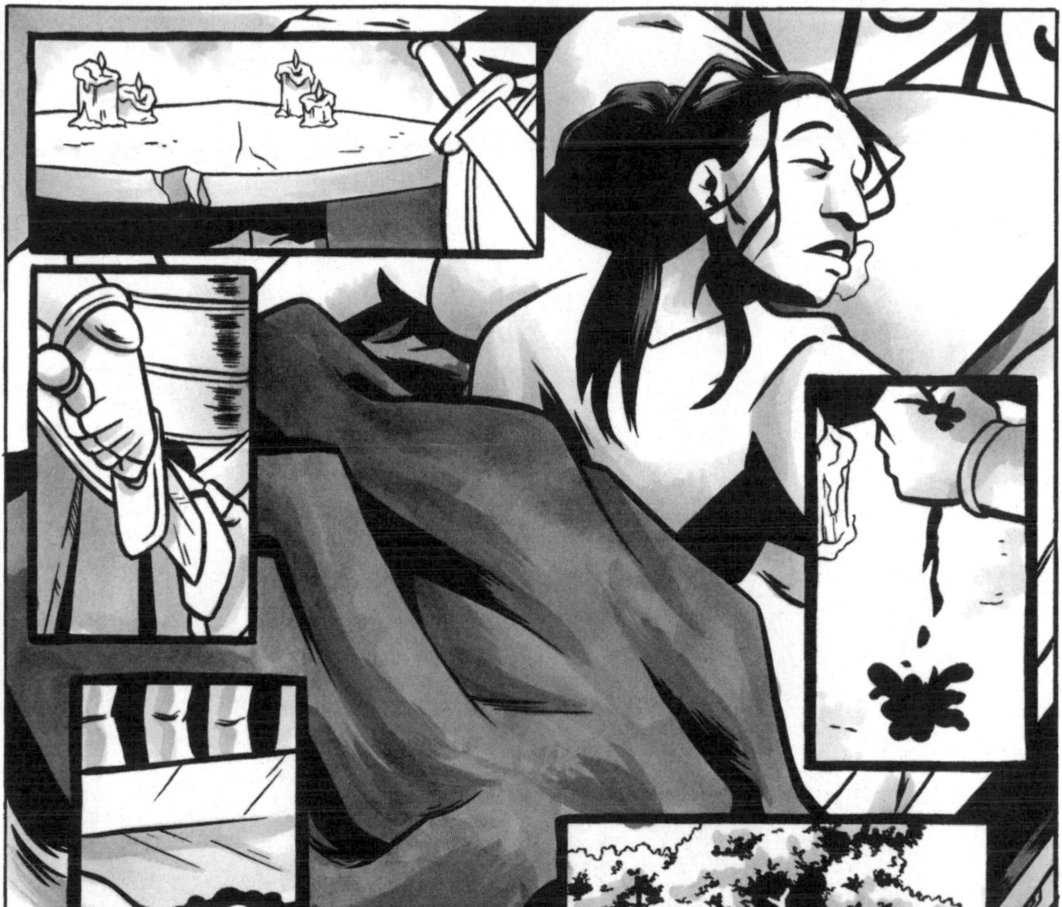

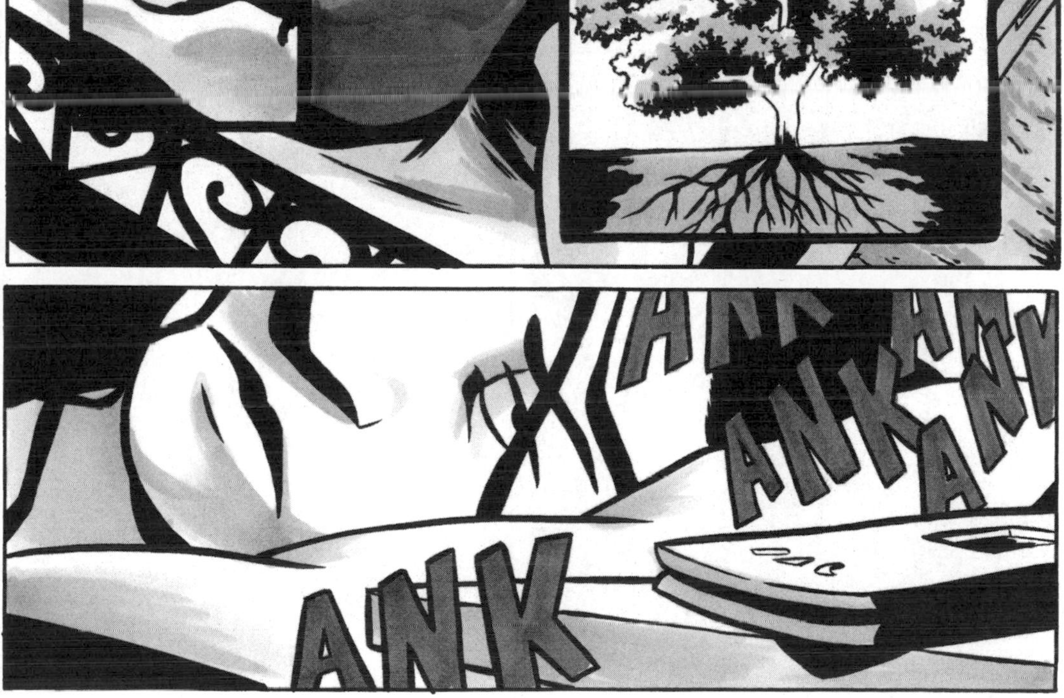
ANK
ANK
ANK

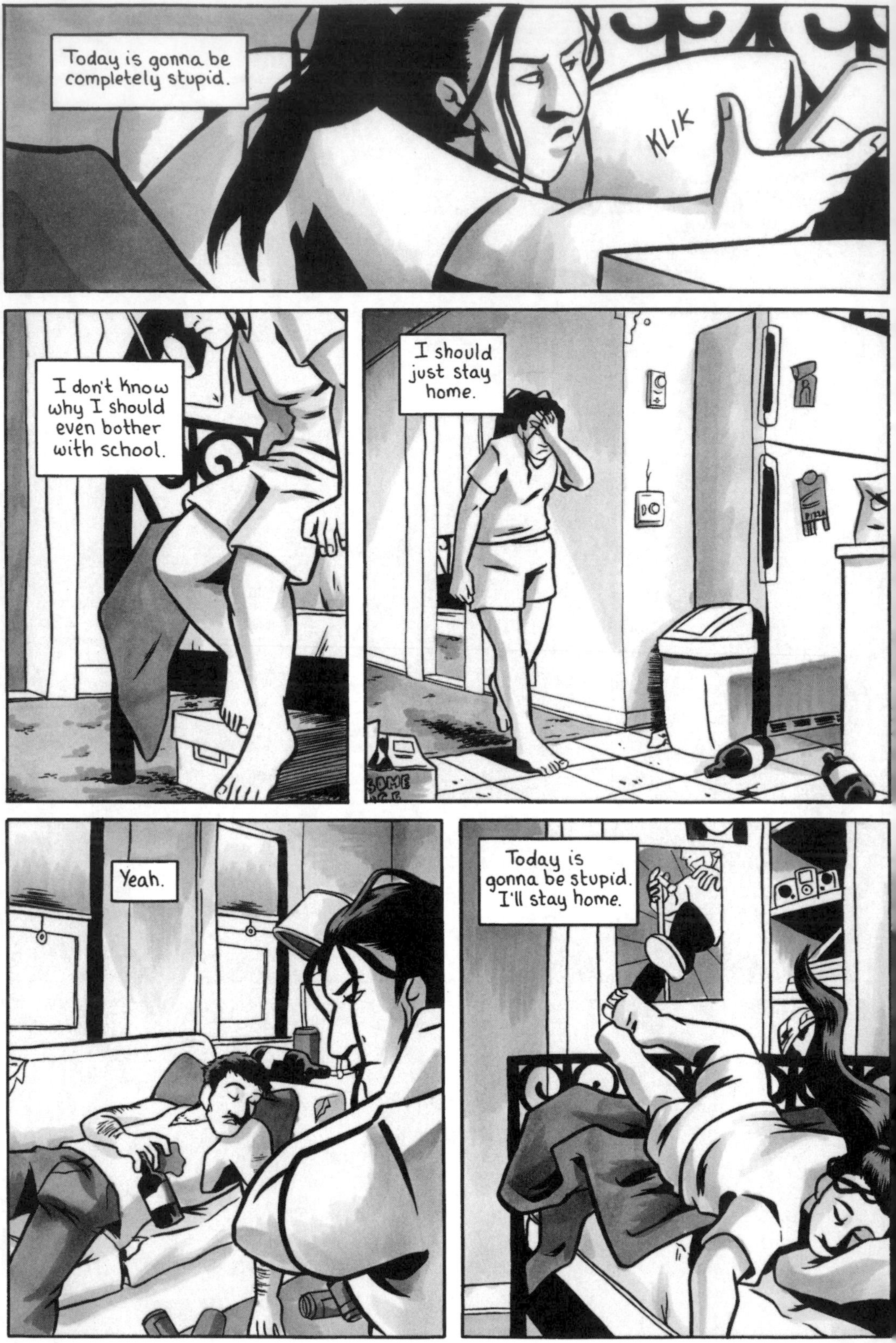
Today is gonna be completely stupid.
KLIK
I don't know why I should even bother with school.
I should just stay home.
Yeah.
Today is gonna be stupid. I'll stay home.

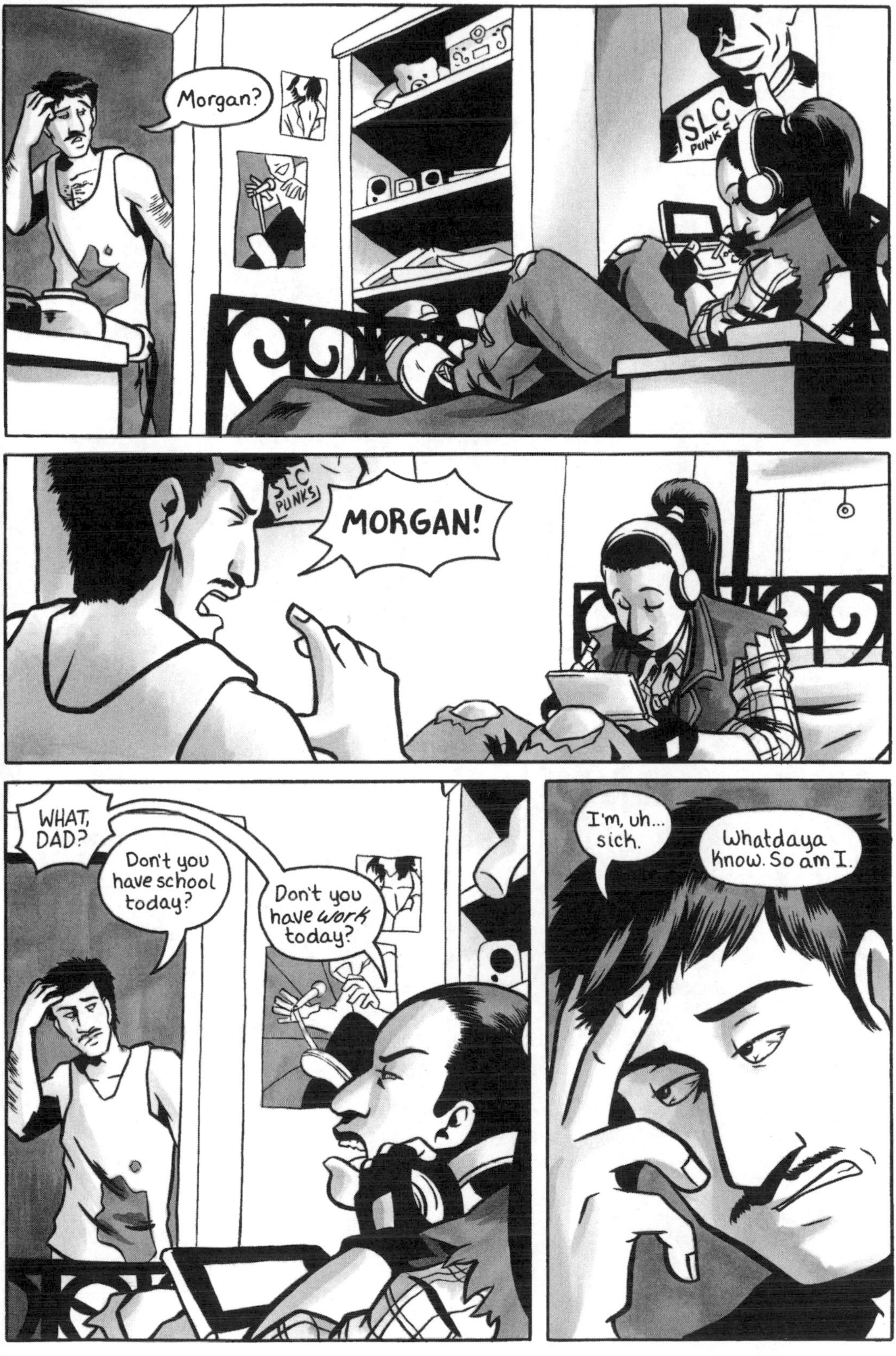
Morgan?
SLC PUNKS
SLC PUNKS
MORGAN!
WHAT, DAD?
Don't you have school today?
Don't you have *work* today?
I'm, uh... sick.
Whatdaya Know. So am I.

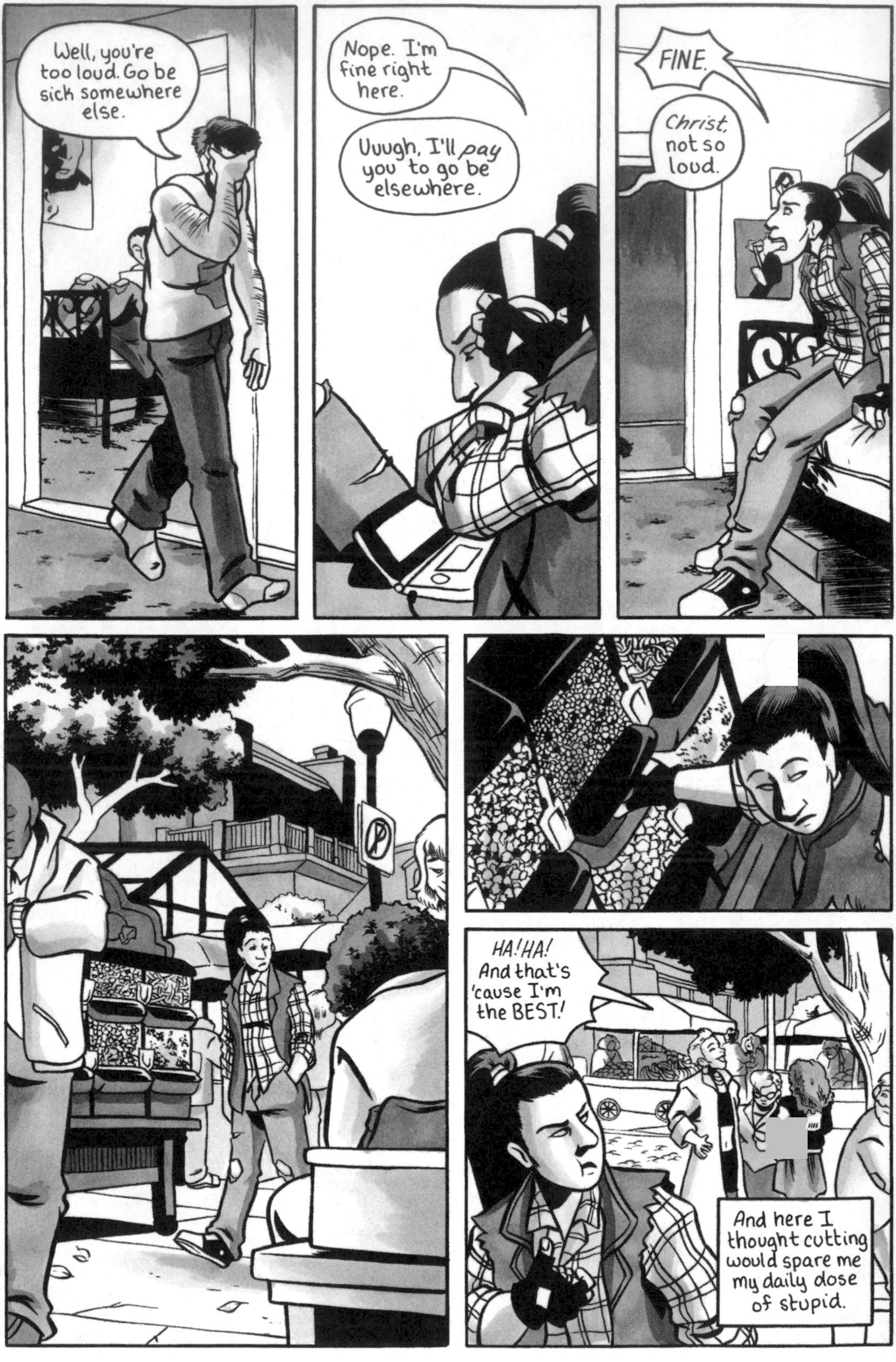
Well, you're too loud. Go be sick somewhere else.
Nope. I'm fine right here.
Uuugh, I'll *pay* you to go be elsewhere.
FINE.
Christ, not so loud.
HA! HA! And that's 'cause I'm the BEST!
And here I thought cutting would spare me my daily dose of stupid.

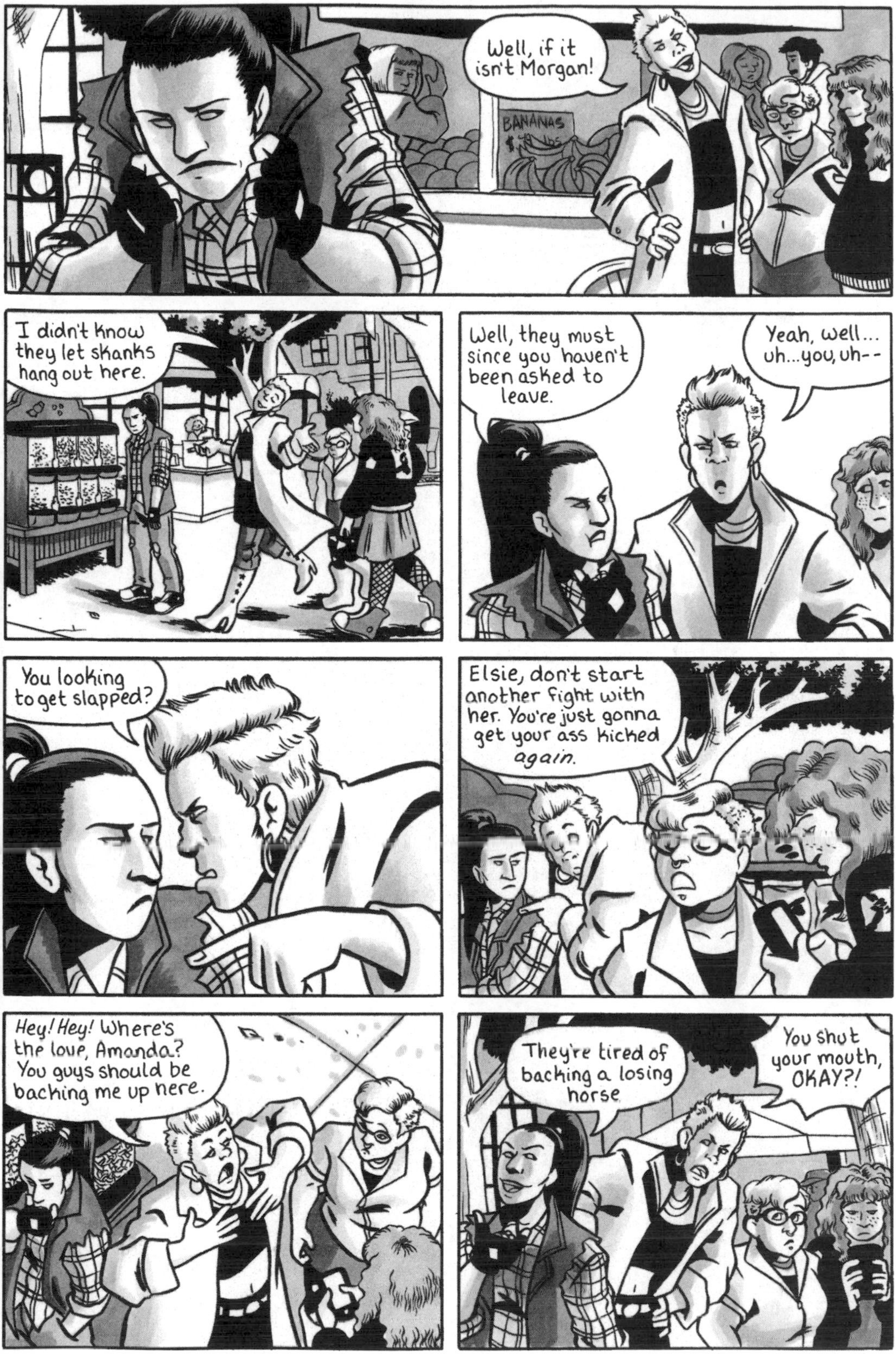
Well, if it isn't Morgan!
BANANAS
I didn't know they let skanks hang out here.
Well, they must since you haven't been asked to leave.
Yeah, well... uh...you, uh--
You looking to get slapped?
Elsie, don't start another fight with her. You're just gonna get your ass kicked *again*.
Hey! Hey! Where's the love, Amanda? You guys should be backing me up here.
They're tired of backing a losing horse.
You shut your mouth, OKAY?!

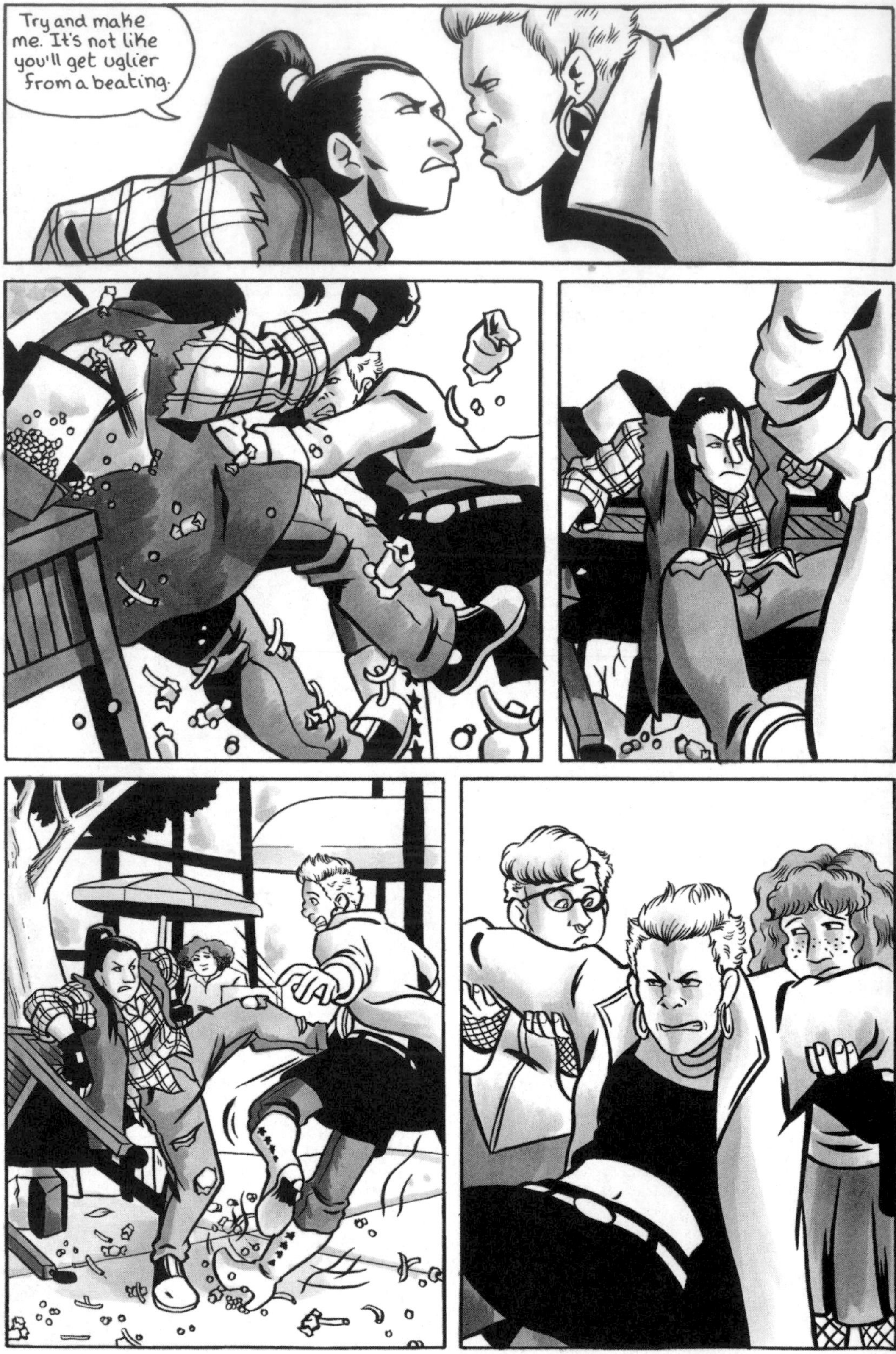
Try and make me. It's not like you'll get uglier from a beating.

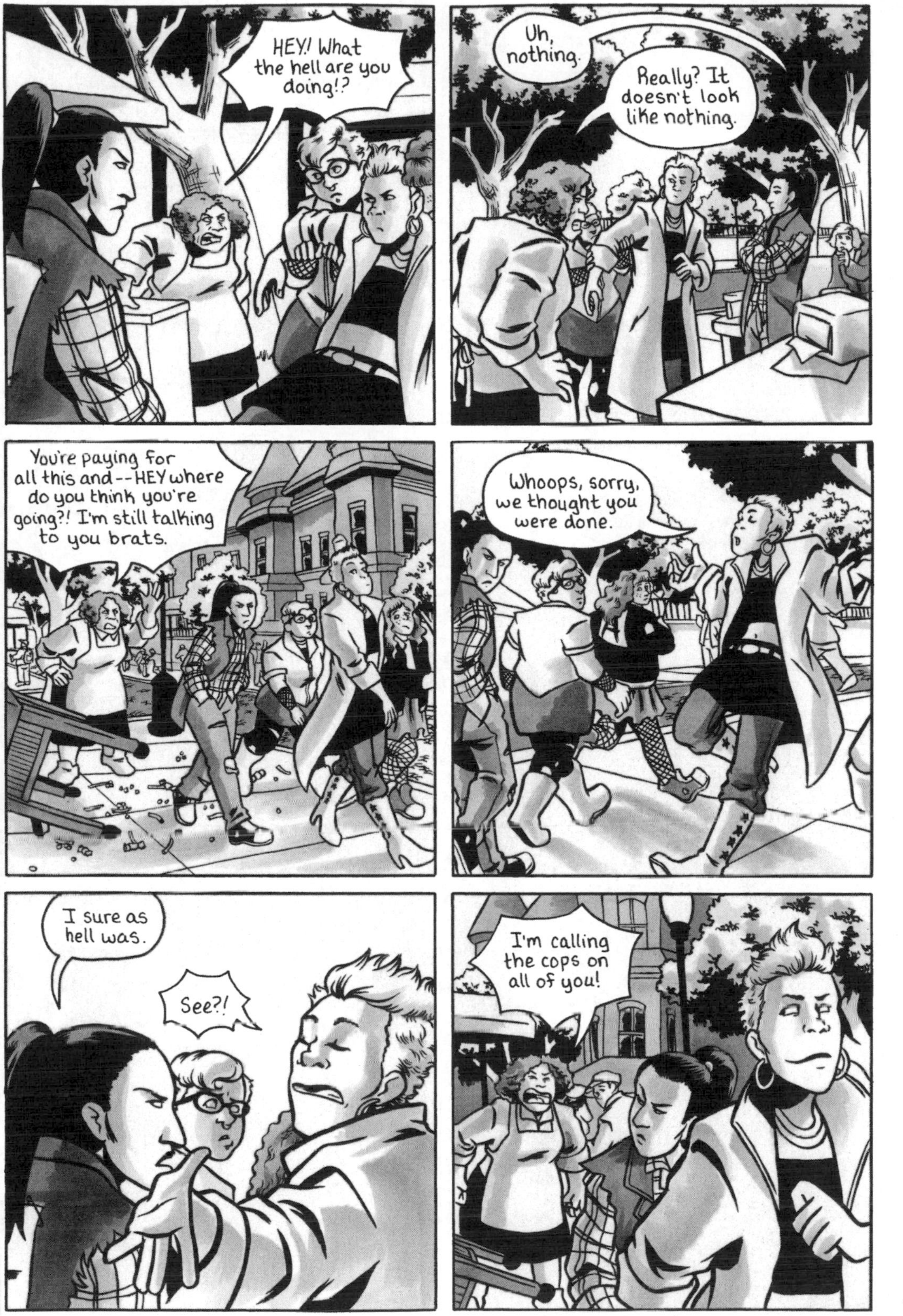
HEY! What the hell are you doing!?
Uh, nothing.
Really? It doesn't look like nothing.
You're paying for all this and--HEY where do you think you're going?! I'm still talking to you brats.
Whoops, sorry, we thought you were done.
I sure as hell was.
See?!
I'm calling the cops on all of you!

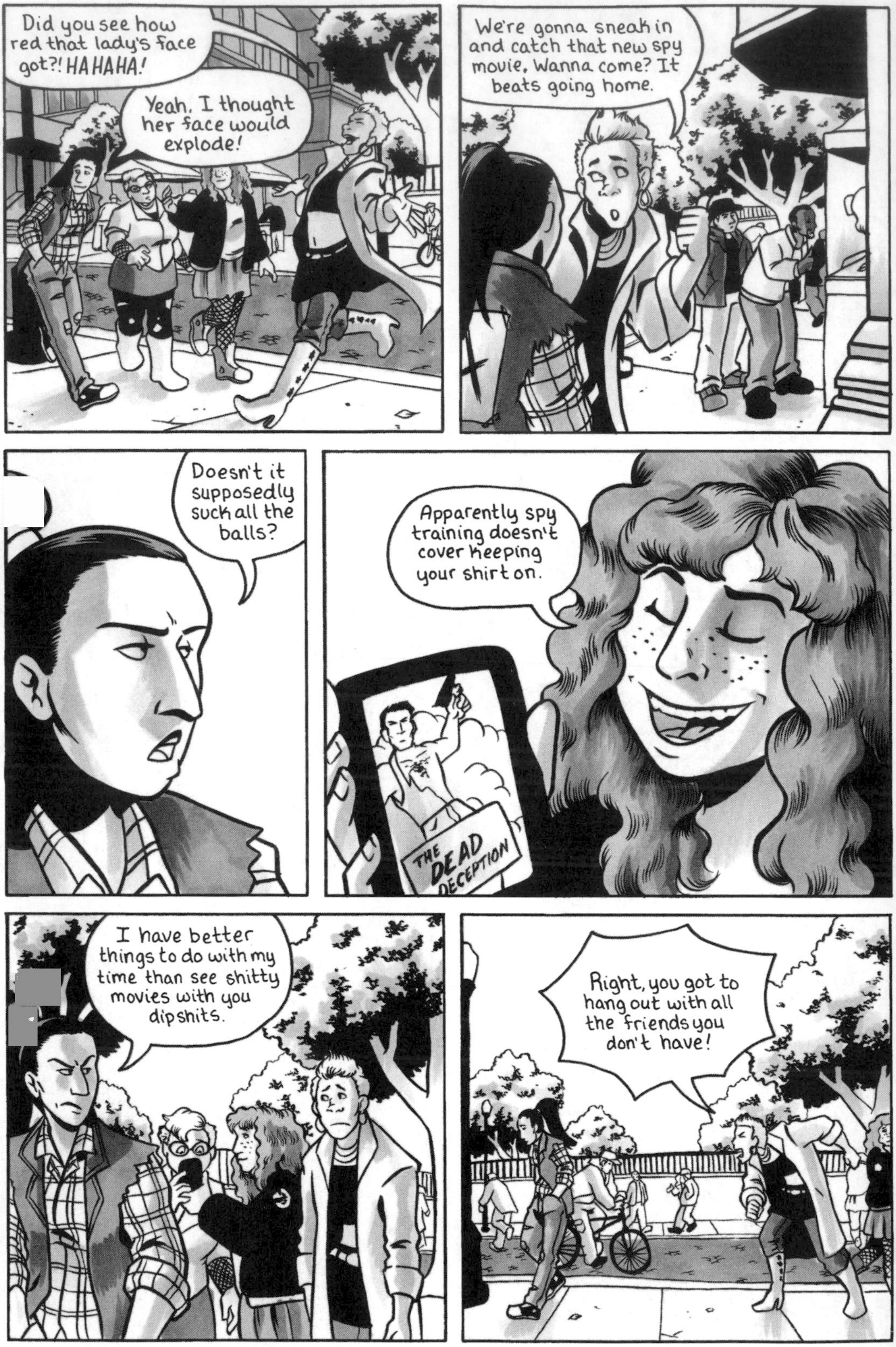
Did you see how red that lady's face got?! HAHAHA!
Yeah. I thought her face would explode!
We're gonna sneak in and catch that new spy movie. Wanna come? It beats going home.
Doesn't it supposedly suck all the balls?
Apparently spy training doesn't cover keeping your shirt on.
THE DEAD DECEPTION
I have better things to do with my time than see shitty movies with you dipshits.
Right, you got to hang out with all the friends you don't have!

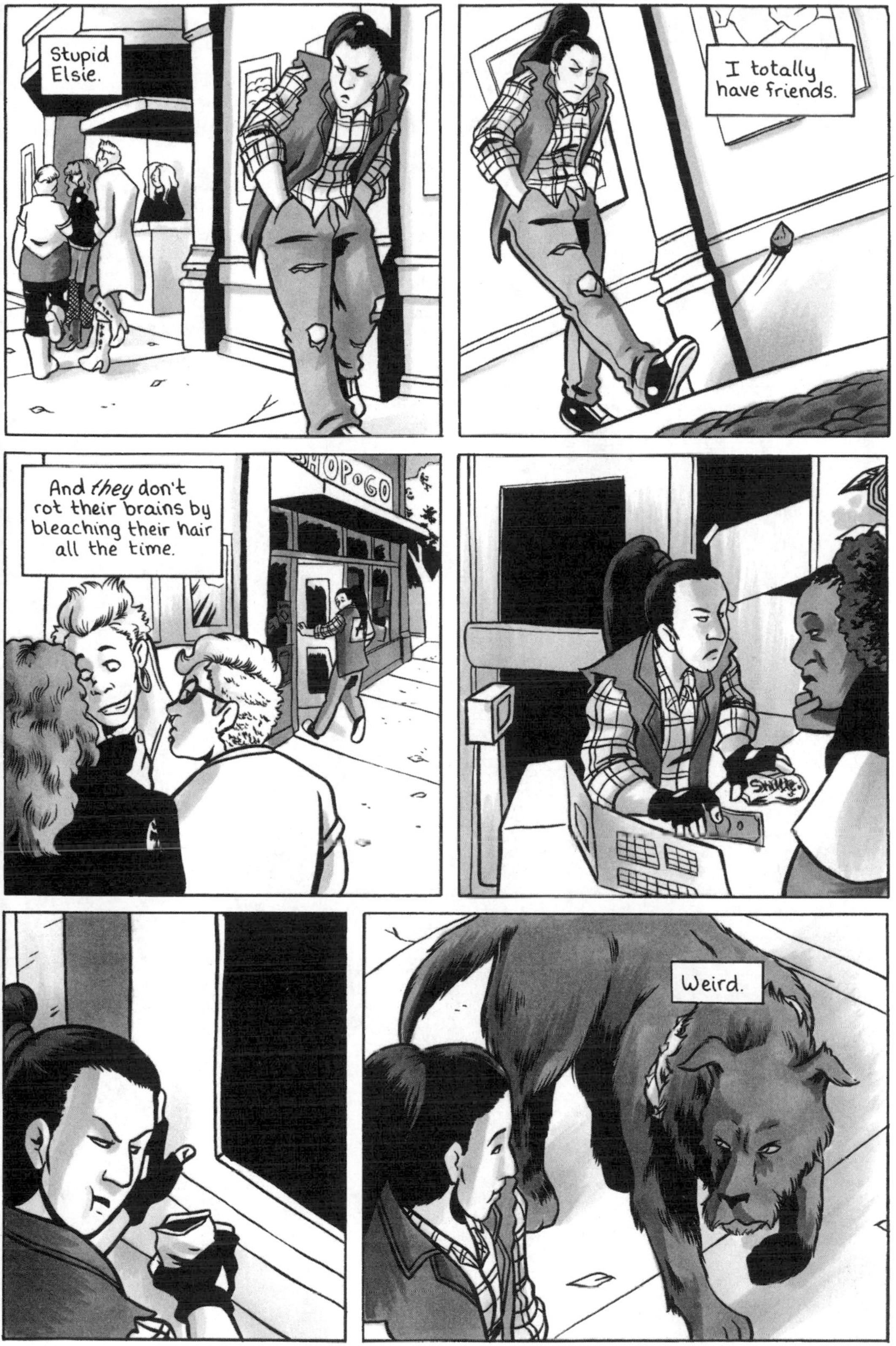
Stupid Elsie.
I totally have friends.
And *they* don't rot their brains by bleaching their hair all the time.
SHOP&GO
Weird.

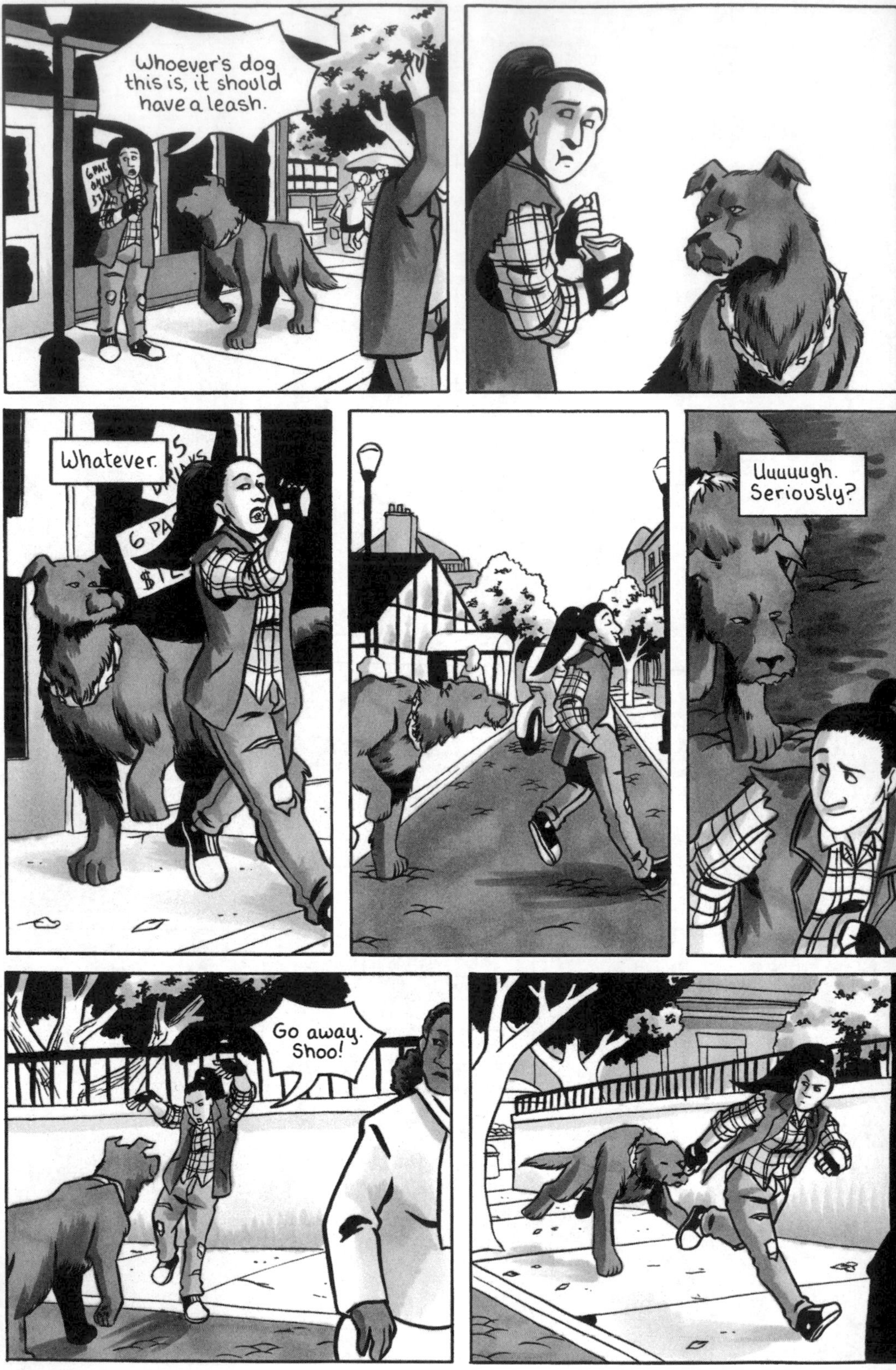
Whoever's dog this is, it should have a leash.
Whatever.
Uuuuugh. Seriously?
Go away. Shoo!

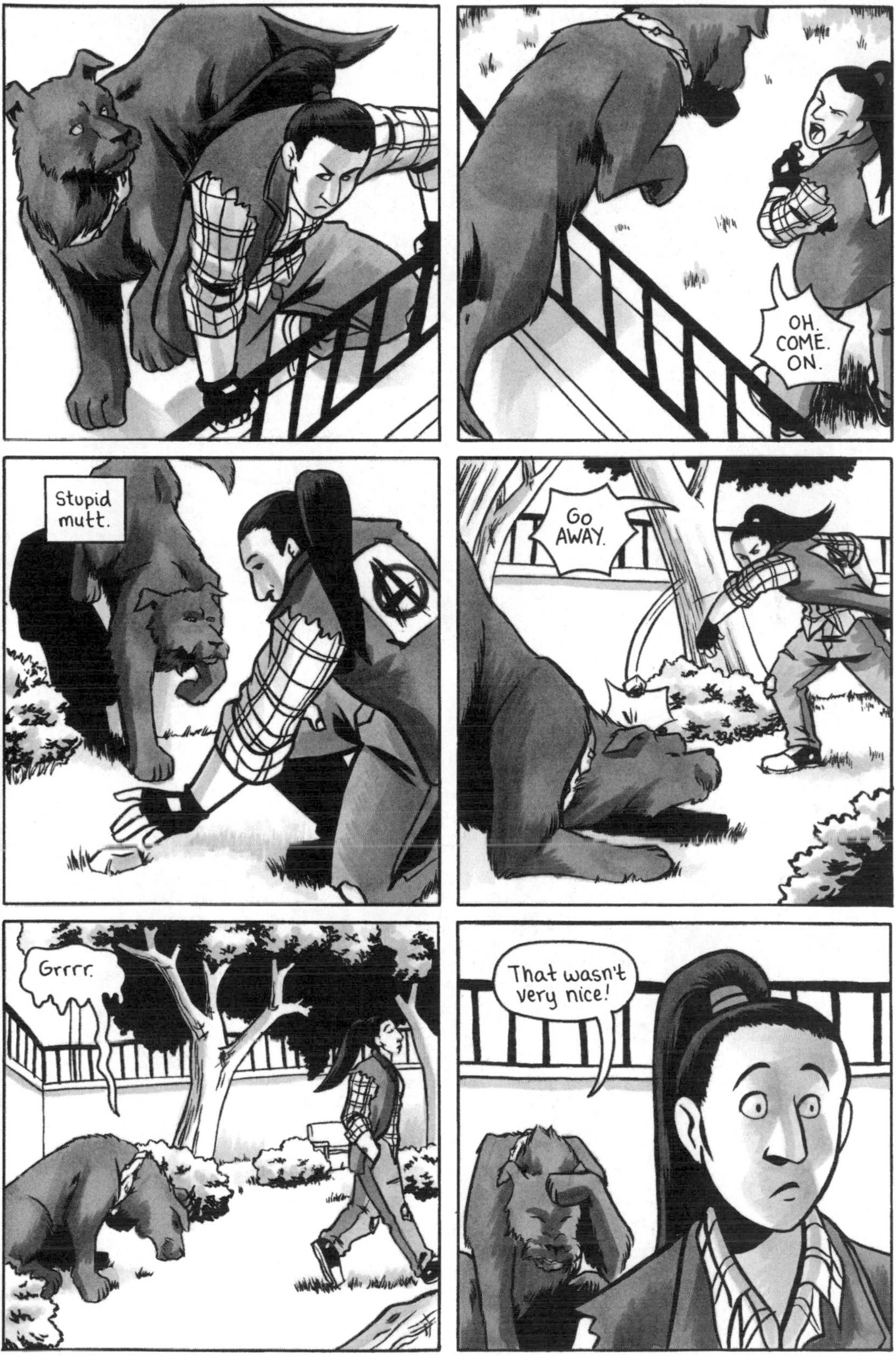
OH. COME. ON.
Stupid mutt.
Go AWAY.
Grrrr.
That wasn't very nice!

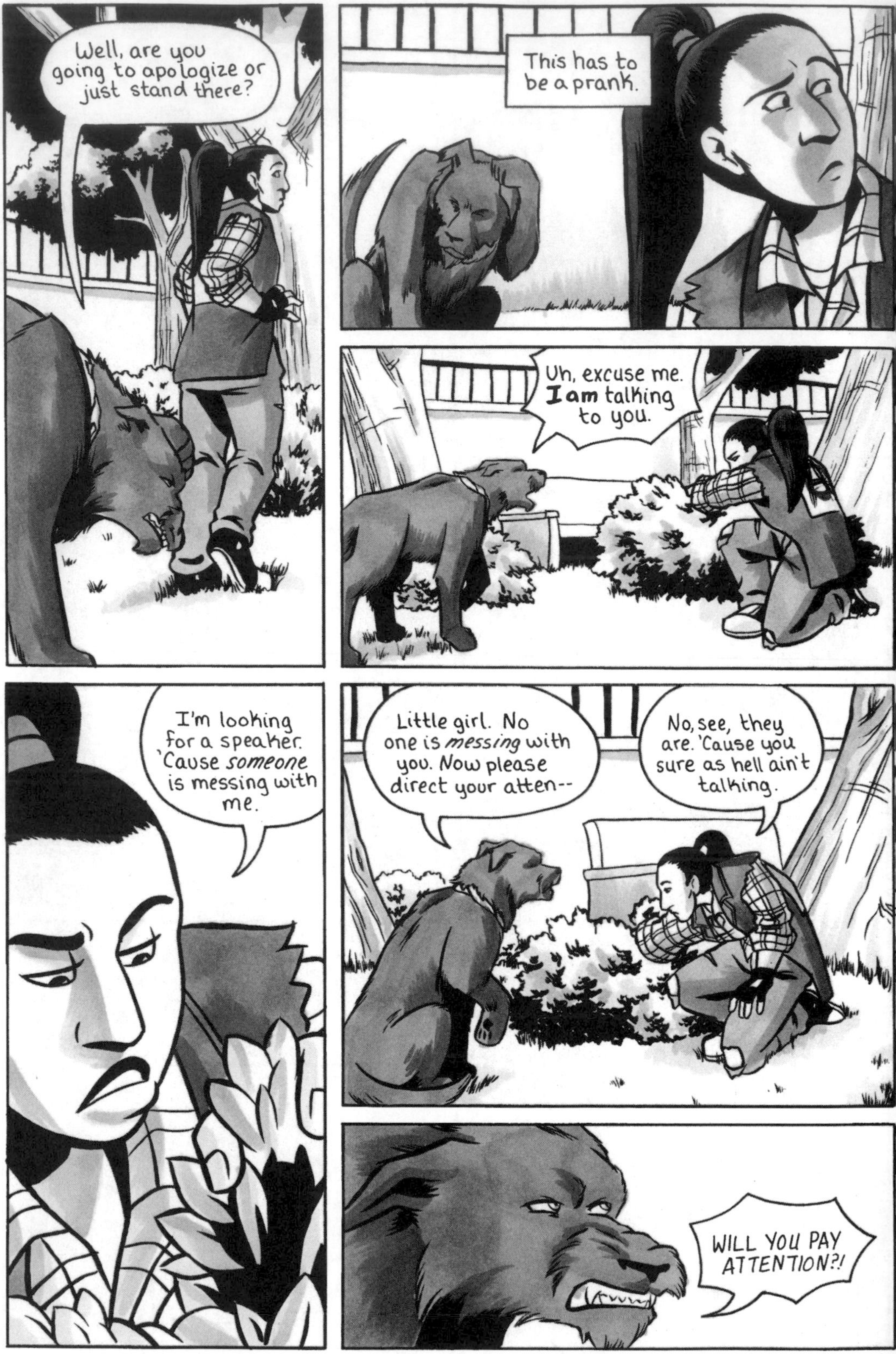
Well, are you going to apologize or just stand there?
This has to be a prank.
Uh, excuse me. **I am** talking to you.
I'm looking for a speaker. 'Cause *someone* is messing with me.
Little girl. No one is *messing* with you. Now please direct your atten--
No, see, they are. 'Cause you sure as hell ain't talking.
WILL YOU PAY ATTENTION?!

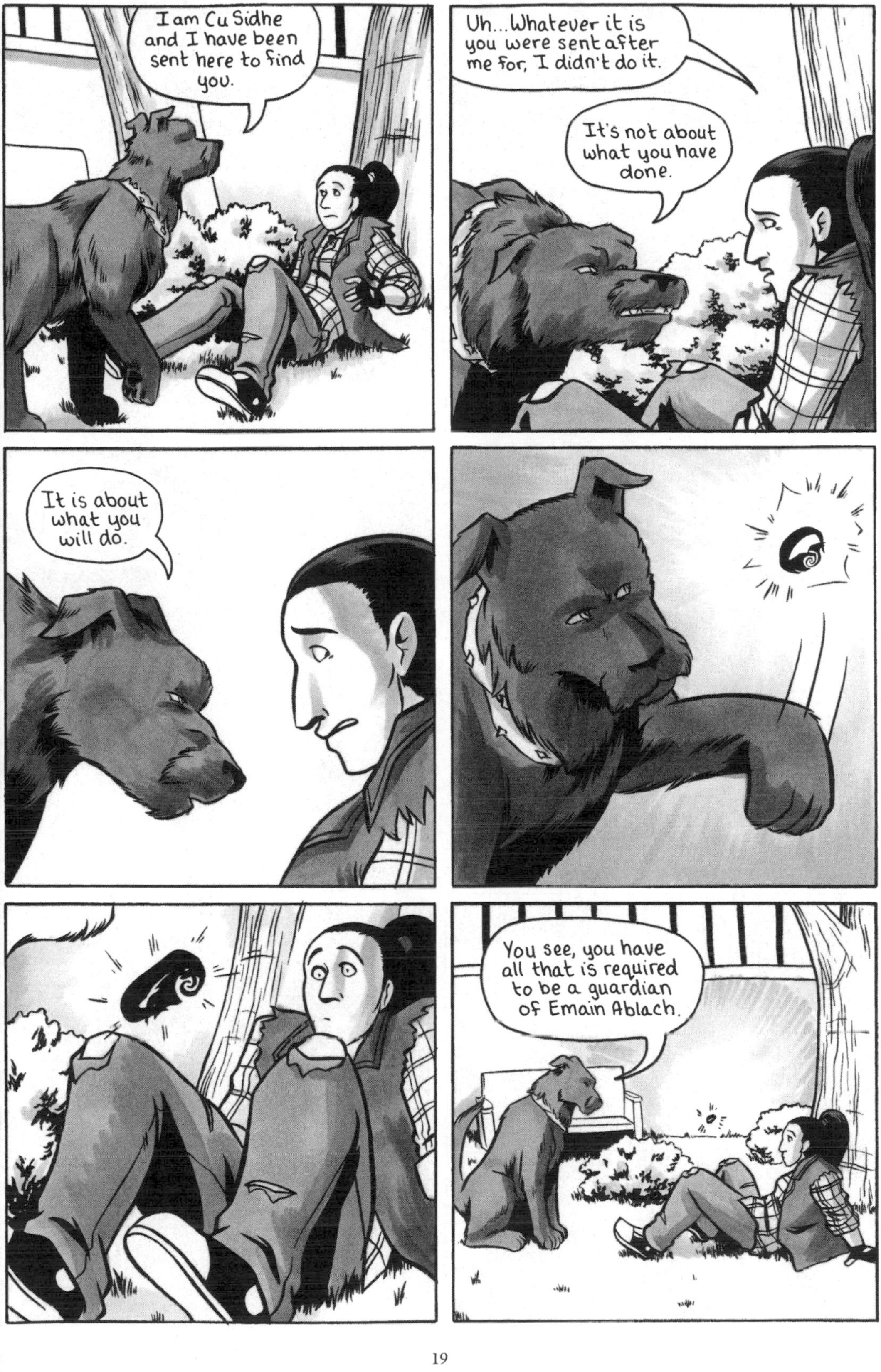
I am Cu Sidhe and I have been sent here to find you.
Uh...Whatever it is you were sent after me for, I didn't do it.
It's not about what you have done.
It is about what you will do.
You see, you have all that is required to be a guardian of Emain Ablach.

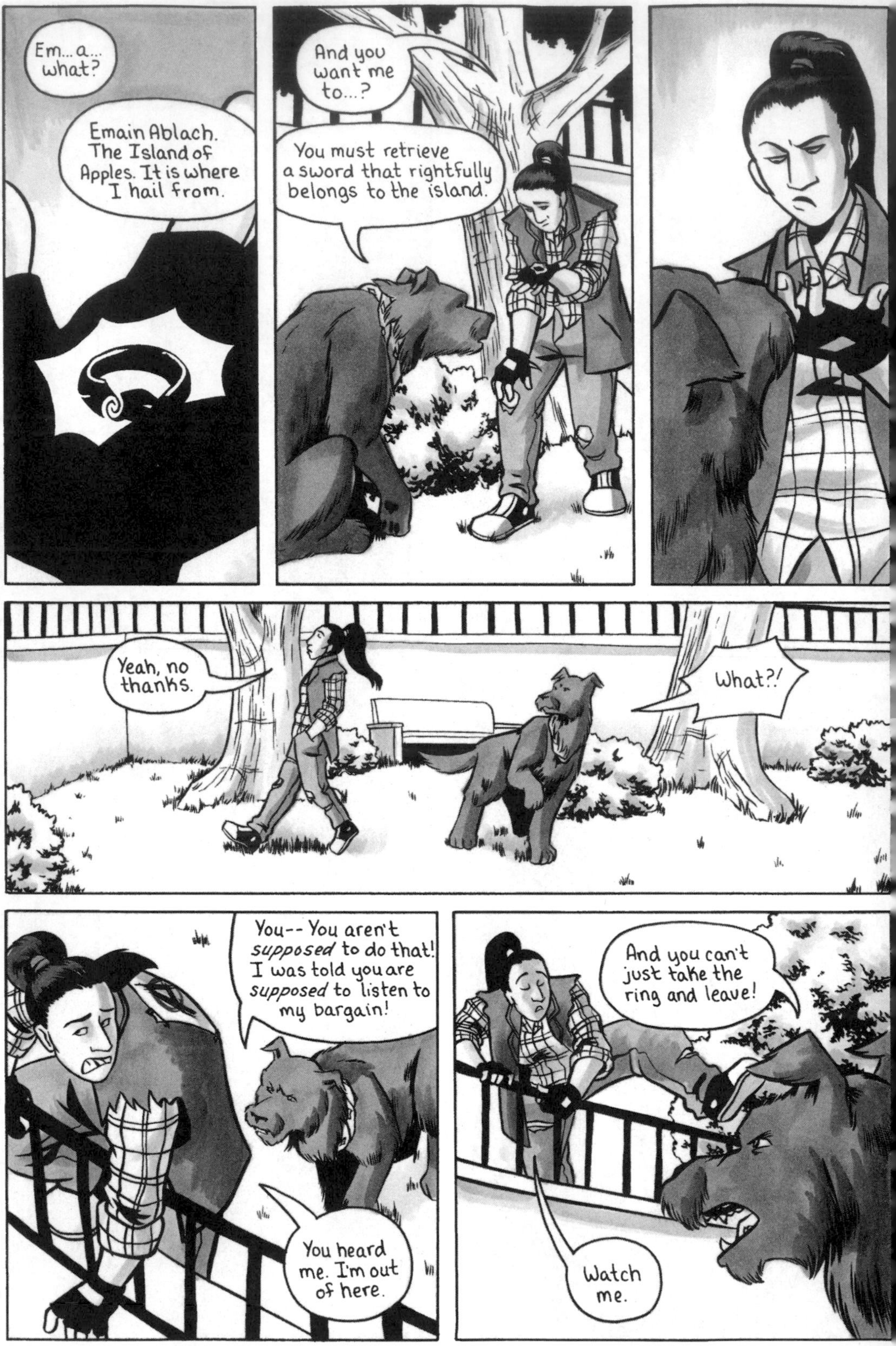
Em... a... what?
Emain Ablach. The Island of Apples. It is where I hail from.
And you want me to...?
You must retrieve a sword that rightfully belongs to the island.
Yeah, no thanks.
What?!
You-- You aren't *supposed* to do that! I was told you are *supposed* to listen to my bargain!
You heard me. I'm out of here.
And you can't just take the ring and leave!
Watch me.

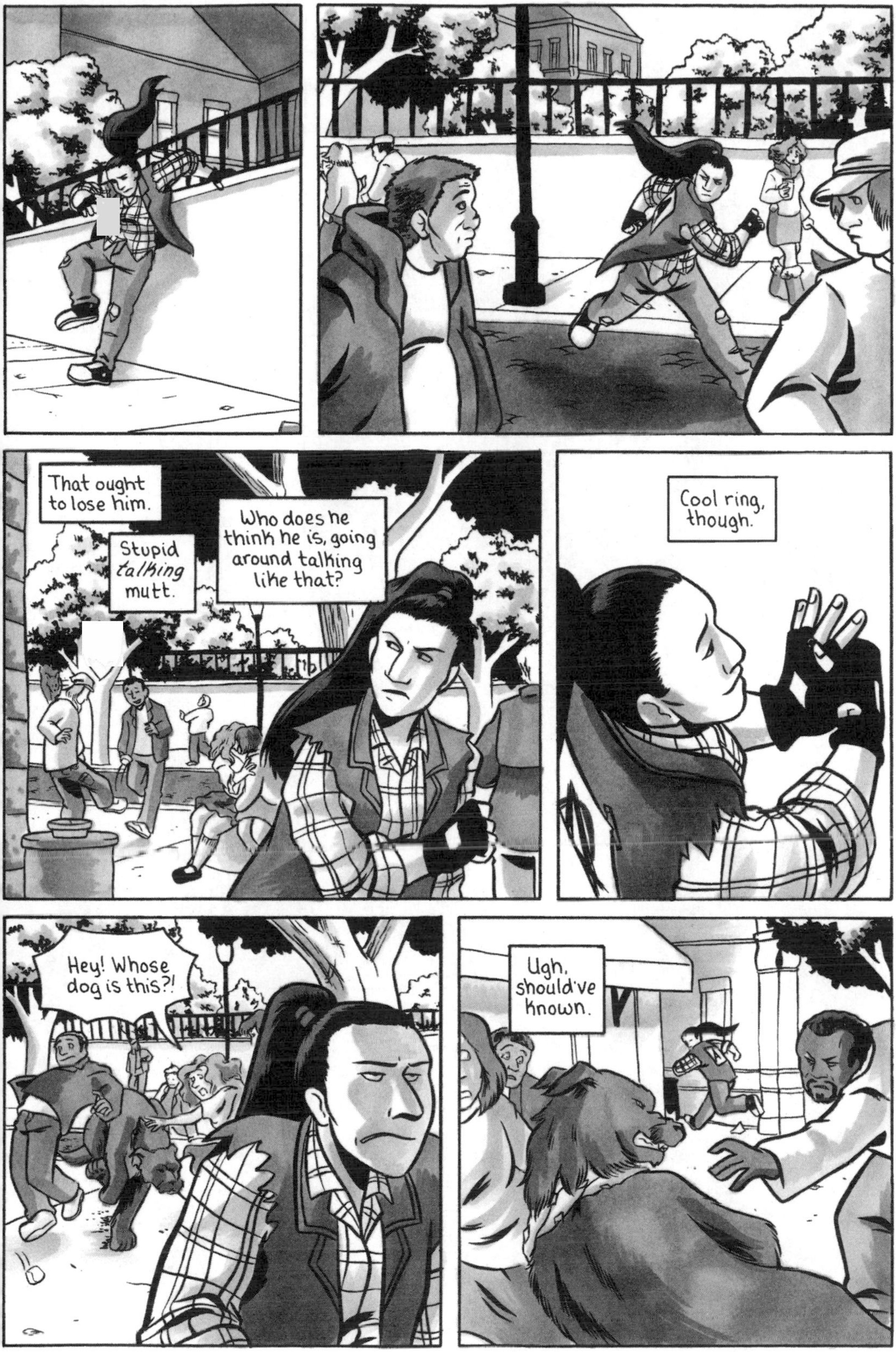
That ought to lose him.
Stupid *talking* mutt.
Who does he think he is, going around talking like that?
Cool ring, though.
Hey! Whose dog is this?!
Ugh, should've known.

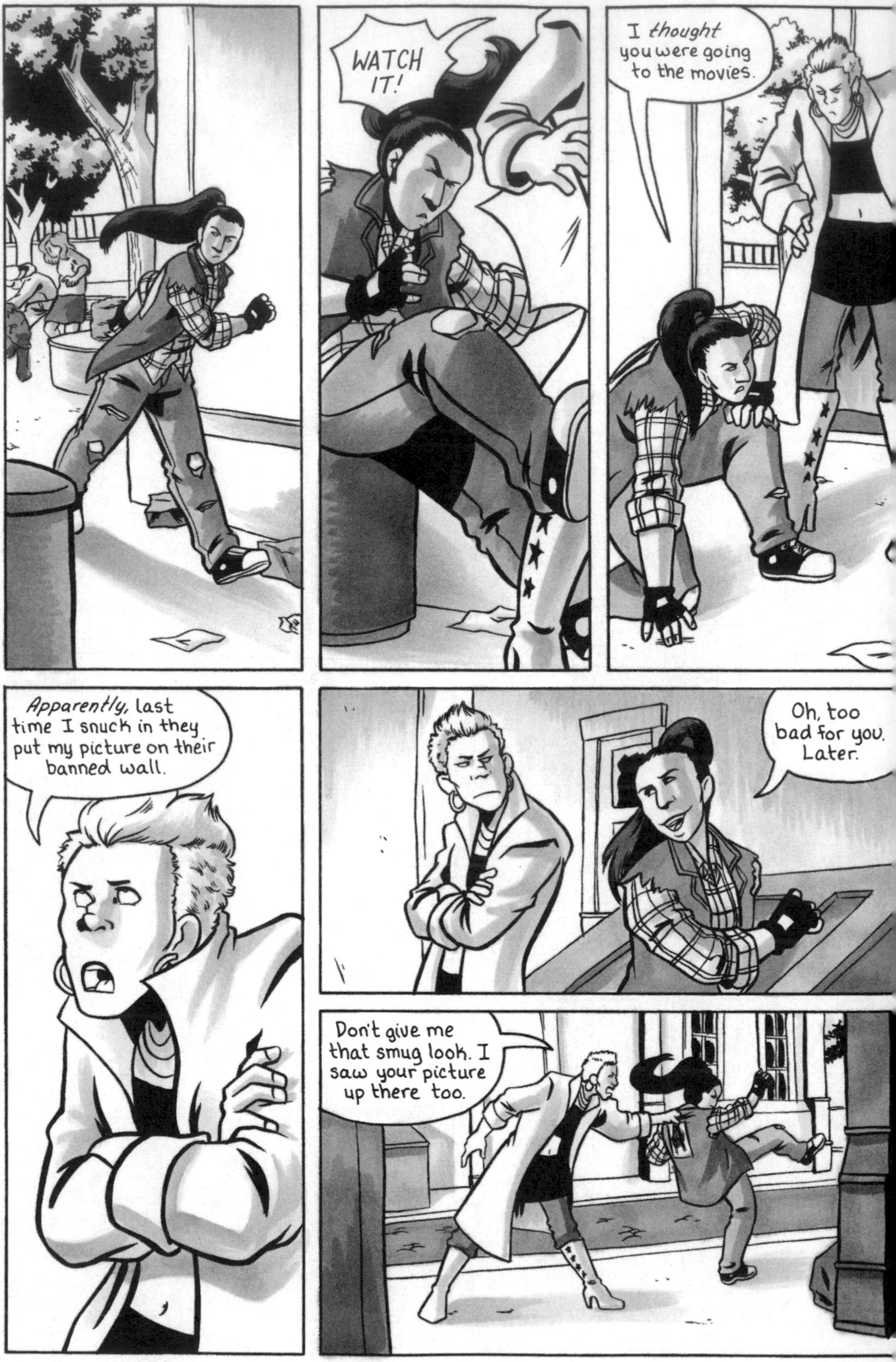
WATCH IT!
I *thought* you were going to the movies.
Apparently, last time I snuck in they put my picture on their banned wall.
Oh, too bad for you. Later.
Don't give me that smug look. I saw your picture up there too.

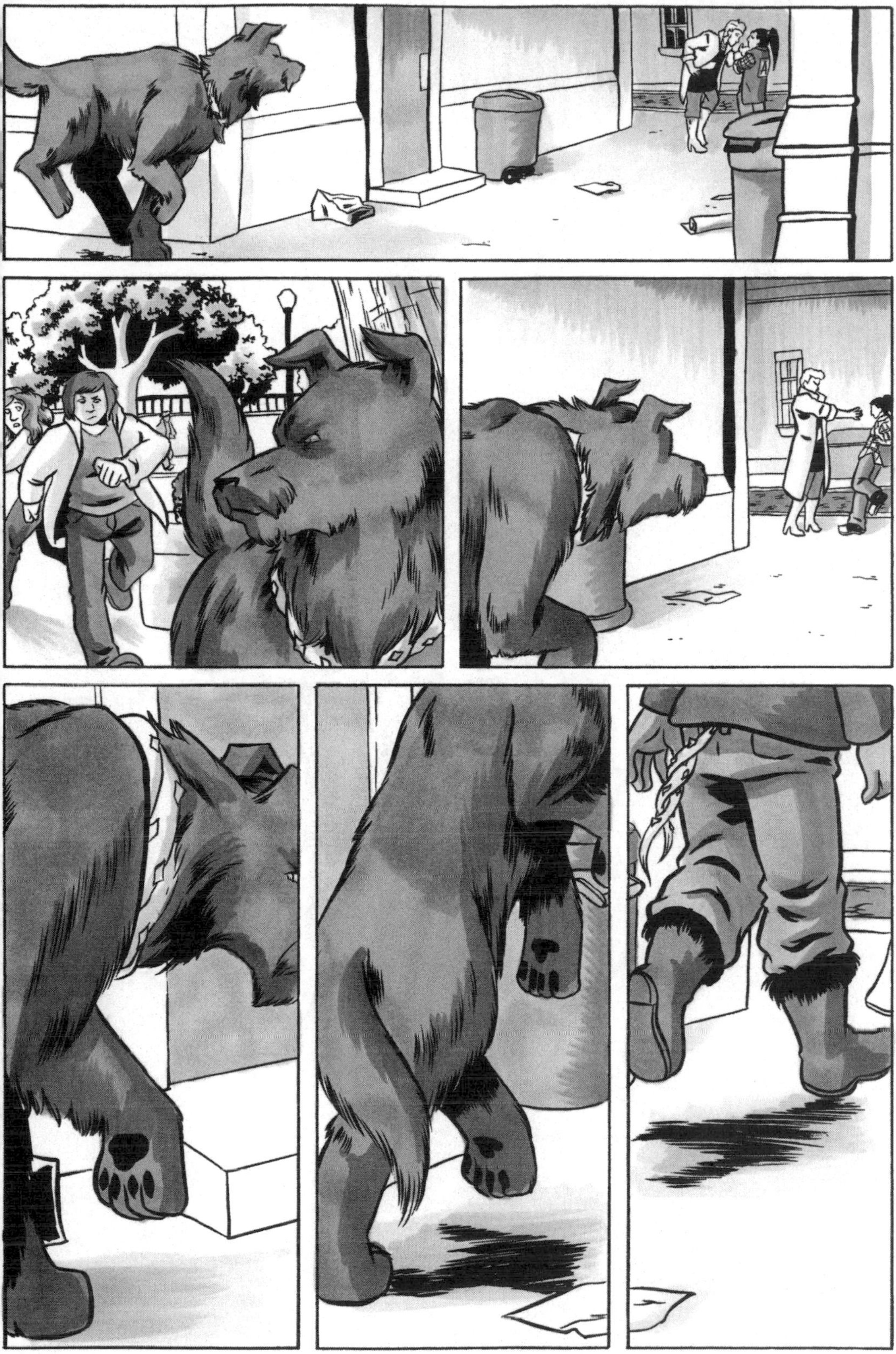

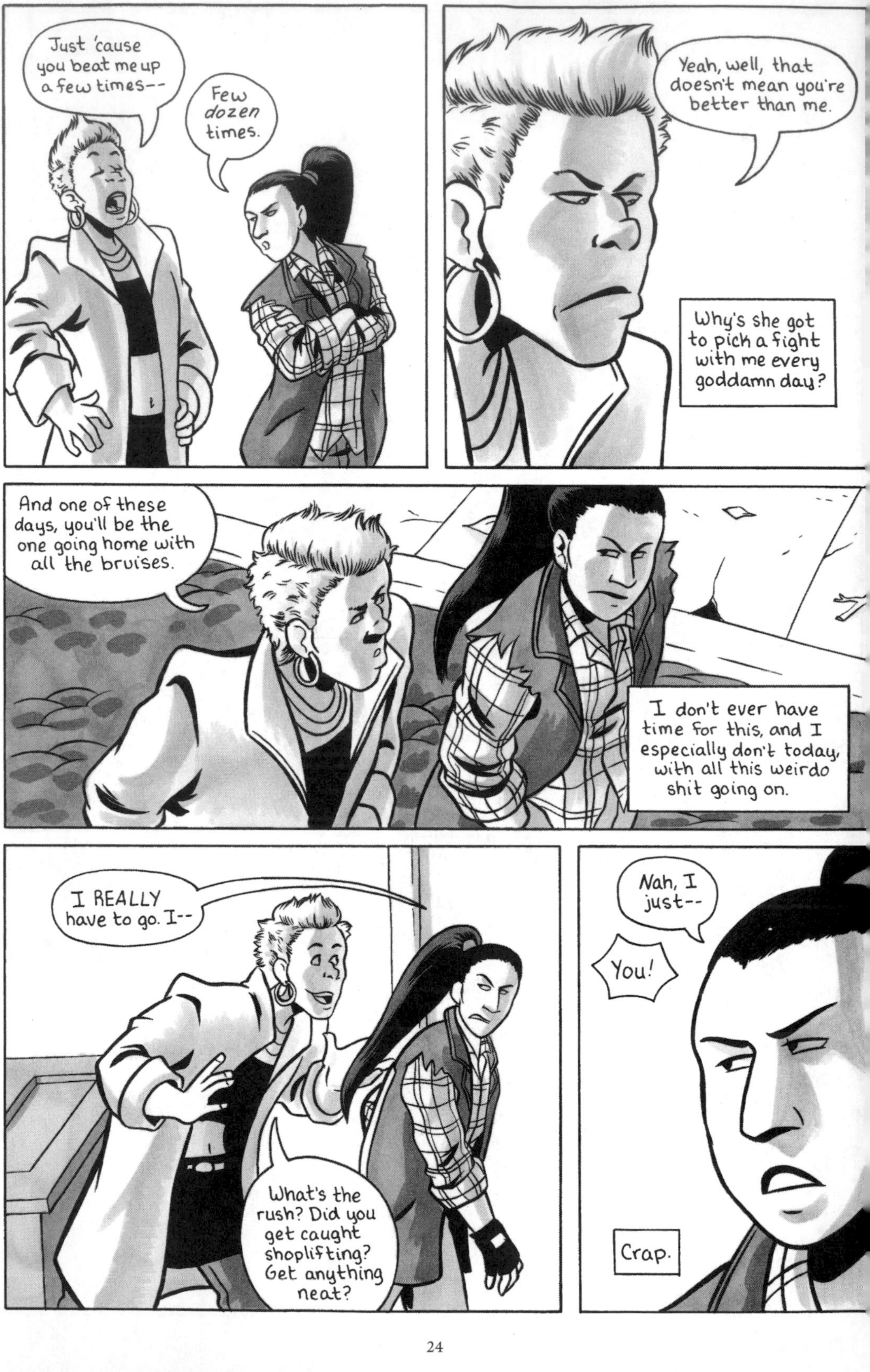
Just 'cause you beat me up a few times--
Few *dozen* times.
Yeah, well, that doesn't mean you're better than me.
Why's she got to pick a fight with me every goddamn day?
And one of these days, you'll be the one going home with all the bruises.
I don't ever have time for this, and I especially don't today, with all this weirdo shit going on.
I REALLY have to go. I--
What's the rush? Did you get caught shoplifting? Get anything neat?
Nah, I just--
You!
Crap.

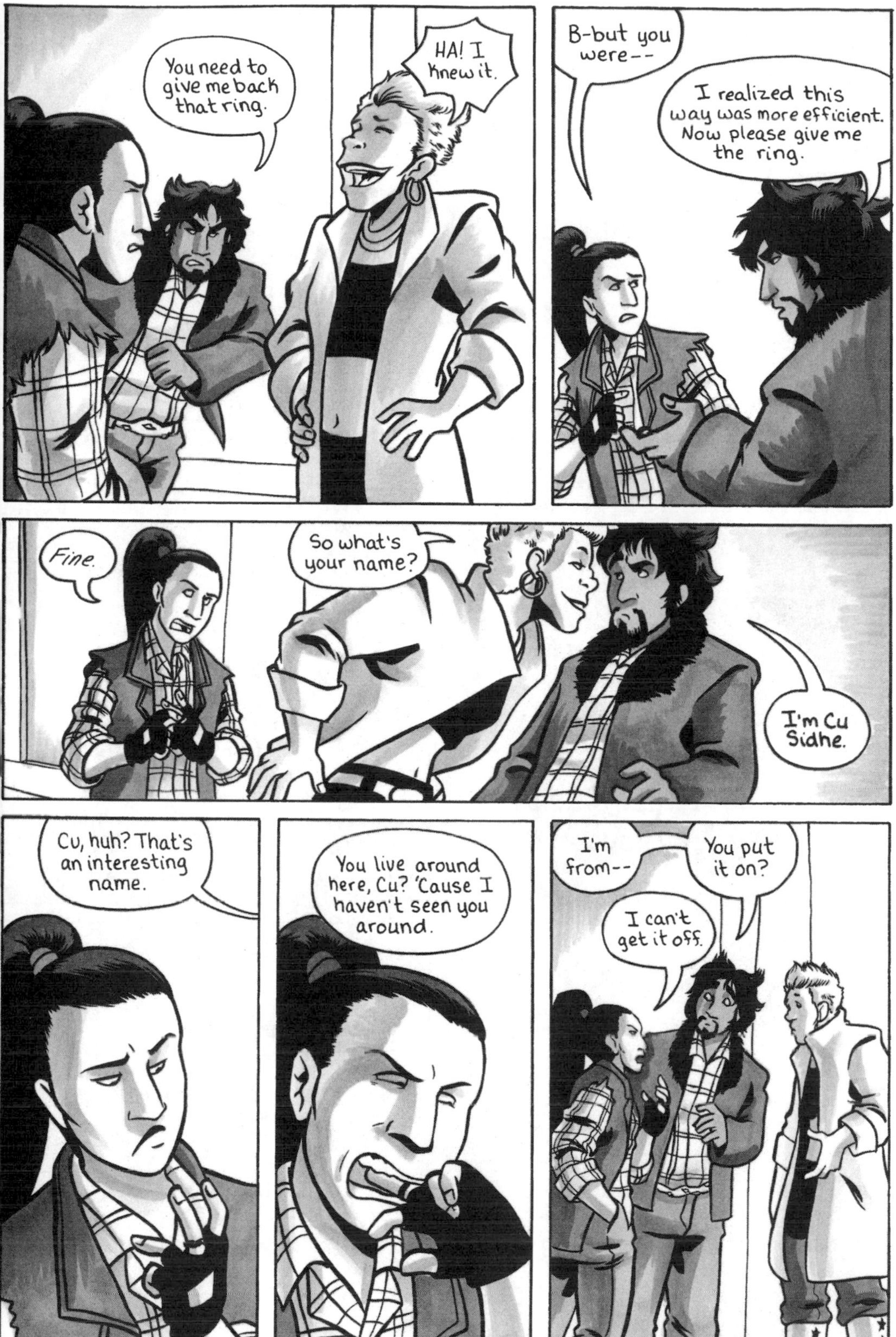
You need to give me back that ring.
HA! I knew it.
B-but you were--
I realized this way was more efficient. Now please give me the ring.
Fine.
So what's your name?
I'm Cu Sidhe.
Cu, huh? That's an interesting name.
You live around here, Cu? 'Cause I haven't seen you around.
I'm from--
You put it on?
I can't get it off.

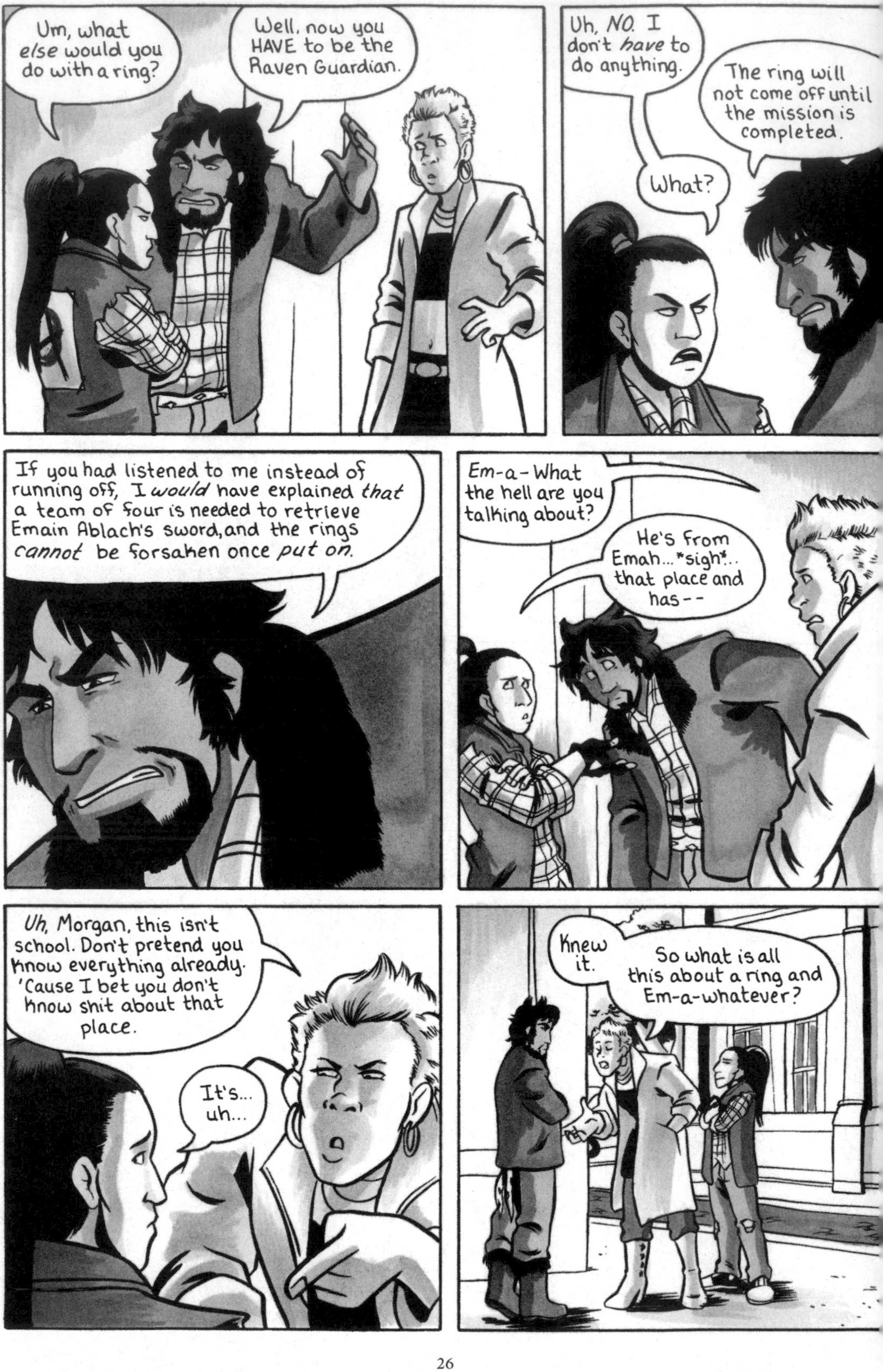
Um, what else would you do with a ring?
Well, now you HAVE to be the Raven Guardian.
Uh, NO. I don't have to do anything.
What?
The ring will not come off until the mission is completed.
If you had listened to me instead of running off, I would have explained that a team of four is needed to retrieve Emain Ablach's sword, and the rings cannot be forsaken once put on.
Em-a-What the hell are you talking about?
He's from Emah... *sigh*... that place and has--
Uh, Morgan, this isn't school. Don't pretend you know everything already. 'Cause I bet you don't know shit about that place.
It's... uh...
Knew it.
So what is all this about a ring and Em-a-whatever?

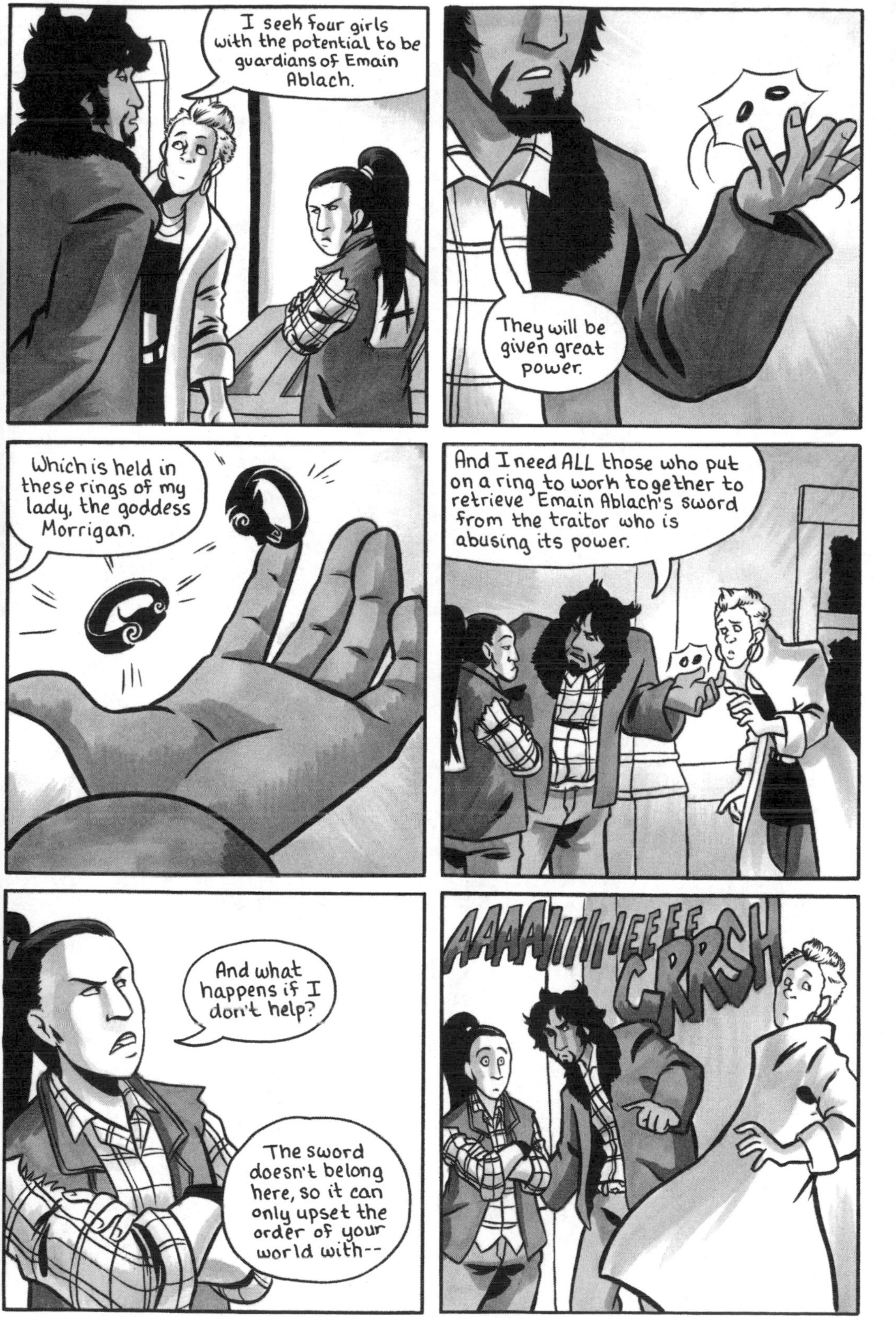
I seek four girls with the potential to be guardians of Emain Ablach.
They will be given great power.
Which is held in these rings of my lady, the goddess Morrigan.
And I need ALL those who put on a ring to work together to retrieve Emain Ablach's sword from the traitor who is abusing its power.
And what happens if I don't help?
The sword doesn't belong here, so it can only upset the order of your world with--
AAAAIIIIIEEEEE
CRRSH

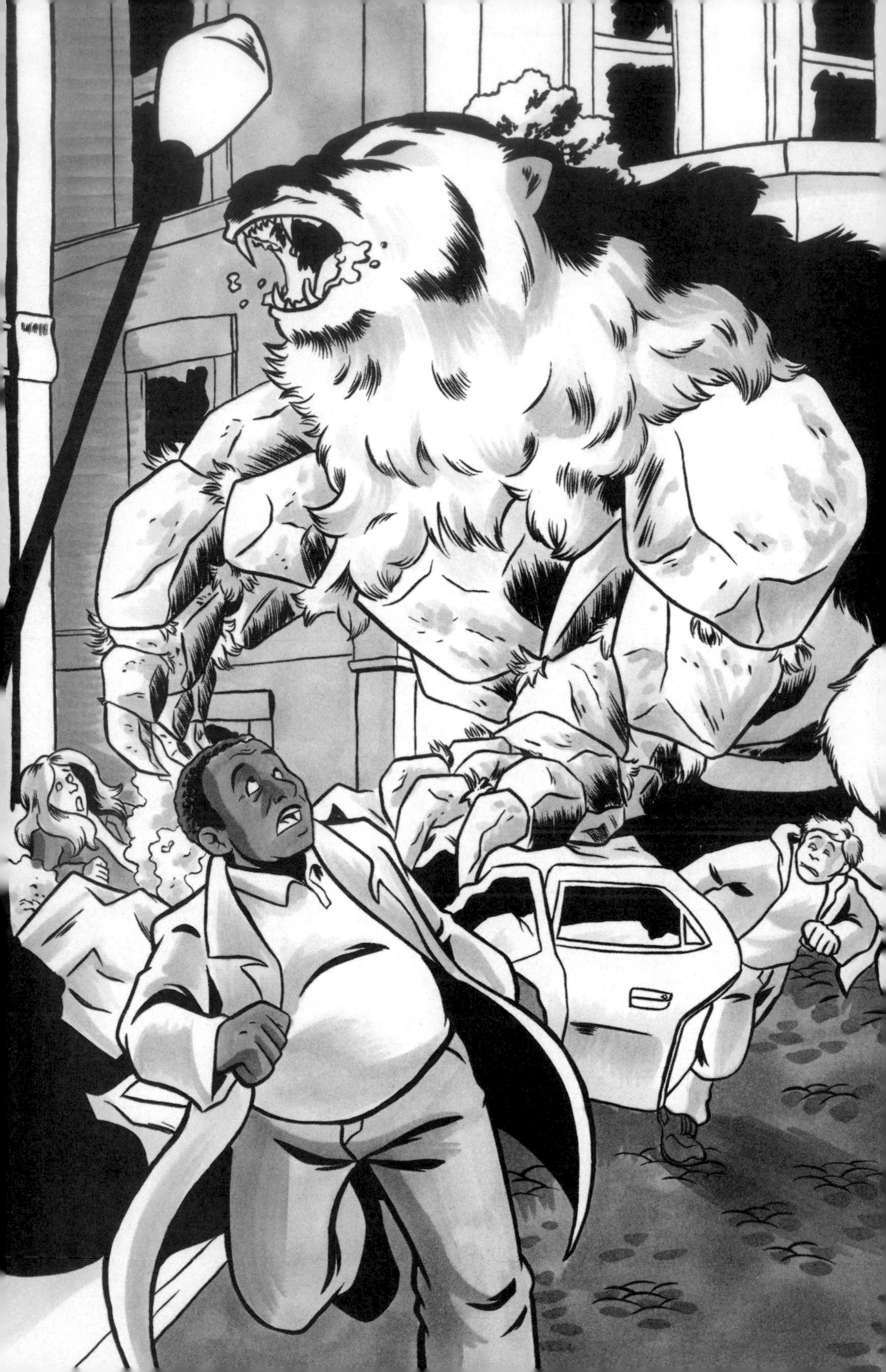

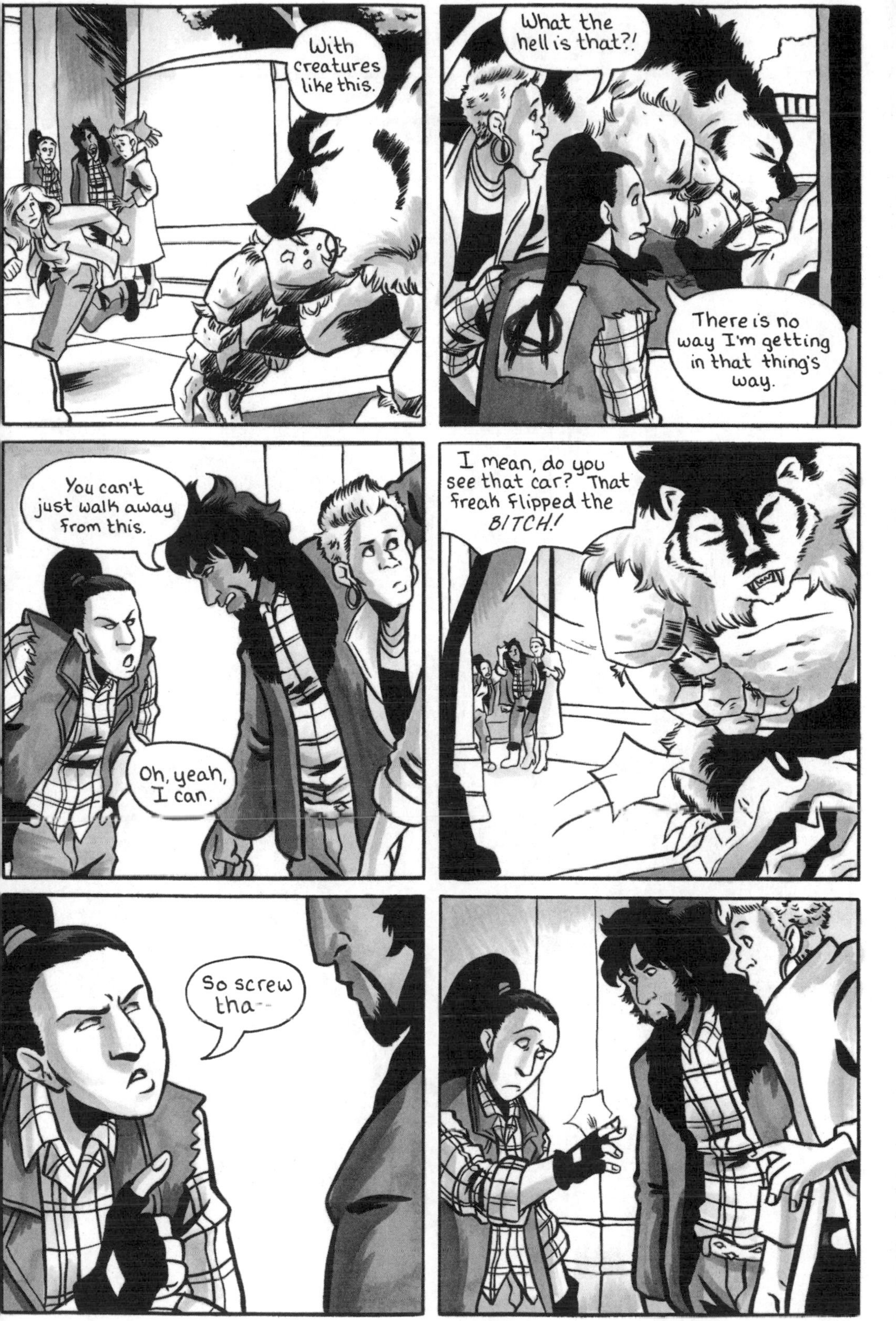
With creatures like this.
What the hell is that?!
There is no way I'm getting in that thing's way.
You can't just walk away from this.
Oh, yeah, I can.
I mean, do you see that car? That freak flipped the BITCH!
So screw tha--

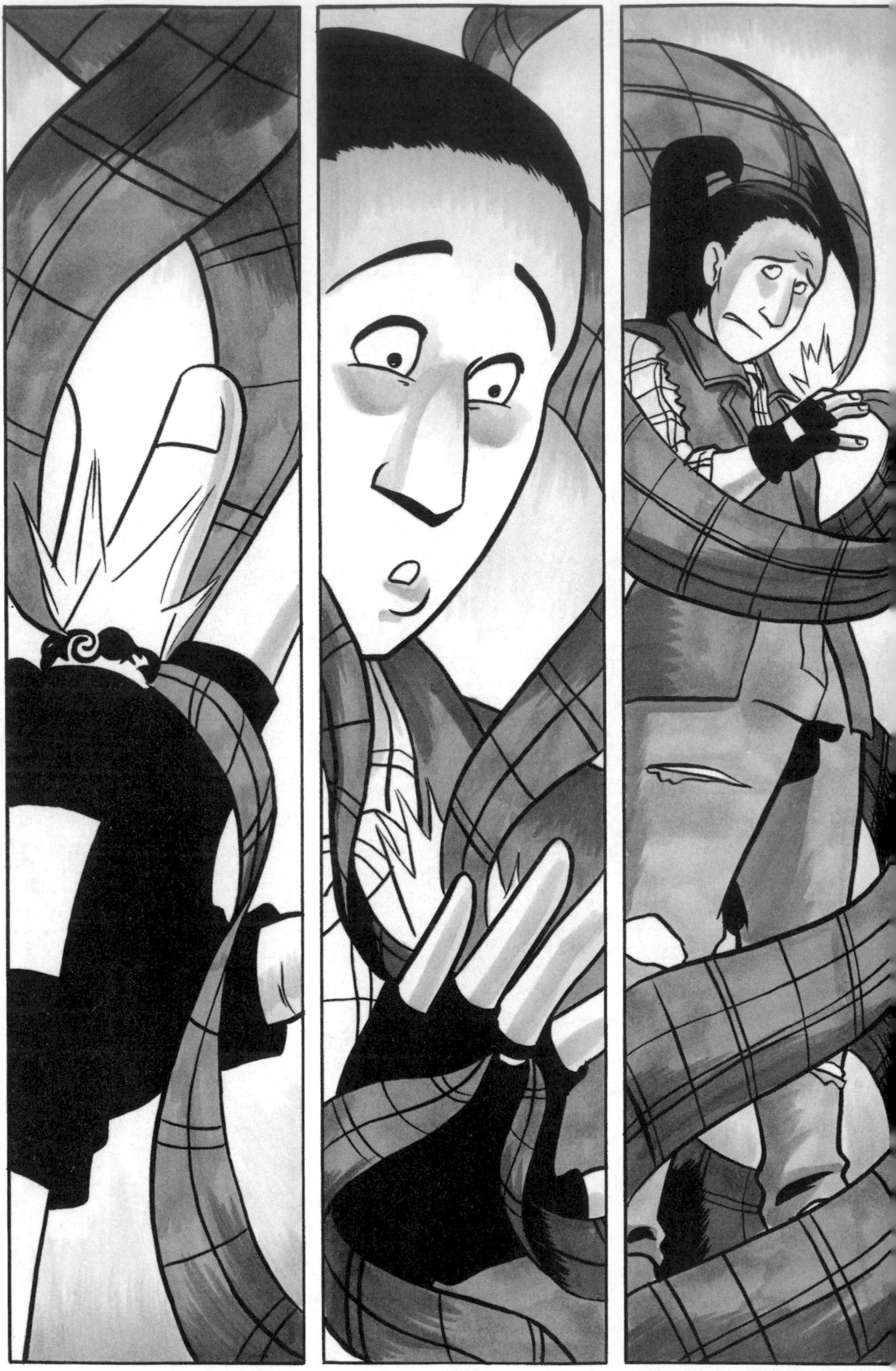

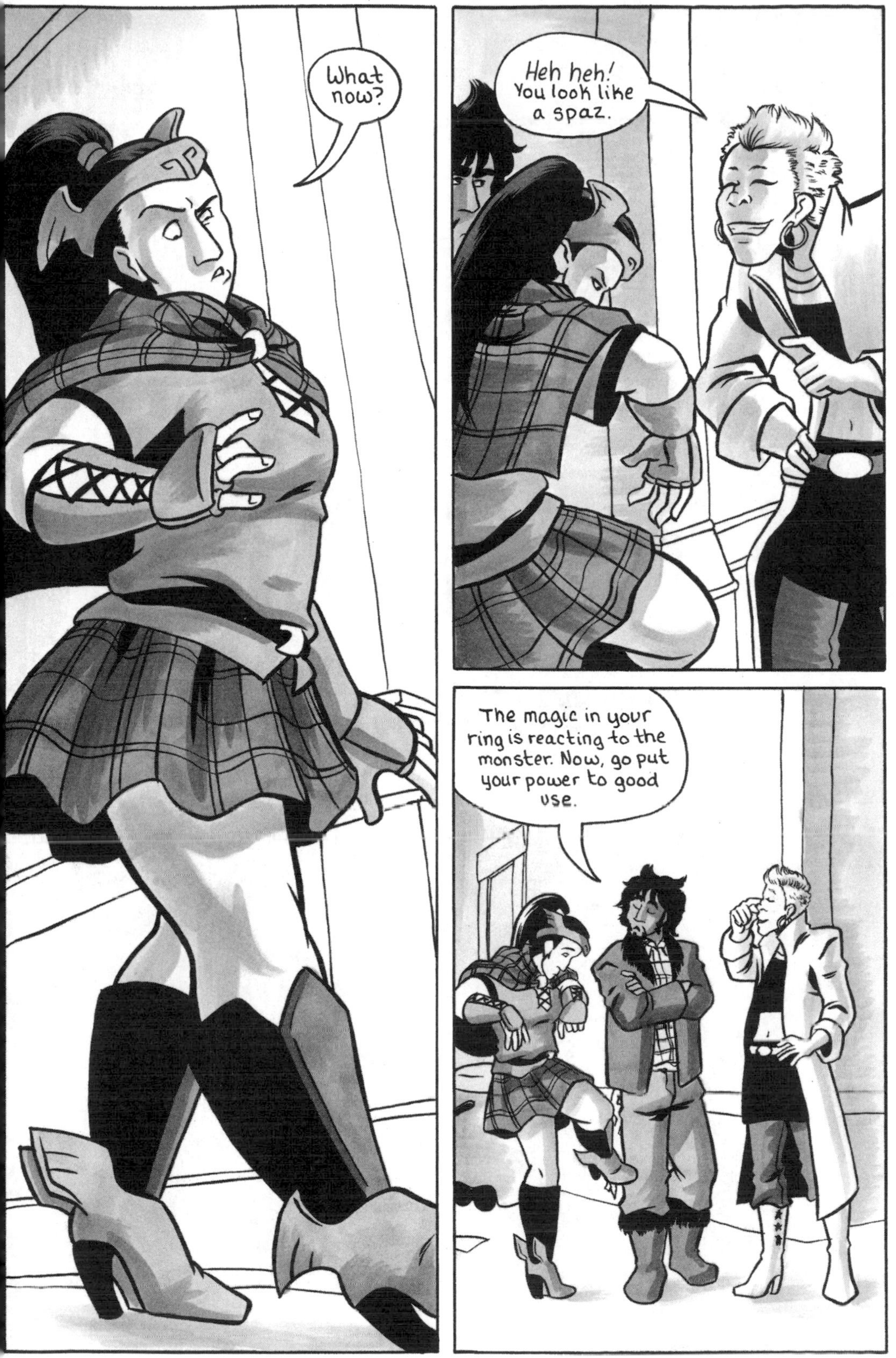
What now?
Heh heh! You look like a spaz.
The magic in your ring is reacting to the monster. Now, go put your power to good use.

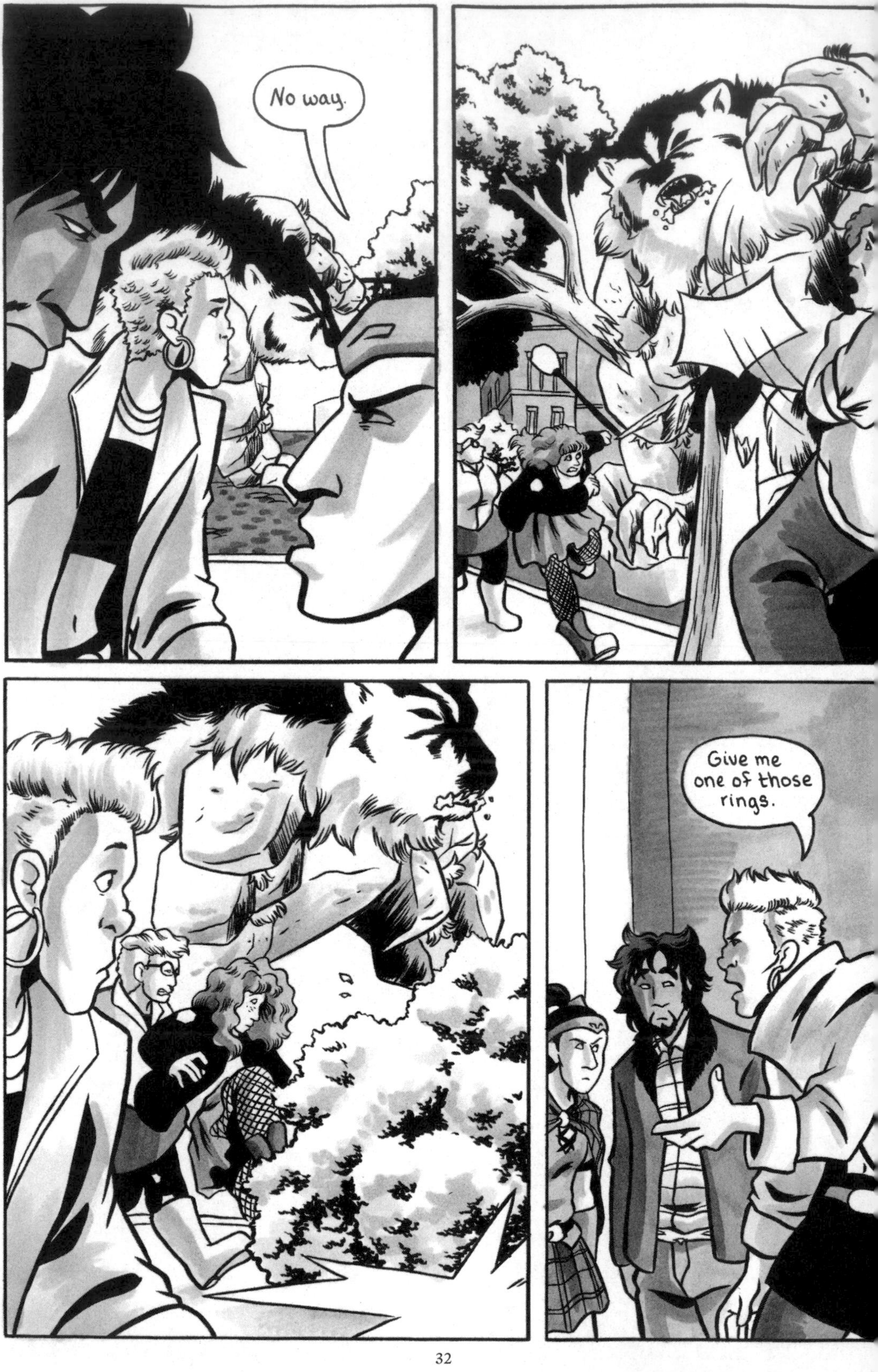
No way.
Give me one of those rings.

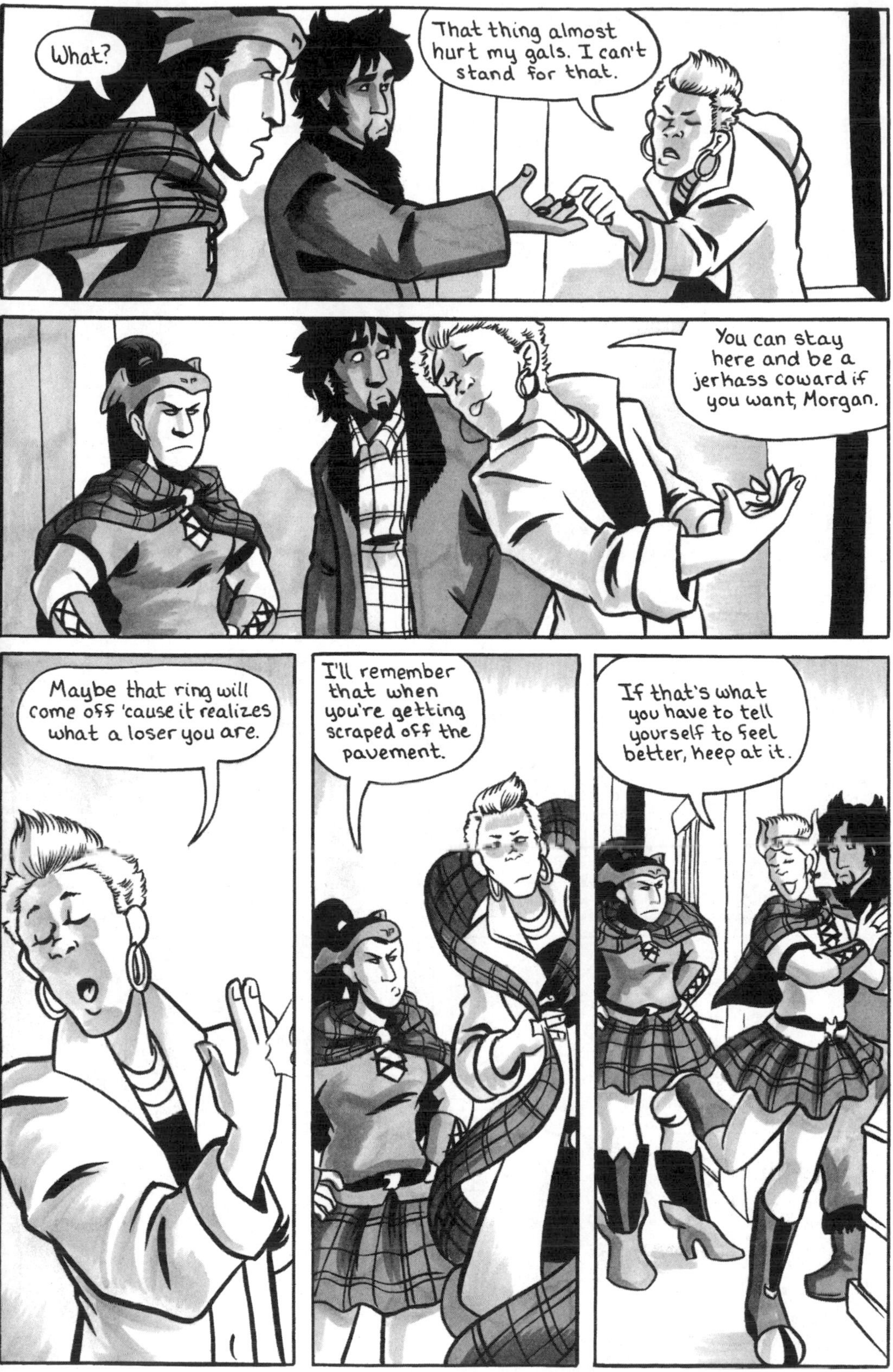
What?
That thing almost hurt my gals. I can't stand for that.
You can stay here and be a jerkass coward if you want, Morgan.
Maybe that ring will come off 'cause it realizes what a loser you are.
I'll remember that when you're getting scraped off the pavement.
If that's what you have to tell yourself to feel better, keep at it.

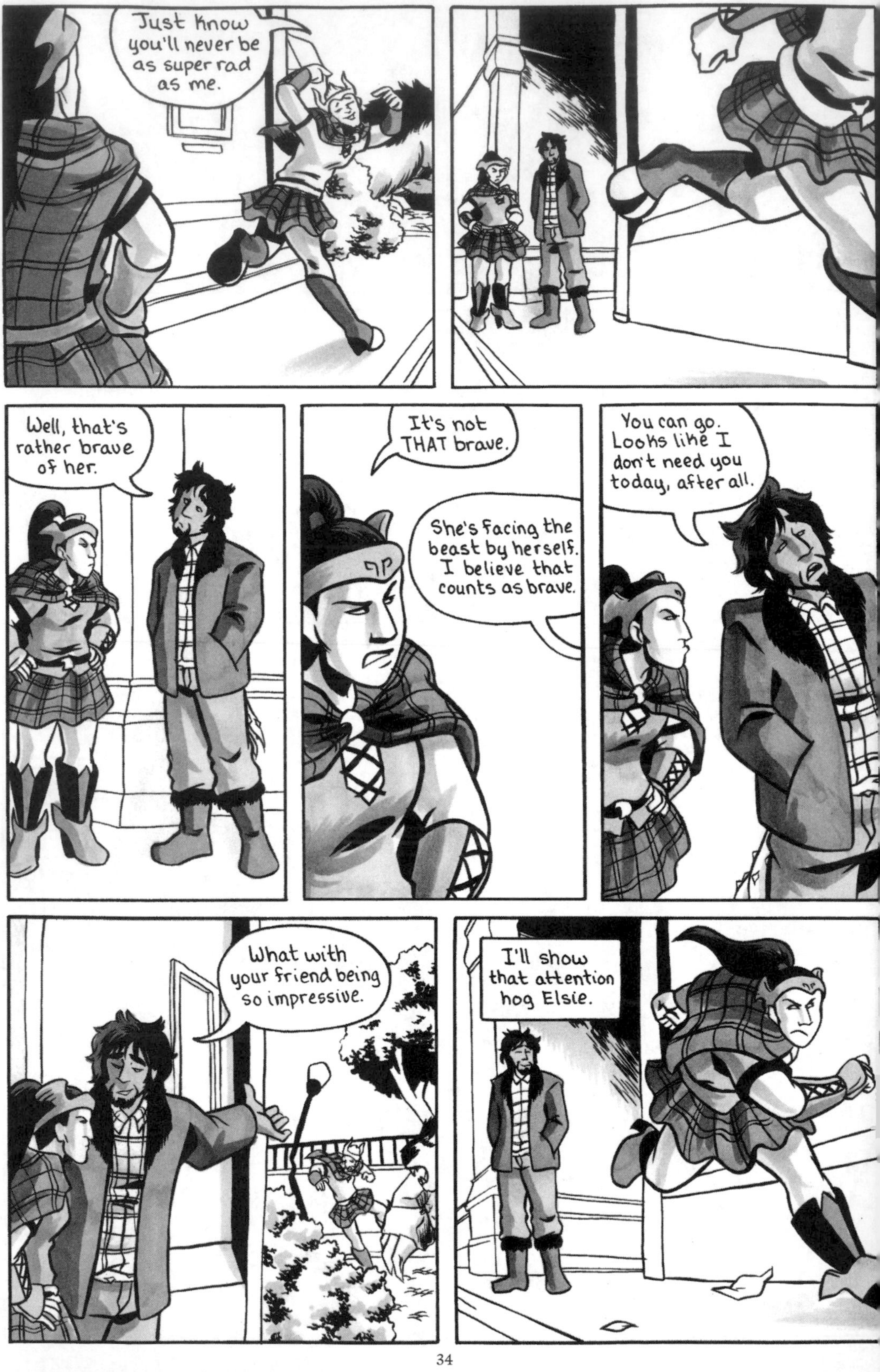
Just know you'll never be as super rad as me.
Well, that's rather brave of her.
It's not THAT brave.
She's facing the beast by herself. I believe that counts as brave.
You can go. Looks like I don't need you today, after all.
What with your friend being so impressive.
I'll show that attention hog Elsie.

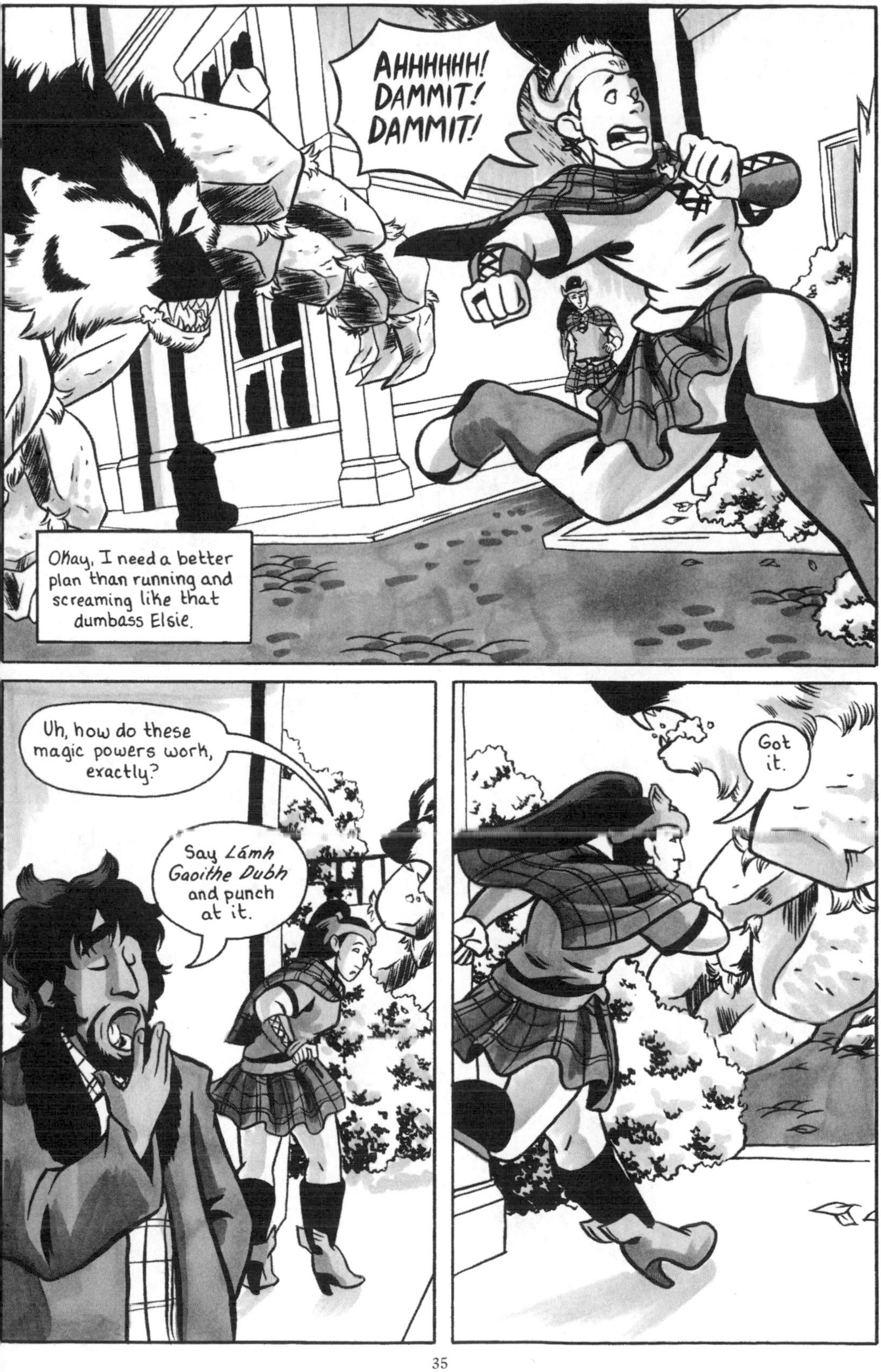
AHHHHHH! DAMMIT! DAMMIT!
Okay, I need a better plan than running and screaming like that dumbass Elsie.
Uh, how do these magic powers work, exactly?
Say *Lámh Gaoithe Dubh* and punch at it.
Got it.

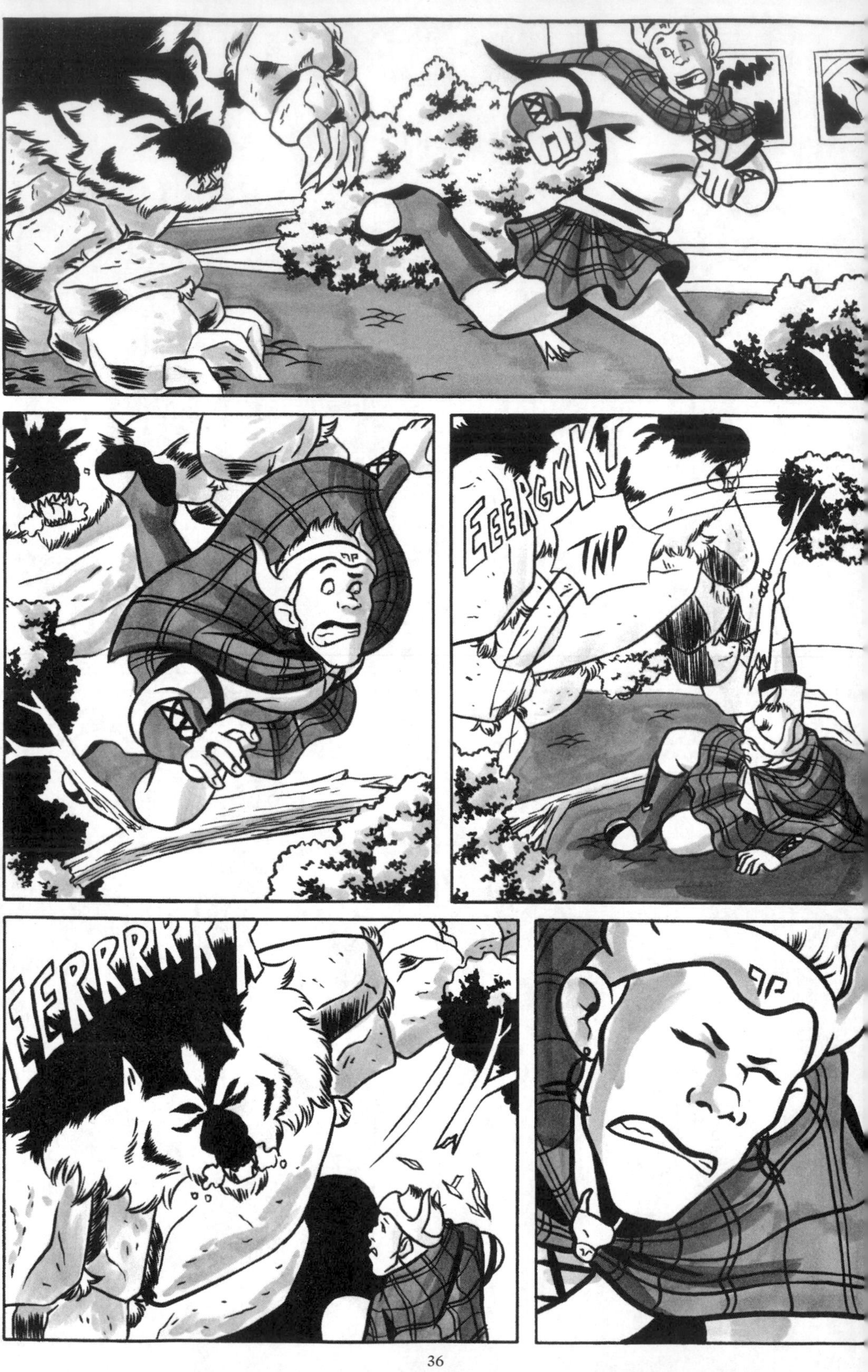
EEERGKKT
TNP
EERRRRKK

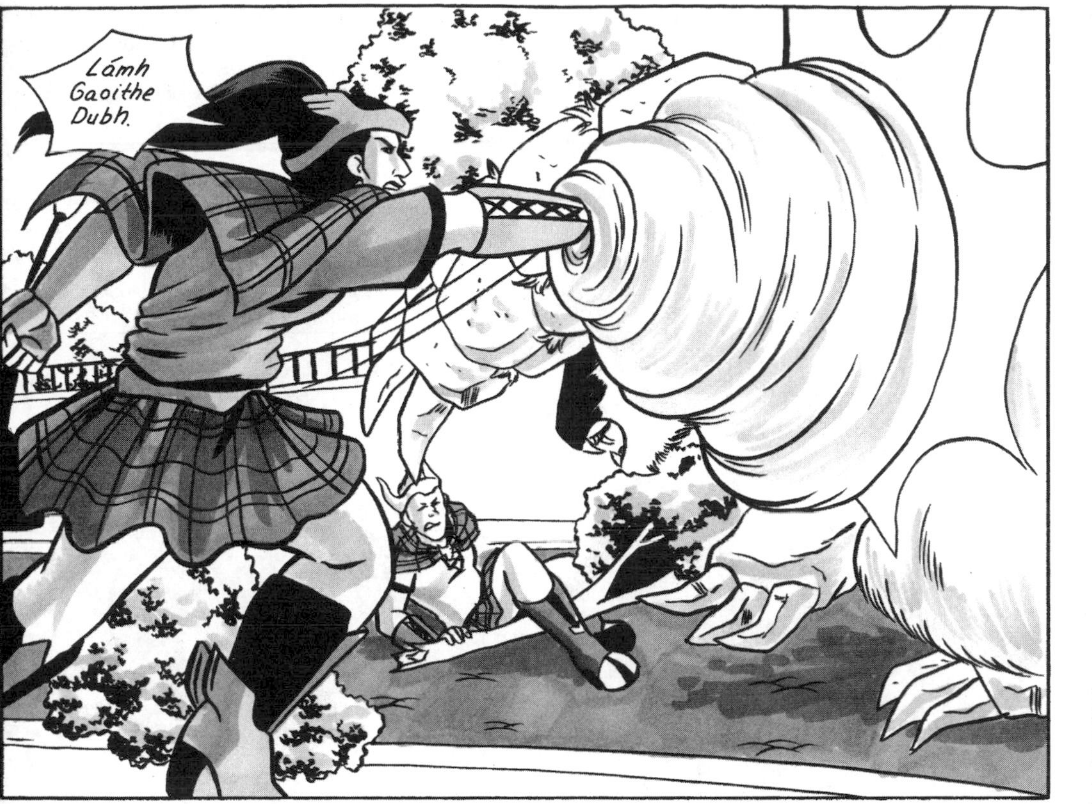
Lámh Gaoithe Dubh.

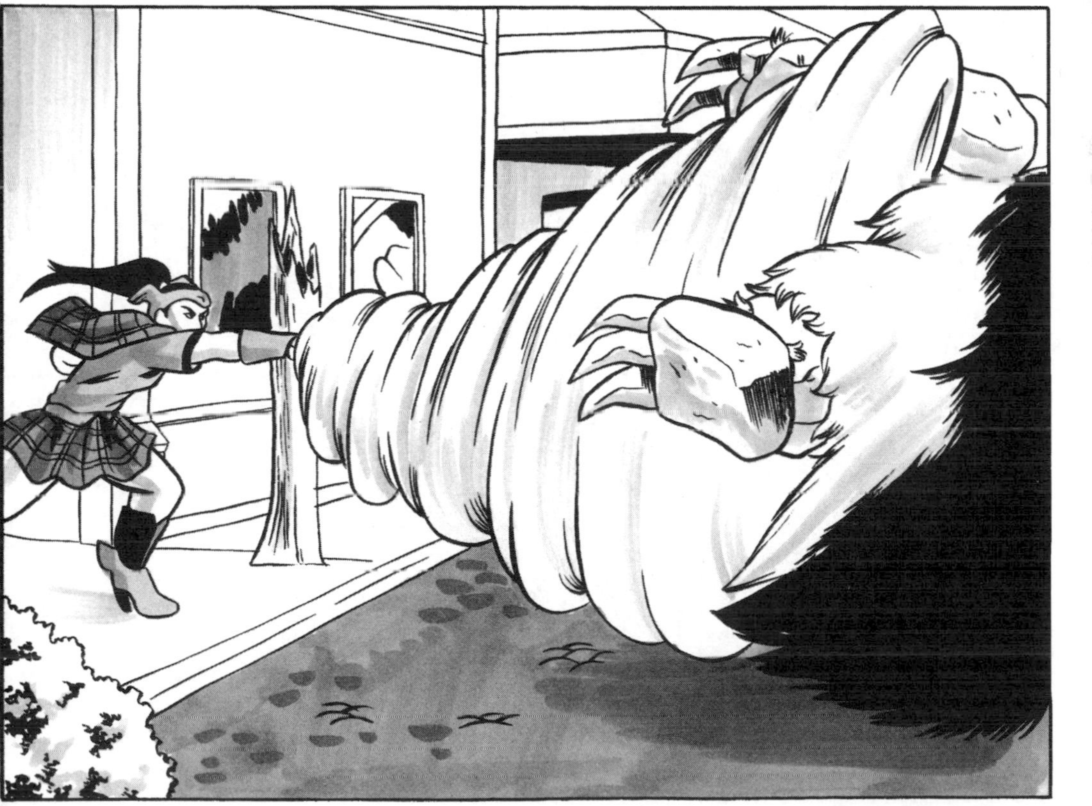

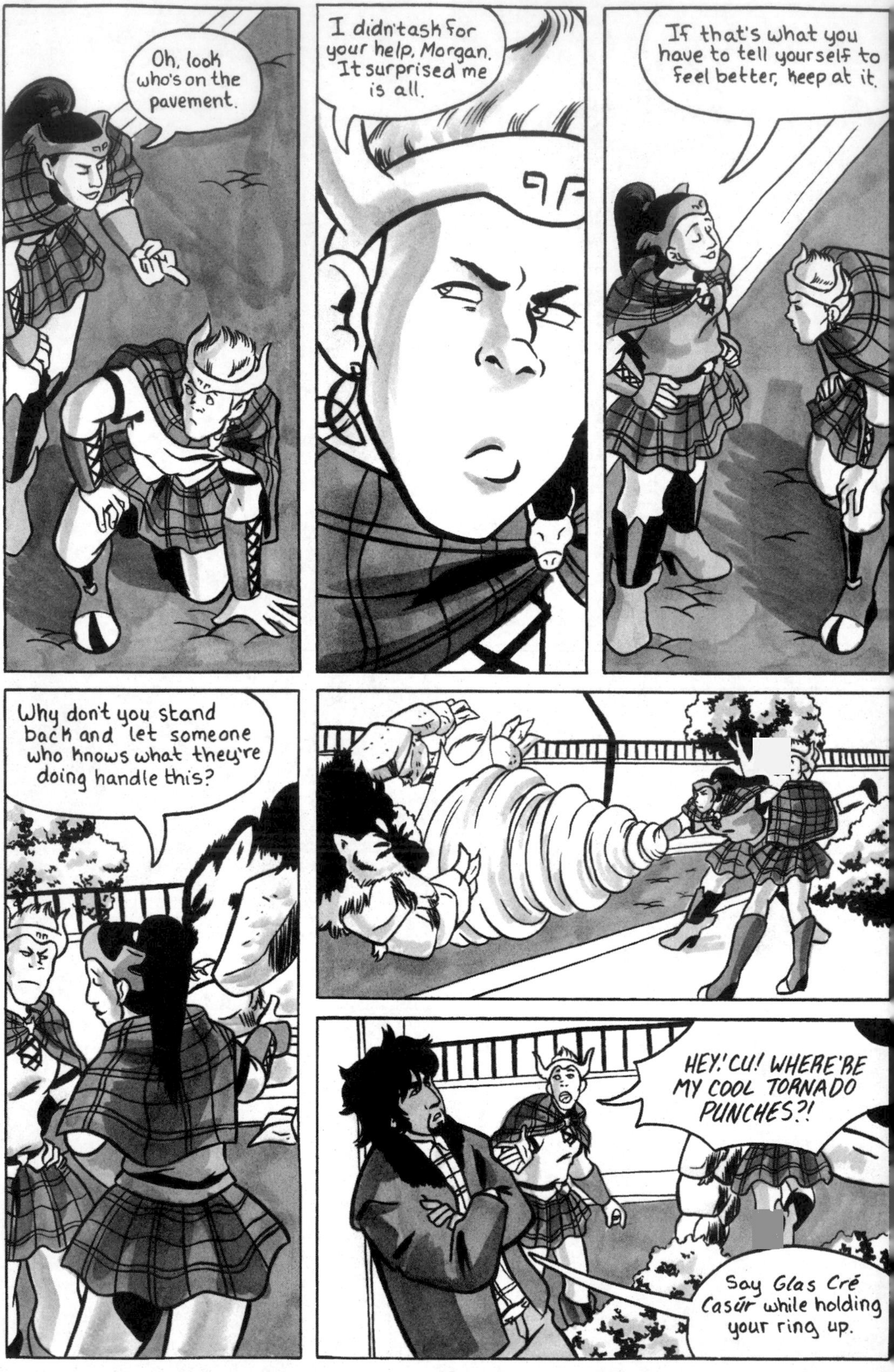
Oh, look who's on the pavement.
I didn't ask for your help, Morgan. It surprised me is all.
If that's what you have to tell yourself to feel better, keep at it.
Why don't you stand back and let someone who knows what they're doing handle this?
HEY! CU! WHERE'RE MY COOL TORNADO PUNCHES?!
Say Glas Cré Casúr while holding your ring up.

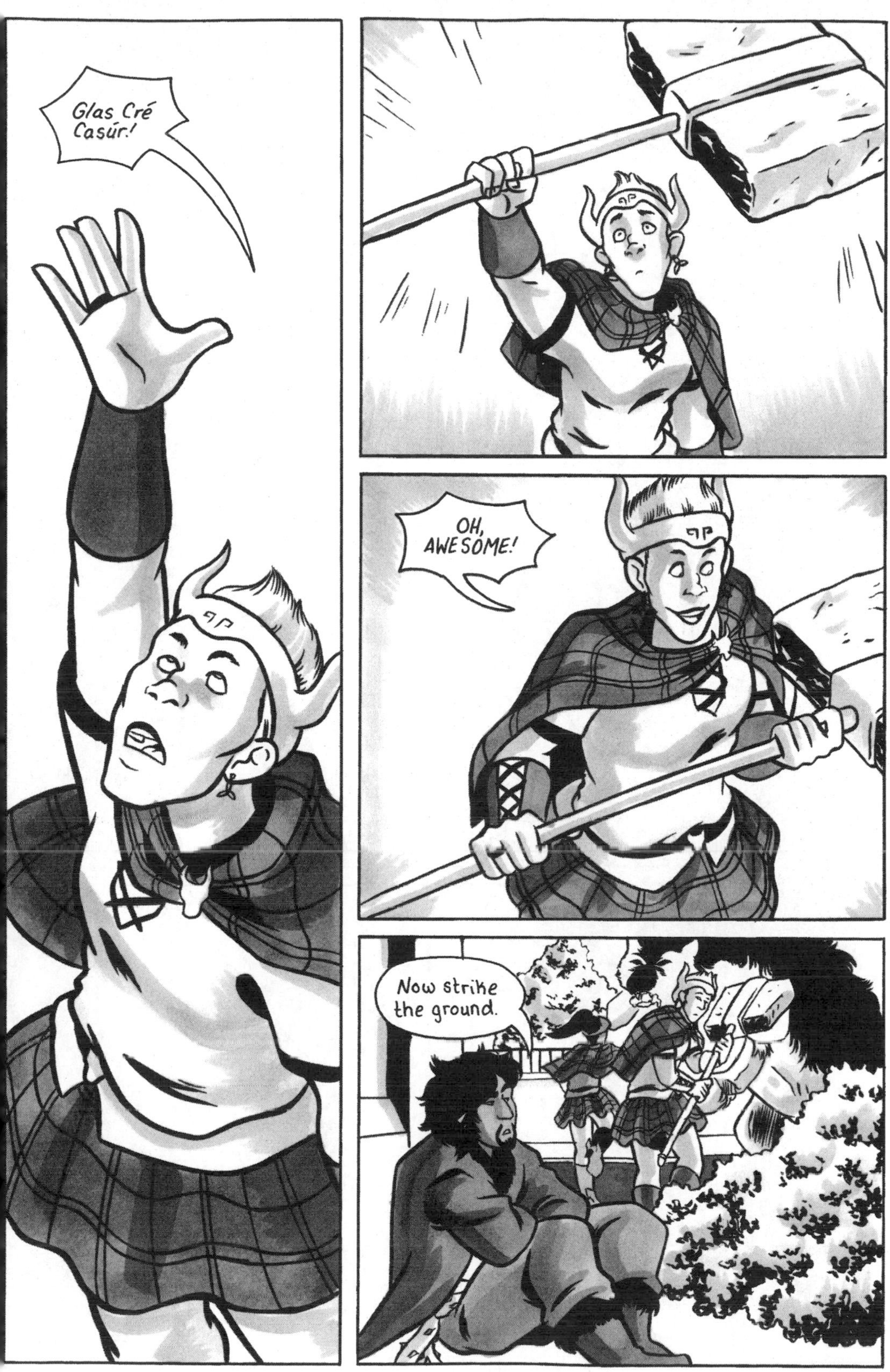
Glas Cré Casúr!
OH, AWESOME!
Now strike the ground.

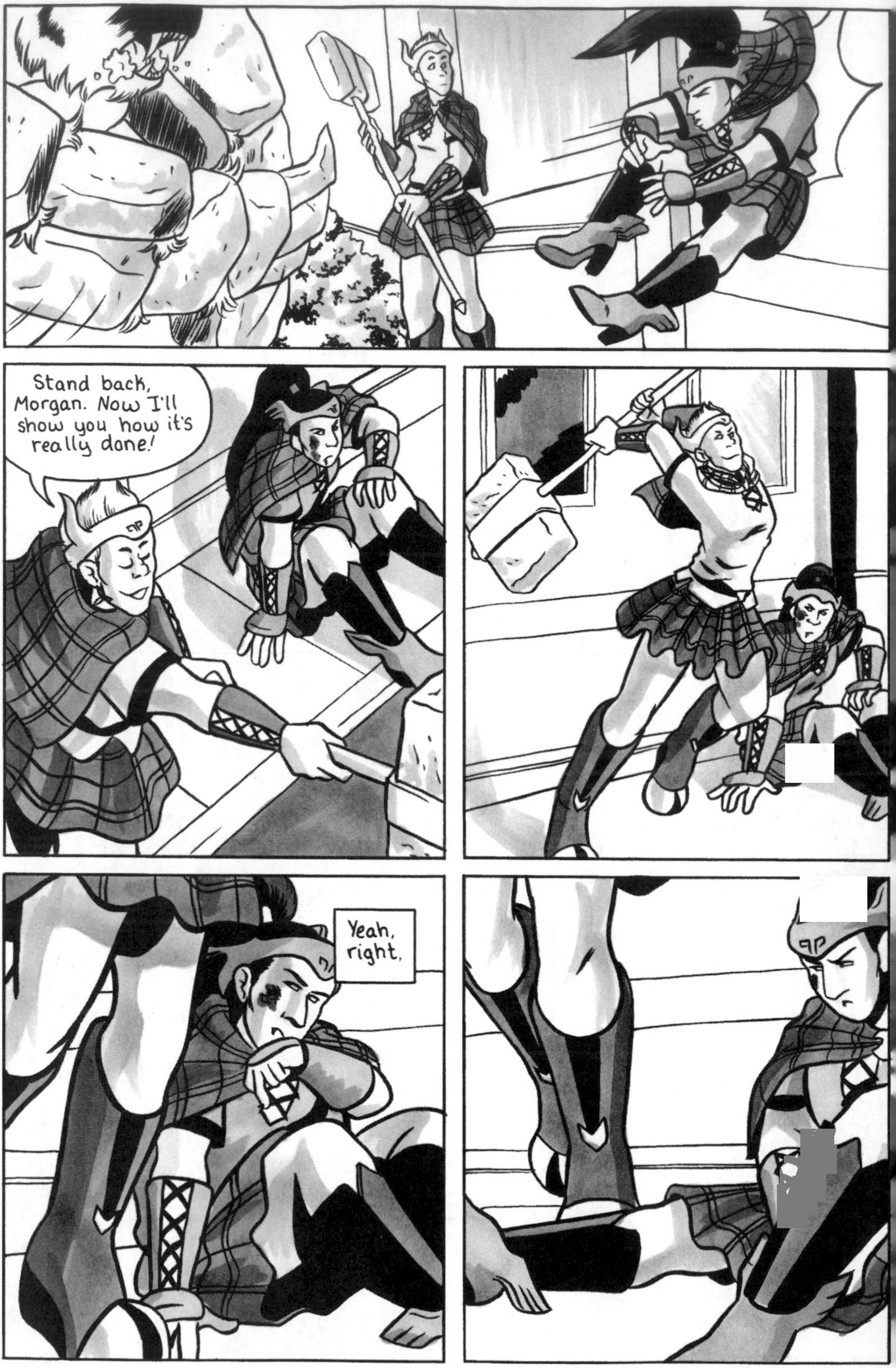

Stand back, Morgan. Now I'll show you how it's really done!
Yeah, right.

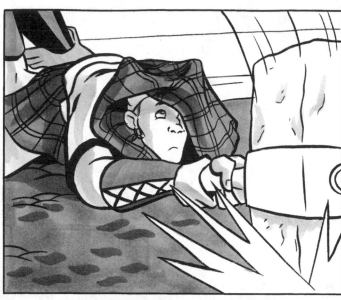

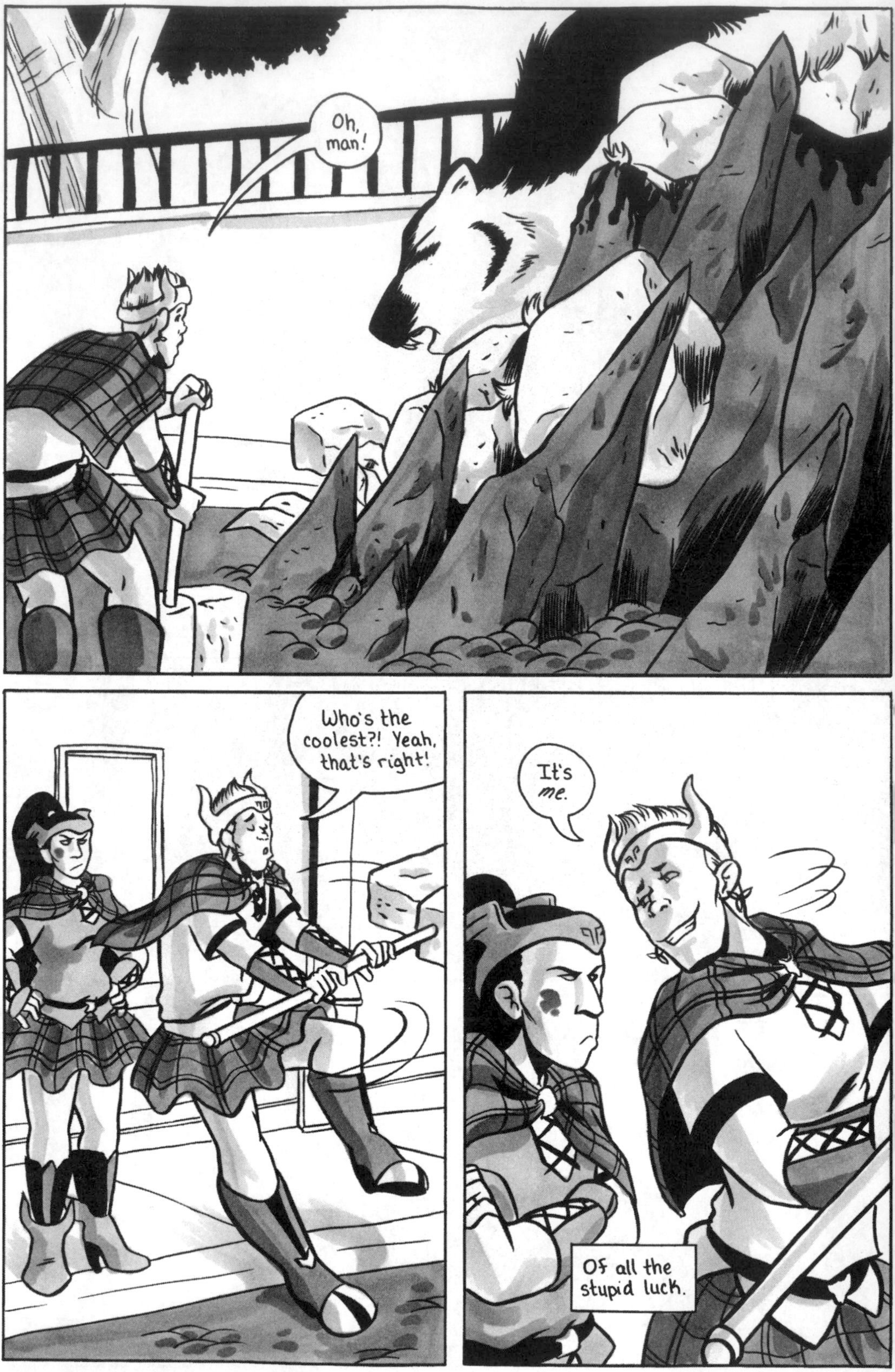

Oh, man!
Who's the coolest?! Yeah, that's right!
It's *me*.
Of all the stupid luck.

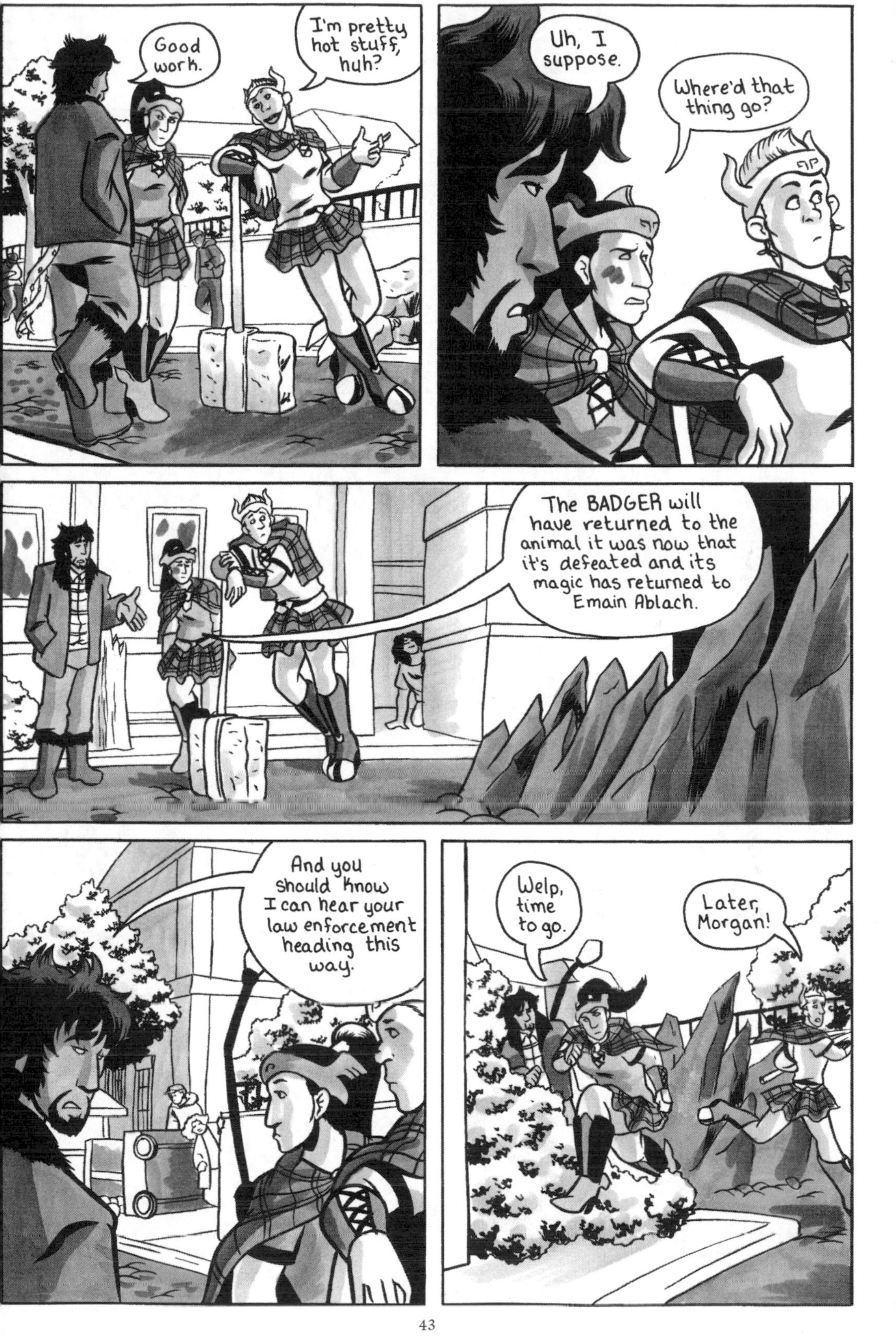
Good work.
I'm pretty hot stuff, huh?
Uh, I suppose.
Where'd that thing go?
The BADGER will have returned to the animal it was now that it's defeated and its magic has returned to Emain Ablach.
And you should know I can hear your law enforcement heading this way.
Welp, time to go.
Later, Morgan!

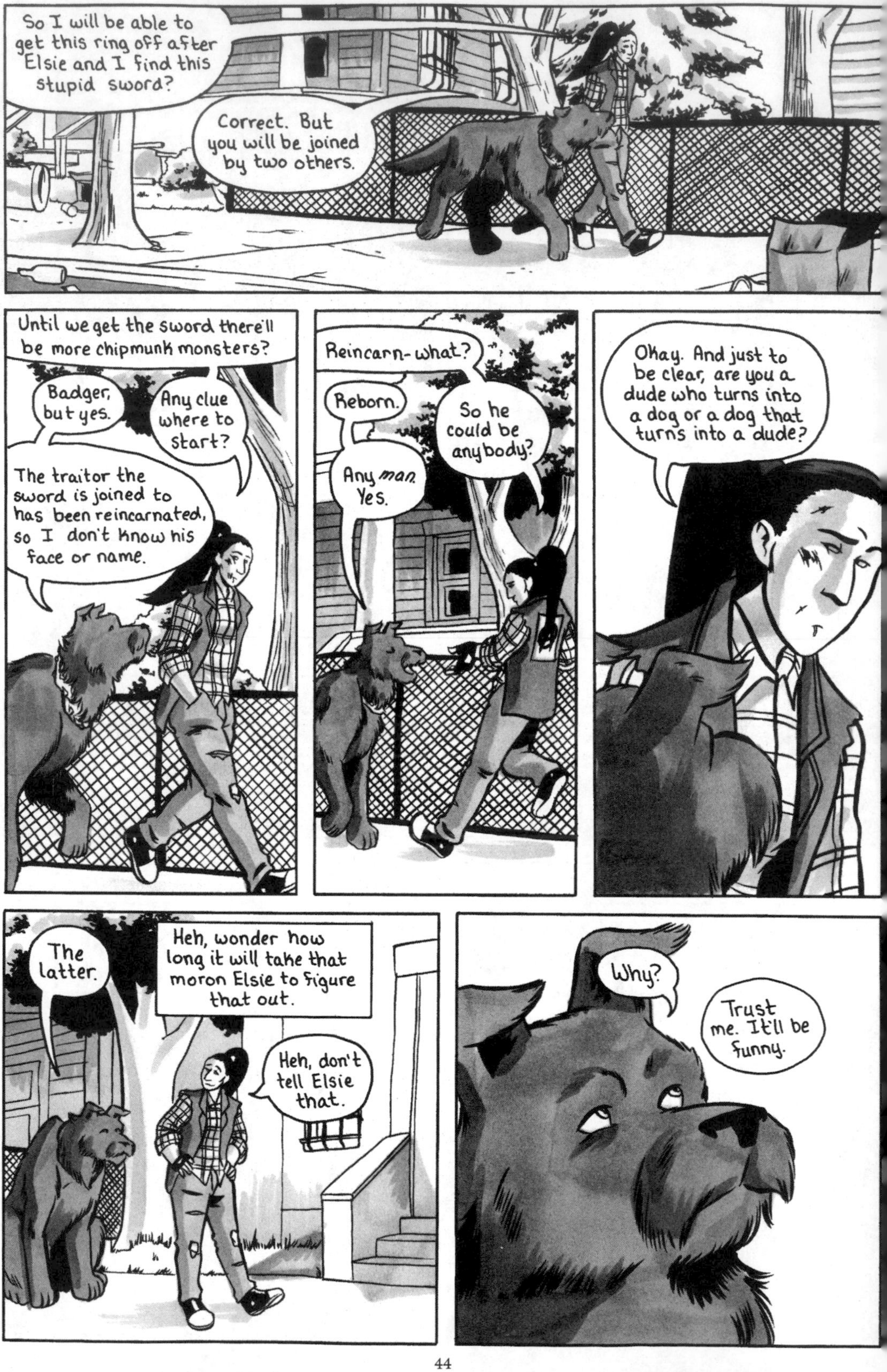
So I will be able to get this ring off after Elsie and I find this stupid sword?
Correct. But you will be joined by two others.
Until we get the sword there'll be more chipmunk monsters?
Badger, but yes.
Any clue where to start?
The traitor the sword is joined to has been reincarnated, so I don't know his face or name.
Reincarn-what?
Reborn.
Any *man*. Yes.
So he could be anybody?
Okay. And just to be clear, are you a dude who turns into a dog or a dog that turns into a dude?
The latter.
Heh, wonder how long it will take that moron Elsie to figure that out.
Heh, don't tell Elsie that.
Why?
Trust me. It'll be funny.

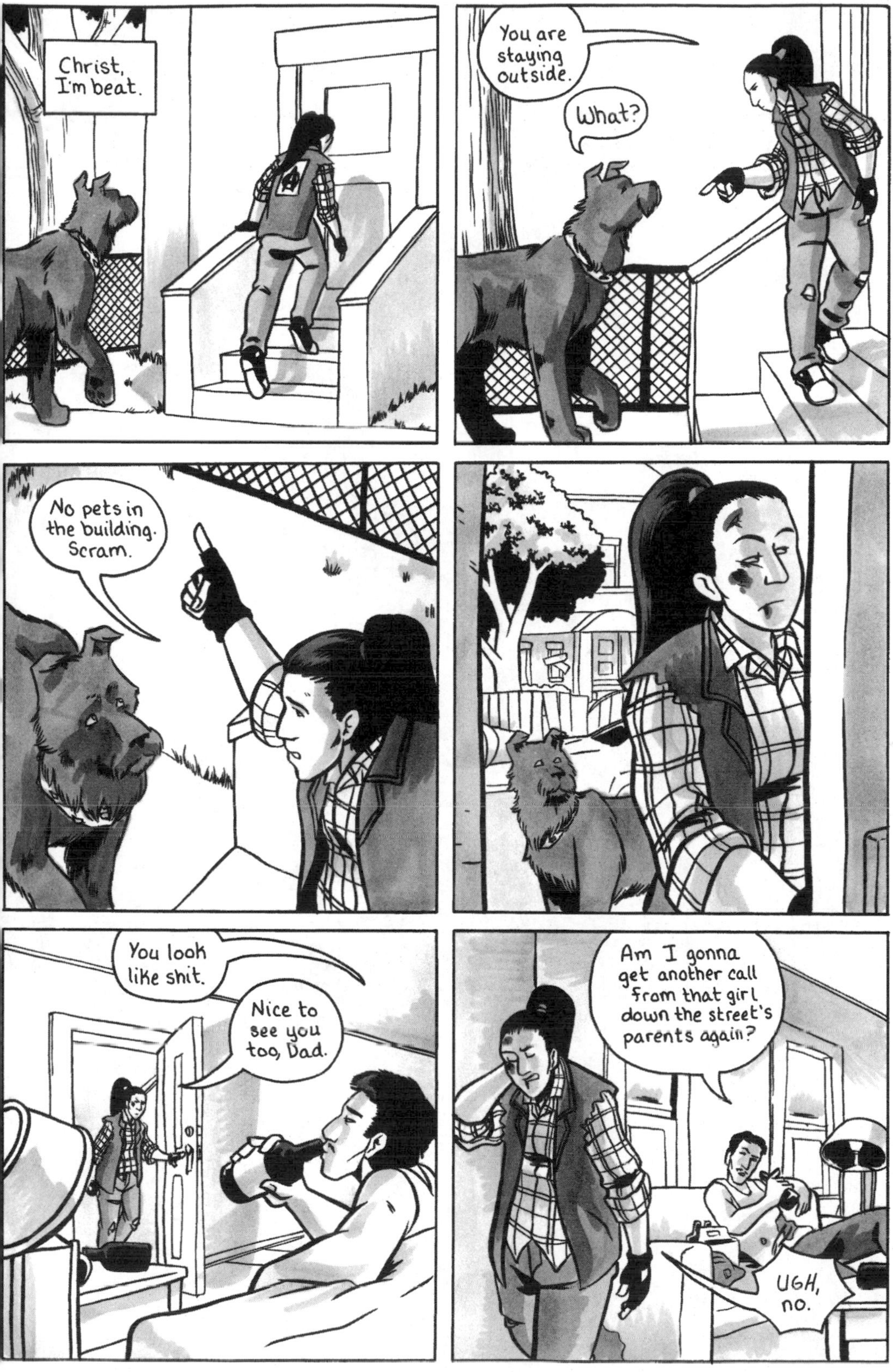
Christ, I'm beat.
You are staying outside.
What?
No pets in the building. Scram.
You look like shit.
Nice to see you too, Dad.
Am I gonna get another call from that girl down the street's parents again?
UGH, no.

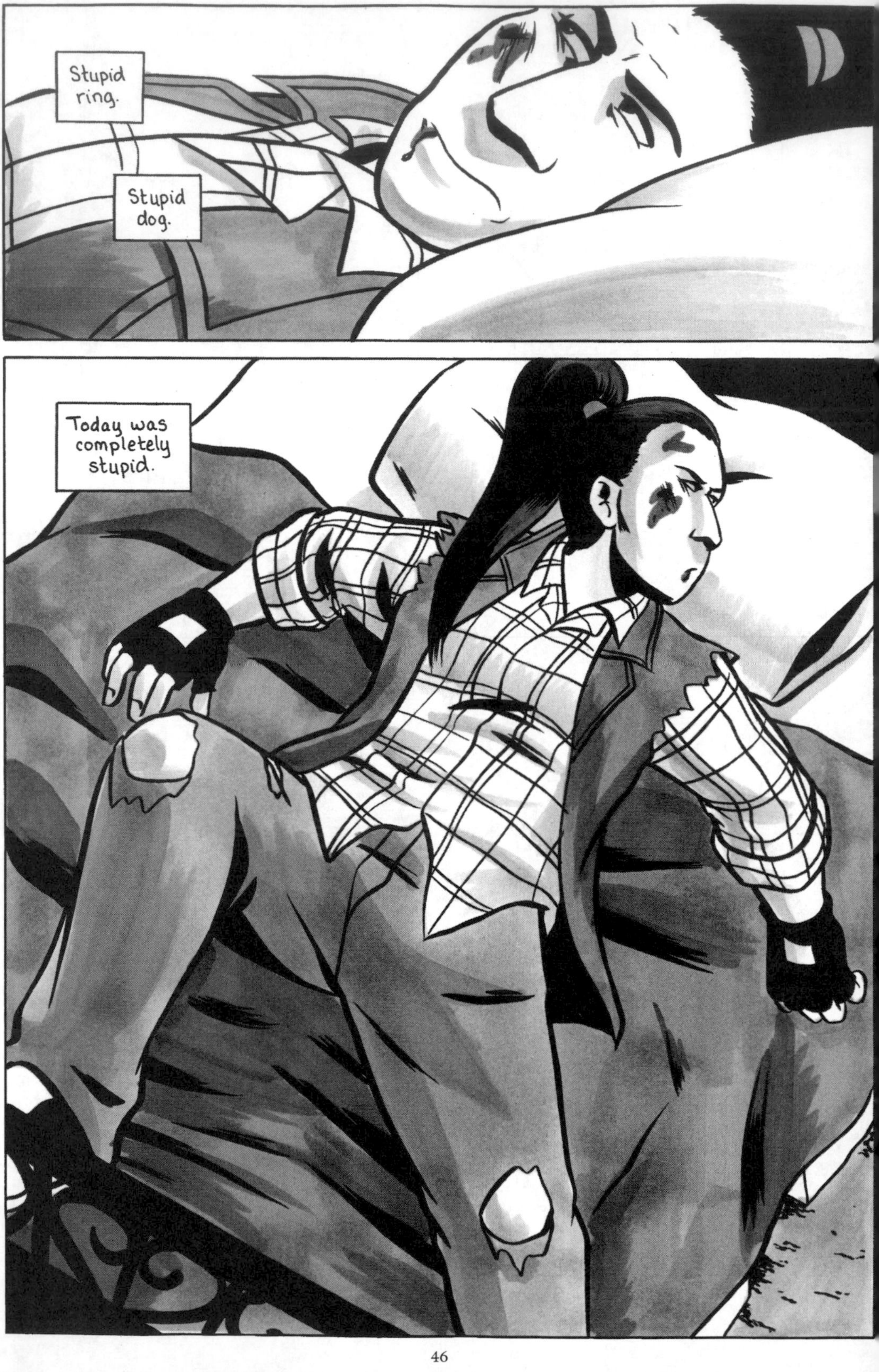
Stupid ring.
Stupid dog.
Today was completely stupid.

CHAPTER 2:

Elsie the Earth Cow

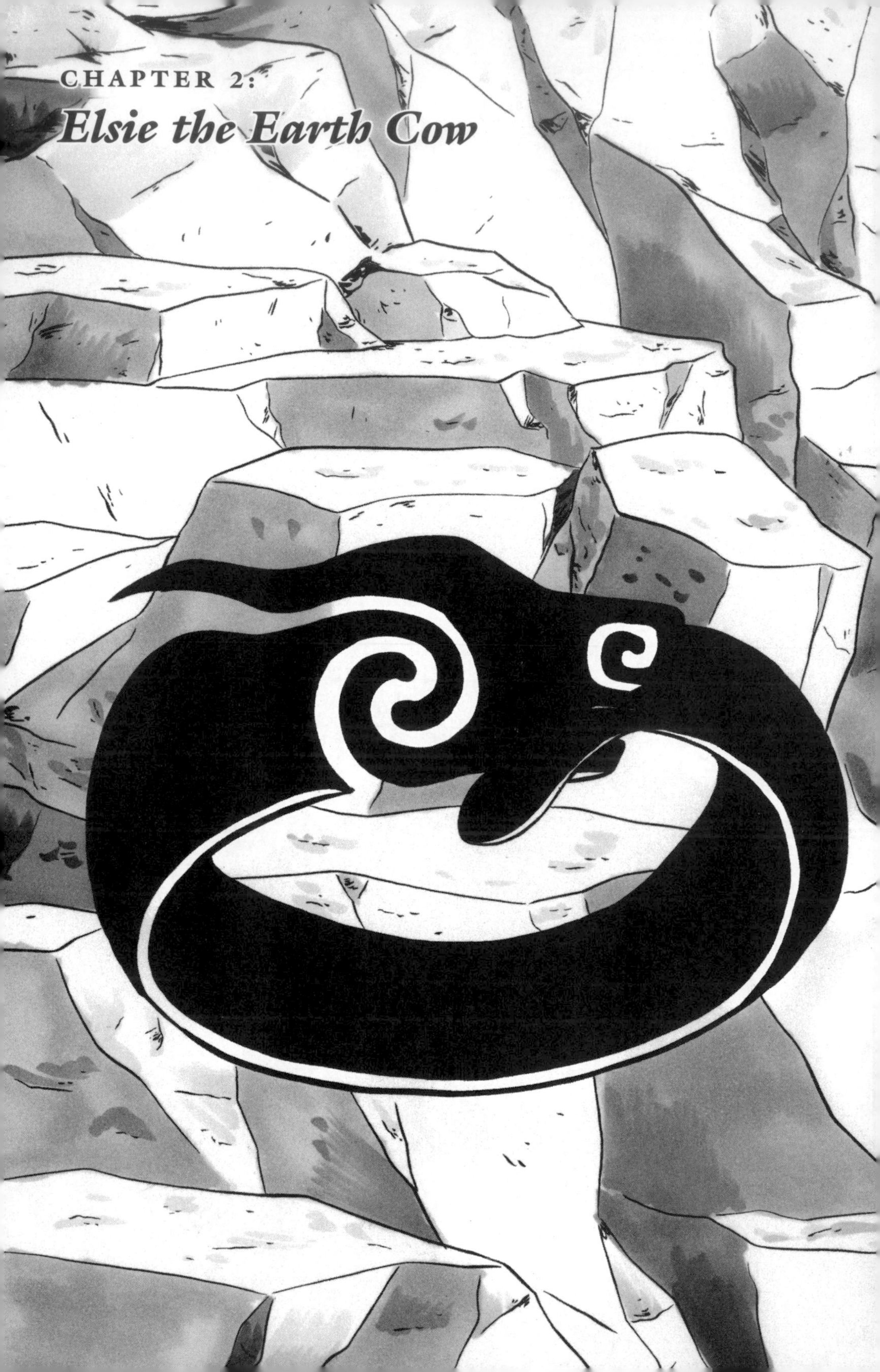

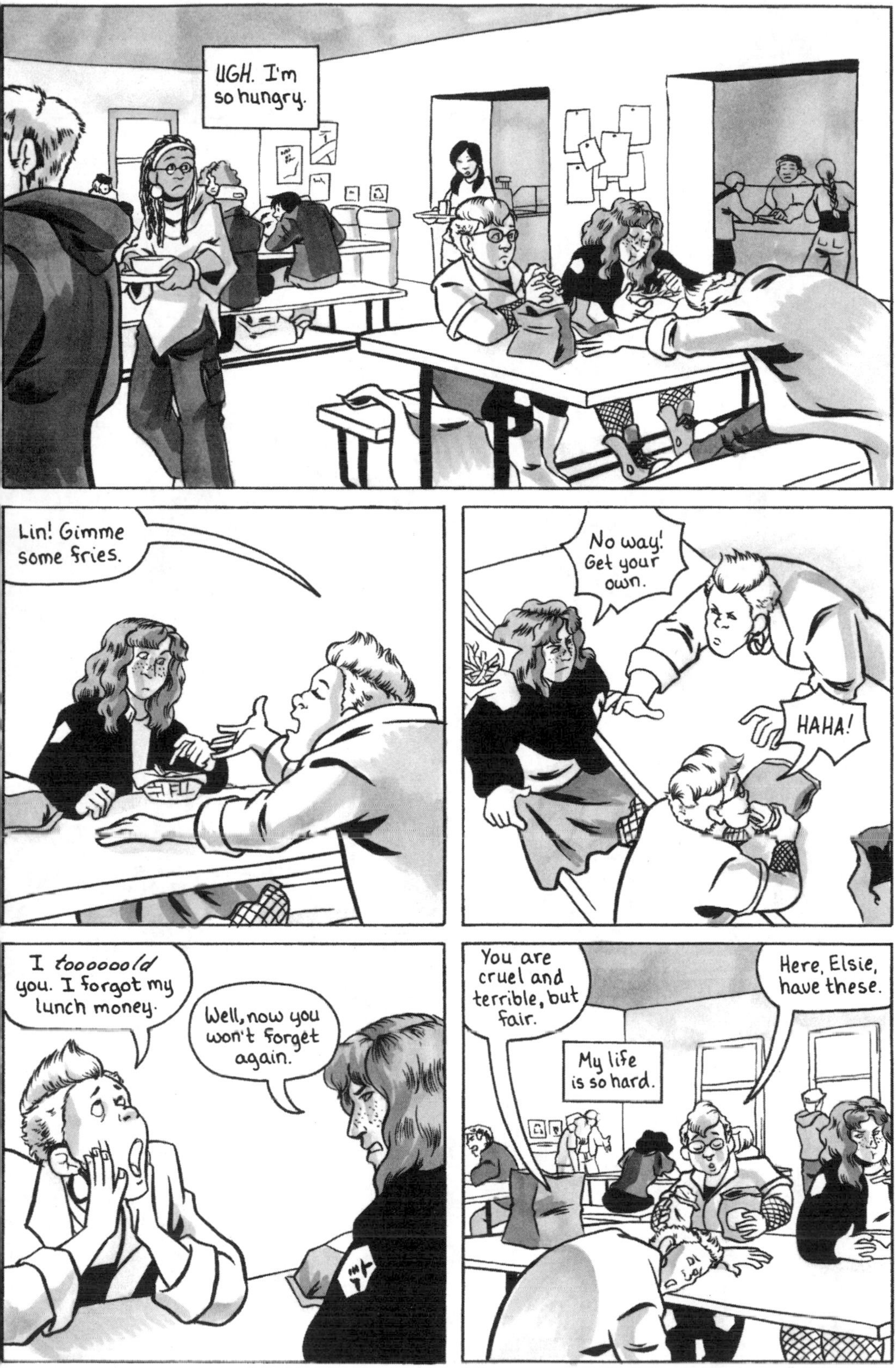
UGH. I'm so hungry.
Lin! Gimme some fries.
No way! Get your own.
HAHA!
I toooooold you. I forgot my lunch money.
Well, now you won't forget again.
You are cruel and terrible, but fair.
My life is so hard.
Here, Elsie, have these.

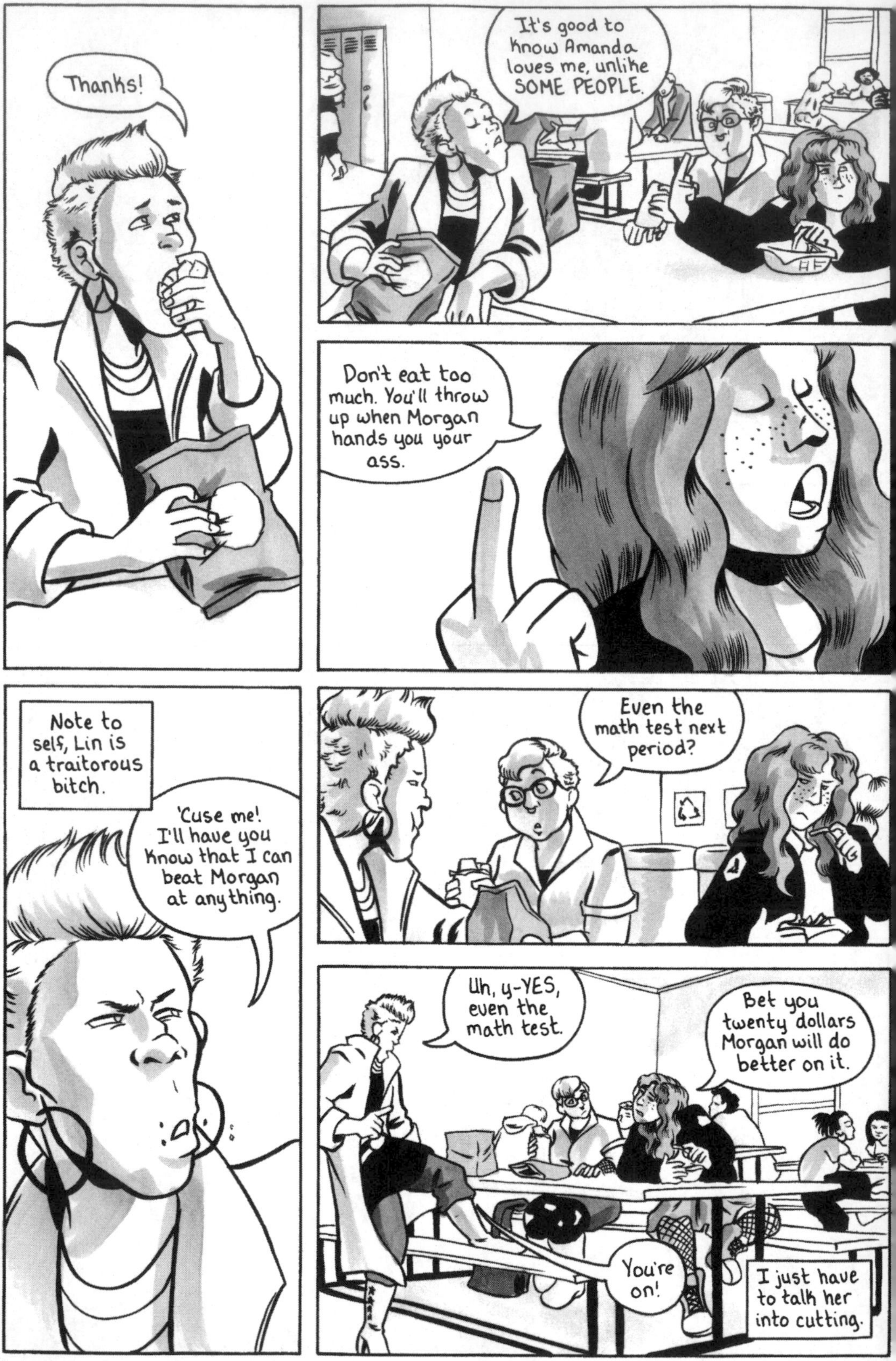

Thanks!
It's good to know Amanda loves me, unlike SOME PEOPLE.
Don't eat too much. You'll throw up when Morgan hands you your ass.
Note to self, Lin is a traitorous bitch.
'Cuse me! I'll have you know that I can beat Morgan at anything.
Even the math test next period?
Uh, y-YES, even the math test.
Bet you twenty dollars Morgan will do better on it.
You're on!
I just have to talk her into cutting.

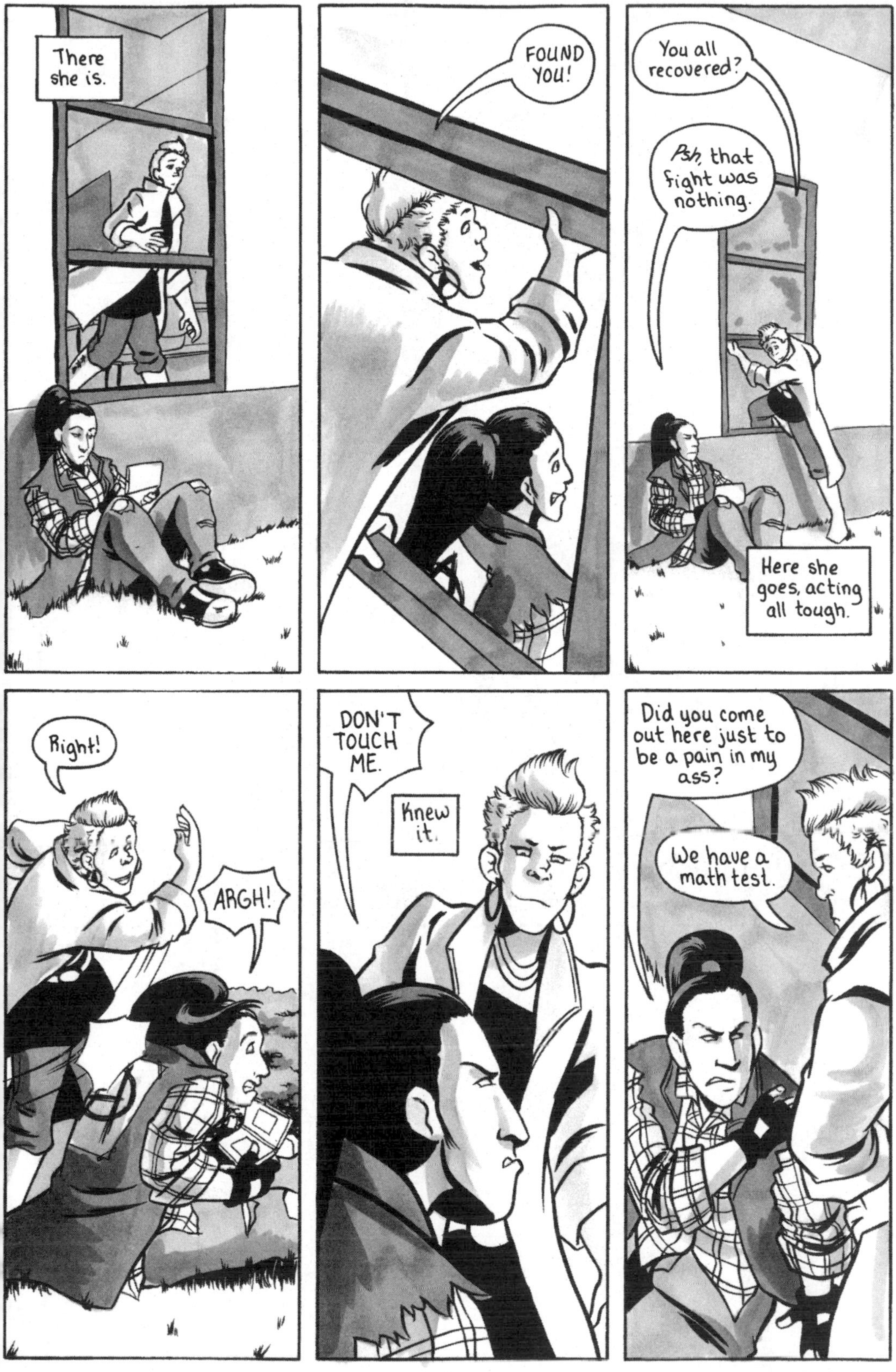
There she is.
FOUND YOU!
You all recovered?
Psh, that fight was nothing.
Here she goes, acting all tough.
Right!
ARGH!
DON'T TOUCH ME.
Knew it.
Did you come out here just to be a pain in my ass?
We have a math test.

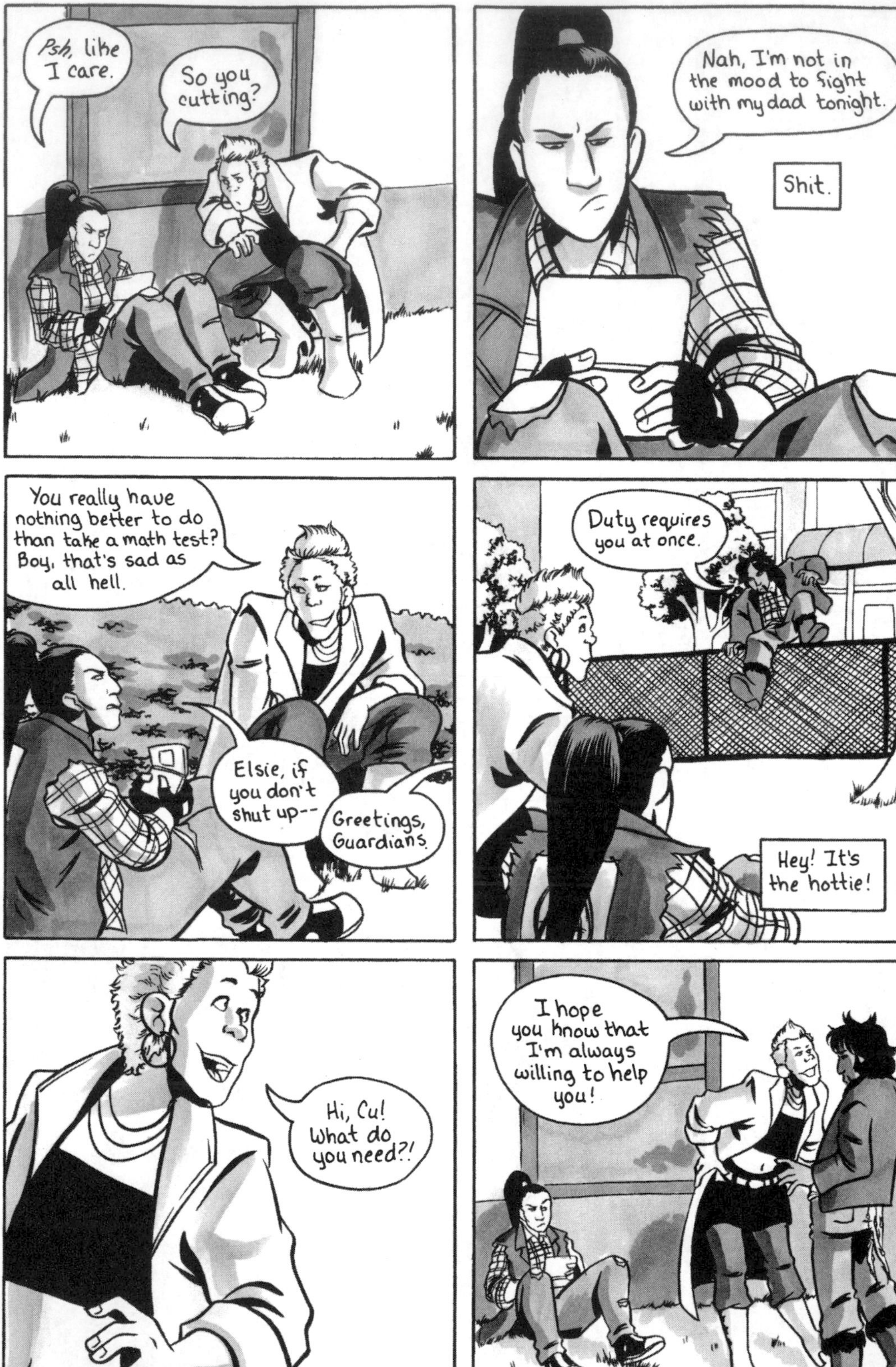
Psh, like I care.
So you cutting?
Nah, I'm not in the mood to fight with my dad tonight.
Shit.
You really have nothing better to do than take a math test? Boy, that's sad as all hell.
Elsie, if you don't shut up--
Greetings, Guardians.
Duty requires you at once.
Hey! It's the hottie!
Hi, Cu! What do you need?!
I hope you know that I'm always willing to help you!

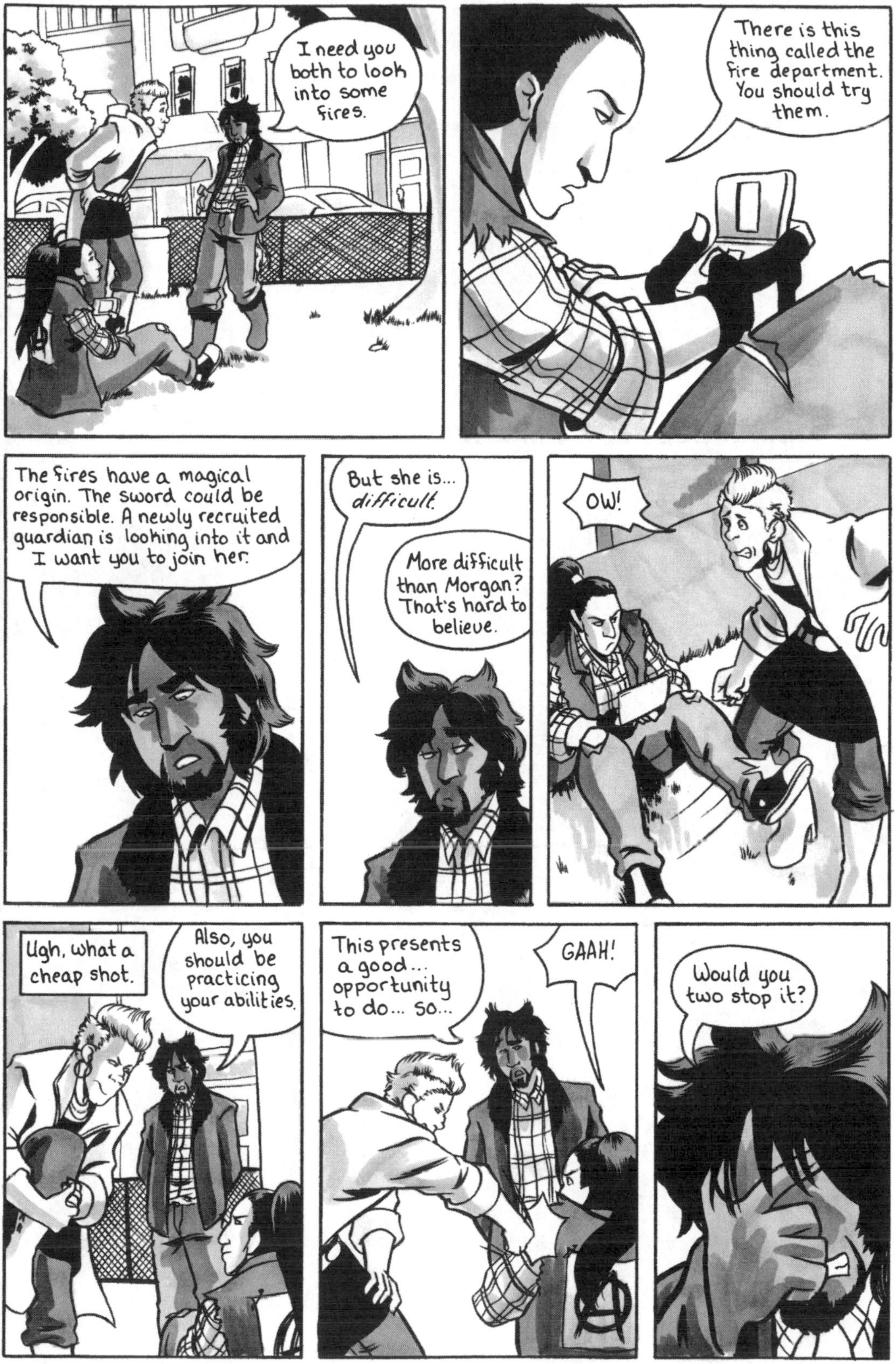

I need you both to look into some fires.
There is this thing called the fire department. You should try them.
The fires have a magical origin. The sword could be responsible. A newly recruited guardian is looking into it and I want you to join her.
But she is... *difficult.*
More difficult than Morgan? That's hard to believe.
OW!
Ugh, what a cheap shot.
Also, you should be practicing your abilities.
This presents a good... opportunity to do... so...
GAAH!
Would you two stop it?

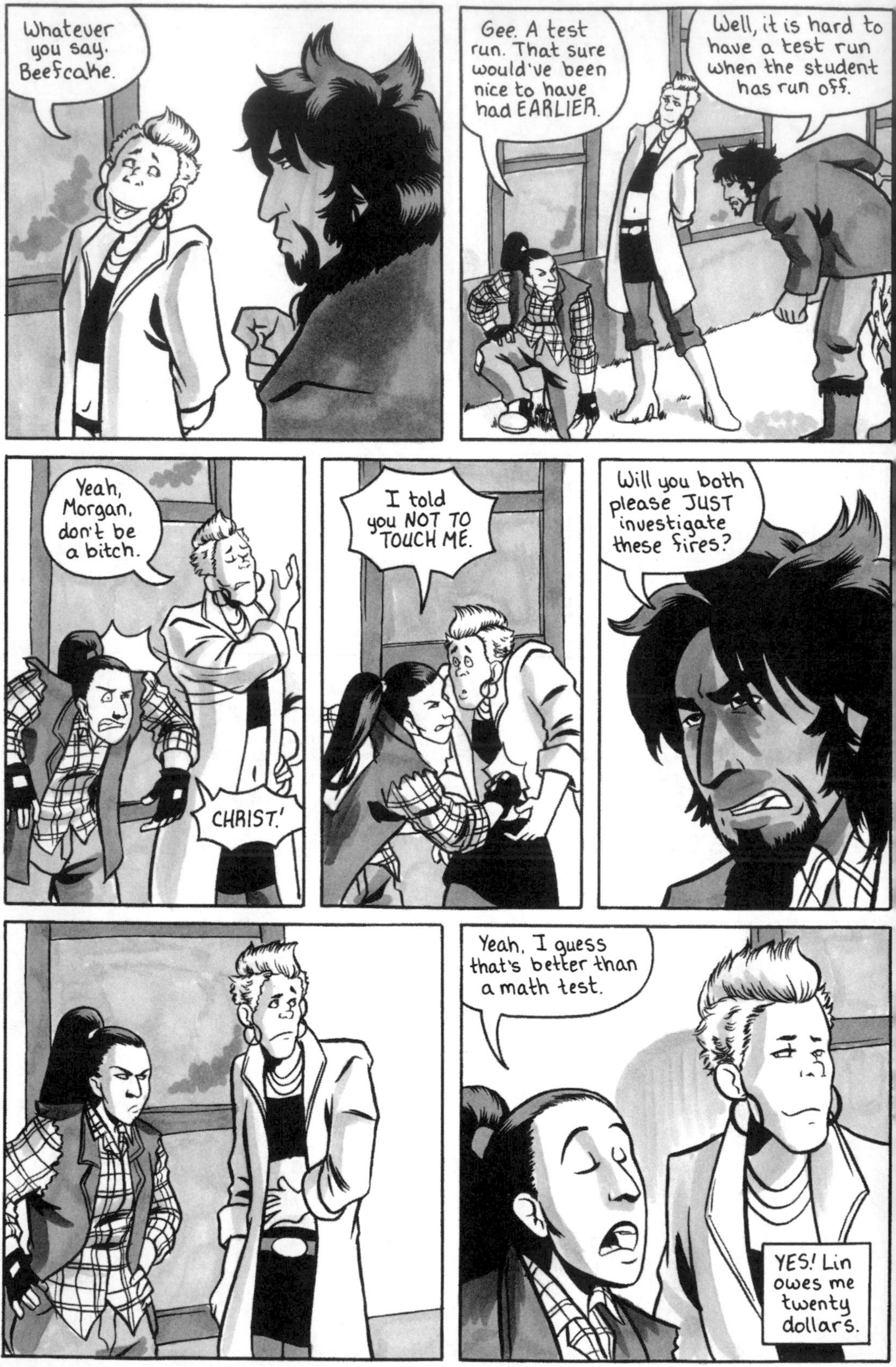
Whatever you say. Beefcake.
Gee. A test run. That sure would've been nice to have had EARLIER.
Well, it is hard to have a test run when the student has run off.
Yeah, Morgan, don't be a bitch.
CHRIST!
I told you NOT TO TOUCH ME.
Will you both please JUST investigate these fires?
Yeah, I guess that's better than a math test.
YES! Lin owes me twenty dollars.

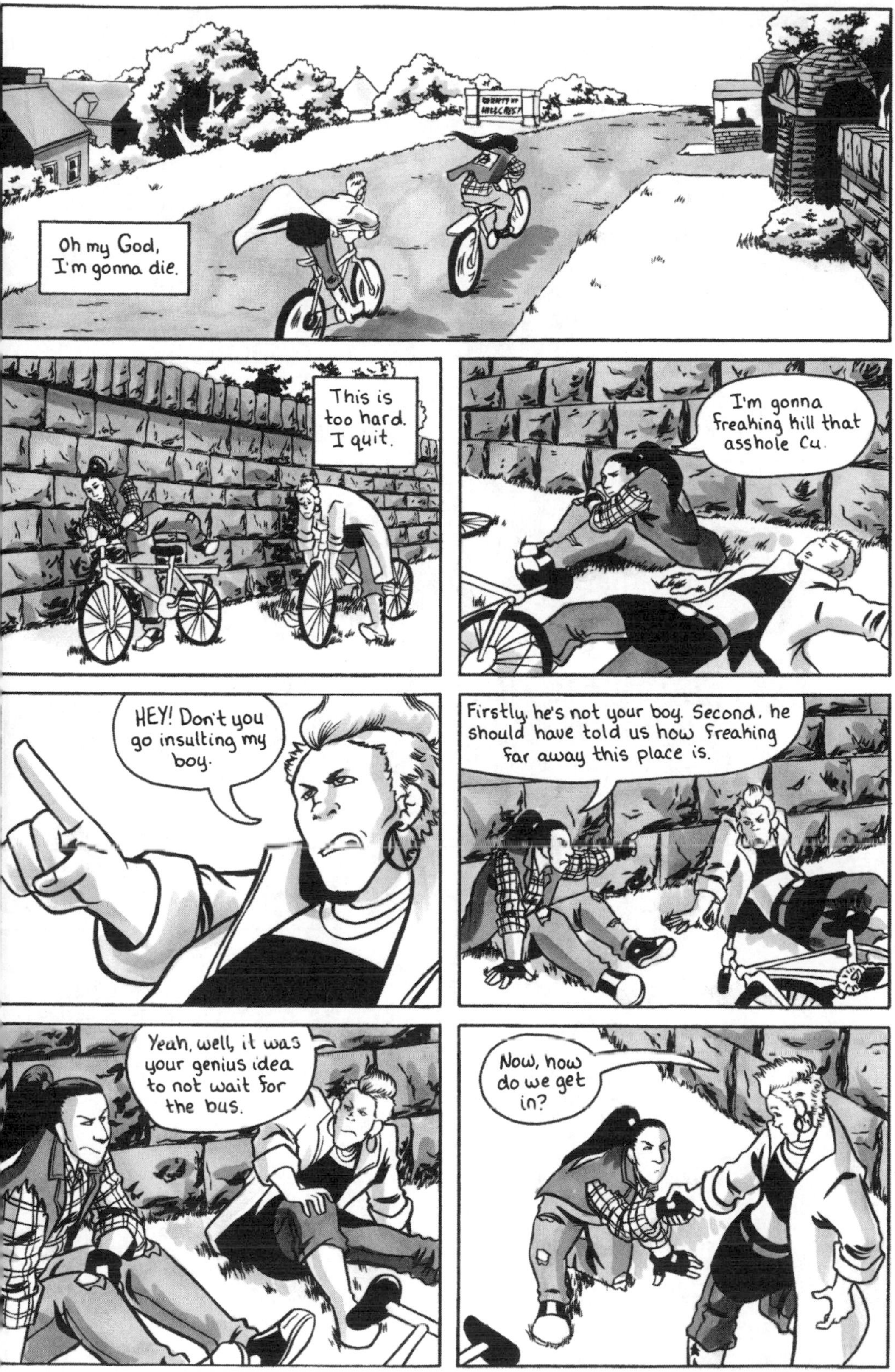
Oh my God, I'm gonna die.
This is too hard. I quit.
I'm gonna freaking kill that asshole Cu.
HEY! Don't you go insulting my boy.
Firstly, he's not your boy. Second, he should have told us how freaking far away this place is.
Yeah, well, it was your genius idea to not wait for the bus.
Now, how do we get in?

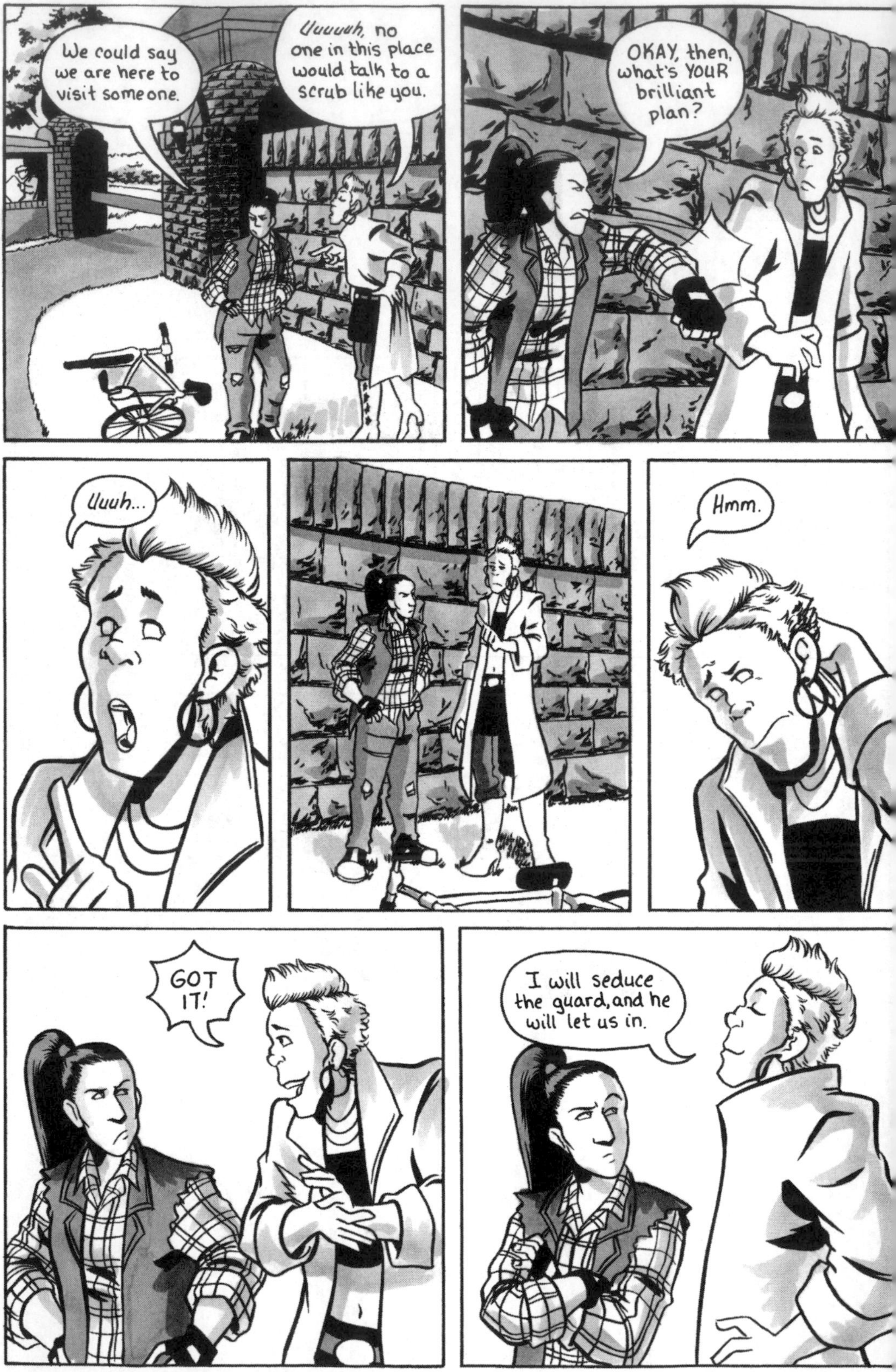
We could say we are here to visit someone.
Uuuuuh, no one in this place would talk to a scrub like you.
OKAY, then, what's YOUR brilliant plan?
Uuuh...
Hmm.
GOT IT!
I will seduce the guard, and he will let us in.

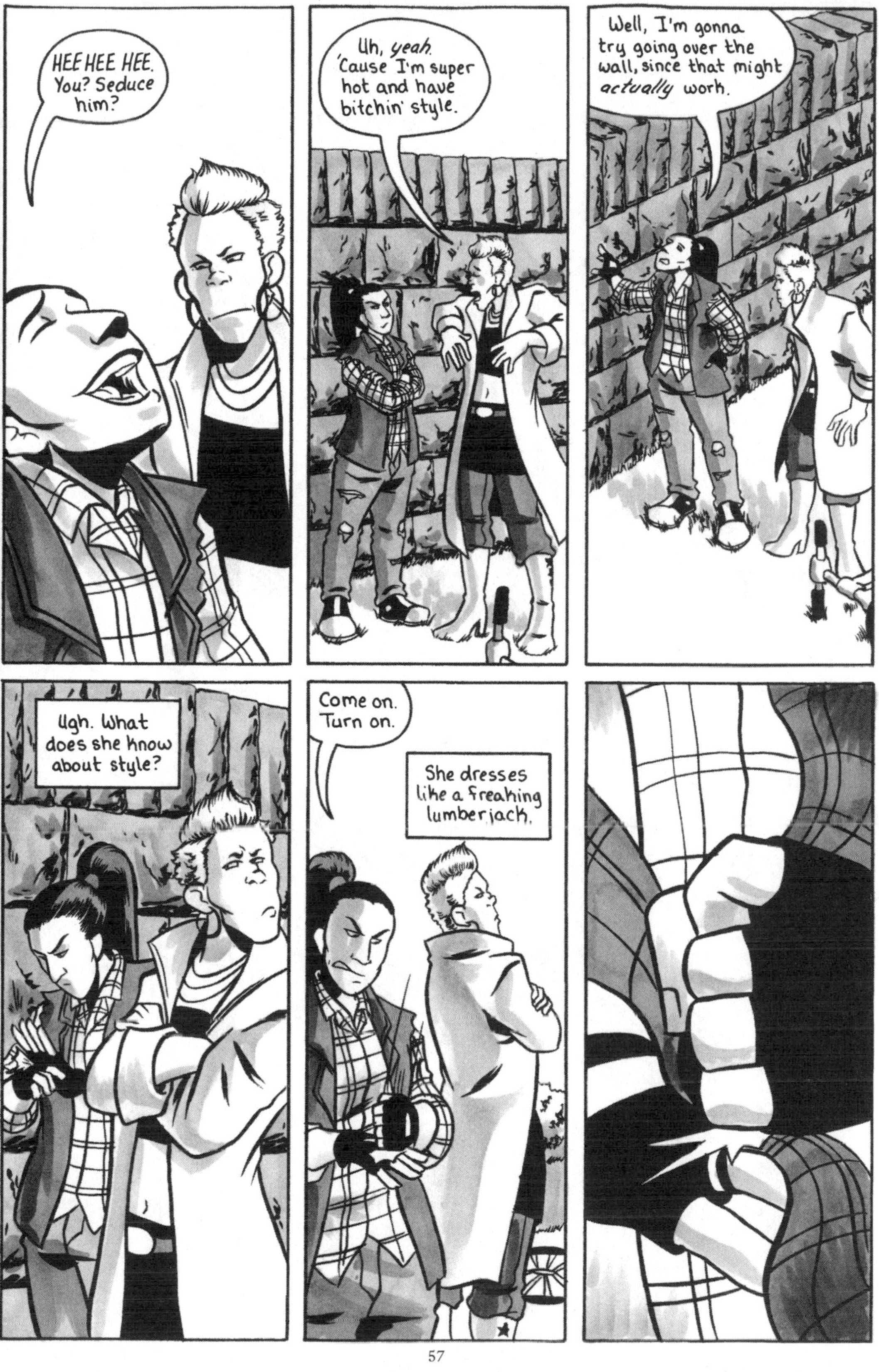
HEE HEE HEE. You? Seduce him?
Uh, yeah. 'Cause I'm super hot and have bitchin' style.
Well, I'm gonna try going over the wall, since that might actually work.
Ugh. What does she know about style?
Come on. Turn on.
She dresses like a freaking lumberjack.

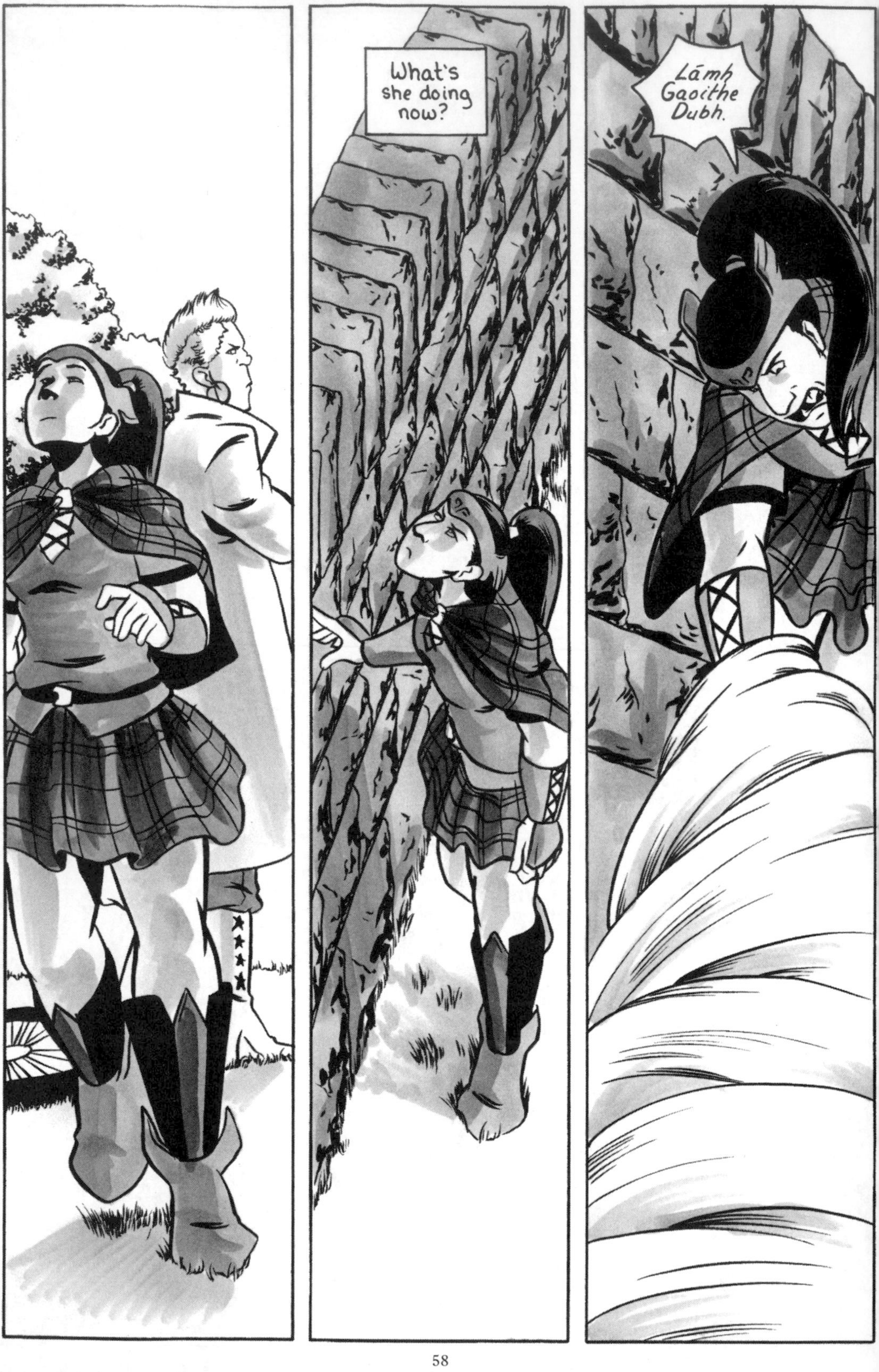
What's she doing now?
Lámh Gaoithe Dubh.

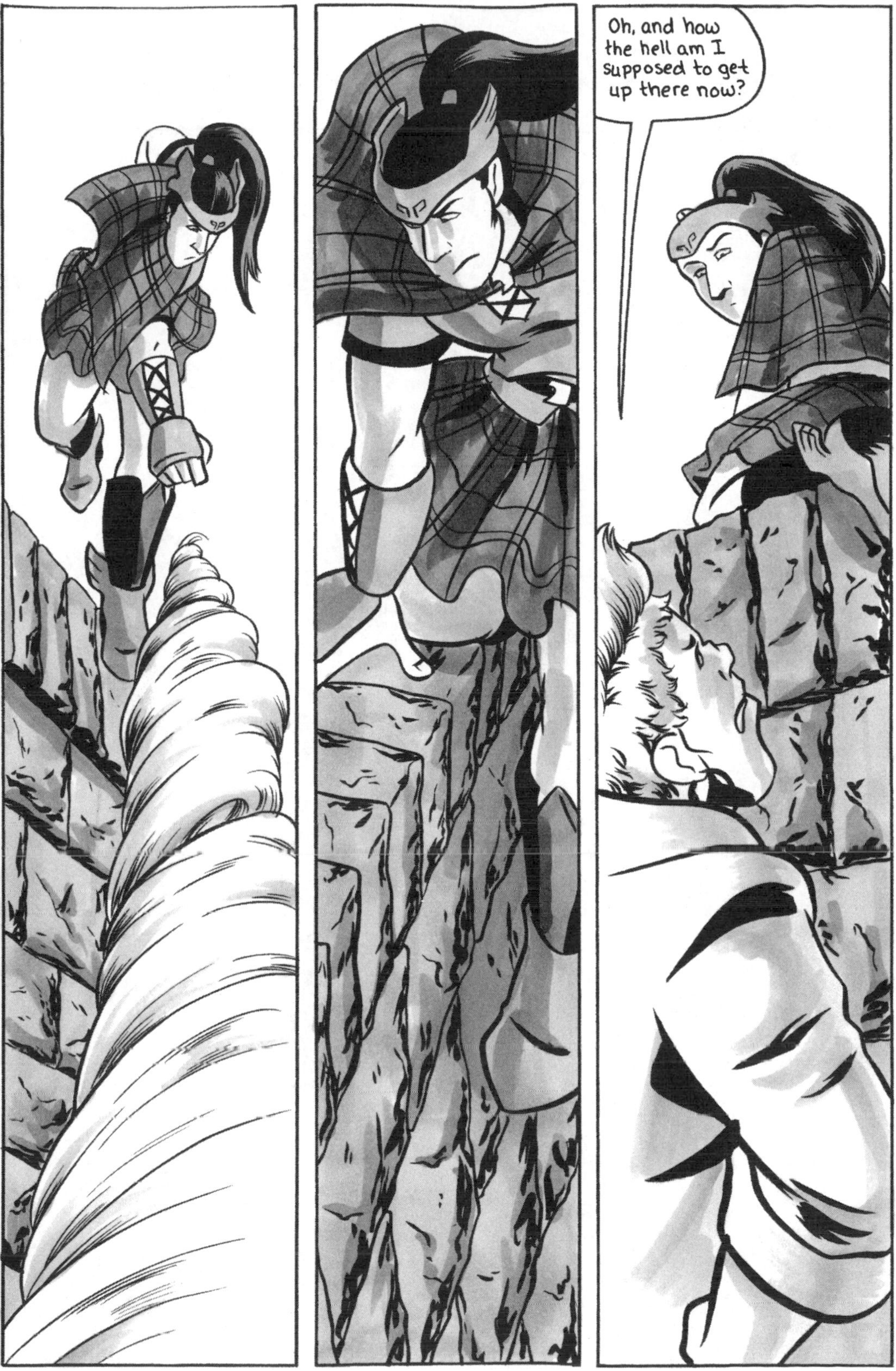
Oh, and how the hell am I supposed to get up there now?

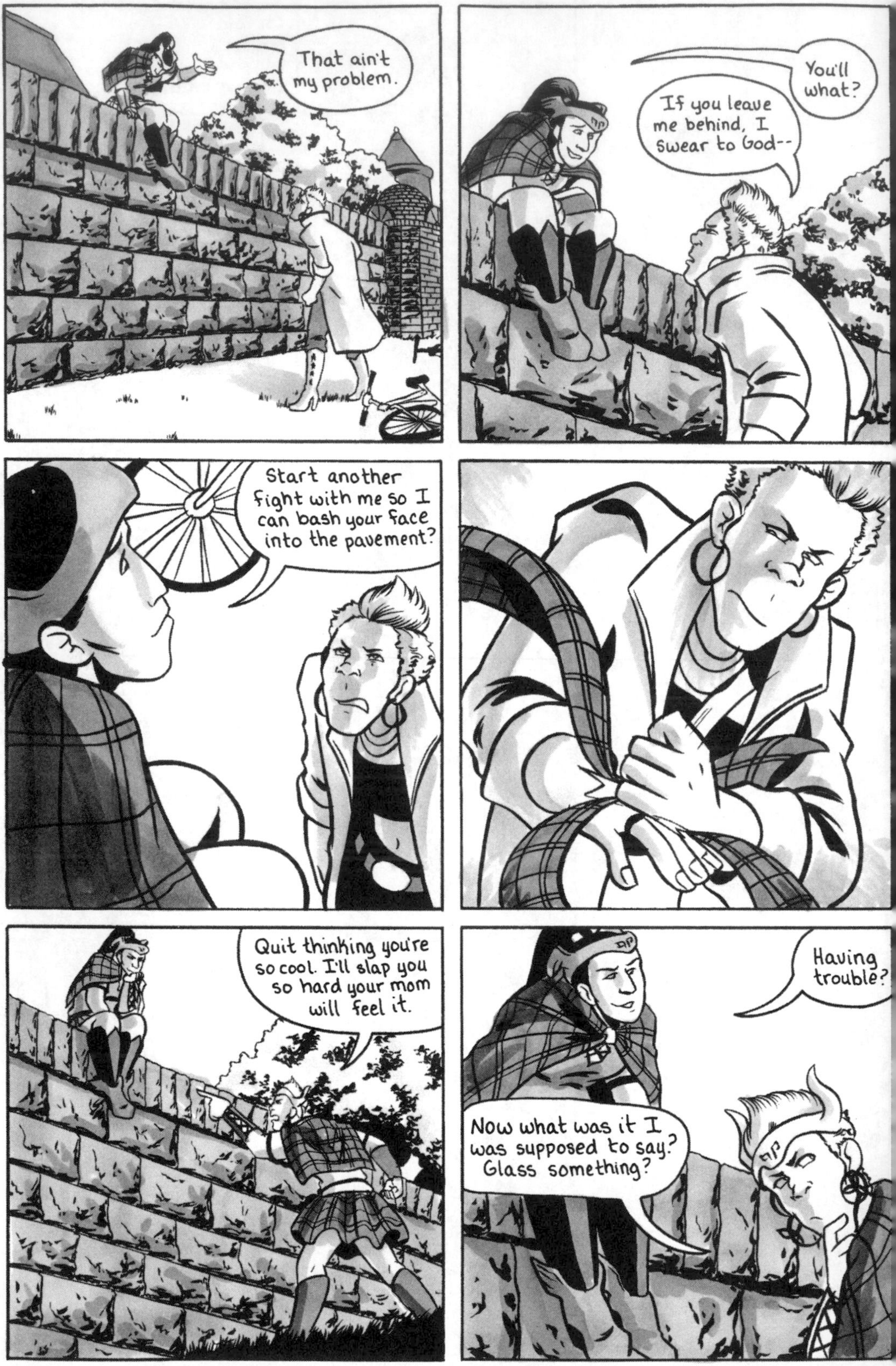
That ain't my problem.
If you leave me behind, I swear to God--
You'll what?
Start another fight with me so I can bash your face into the pavement?
Quit thinking you're so cool. I'll slap you so hard your mom will feel it.
Having trouble?
Now what was it I was supposed to say? Glass something?

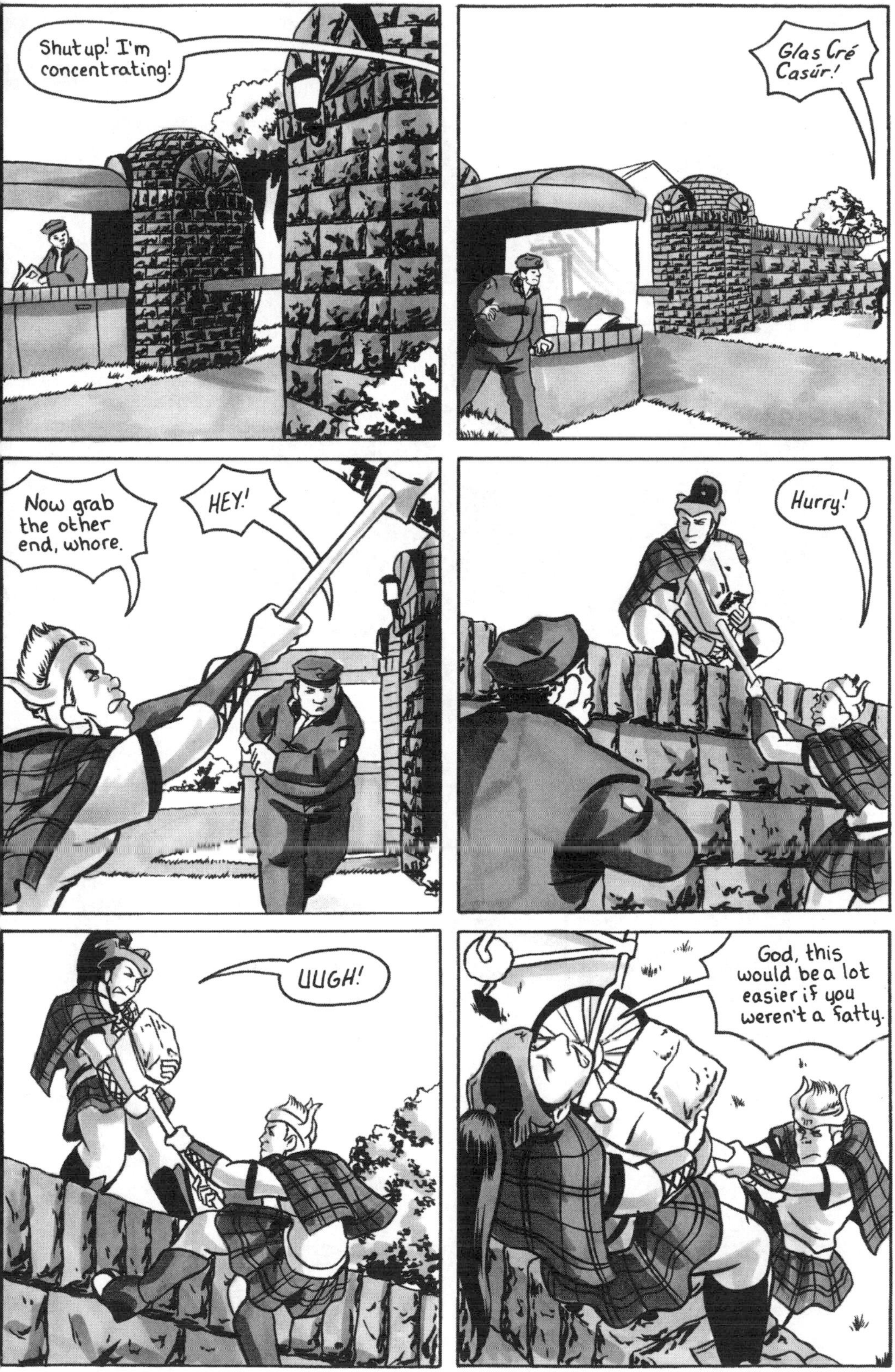
Shut up! I'm concentrating!
Glas Cré Casúr!
Now grab the other end, whore.
HEY!
Hurry!
UUGH!
God, this would be a lot easier if you weren't a fatty.

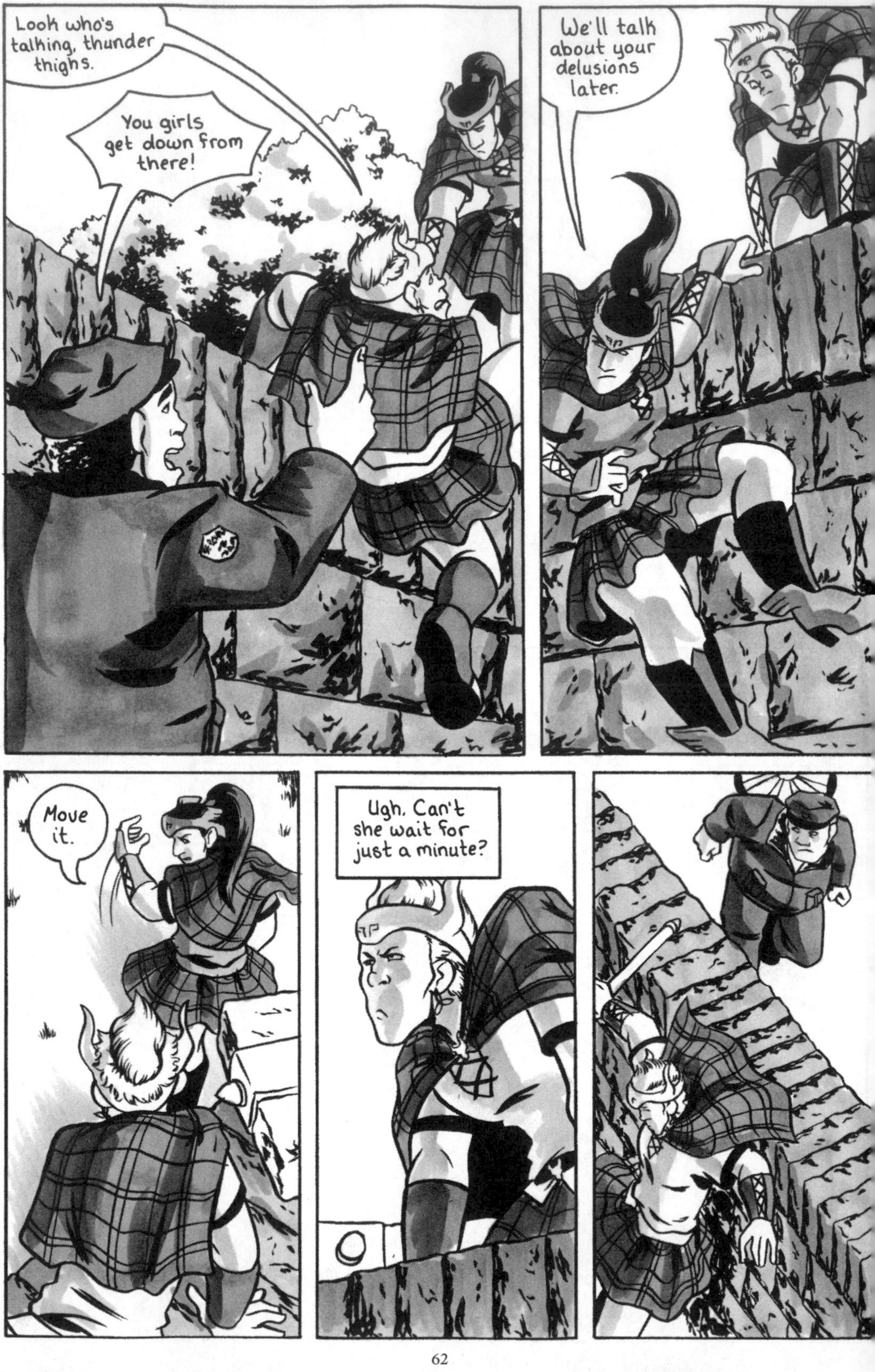

Look who's talking, thunder thighs.
You girls get down from there!
We'll talk about your delusions later.
Move it.
Ugh. Can't she wait for just a minute?

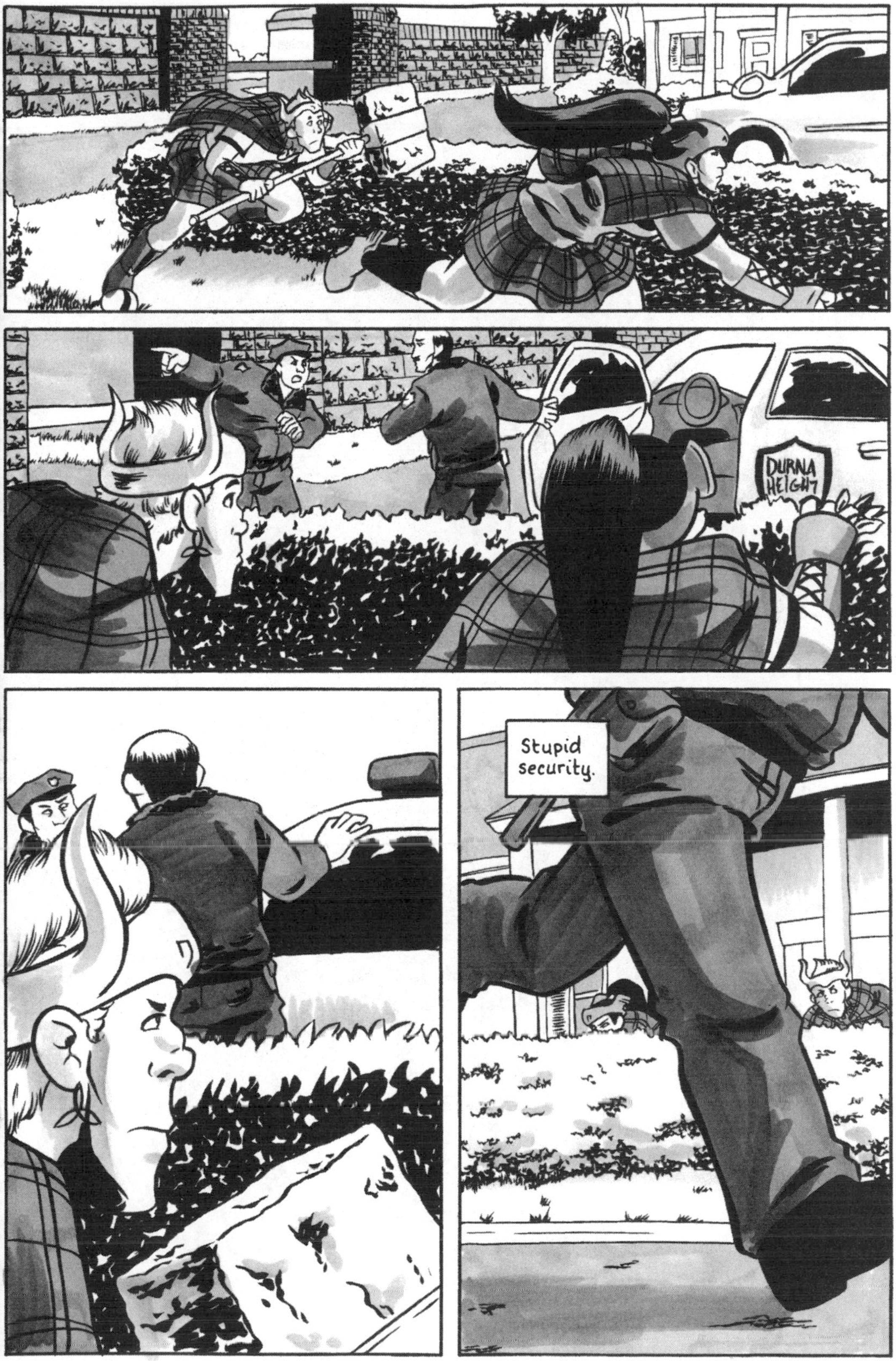
DURNA HEIGHTS
Stupid security.

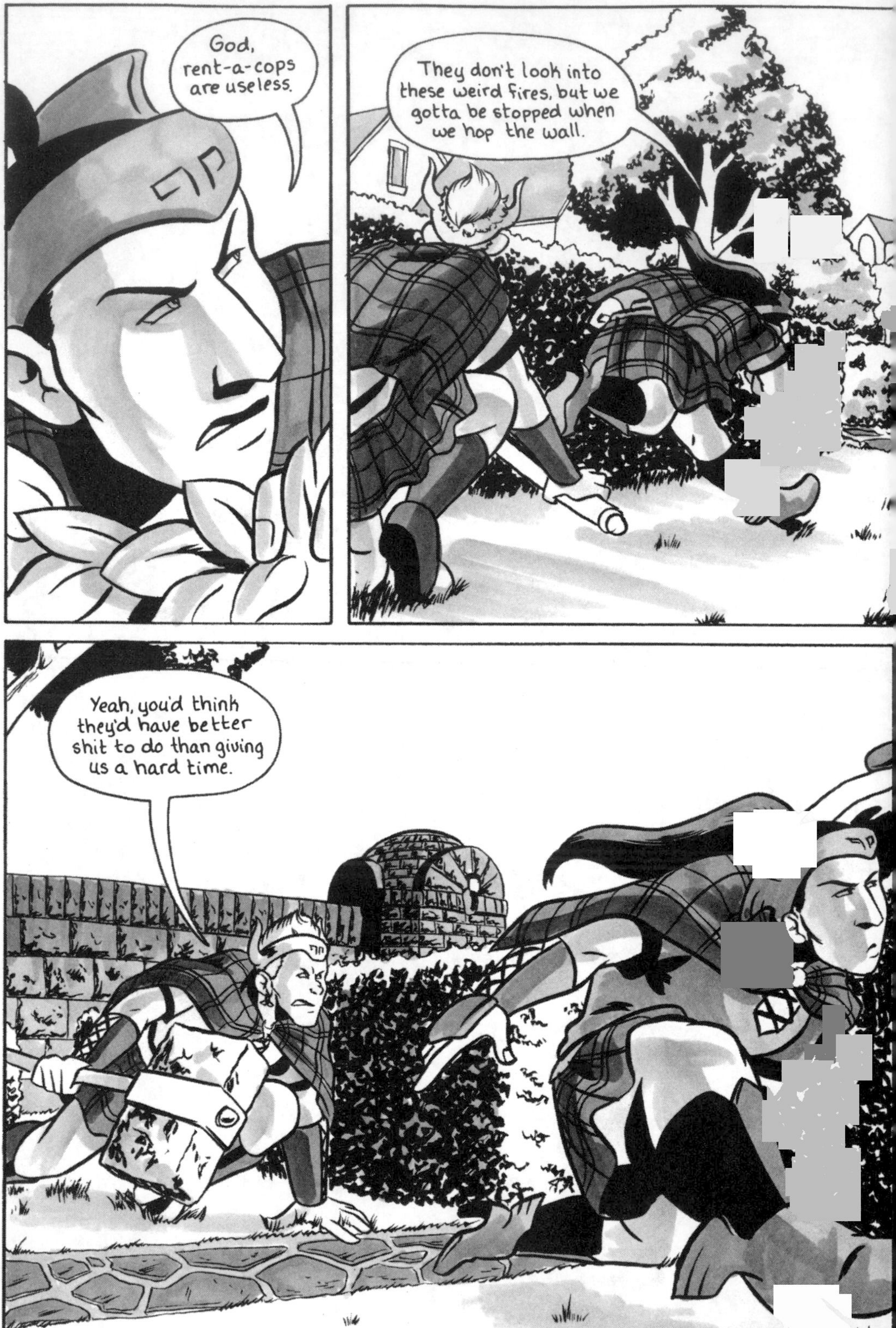
God, rent-a-cops are useless.
They don't look into these weird fires, but we gotta be stopped when we hop the wall.
Yeah, you'd think they'd have better shit to do than giving us a hard time.

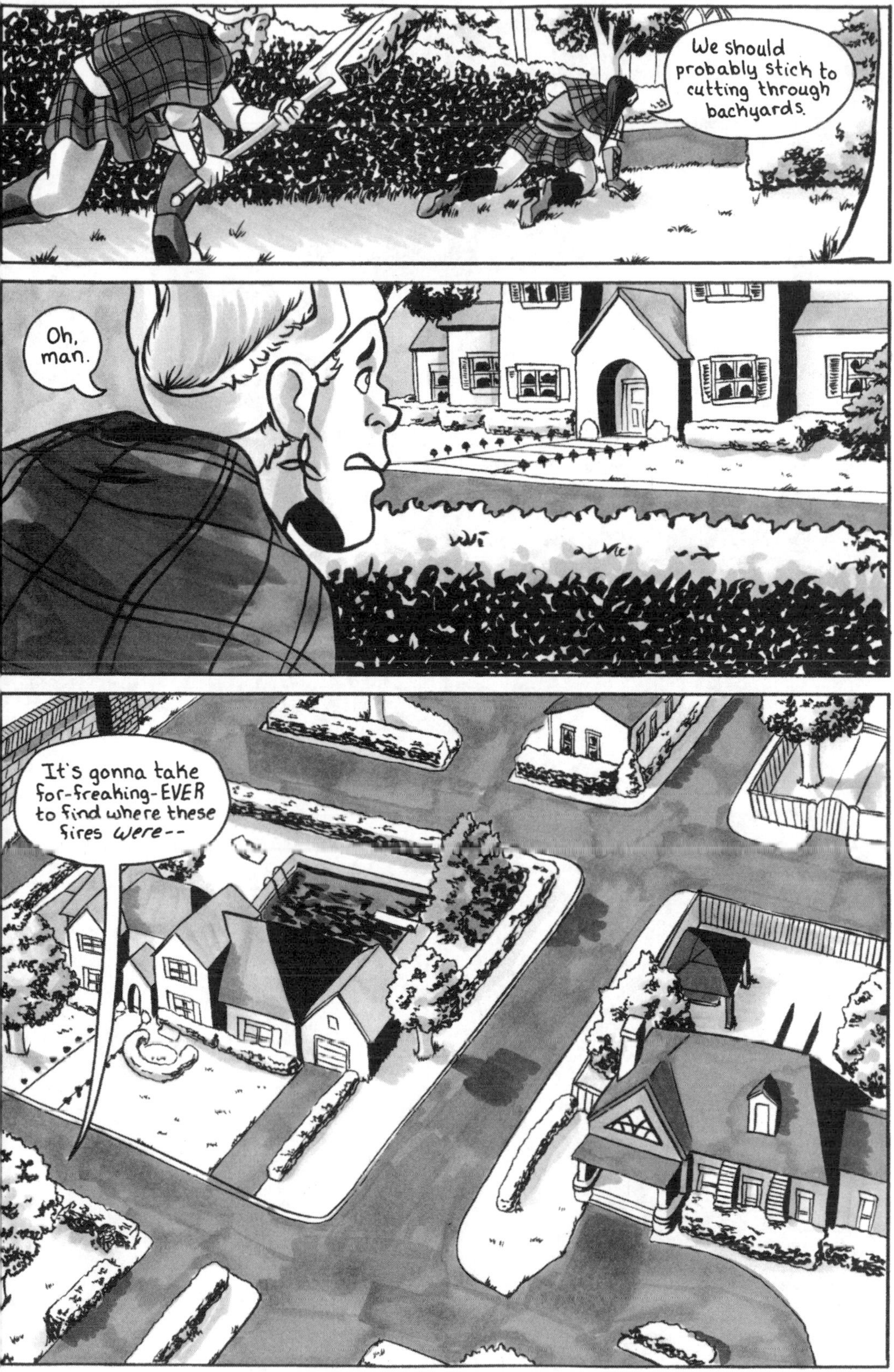
We should probably stick to cutting through backyards.
Oh, man.
It's gonna take for-freaking-EVER to find where these fires were--

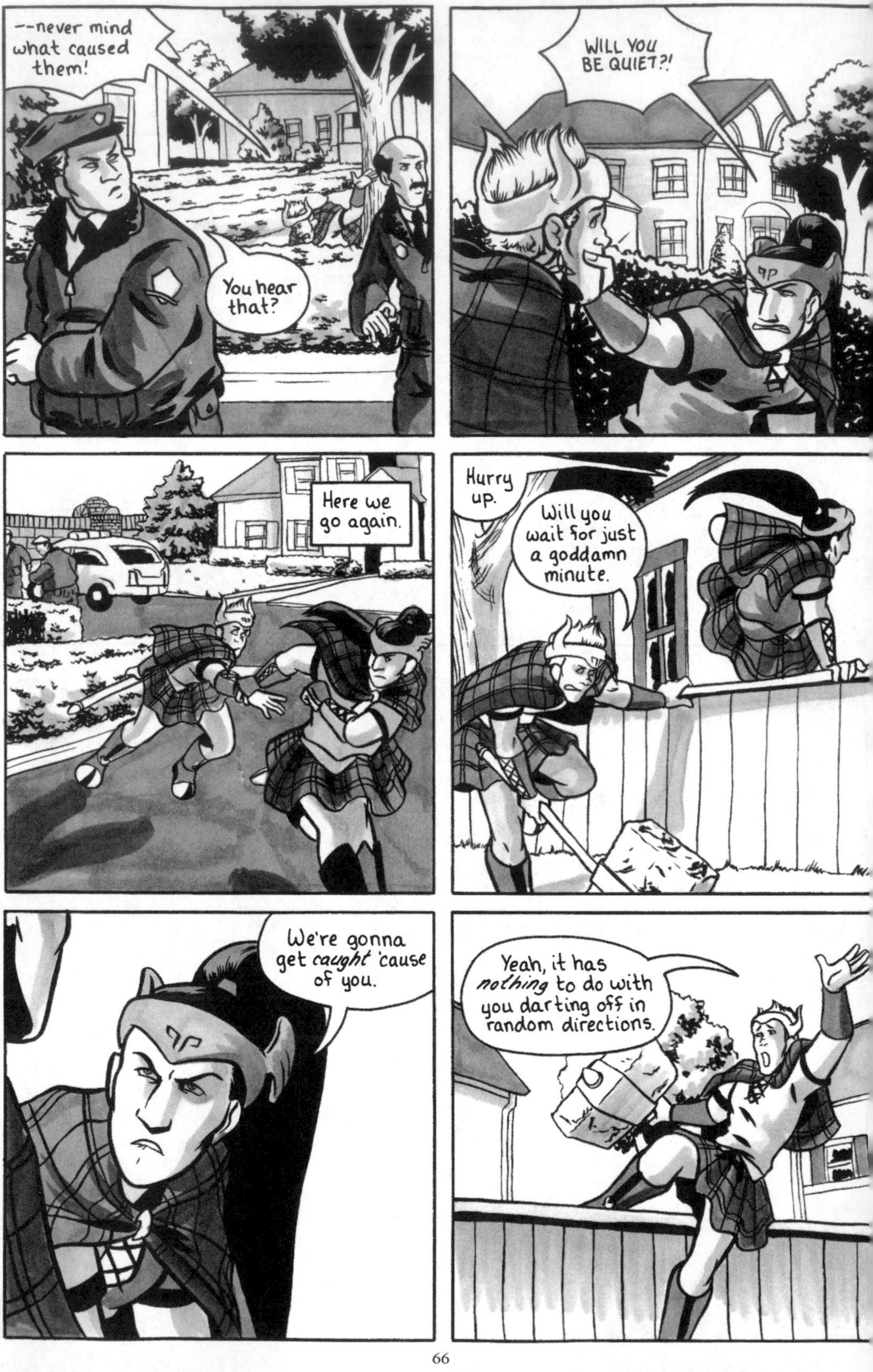
--never mind what caused them!
You hear that?
WILL YOU BE QUIET?!
Here we go again.
Hurry up.
Will you wait for just a goddamn minute.
We're gonna get *caught* 'cause of you.
Yeah, it has *nothing* to do with you darting off in random directions.

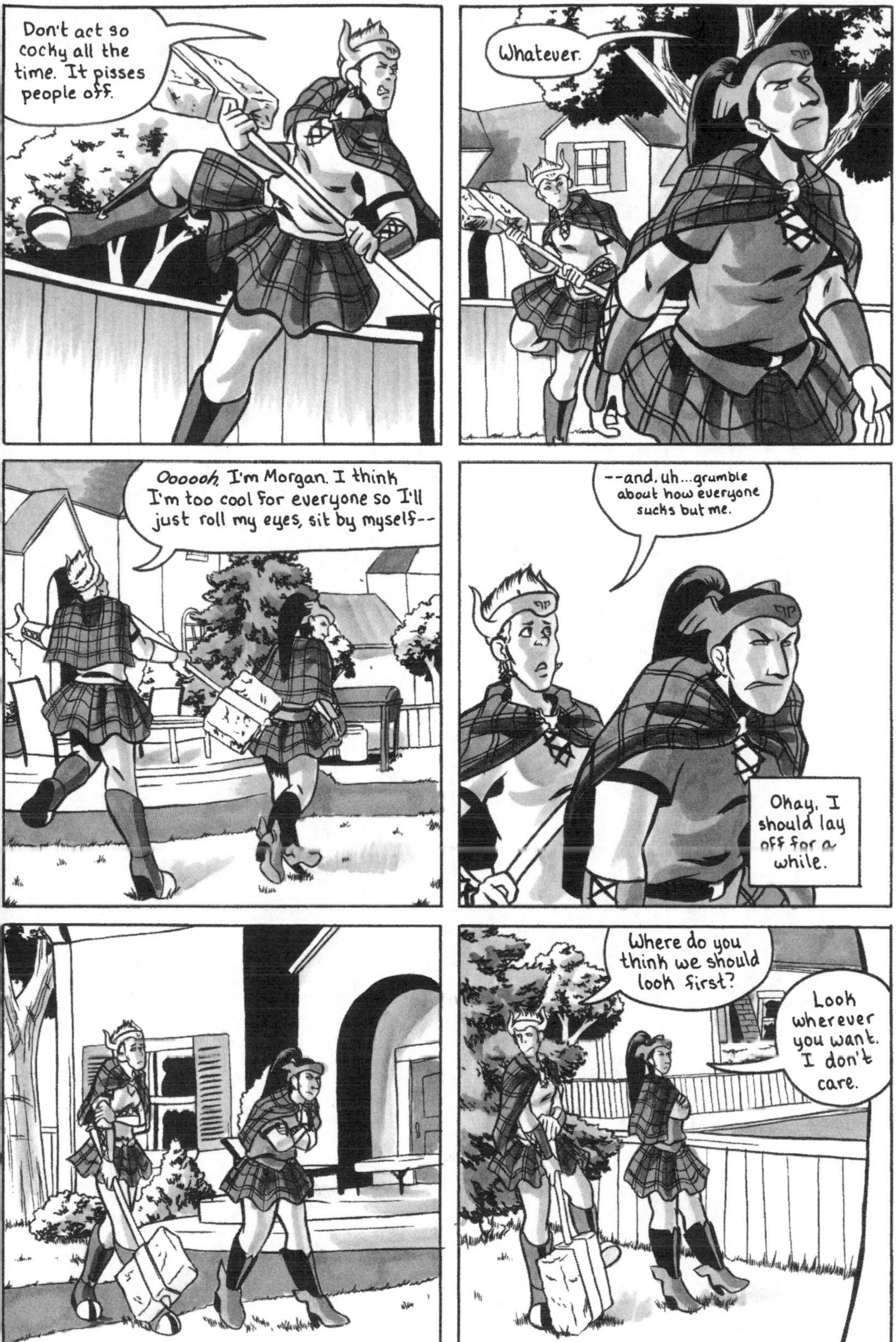
Don't act so cocky all the time. It pisses people off.
Whatever.
Oooooh, I'm Morgan. I think I'm too cool for everyone so I'll just roll my eyes, sit by myself--
--and, uh...grumble about how everyone sucks but me.
Okay, I should lay off for a while.
Where do you think we should look first?
Look wherever you want. I don't care.

Hold this. I'ma get a better look from that tree. Maybe I'll see smoke or something fiery.

Christ, this thing is heavy.

Not when you're a buff babe like me!

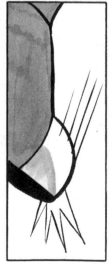

GAH!

HAHA!

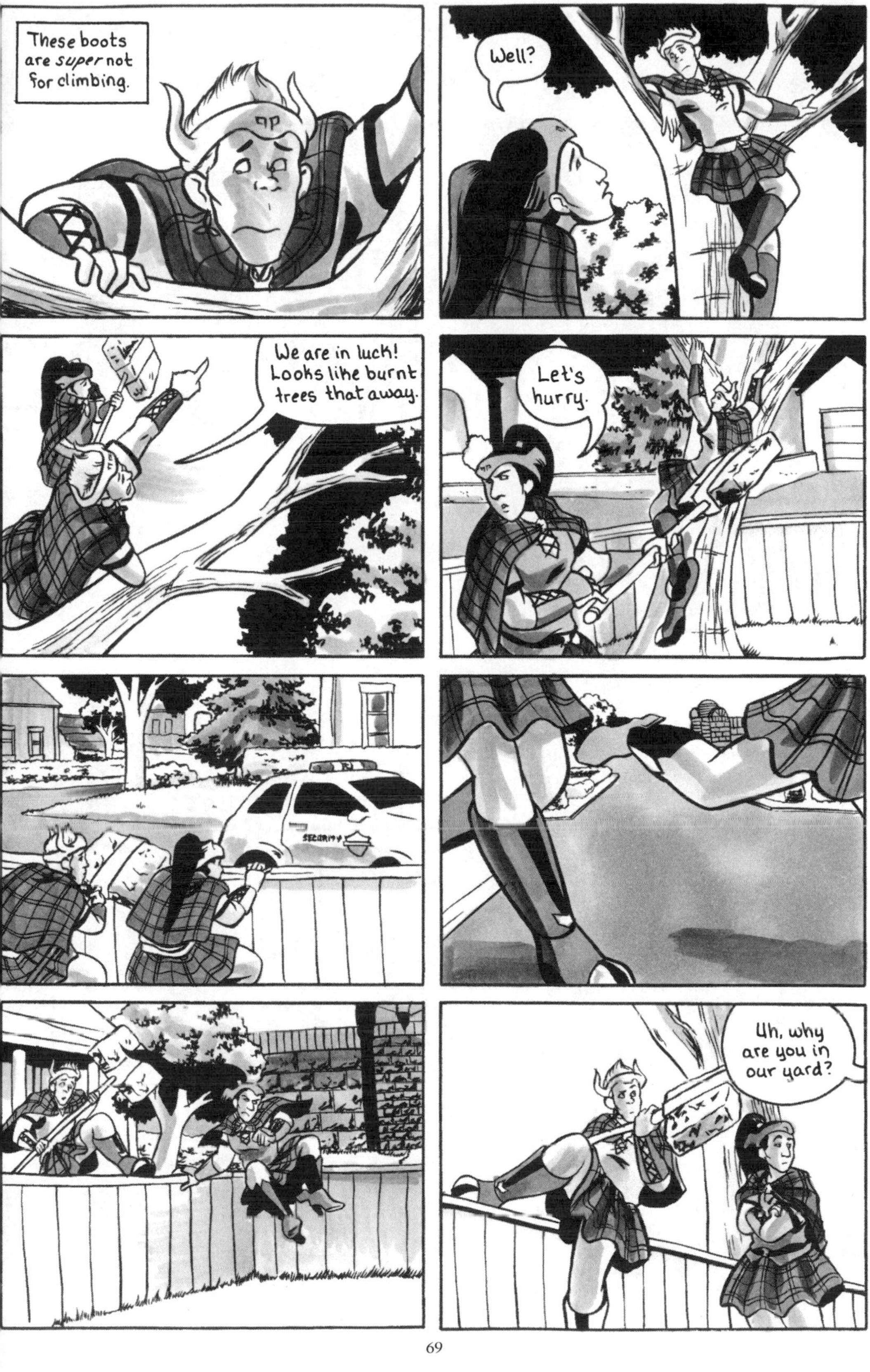
These boots are *super* not for climbing.
Well?
We are in luck! Looks like burnt trees that away.
Let's hurry.
SECURITY
Uh, why are you in our yard?

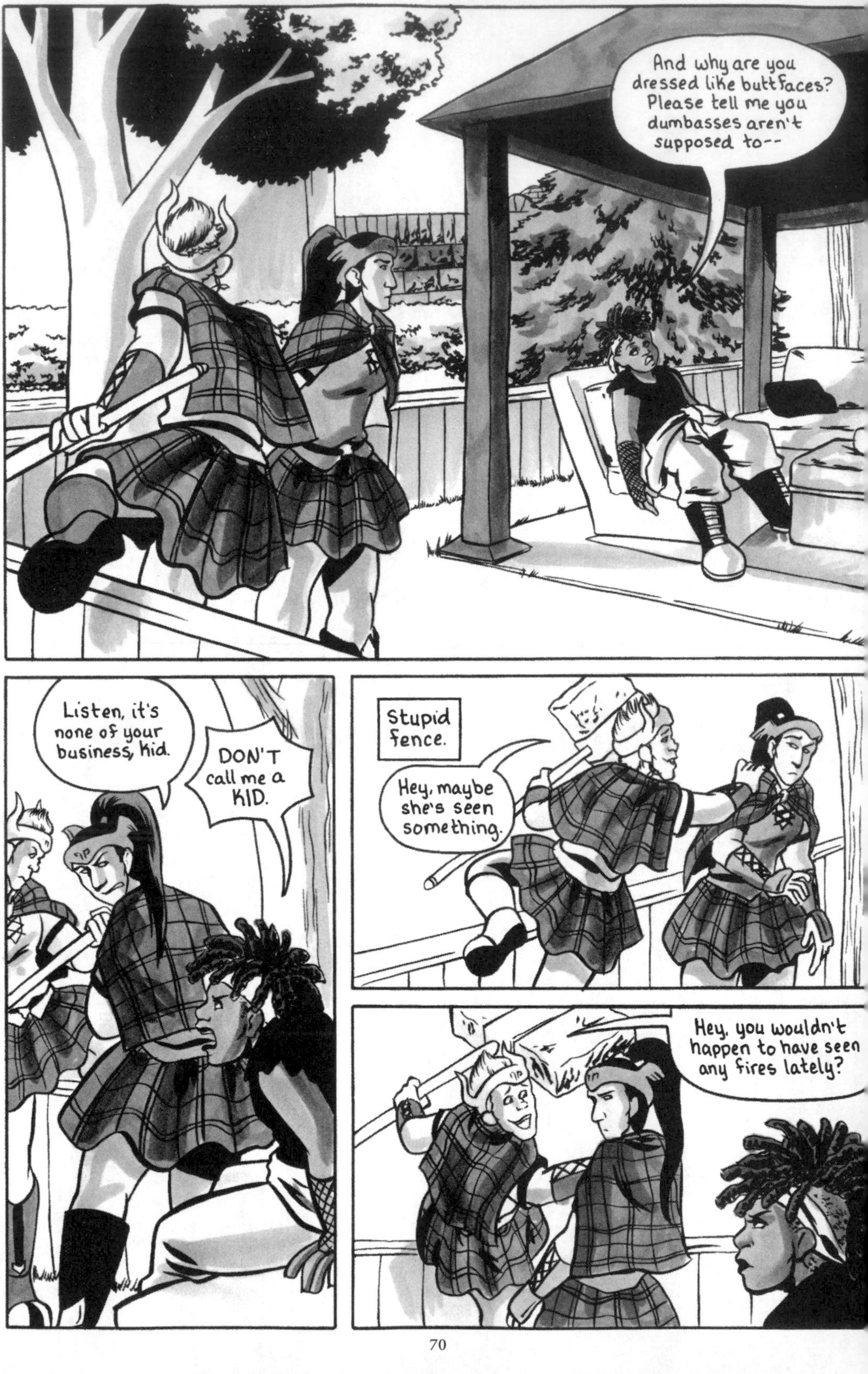
And why are you dressed like buttfaces? Please tell me you dumbasses aren't supposed to--
Listen, it's none of your business, kid.
DON'T call me a KID.
Stupid fence.
Hey, maybe she's seen something.
Hey, you wouldn't happen to have seen any fires lately?

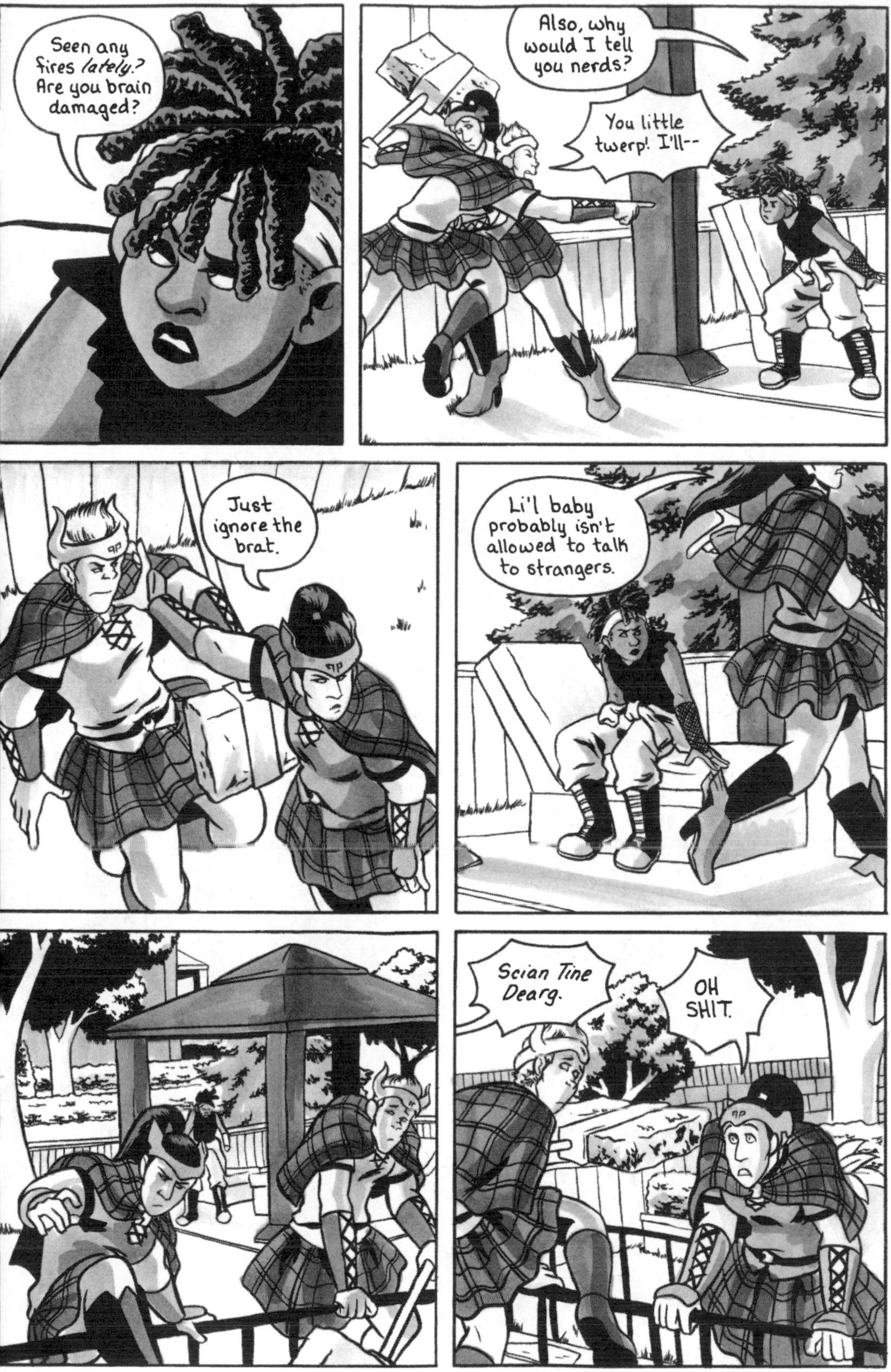
Seen any fires *lately?* Are you brain damaged?
Also, why would I tell you nerds?
You little twerp! I'll--
Just ignore the brat.
Li'l baby probably isn't allowed to talk to strangers.
Scian Tine Dearg.
OH SHIT.

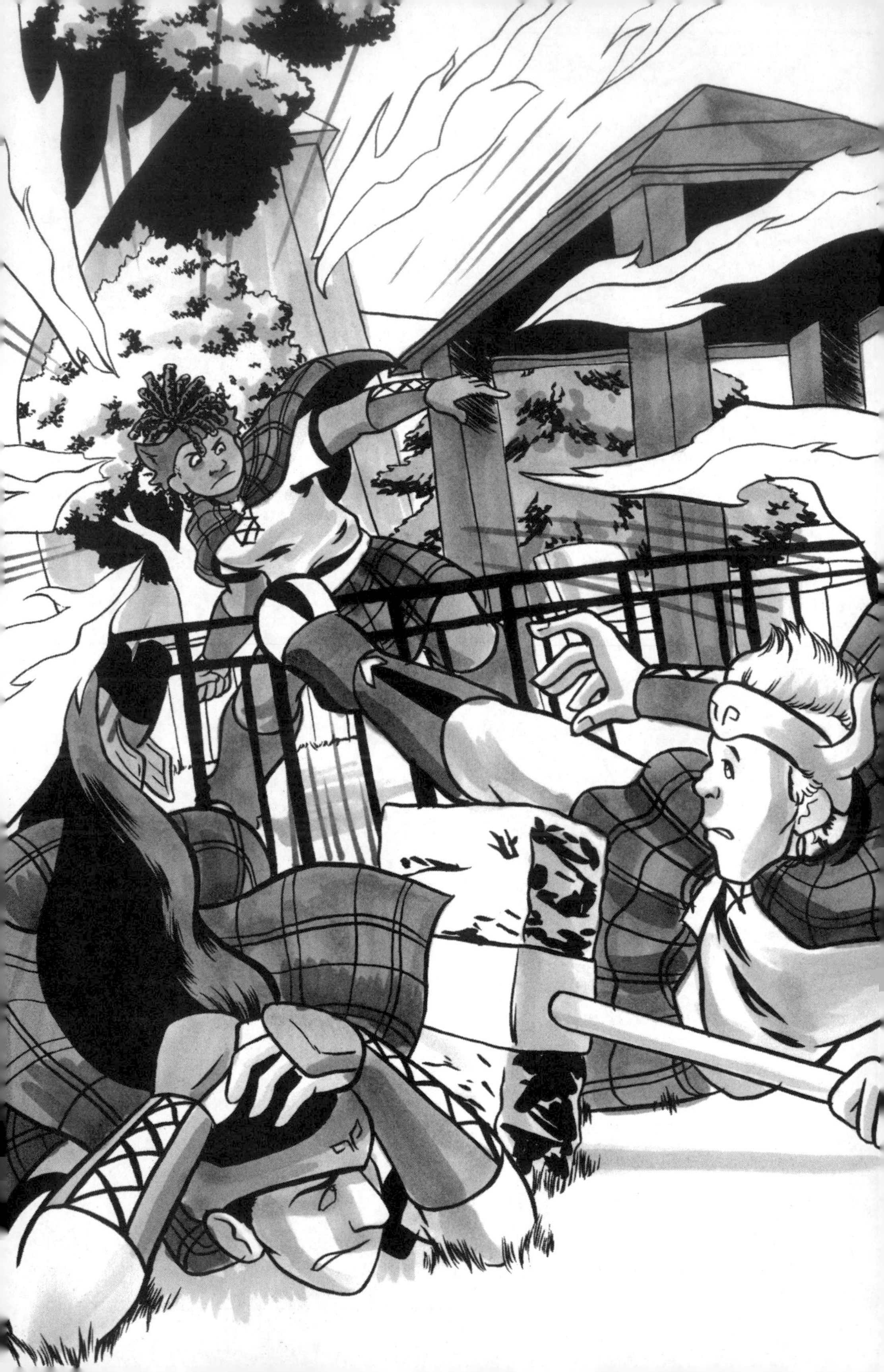

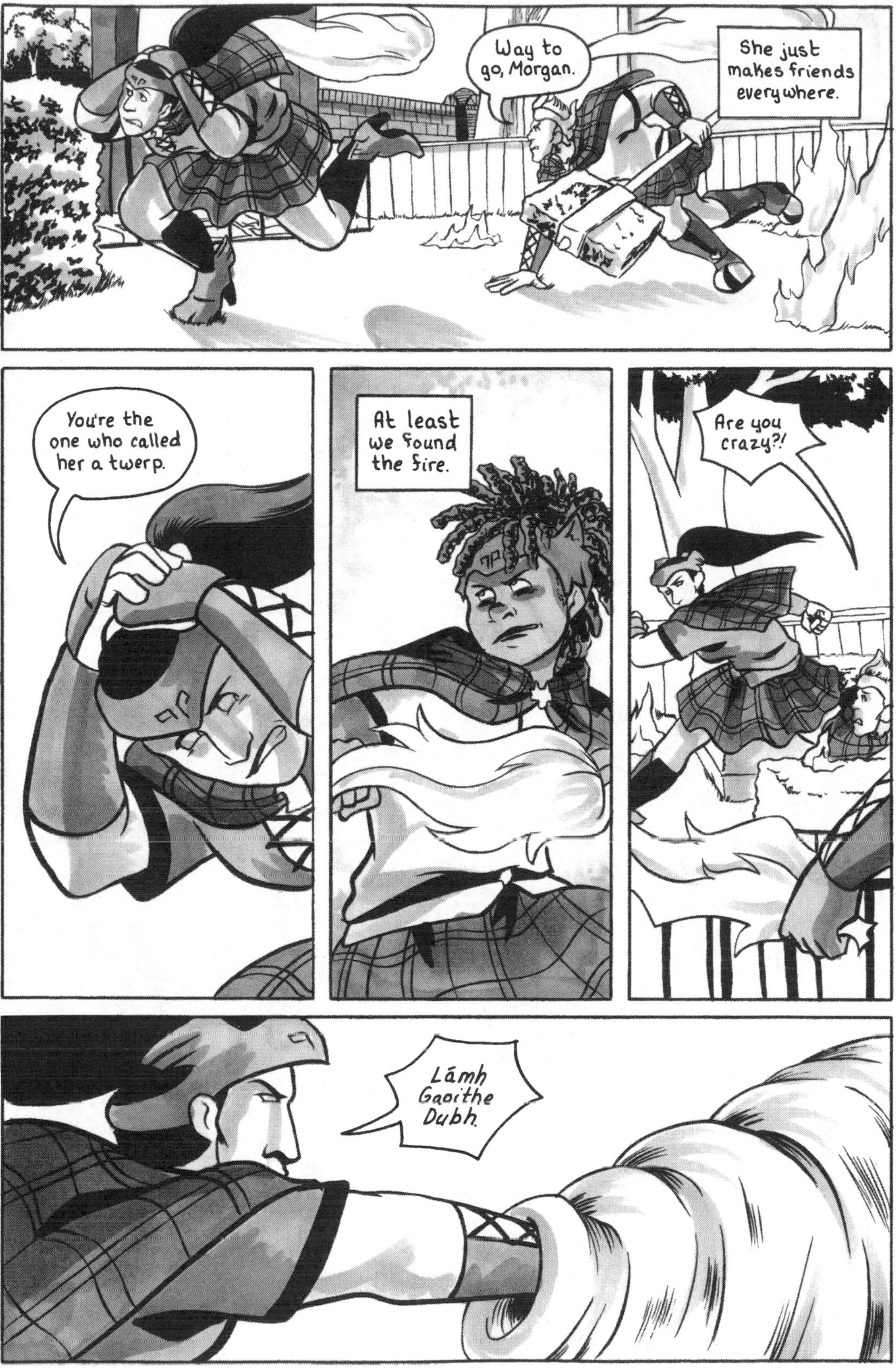
Way to go, Morgan.
She just makes friends everywhere.
You're the one who called her a twerp.
At least we found the fire.
Are you crazy?!
Lámh Gaoithe Dubh.

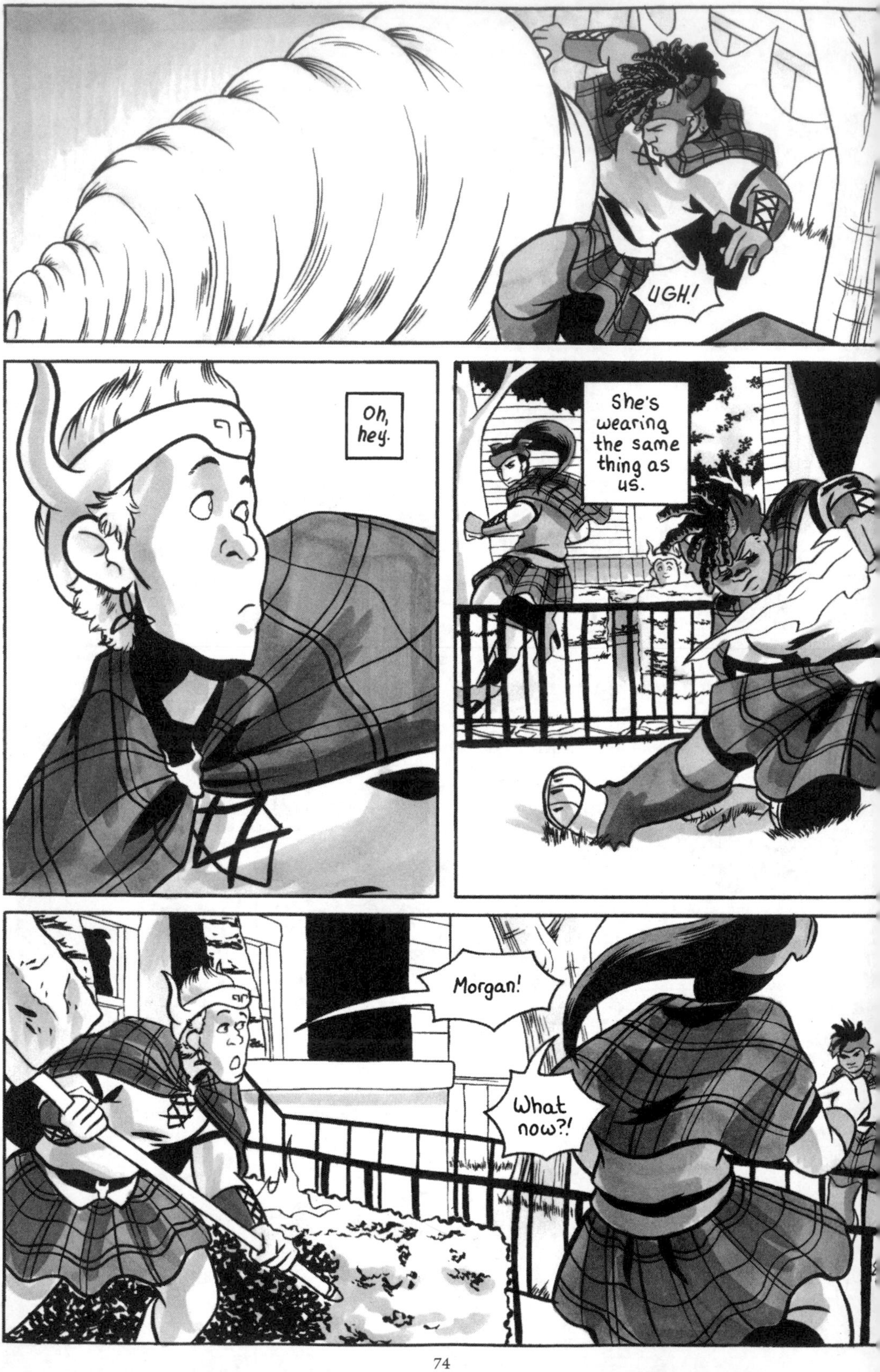
UGH!
Oh, hey.
She's wearing the same thing as us.
Morgan!
What now?!

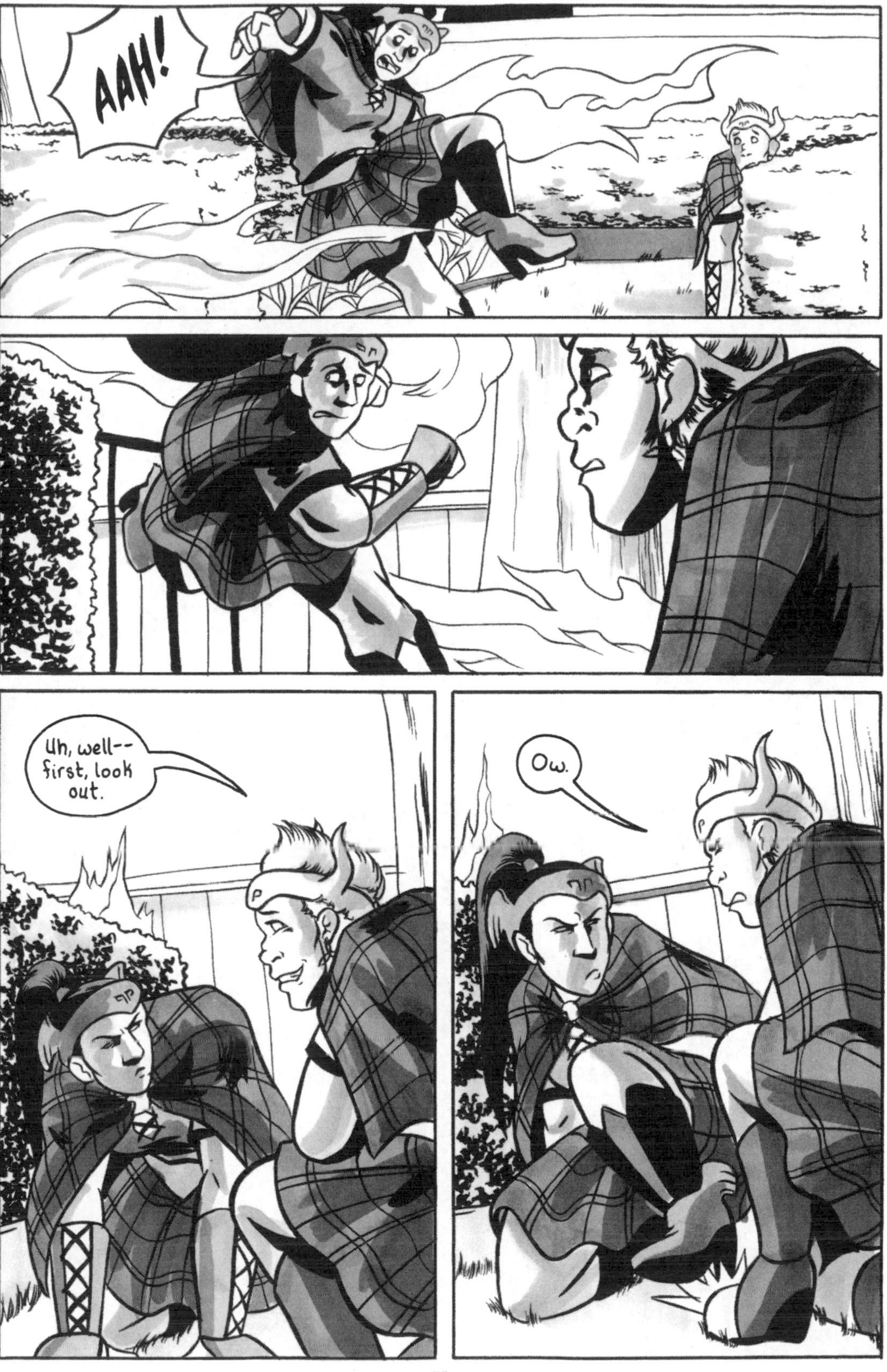
AAH!
Uh, well--
first, look
out.
Ow.

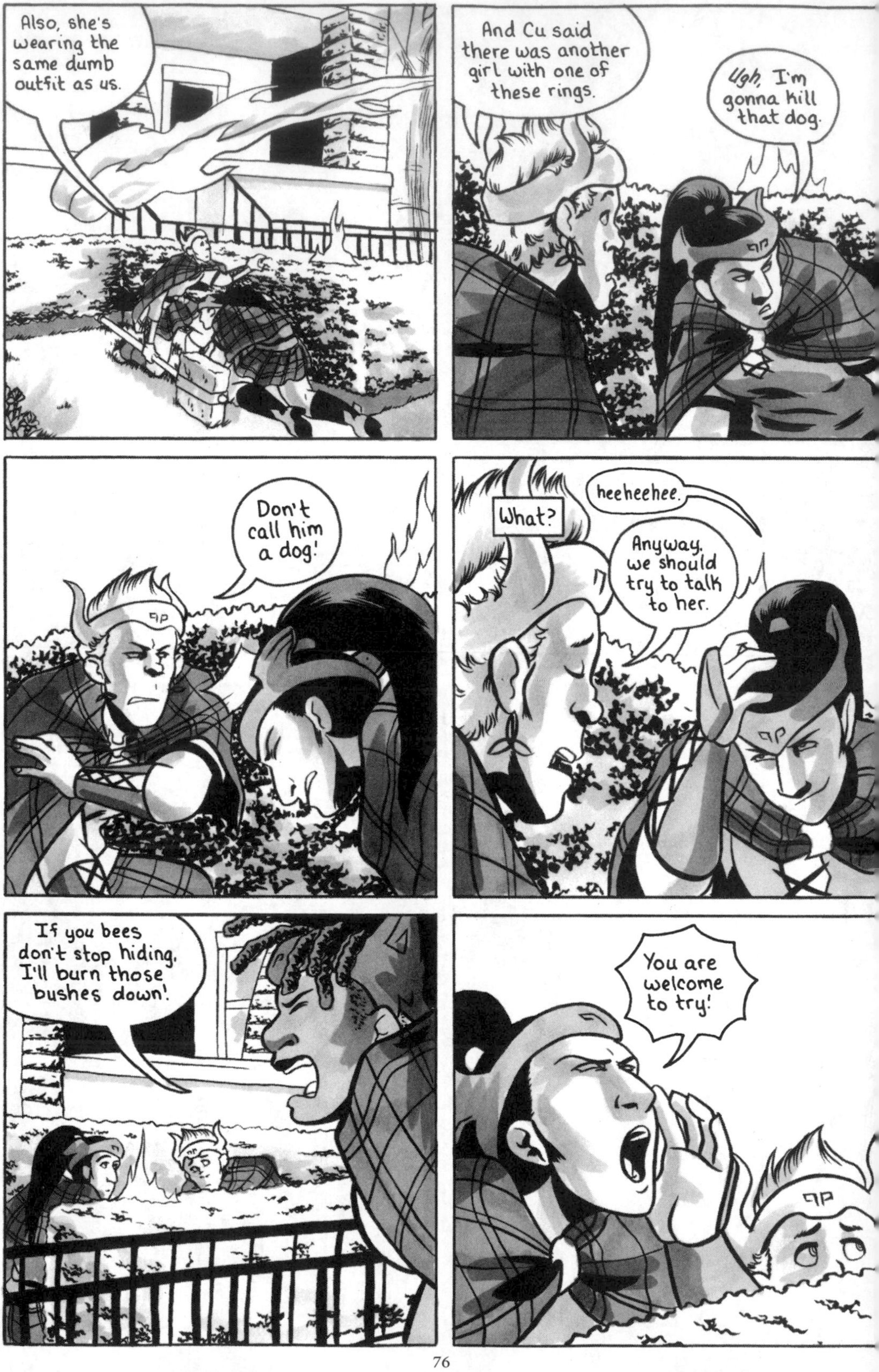
Also, she's wearing the same dumb outfit as us.
And Cu said there was another girl with one of these rings.
Ugh, I'm gonna kill that dog.
Don't call him a dog!
What?
heeheehee.
Anyway, we should try to talk to her.
If you bees don't stop hiding, I'll burn those bushes down!
You are welcome to try!

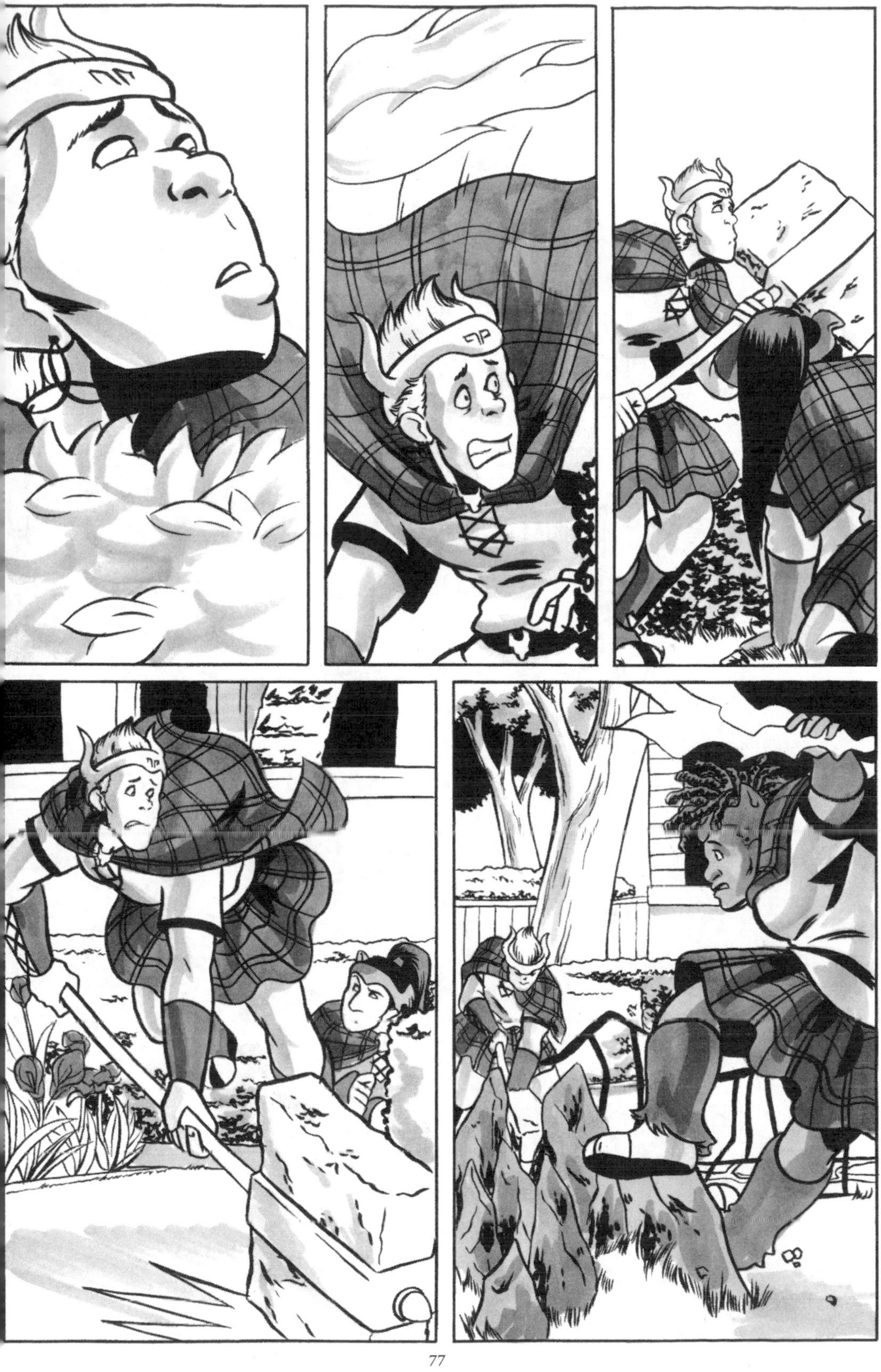

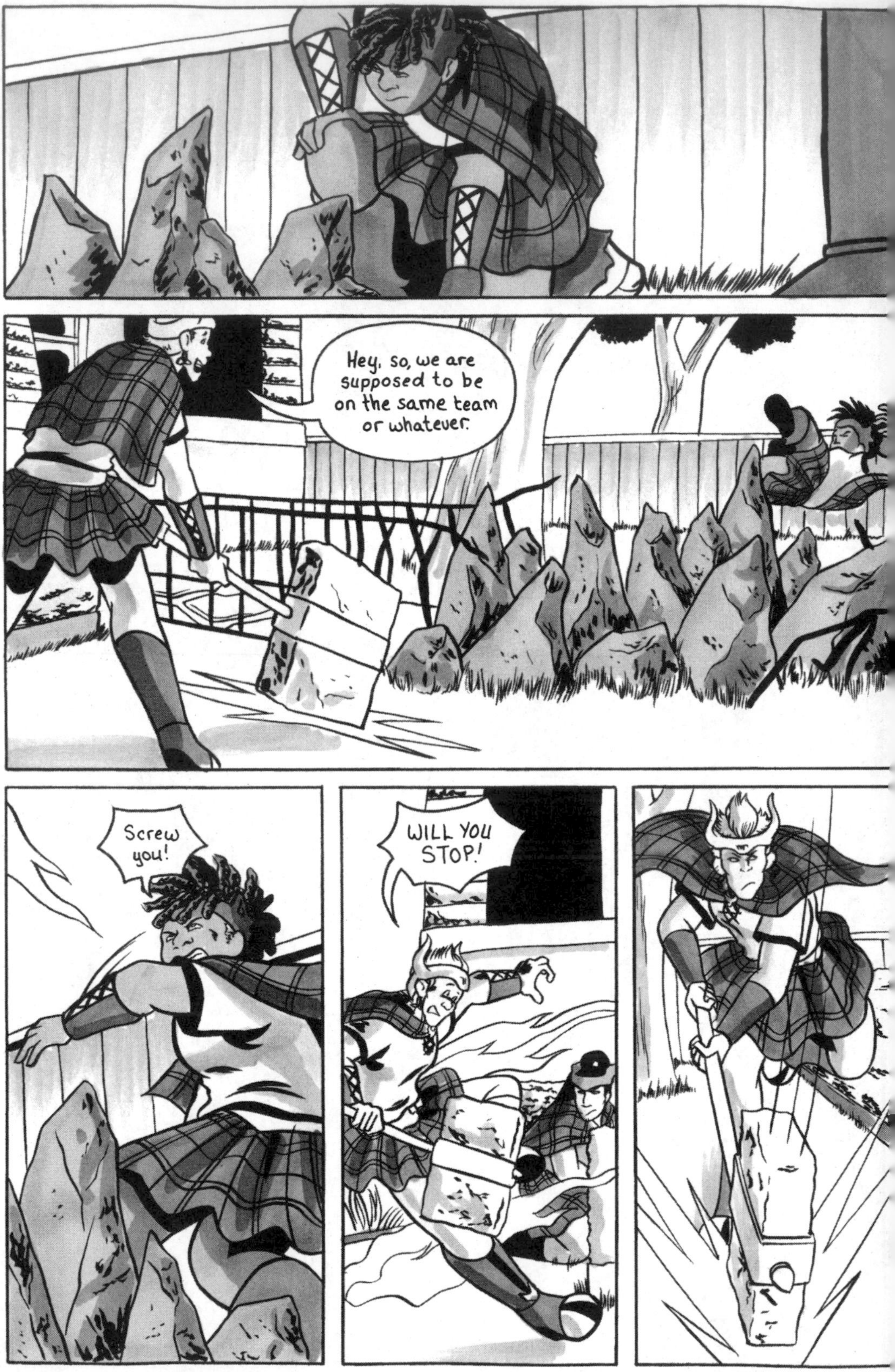
Hey, so, we are supposed to be on the same team or whatever.
Screw you!
WILL YOU STOP!

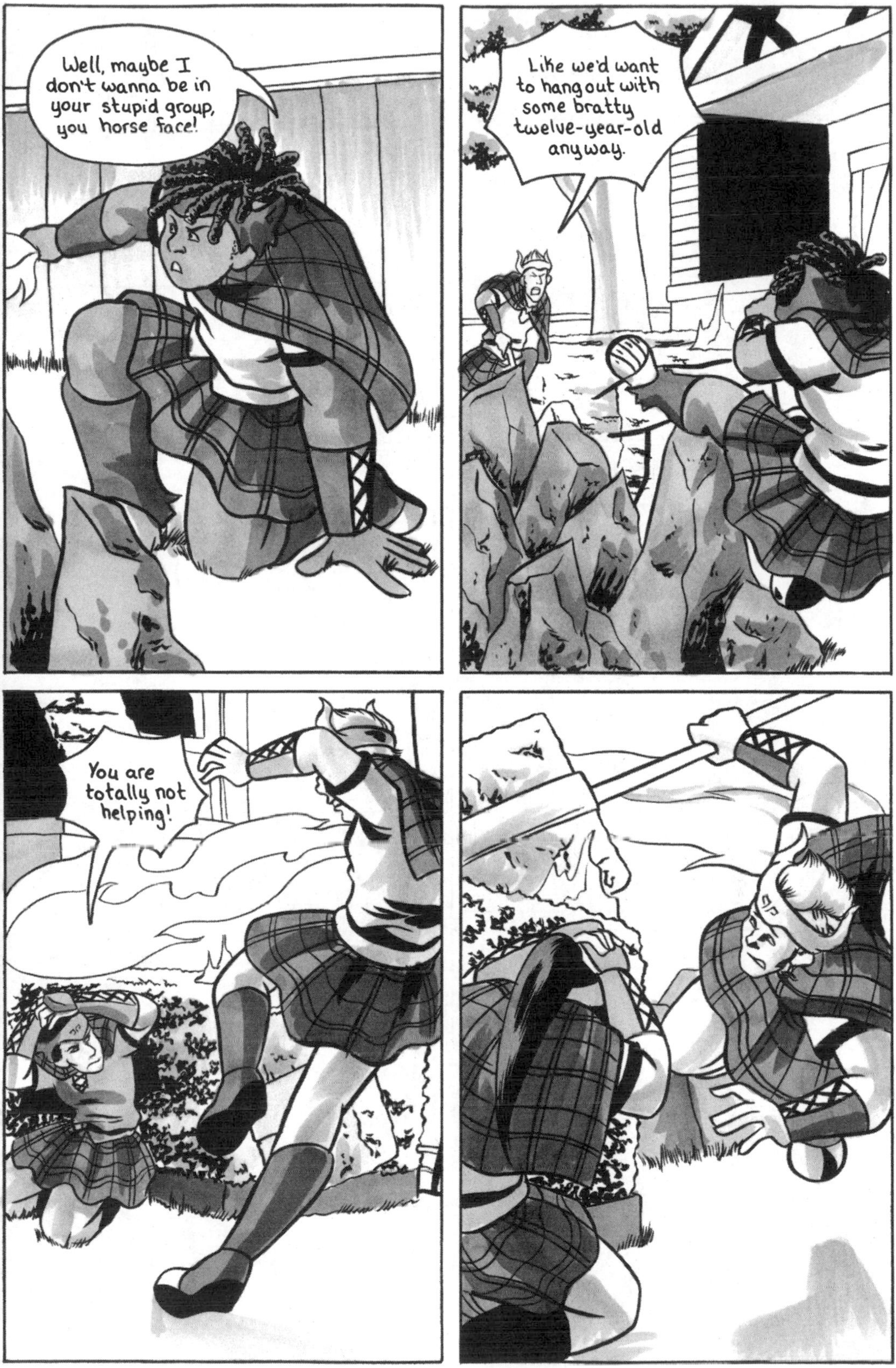
Well, maybe I don't wanna be in your stupid group, you horse face!
Like we'd want to hangout with some bratty twelve-year-old anyway.
You are totally not helping!

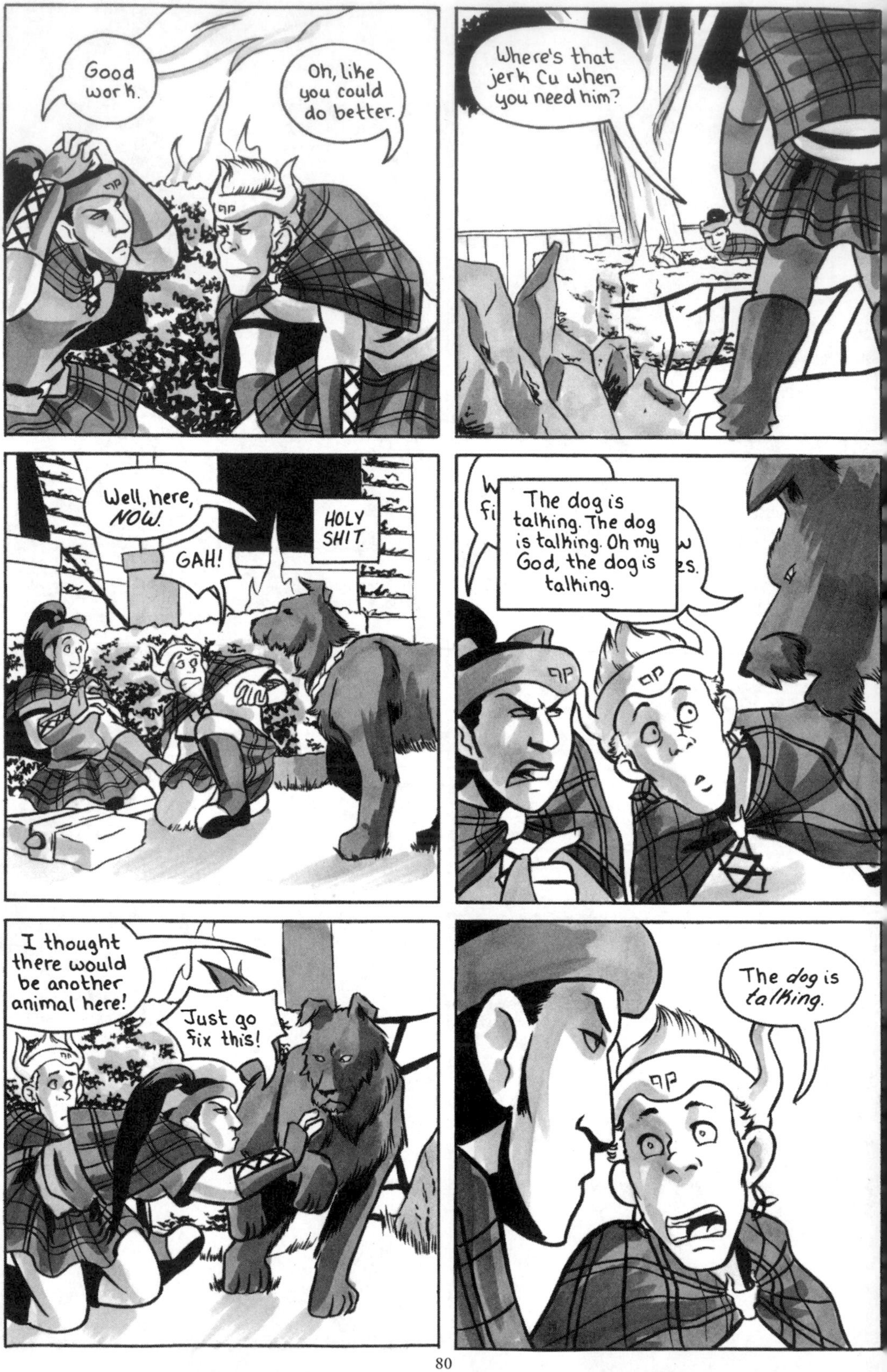
Good work.
Oh, like you could do better.
Where's that jerk Cu when you need him?
Well, here, *NOW*.
GAH!
HOLY SHIT.
The dog is talking. The dog is talking. Oh my God, the dog is talking.
I thought there would be another animal here!
Just go fix this!
The *dog* is *talking*.

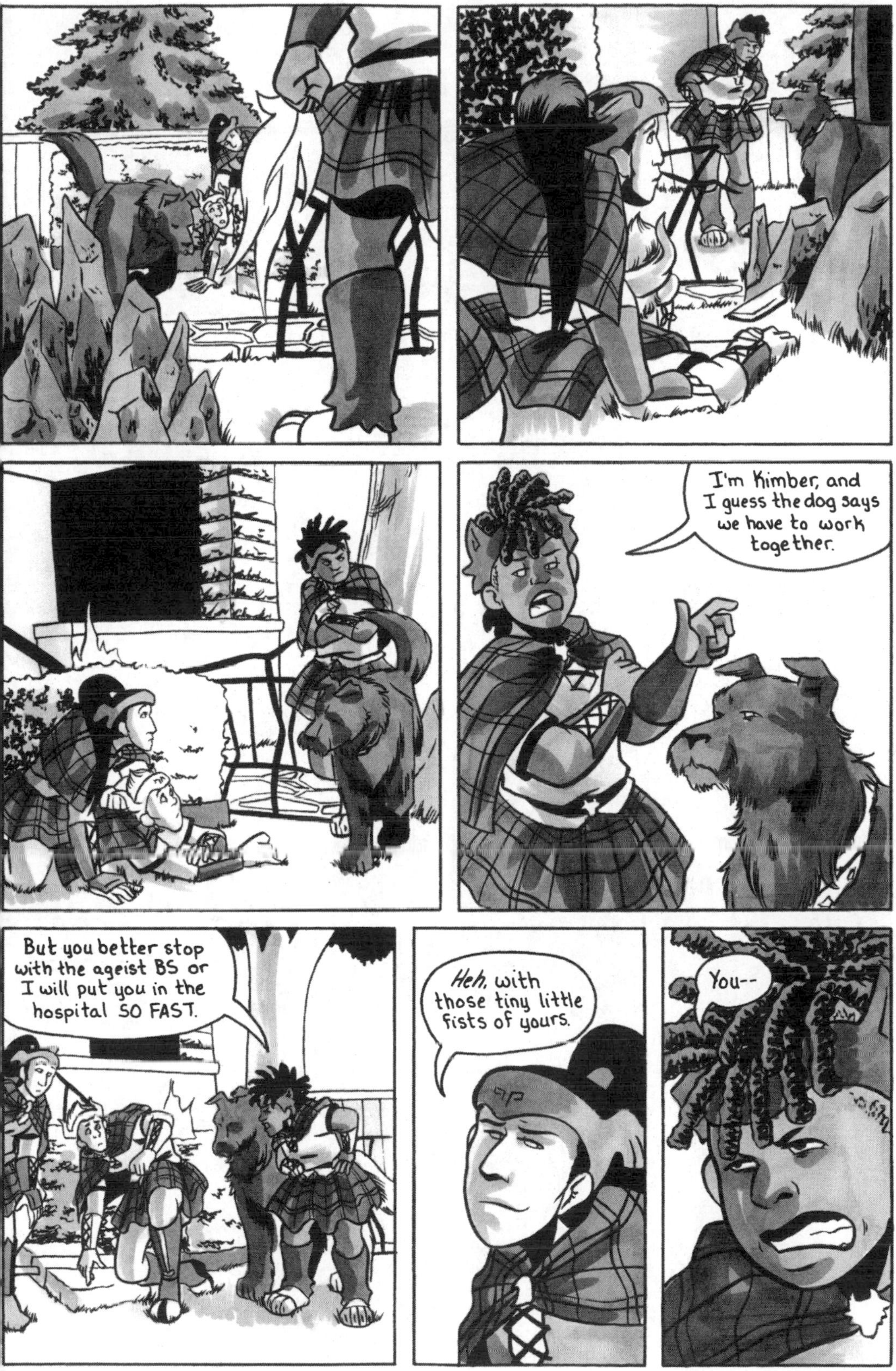
I'm Kimber, and I guess the dog says we have to work together.
But you better stop with the ageist BS or I will put you in the hospital SO FAST.
Heh, with those tiny little fists of yours.
You--

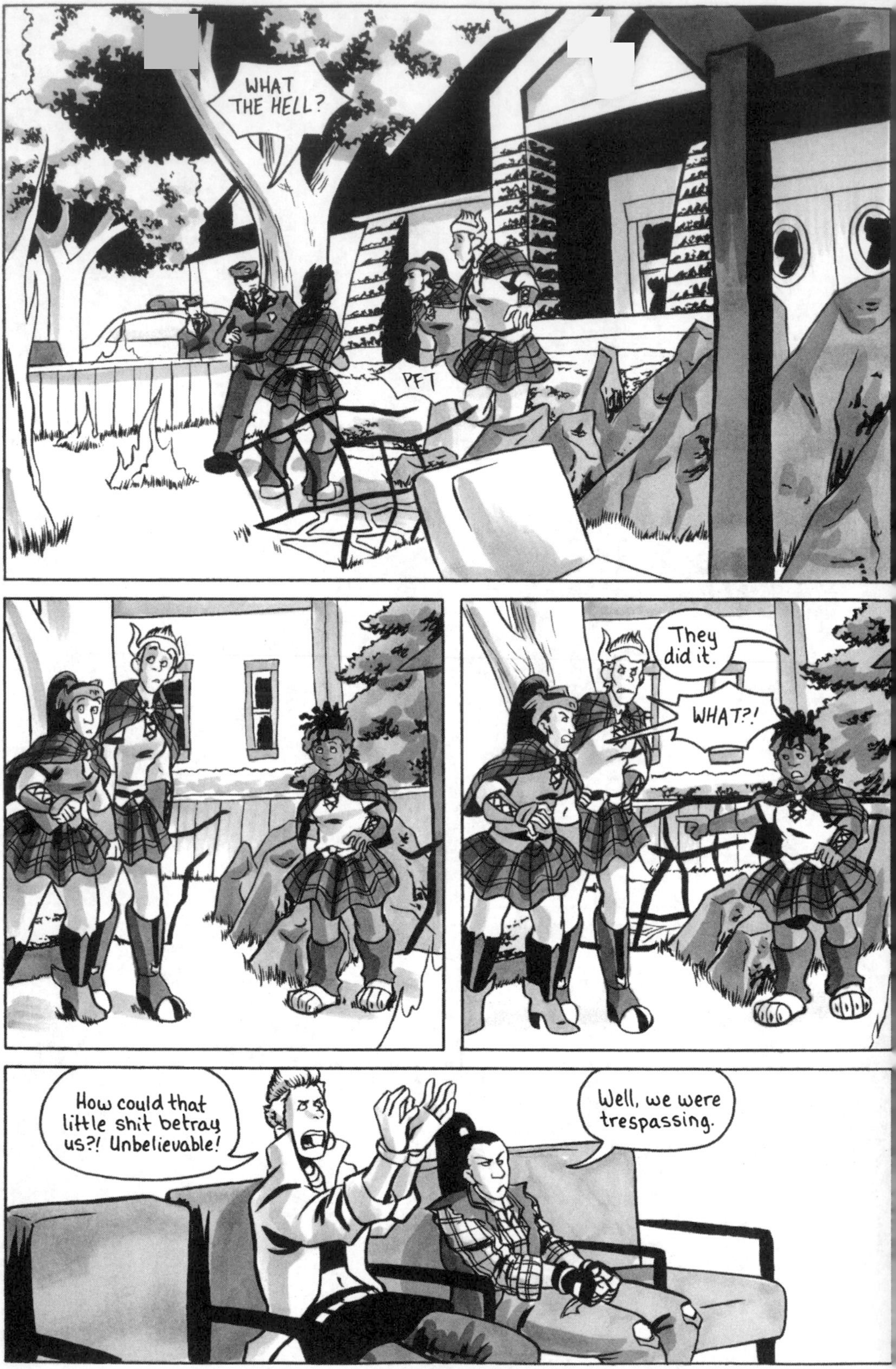
WHAT THE HELL?
PFT
They did it.
WHAT?!
How could that little shit betray us?! Unbelievable!
Well, we were trespassing.

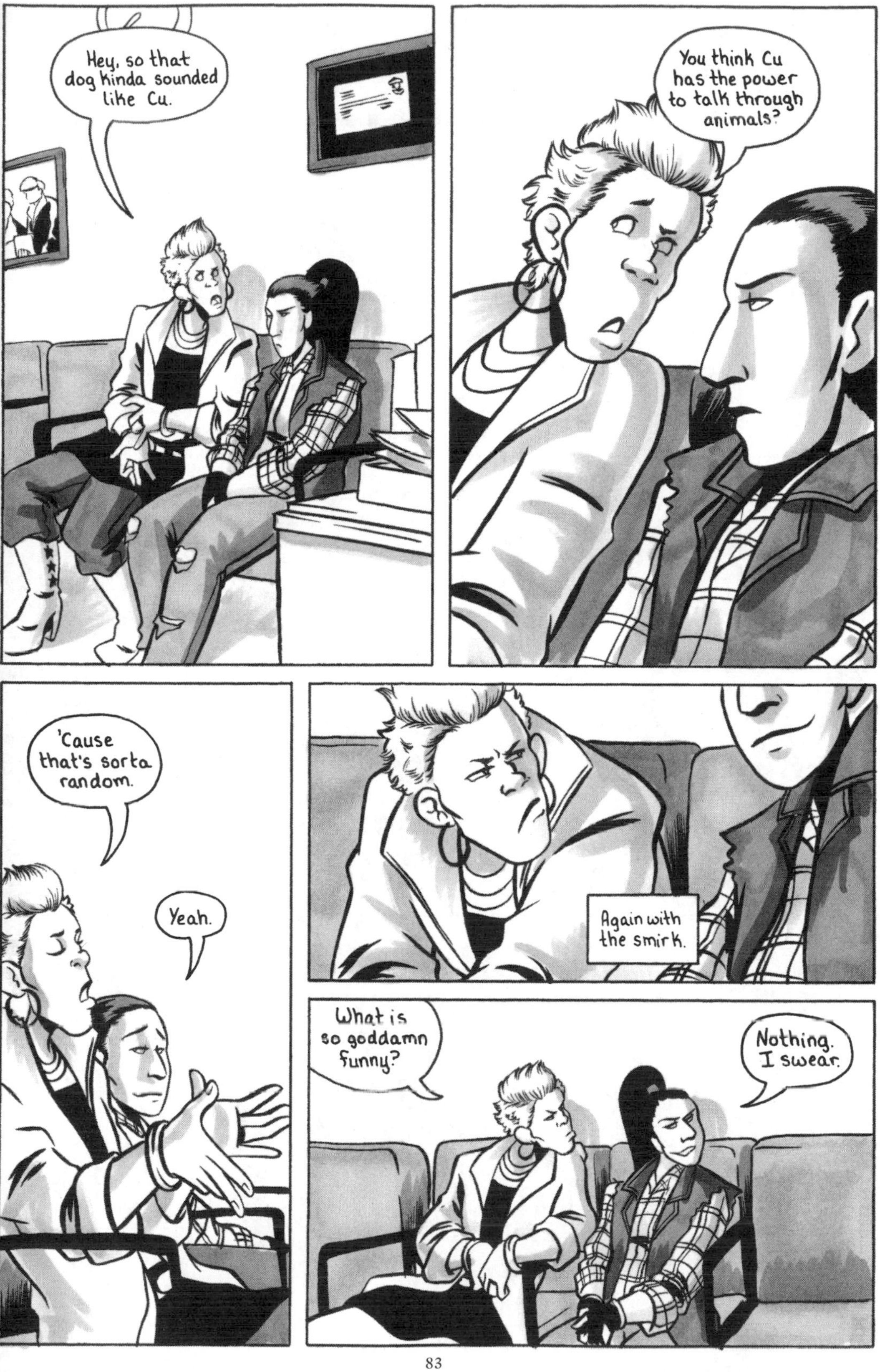
Hey, so that dog kinda sounded like Cu.
You think Cu has the power to talk through animals?
'Cause that's sorta random.
Yeah.
Again with the smirk.
What is so goddamn funny?
Nothing. I swear.

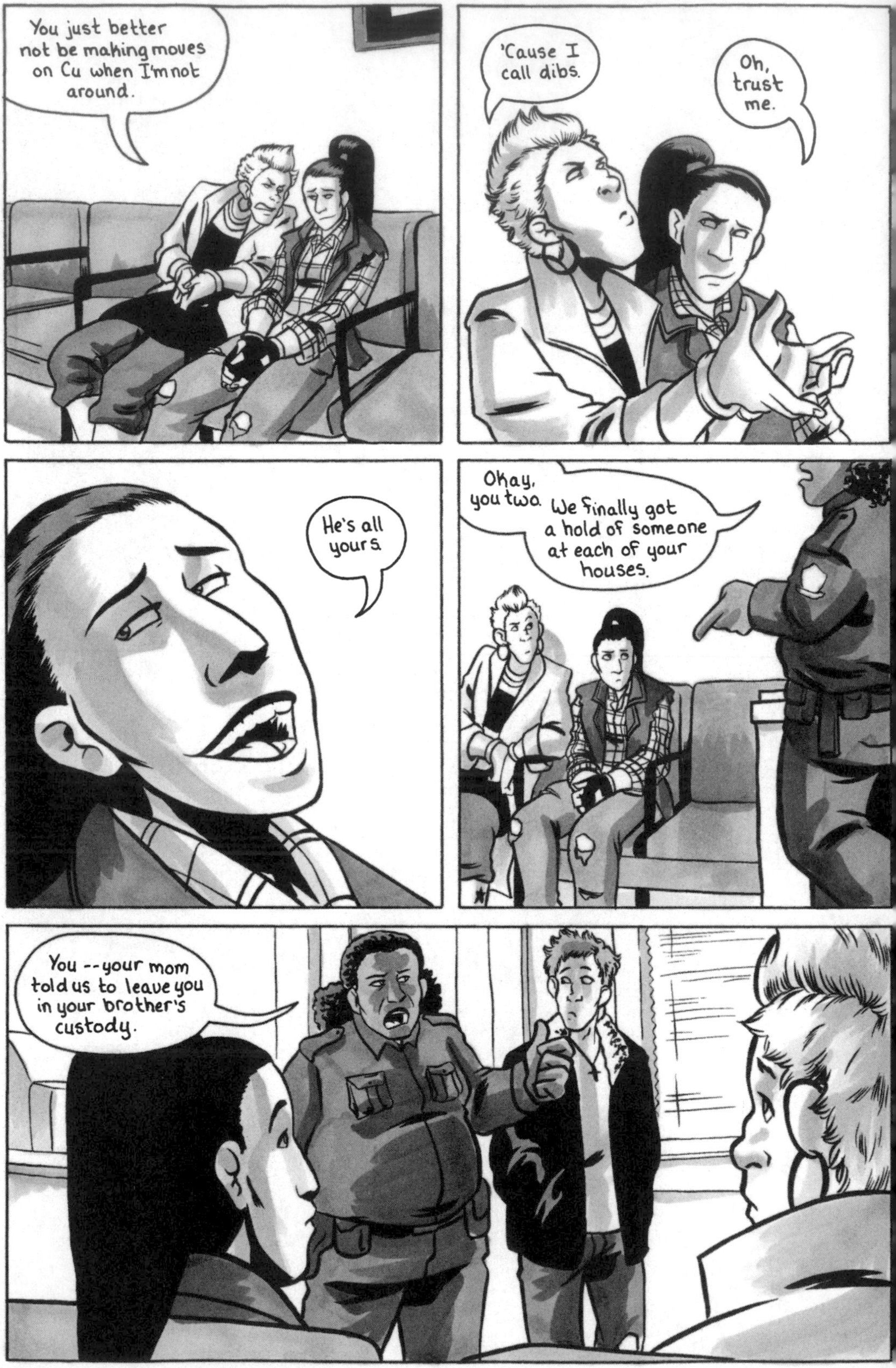
You just better not be making moves on Cu when I'm not around.
'Cause I call dibs.
Oh, trust me.
He's all yours.
Okay, you two.
We finally got a hold of someone at each of your houses.
You --your mom told us to leave you in your brother's custody.

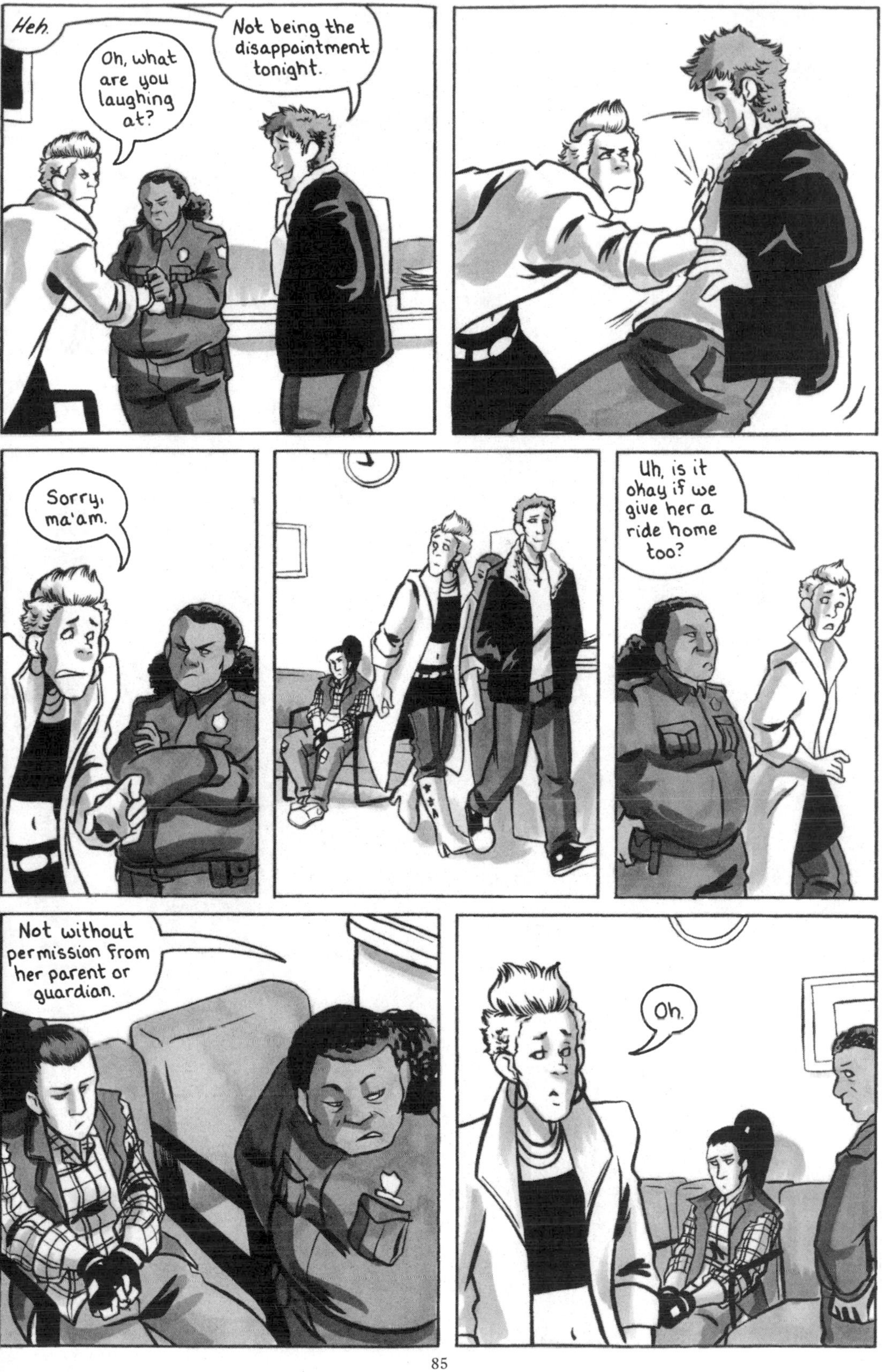
Heh.
Oh, what are you laughing at?
Not being the disappointment tonight.
Sorry, ma'am.
Uh, is it okay if we give her a ride home too?
Not without permission from her parent or guardian.
Oh.

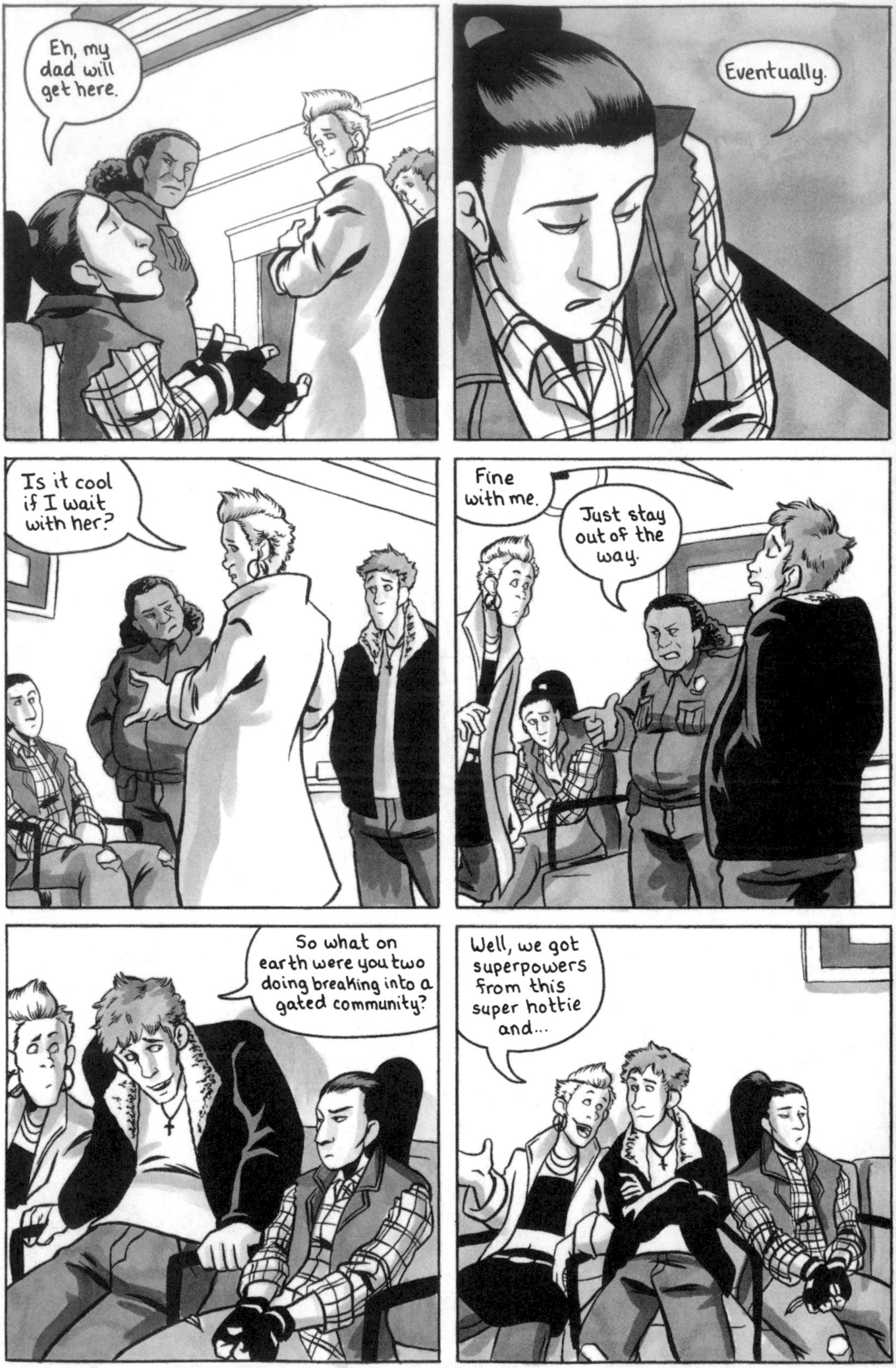
Eh, my dad will get here.
Eventually.
Is it cool if I wait with her?
Fine with me.
Just stay out of the way.
So what on earth were you two doing breaking into a gated community?
Well, we got superpowers from this super hottie and...

CHAPTER 3:

Kimber the Fire Wolf

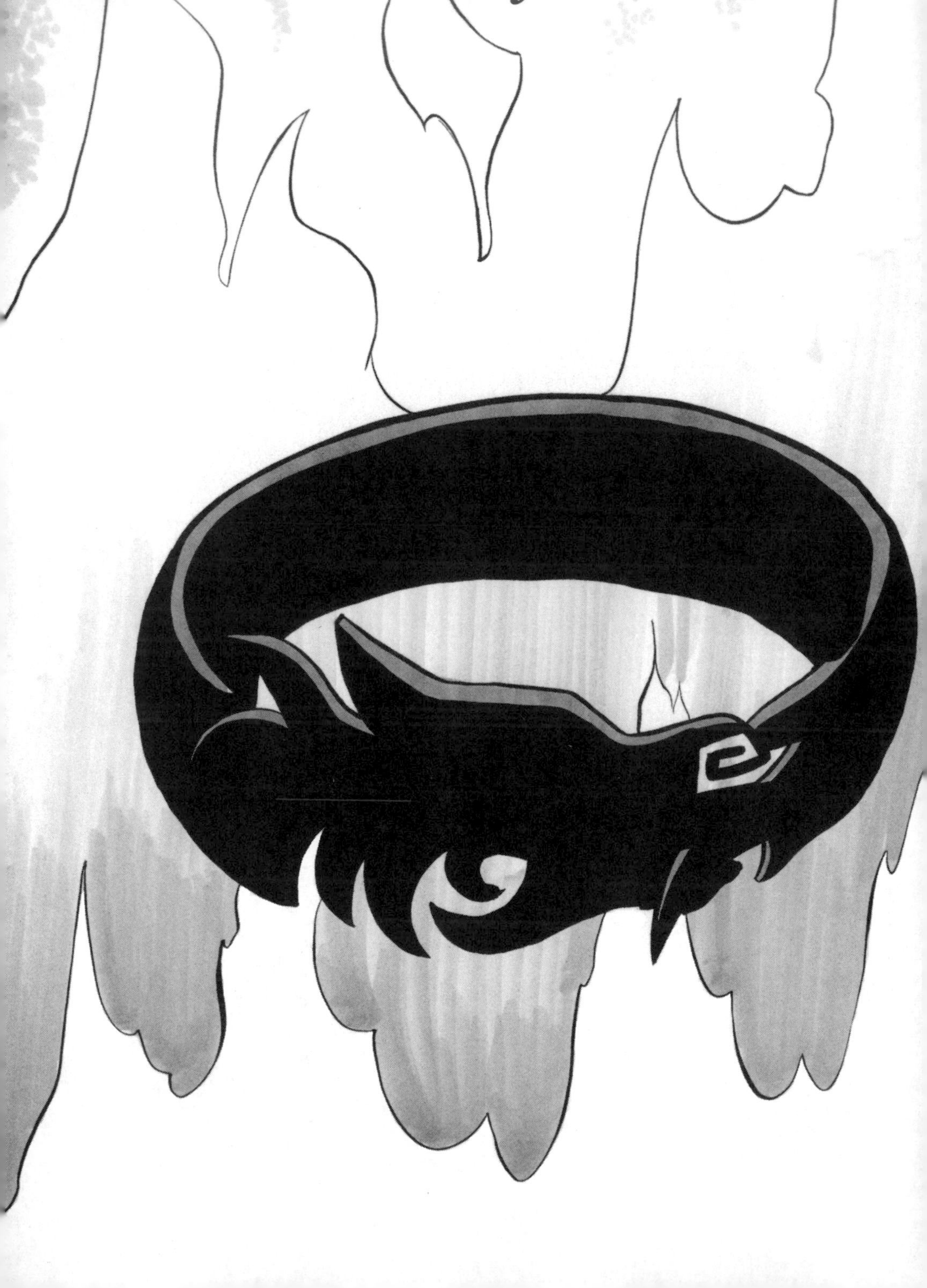

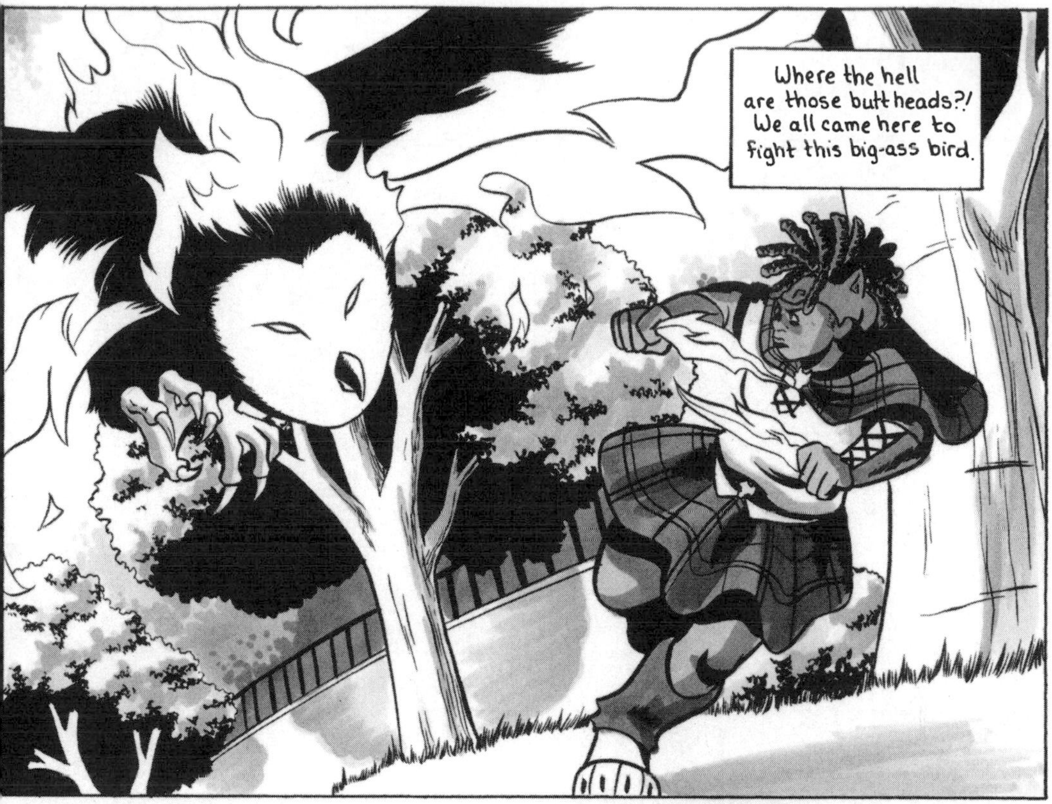
Where the hell are those buttheads?! We all came here to fight this big-ass bird.

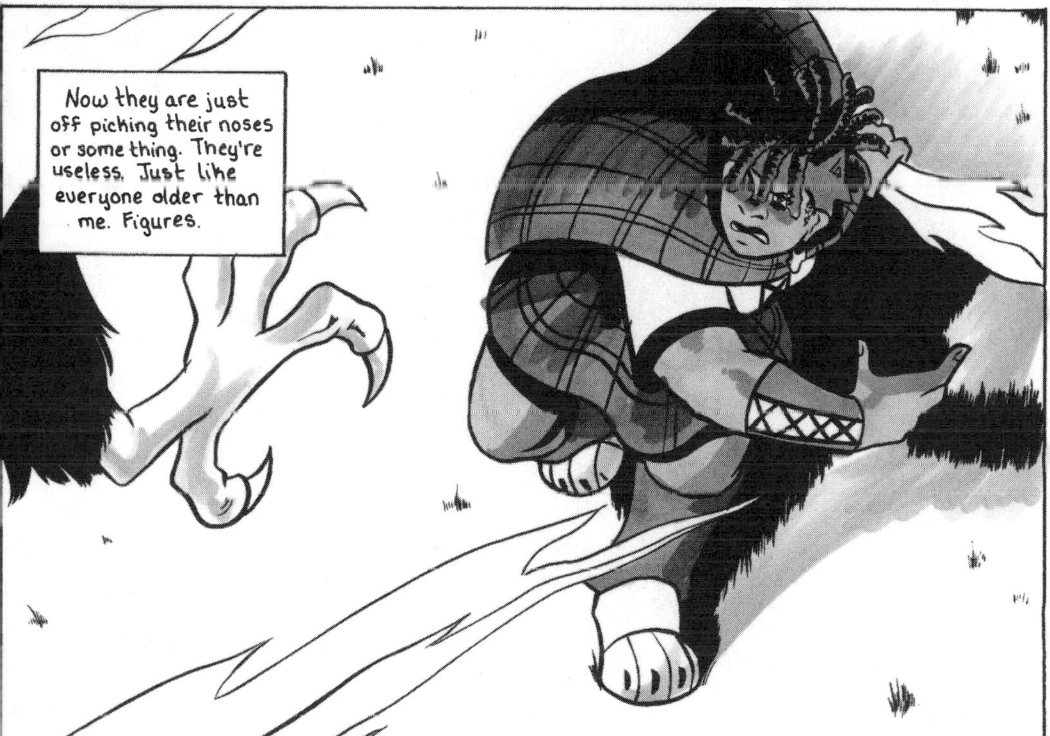
Now they are just off picking their noses or some thing. They're useless. Just like everyone older than me. Figures.

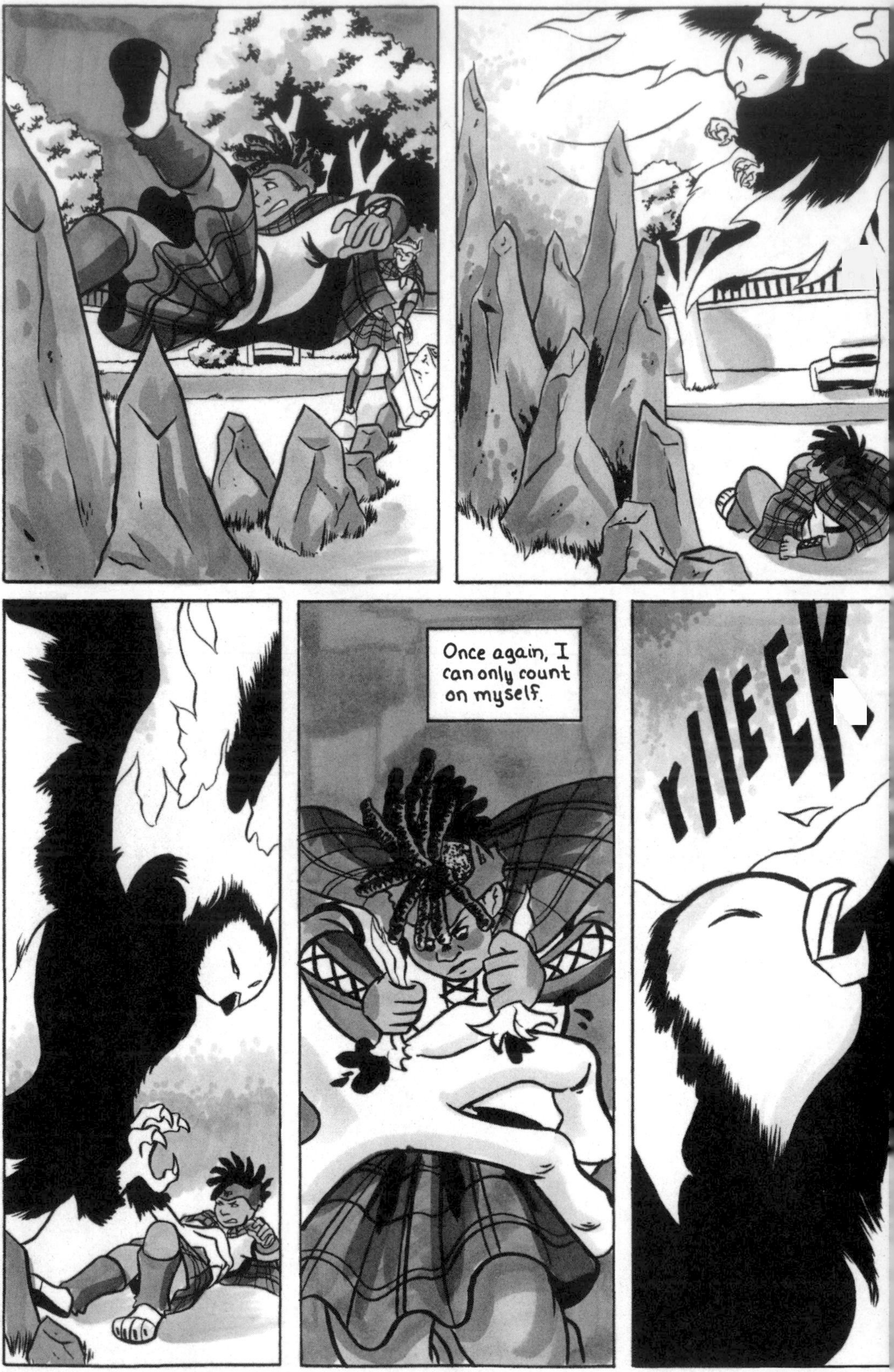
Once again, I can only count on myself.
rIIEEK

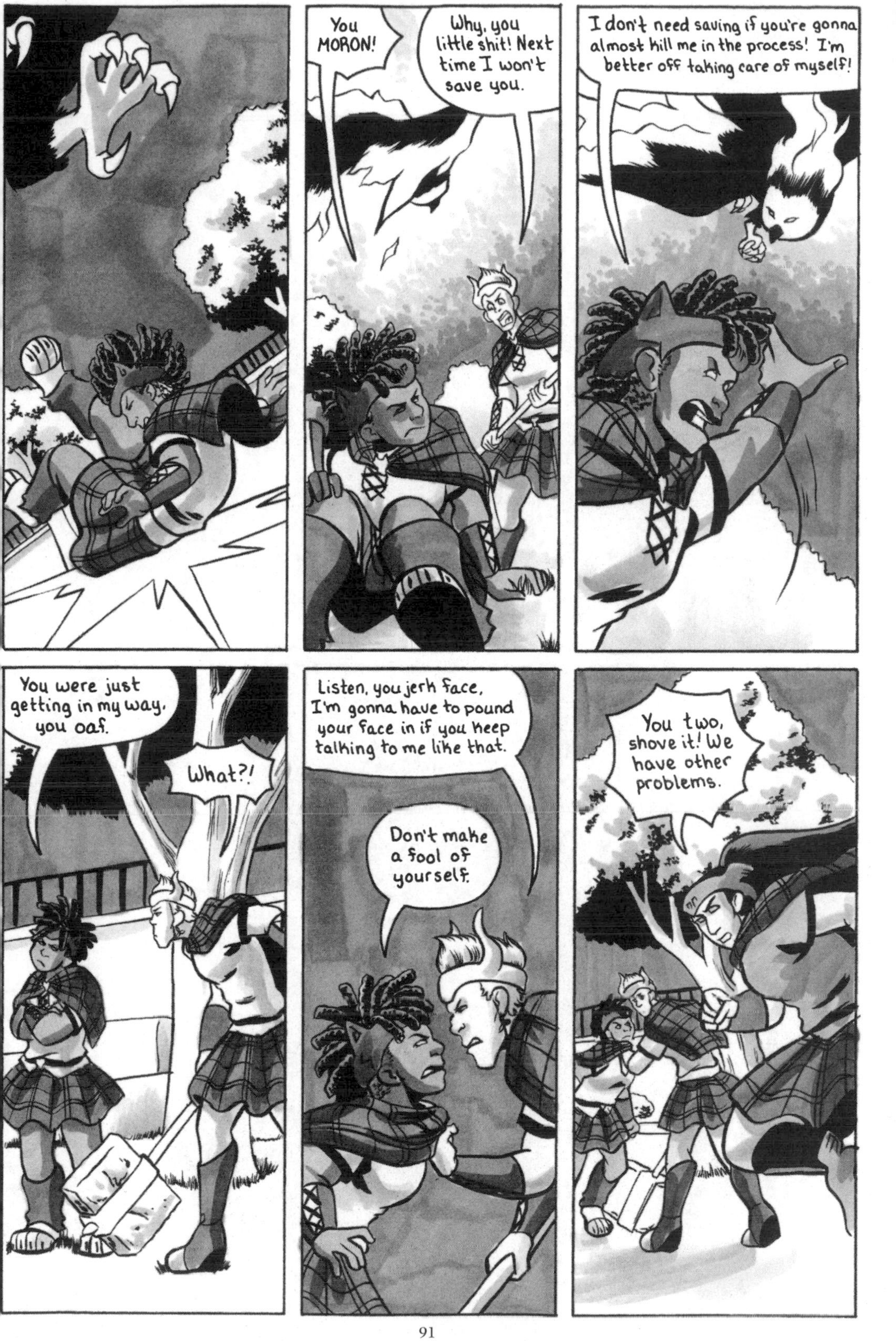
You MORON!
Why, you little shit! Next time I won't save you.
I don't need saving if you're gonna almost kill me in the process! I'm better off taking care of myself!
You were just getting in my way, you oaf.
What?!
Listen, you jerk face, I'm gonna have to pound your face in if you keep talking to me like that.
Don't make a fool of yourself.
You two, shove it! We have other problems.

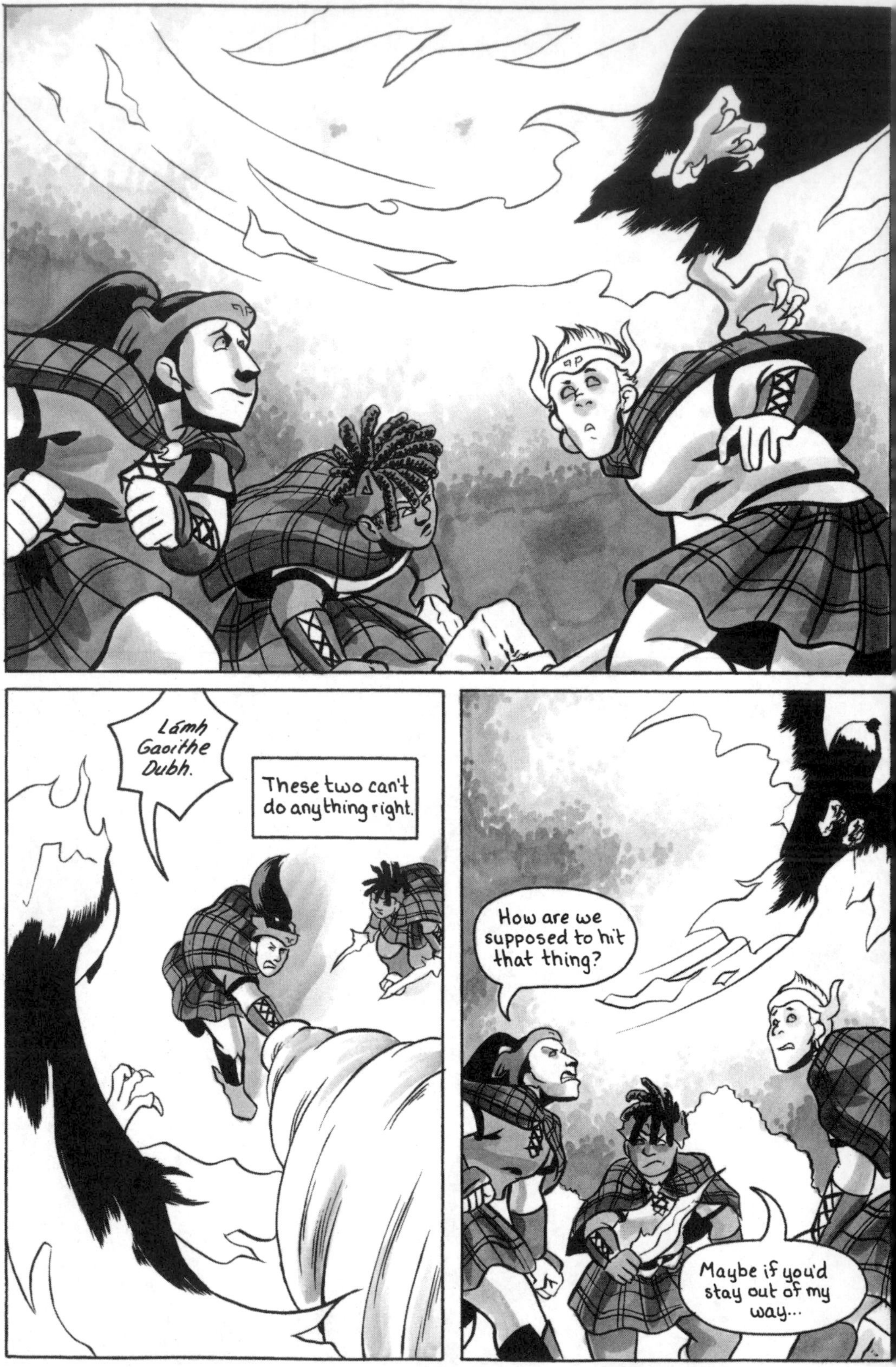
Lámh Gaoithe Dubh.
These two can't do anything right.
How are we supposed to hit that thing?
Maybe if you'd stay out of my way...

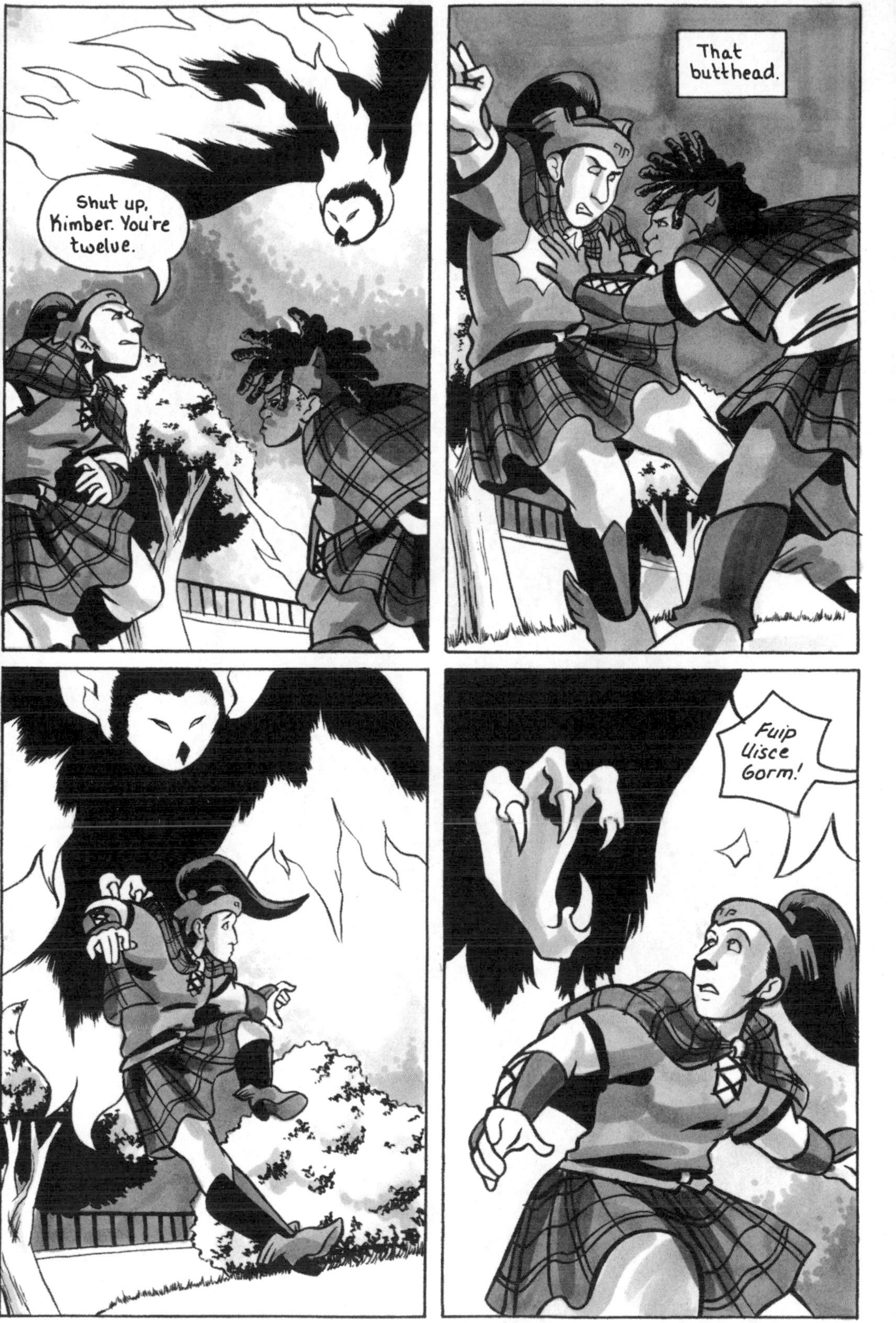
Shut up, Kimber. You're twelve.
That butthead.
Fuip Uisce Gorm!

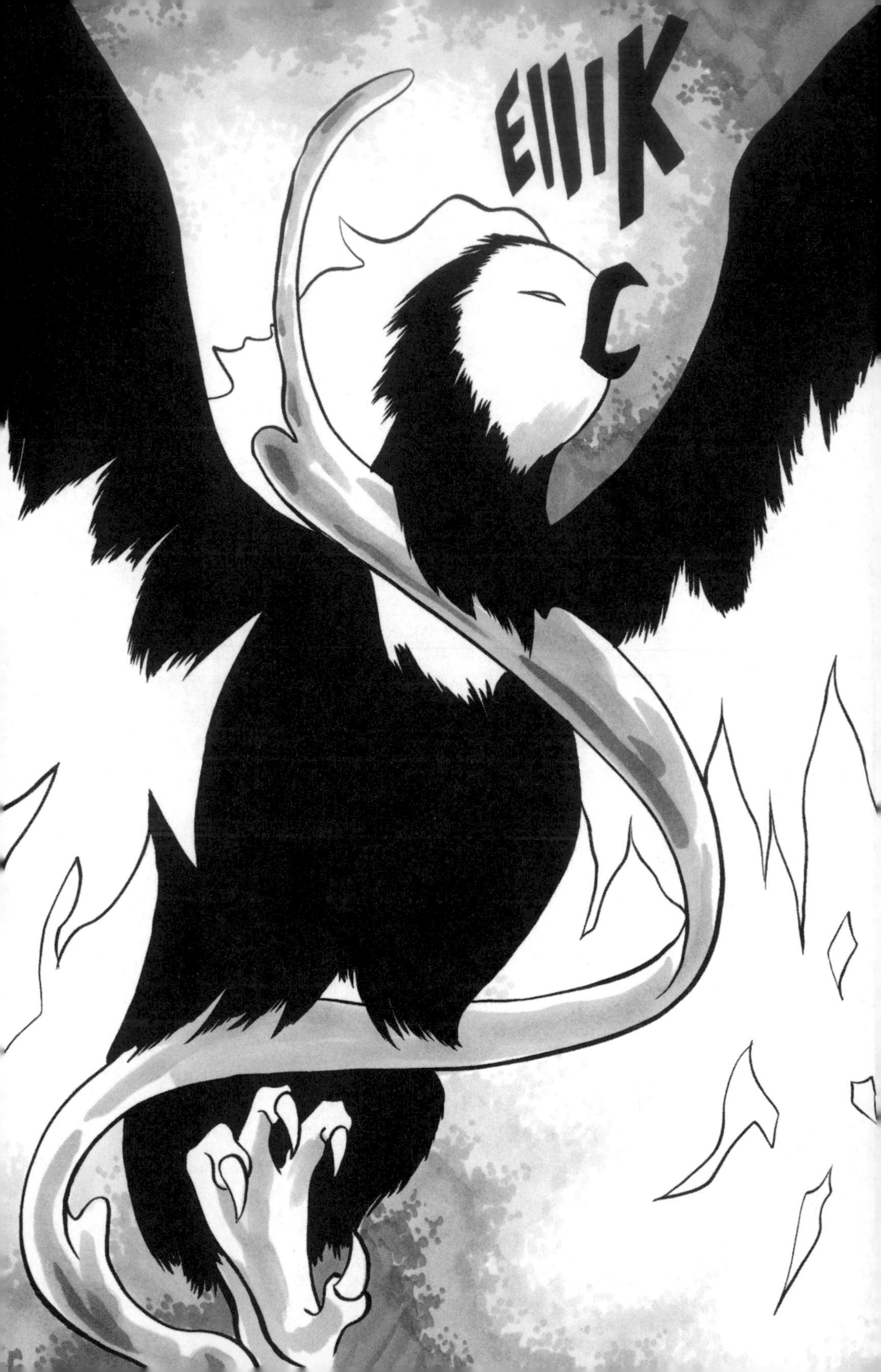
EIIIK

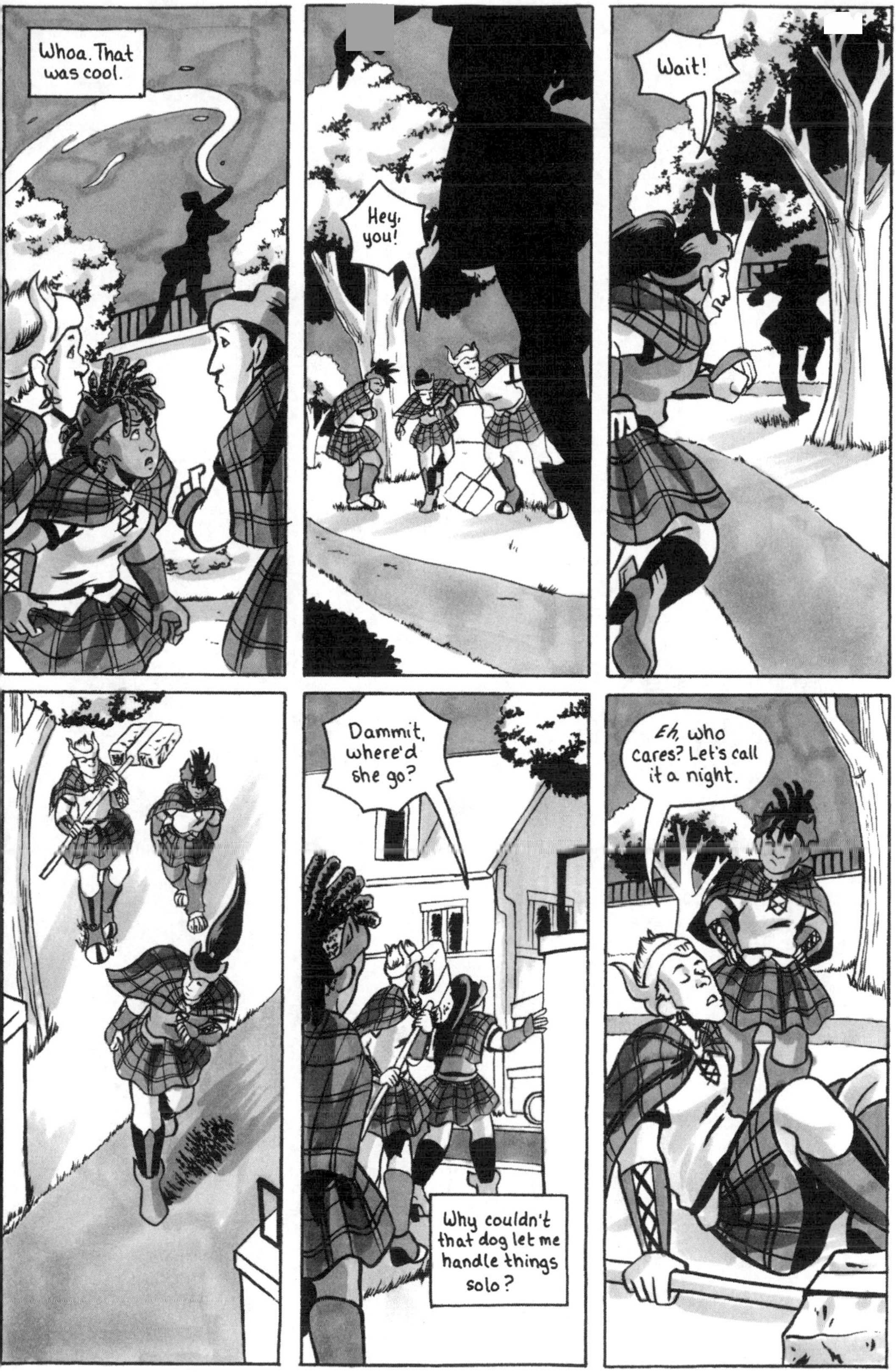
Whoa. That was cool.
Hey, you!
Wait!
Dammit, where'd she go?
Why couldn't that dog let me handle things solo?
Eh, who cares? Let's call it a night.

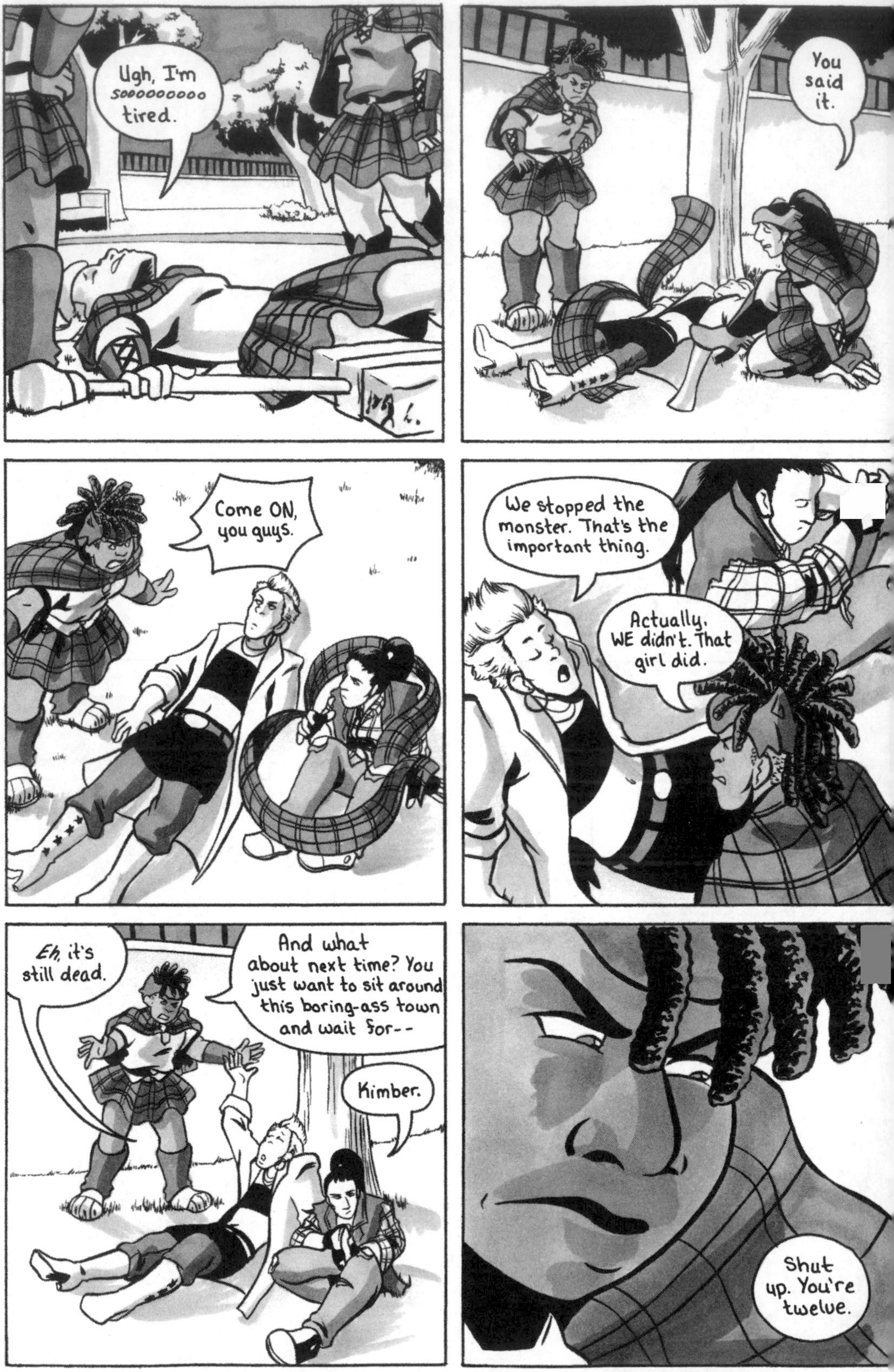
Ugh, I'm sooooooooo tired.
You said it.
Come ON, you guys.
We stopped the monster. That's the important thing.
Actually, WE didn't. That girl did.
Eh, it's still dead.
And what about next time? You just want to sit around this boring-ass town and wait for--
Kimber.
Shut up. You're twelve.

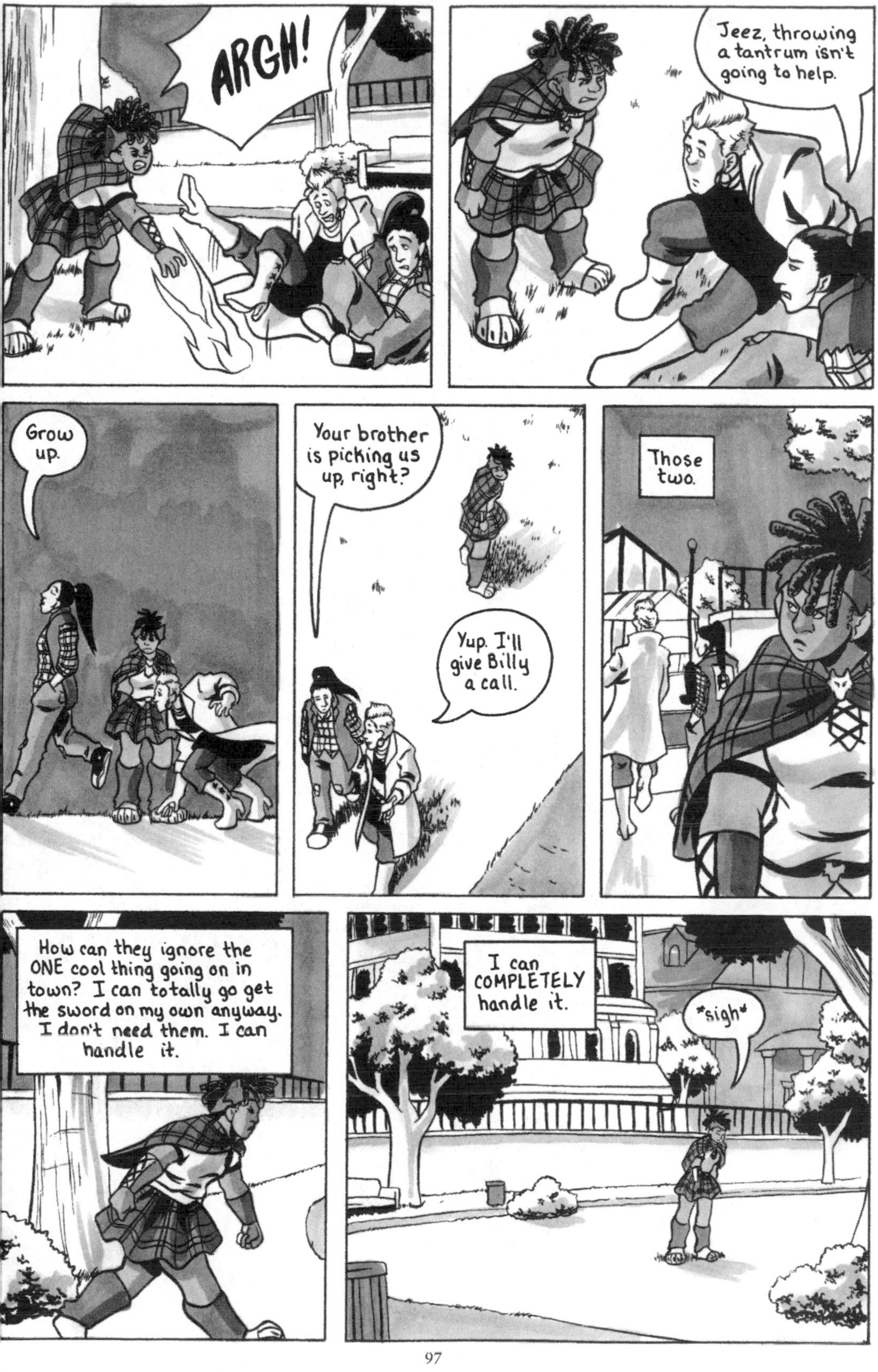
ARGH!
Jeez, throwing a tantrum isn't going to help.
Grow up.
Your brother is picking us up, right?
Yup. I'll give Billy a call.
Those two.
How can they ignore the ONE cool thing going on in town? I can totally go get the sword on my own anyway. I don't need them. I can handle it.
I can COMPLETELY handle it.
sigh

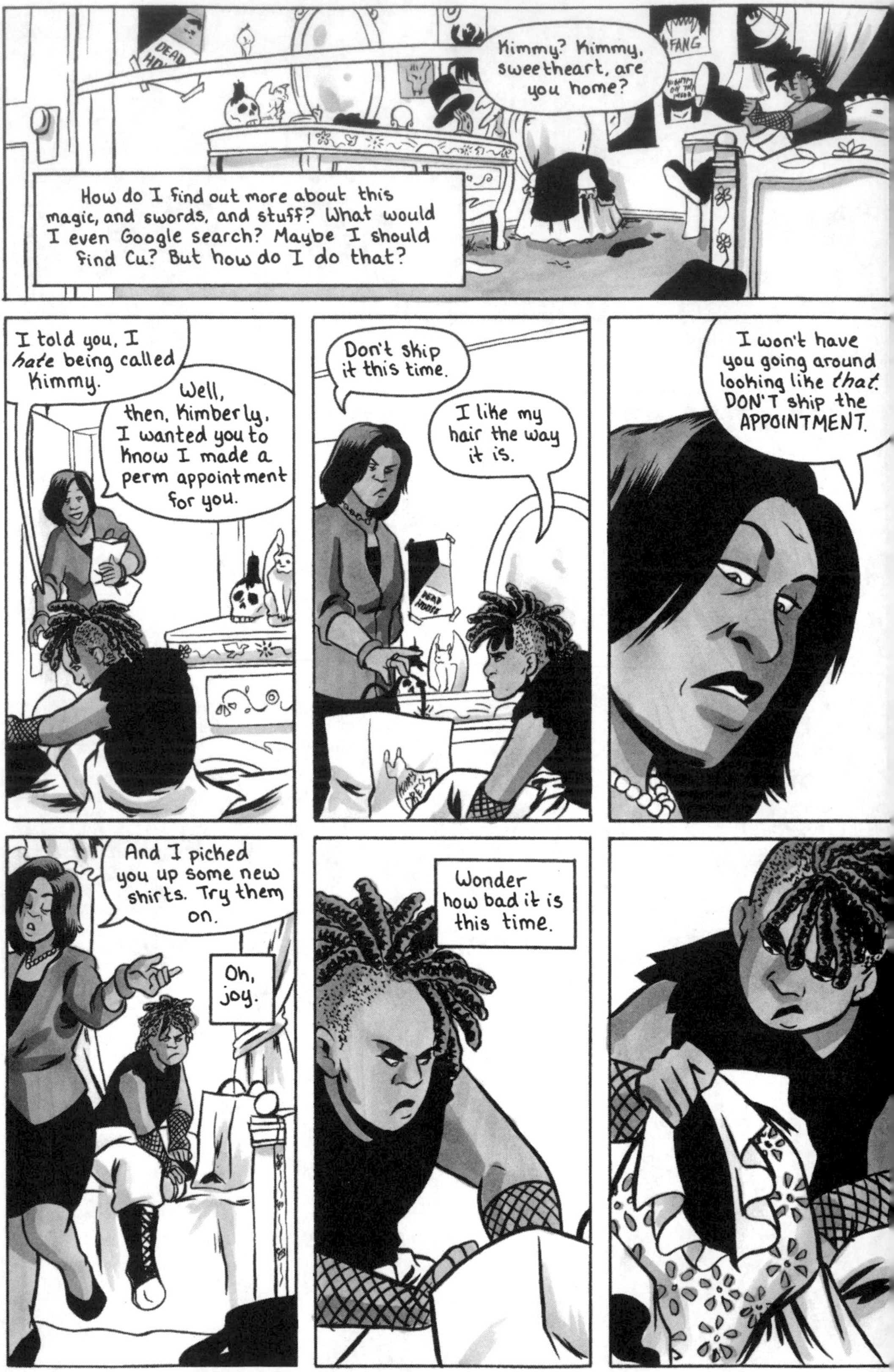
Kimmy? Kimmy, sweetheart, are you home?
How do I find out more about this magic, and swords, and stuff? What would I even Google search? Maybe I should find Cu? But how do I do that?
I told you, I *hate* being called Kimmy.
Well, then, Kimberly, I wanted you to know I made a perm appointment for you.
Don't skip it this time.
I like my hair the way it is.
I won't have you going around looking like *that*. DON'T skip the APPOINTMENT.
And I picked you up some new shirts. Try them on.
Oh, joy.
Wonder how bad it is this time.

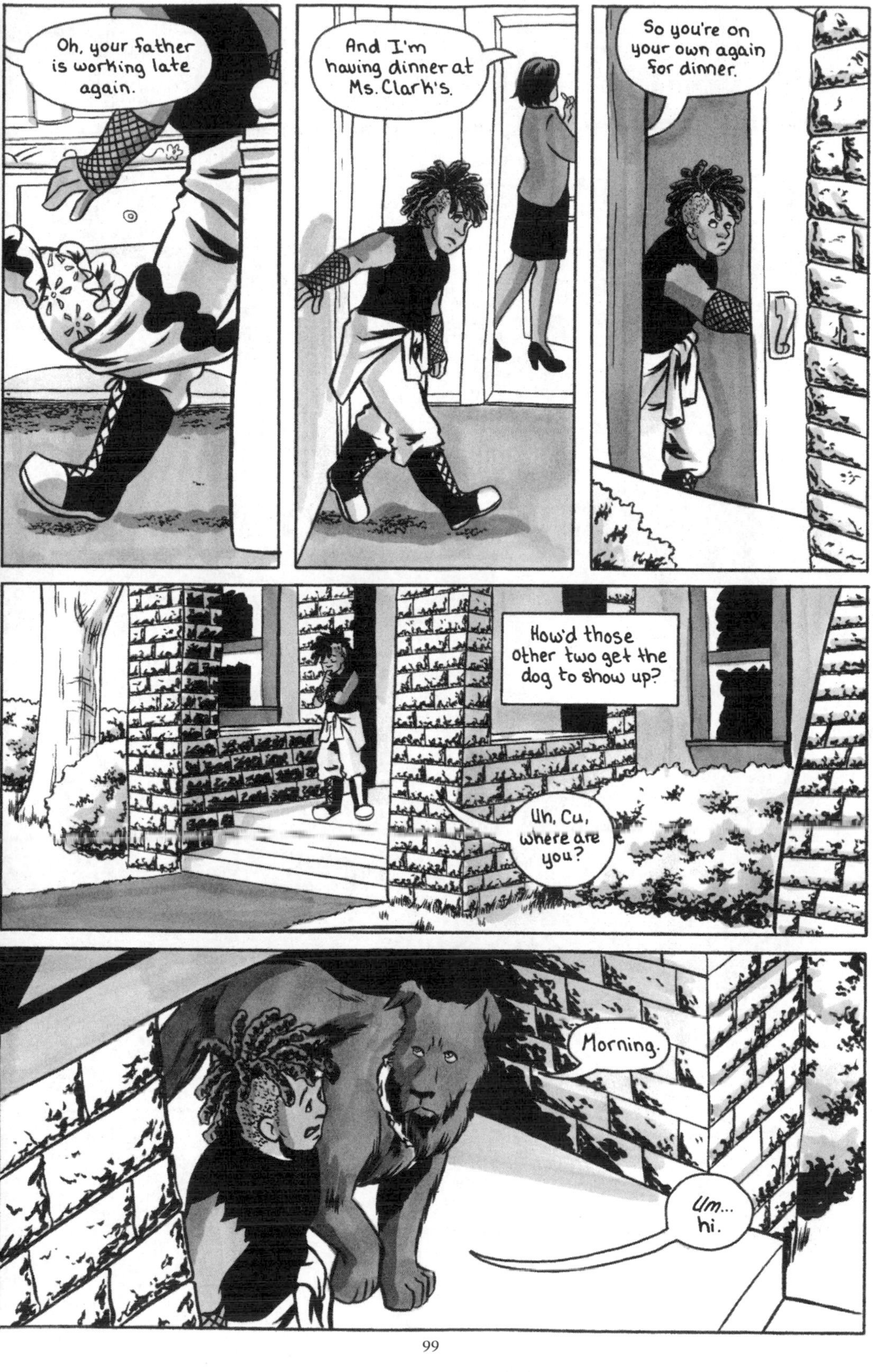
Oh, your father is working late again.
And I'm having dinner at Ms. Clark's.
So you're on your own again for dinner.
How'd those other two get the dog to show up?
Uh, Cu, where are you?
Morning.
Um... hi.

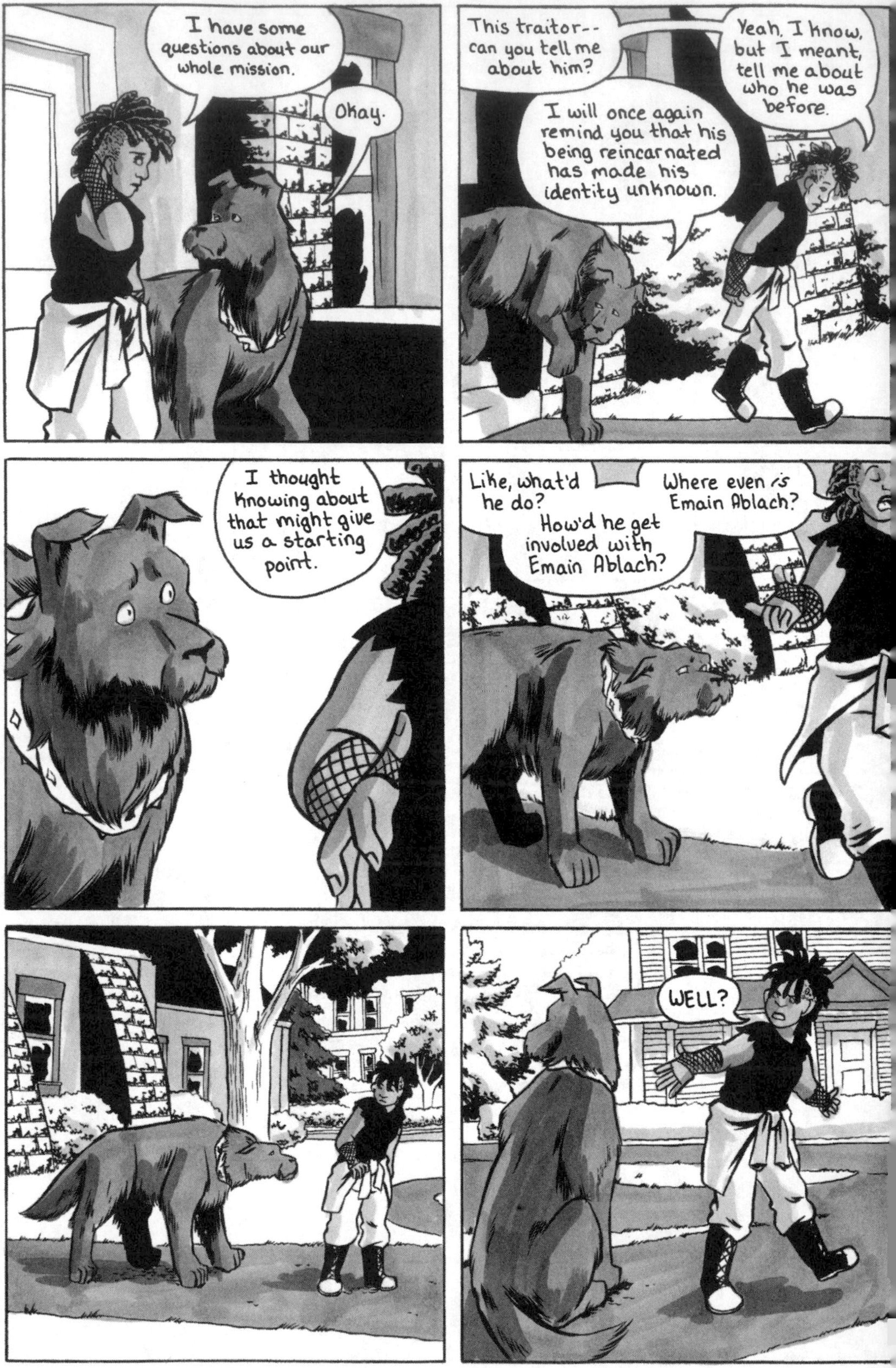

I have some questions about our whole mission.
Okay.
This traitor-- can you tell me about him?
I will once again remind you that his being reincarnated has made his identity unknown.
Yeah, I know, but I meant, tell me about who he was before.
I thought knowing about that might give us a starting point.
Like, what'd he do?
How'd he get involved with Emain Ablach?
Where even is Emain Ablach?
WELL?

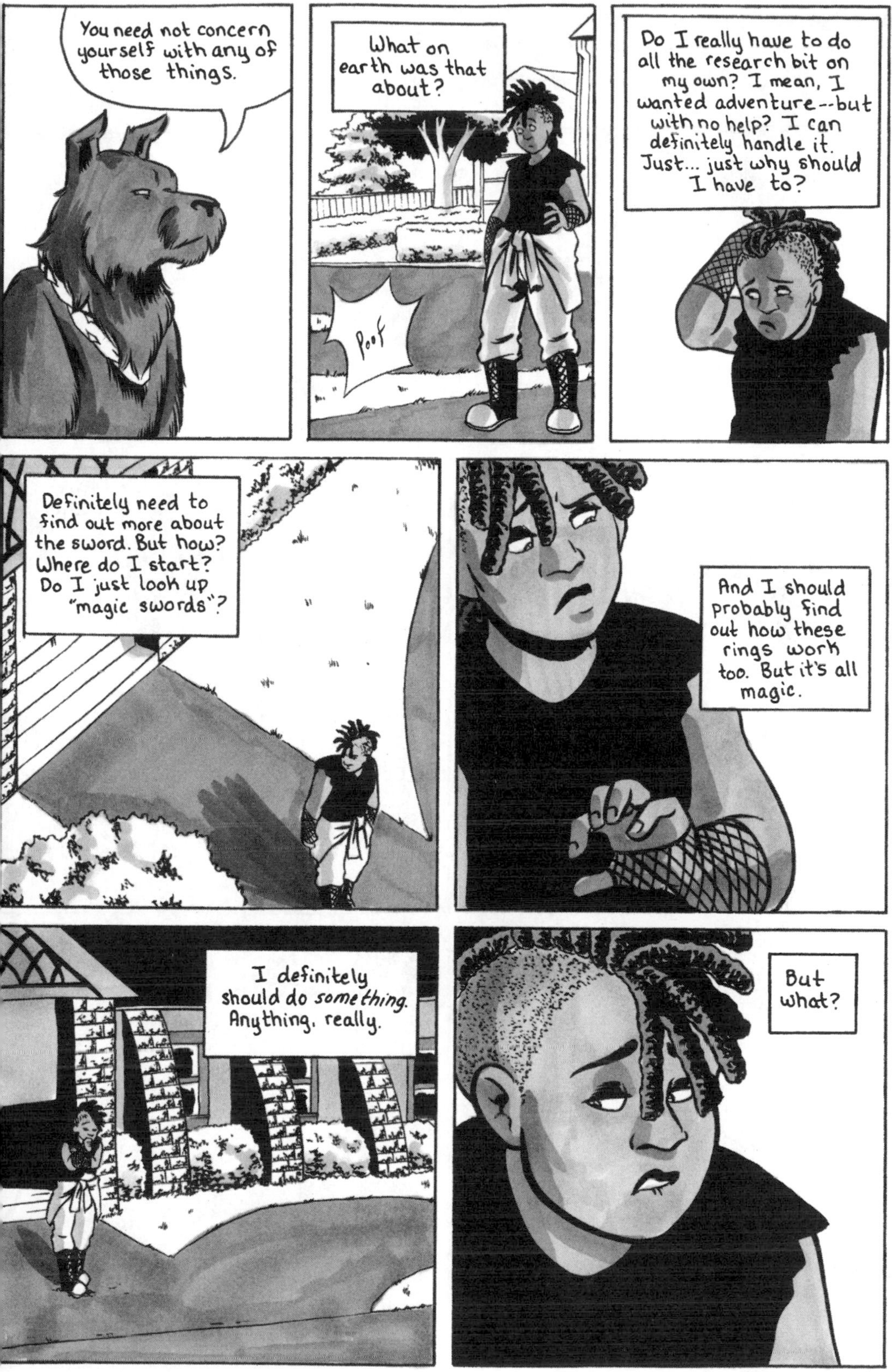
You need not concern yourself with any of those things.
What on earth was that about?
Poof
Do I really have to do all the research bit on my own? I mean, I wanted adventure--but with no help? I can definitely handle it. Just... just why should I have to?
Definitely need to find out more about the sword. But how? Where do I start? Do I just look up "magic swords"?
And I should probably find out how these rings work too. But it's all magic.
I definitely should do *something*. Anything, really.
But what?

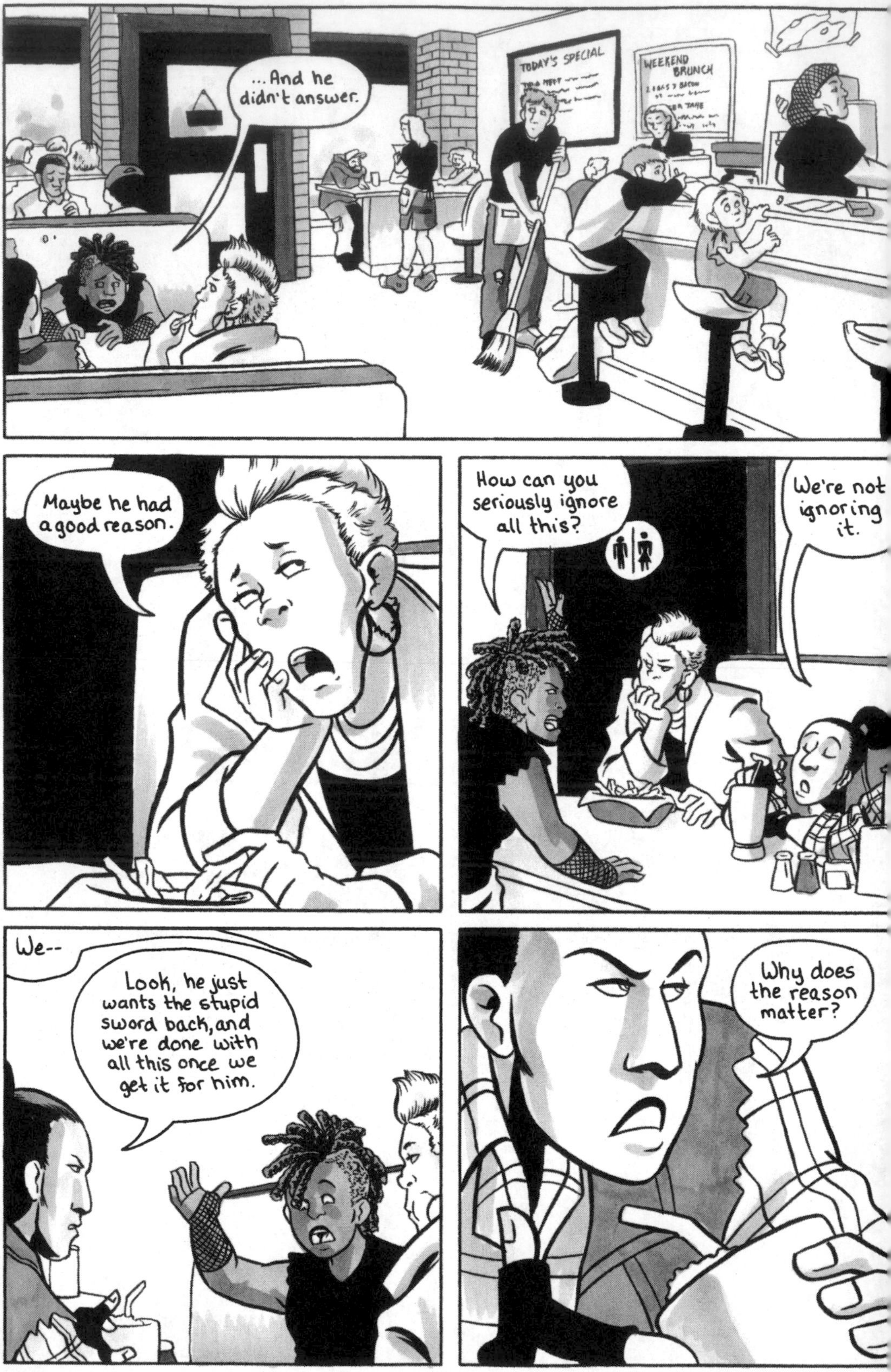
...And he didn't answer.
TODAY'S SPECIAL
WEEKEND BRUNCH
Maybe he had a good reason.
How can you seriously ignore all this?
We're not ignoring it.
We--
Look, he just wants the stupid sword back, and we're done with all this once we get it for him.
Why does the reason matter?

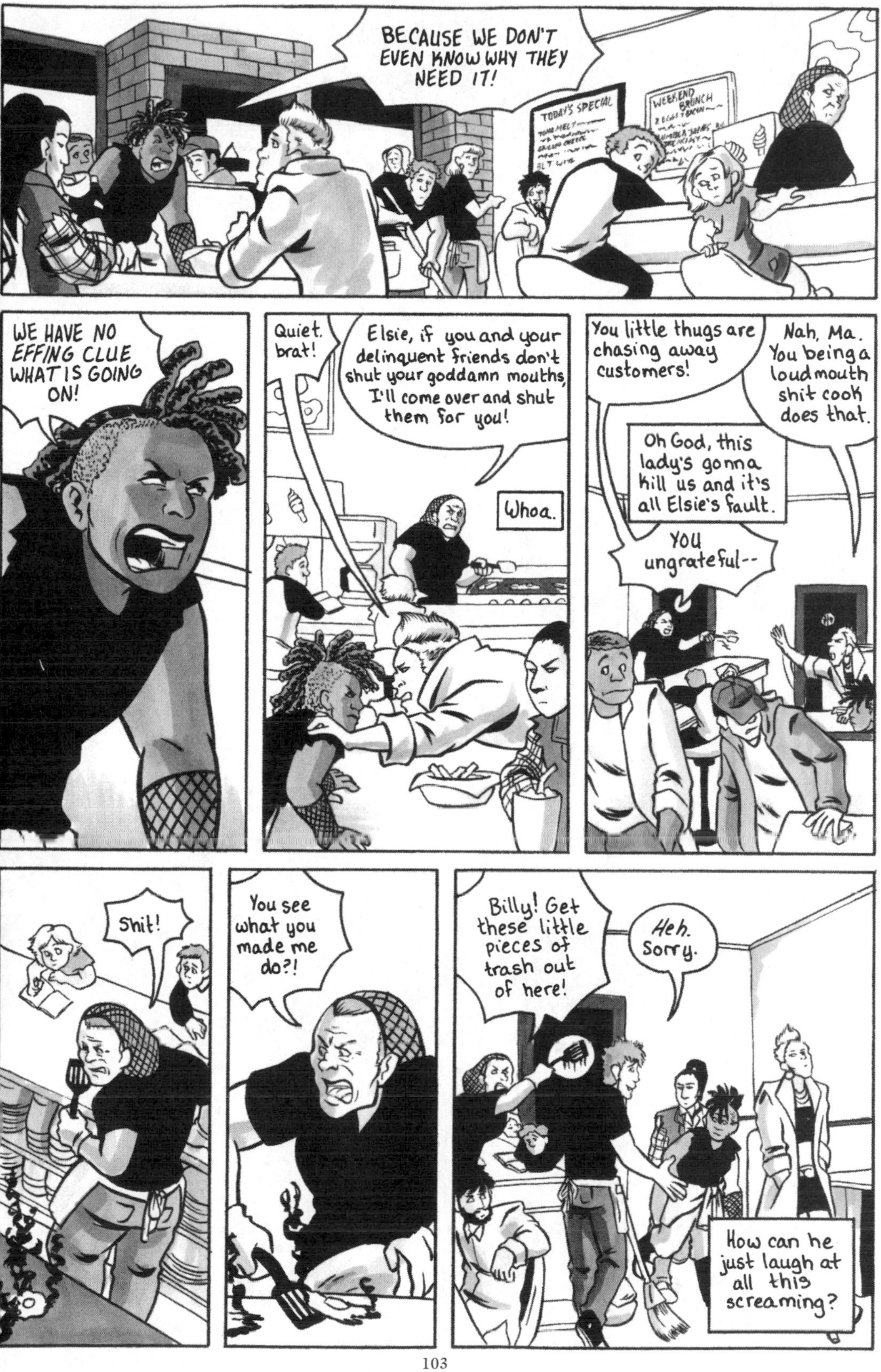
BECAUSE WE DON'T EVEN KNOW WHY THEY NEED IT!
WE HAVE NO EFFING CLUE WHAT IS GOING ON!
Quiet, brat!
Elsie, if you and your delinquent friends don't shut your goddamn mouths, I'll come over and shut them for you!
Whoa.
You little thugs are chasing away customers!
Nah, Ma. You being a loudmouth shit cook does that.
Oh God, this lady's gonna kill us and it's all Elsie's fault.
YOU ungrateful--
Shit!
You see what you made me do?!
Billy! Get these little pieces of trash out of here!
Heh. Sorry.
How can he just laugh at all this screaming?

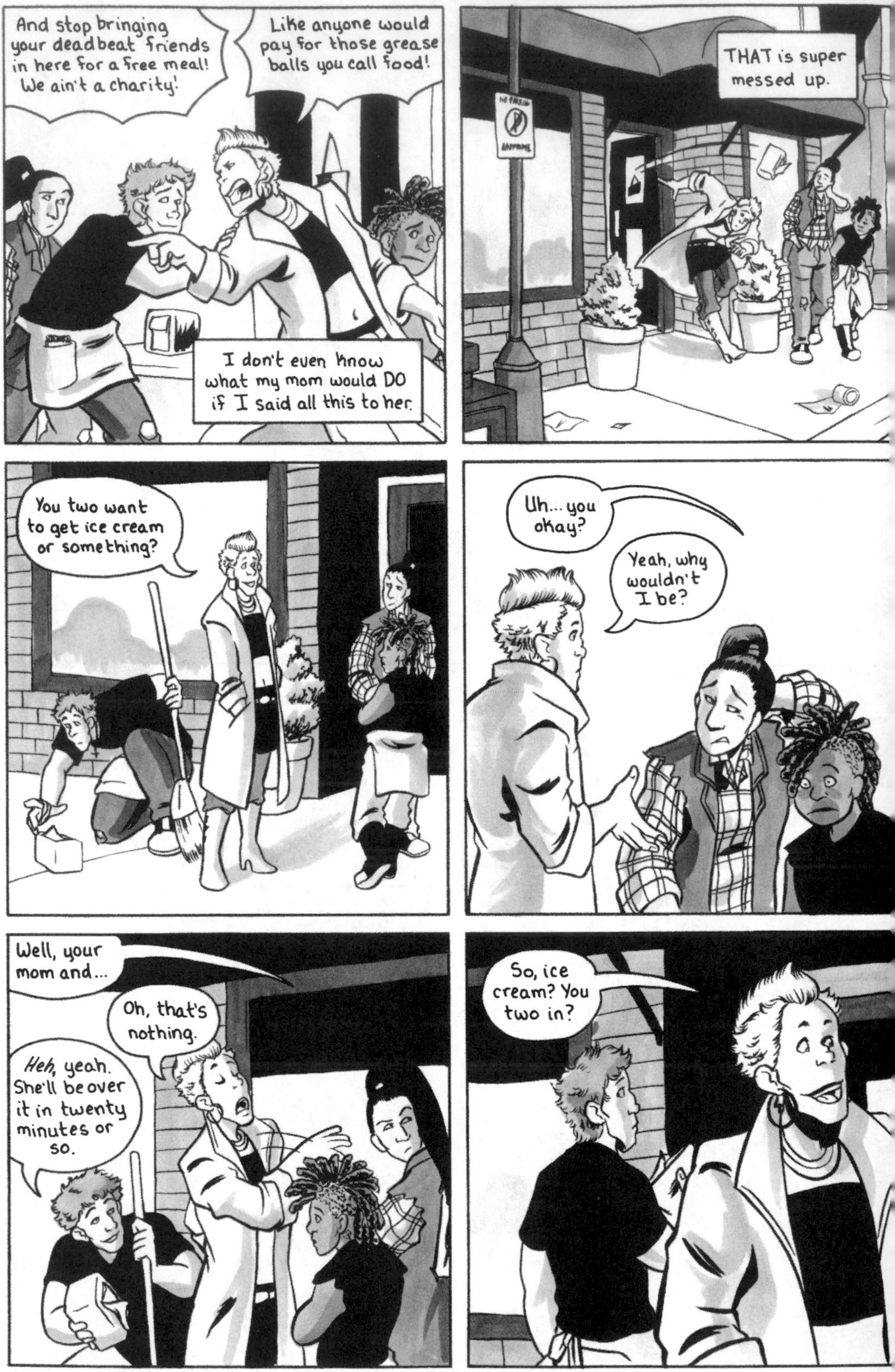
And stop bringing your deadbeat friends in here for a free meal! We ain't a charity!
Like anyone would pay for those grease balls you call food!
I don't even know what my mom would DO if I said all this to her.
THAT is super messed up.
You two want to get ice cream or something?
Uh... you okay?
Yeah, why wouldn't I be?
Well, your mom and...
Oh, that's nothing.
Heh, yeah. She'll be over it in twenty minutes or so.
So, ice cream? You two in?

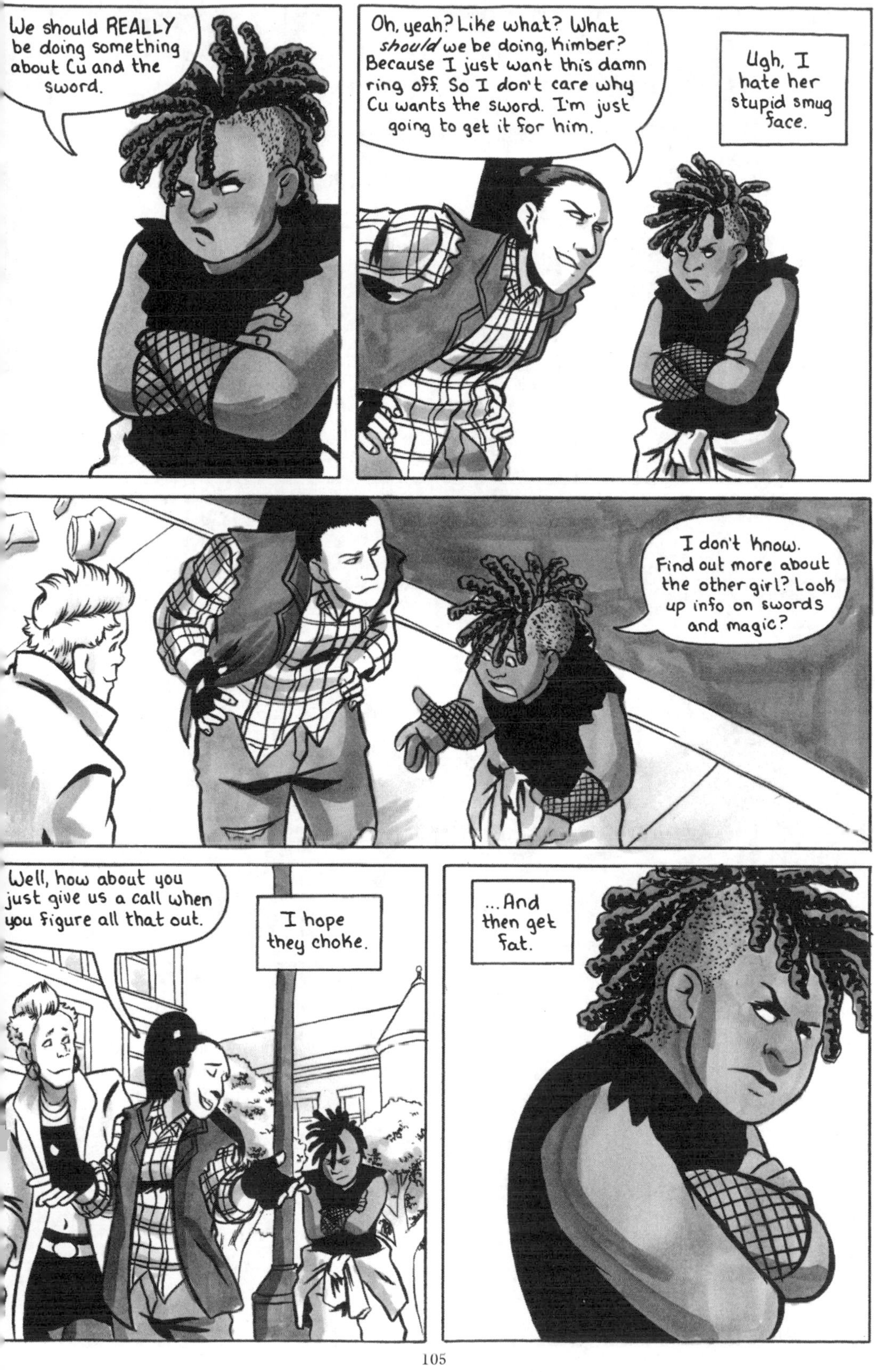
We should REALLY be doing something about Cu and the sword.
Oh, yeah? Like what? What *should* we be doing, Kimber? Because I just want this damn ring off. So I don't care why Cu wants the sword. I'm just going to get it for him.
Ugh, I hate her stupid smug face.
I don't know. Find out more about the other girl? Look up info on swords and magic?
Well, how about you just give us a call when you figure all that out.
I hope they choke.
...And then get fat.

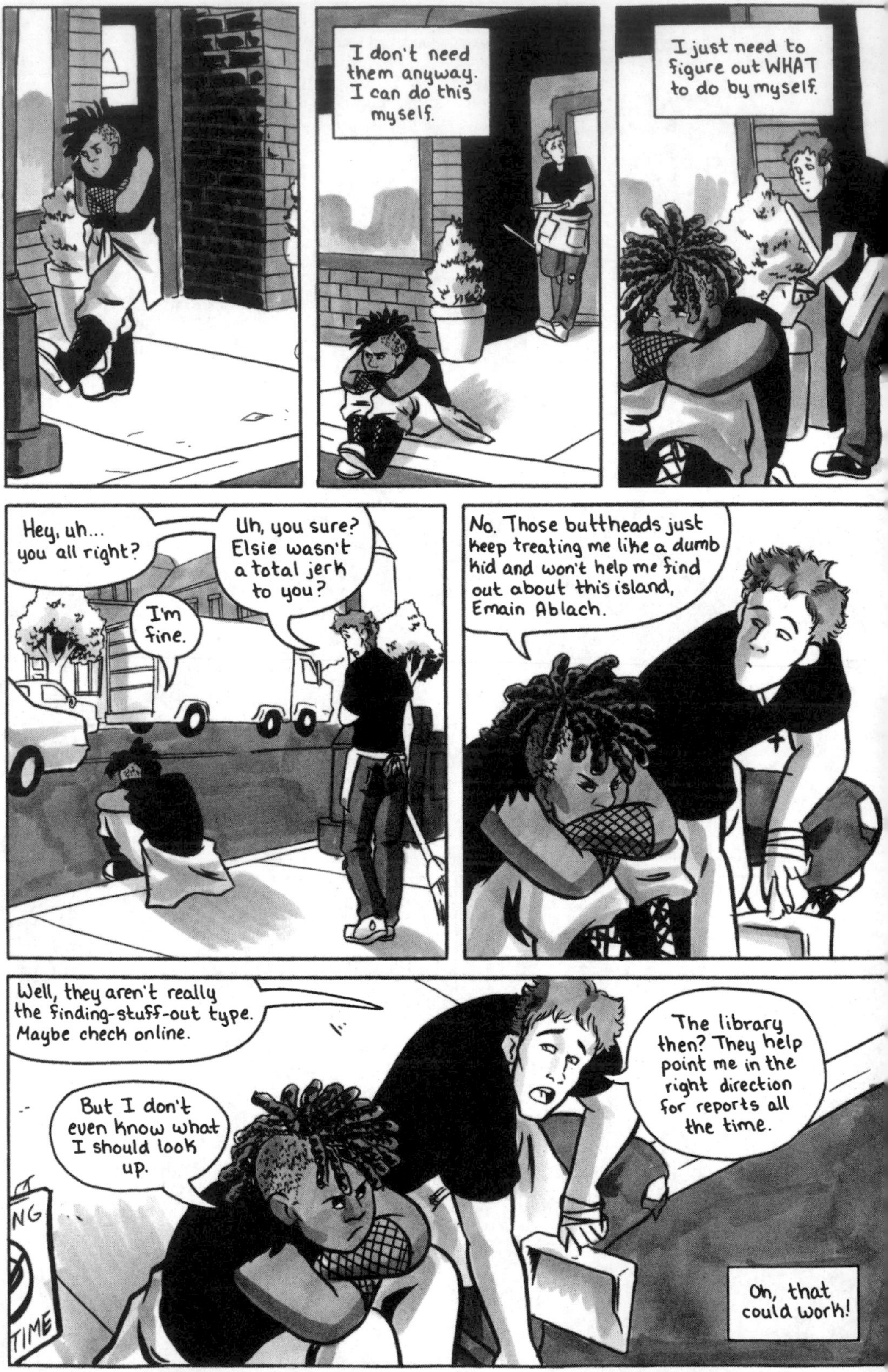
I don't need them anyway. I can do this myself.
I just need to figure out WHAT to do by myself.
Hey, uh... you all right?
I'm fine.
Uh, you sure? Elsie wasn't a total jerk to you?
No. Those buttheads just keep treating me like a dumb kid and won't help me find out about this island, Emain Ablach.
Well, they aren't really the finding-stuff-out type. Maybe check online.
But I don't even know what I should look up.
The library then? They help point me in the right direction for reports all the time.
Oh, that could work!
NG
TIME

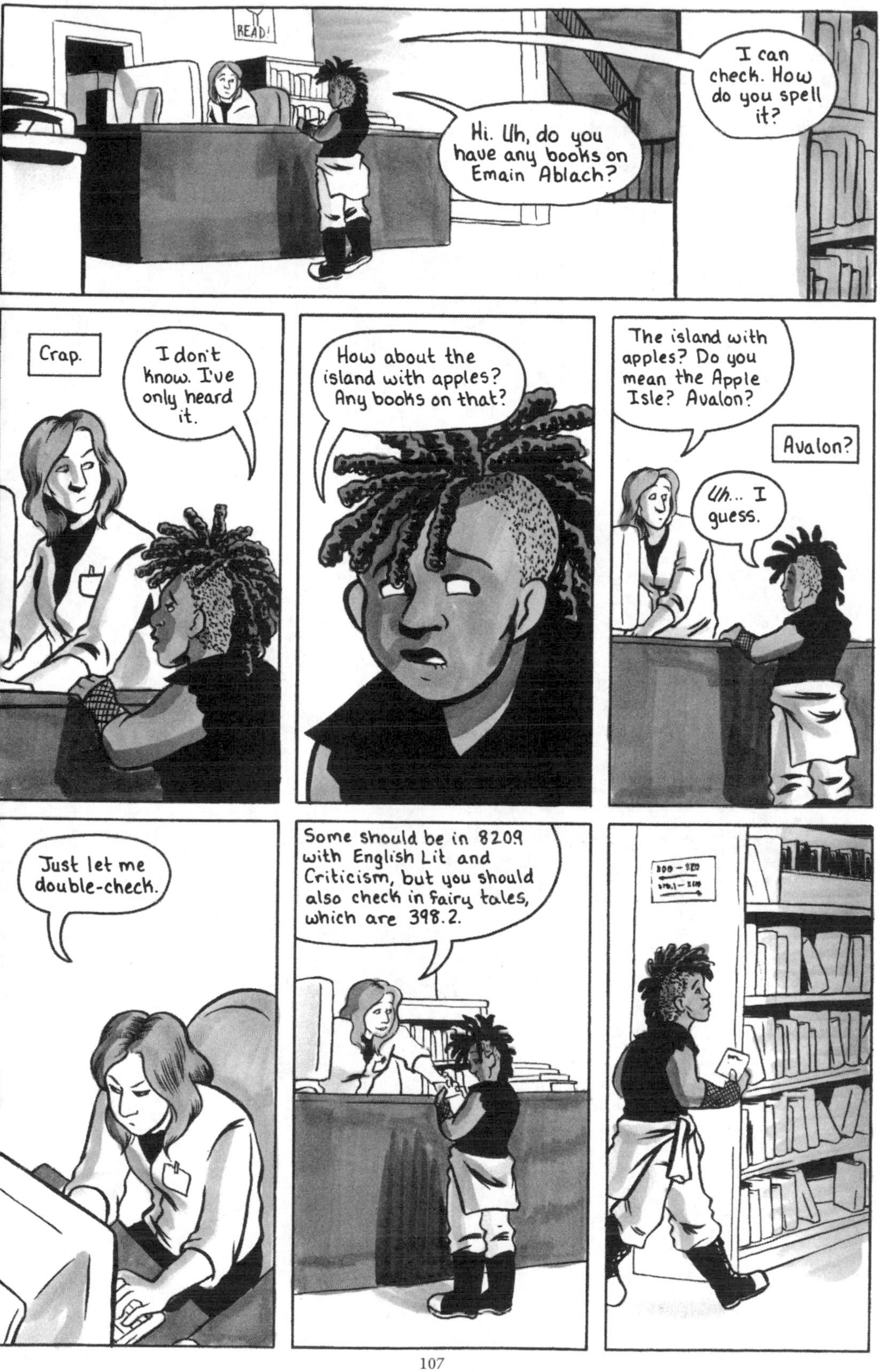
READ!
Hi. Uh, do you have any books on Emain Ablach?
I can check. How do you spell it?
Crap.
I don't know. I've only heard it.
How about the island with apples? Any books on that?
The island with apples? Do you mean the Apple Isle? Avalon?
Avalon?
Uh... I guess.
Just let me double-check.
Some should be in 820.9 with English Lit and Criticism, but you should also check in fairy tales, which are 398.2.

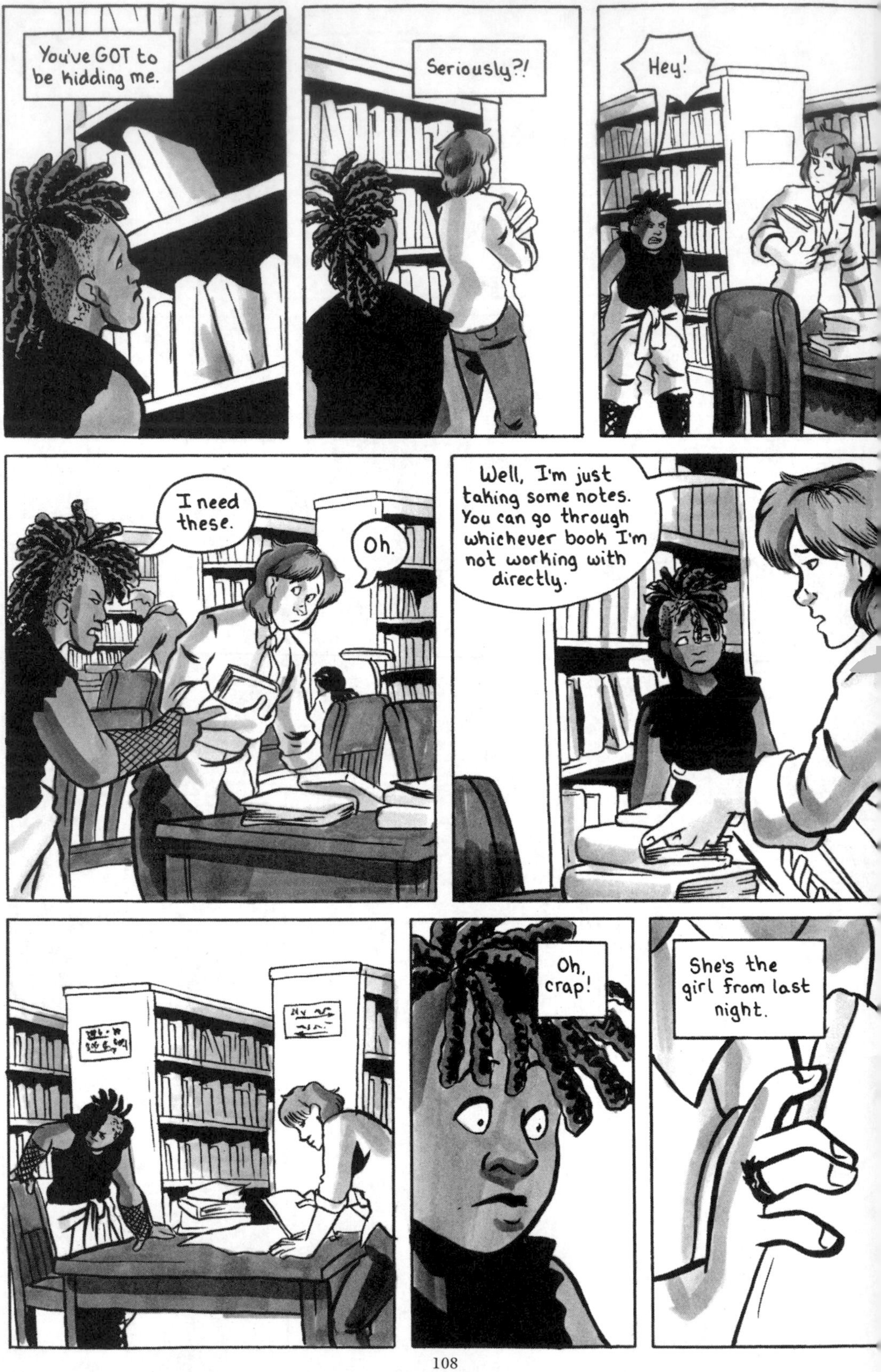
You've GOT to be kidding me.
Seriously?!
Hey!
I need these.
Oh.
Well, I'm just taking some notes. You can go through whichever book I'm not working with directly.
Oh, crap!
She's the girl from last night.

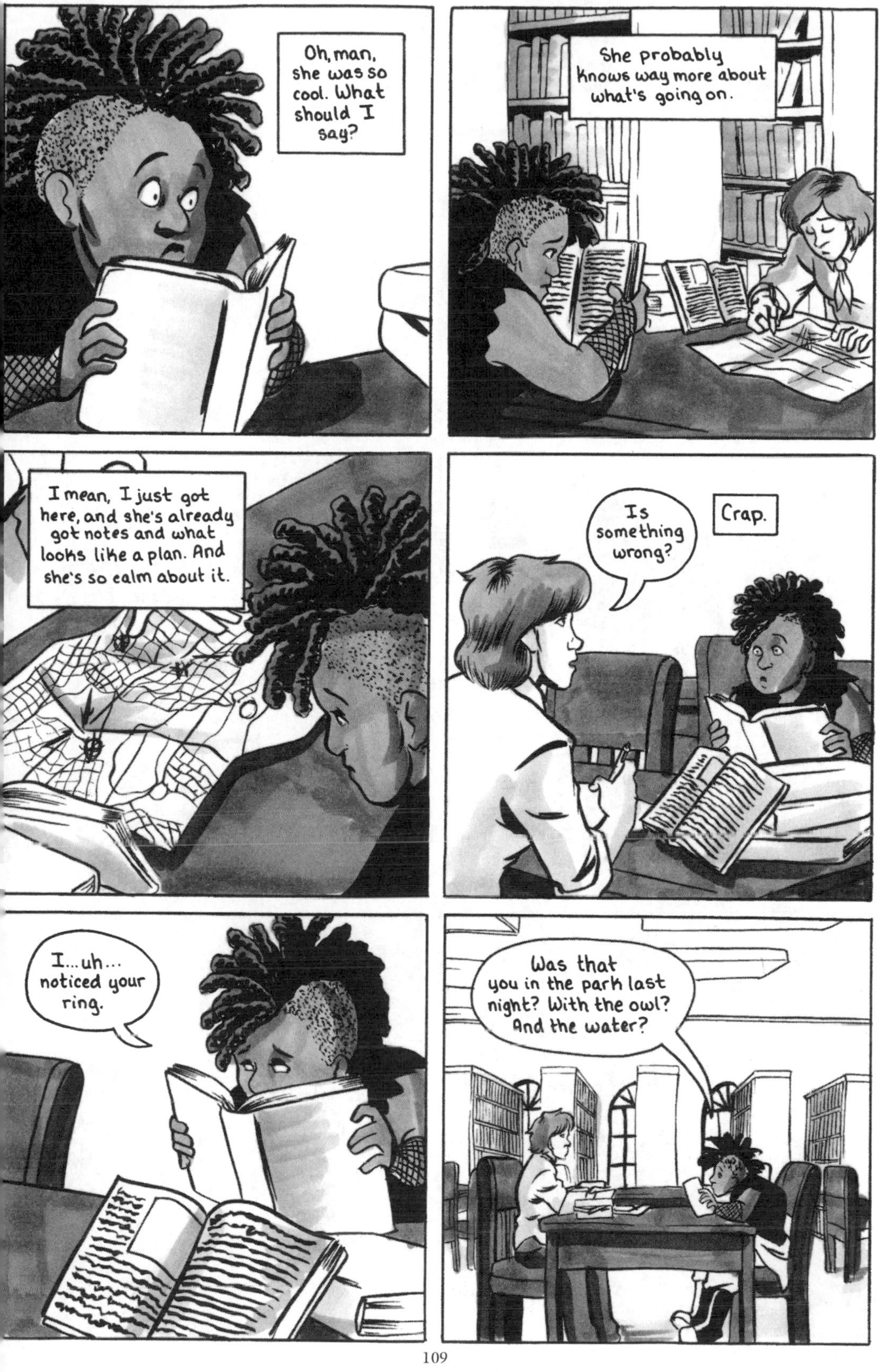
Oh, man, she was so cool. What should I say?
She probably knows way more about what's going on.
I mean, I just got here, and she's already got notes and what looks like a plan. And she's so calm about it.
Is something wrong?
Crap.
I... uh... noticed your ring.
Was that you in the park last night? With the owl? And the water?

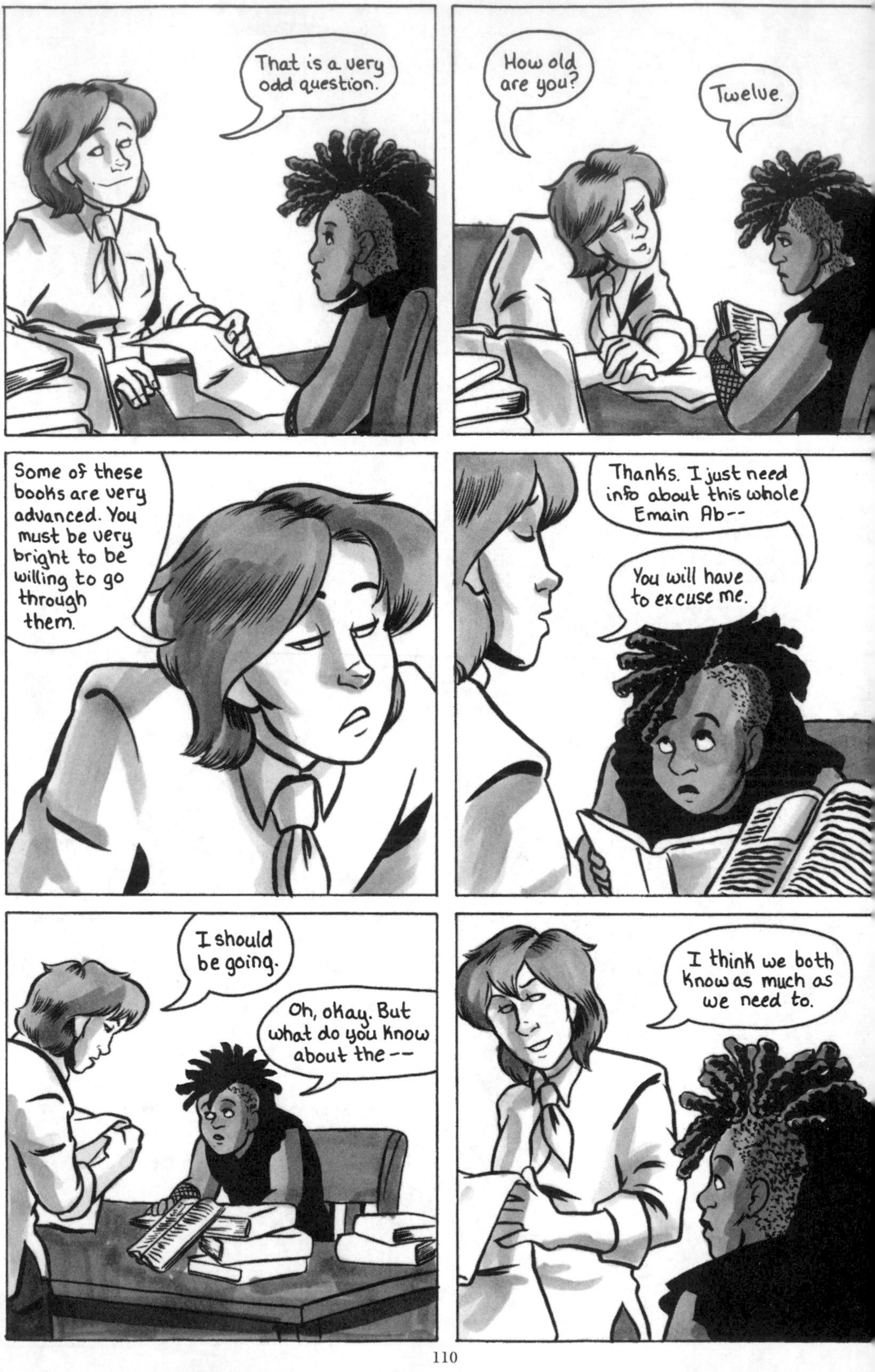
That is a very odd question.
How old are you?
Twelve.
Some of these books are very advanced. You must be very bright to be willing to go through them.
Thanks. I just need info about this whole Emain Ab--
You will have to excuse me.
I should be going.
Oh, okay. But what do you know about the --
I think we both know as much as we need to.

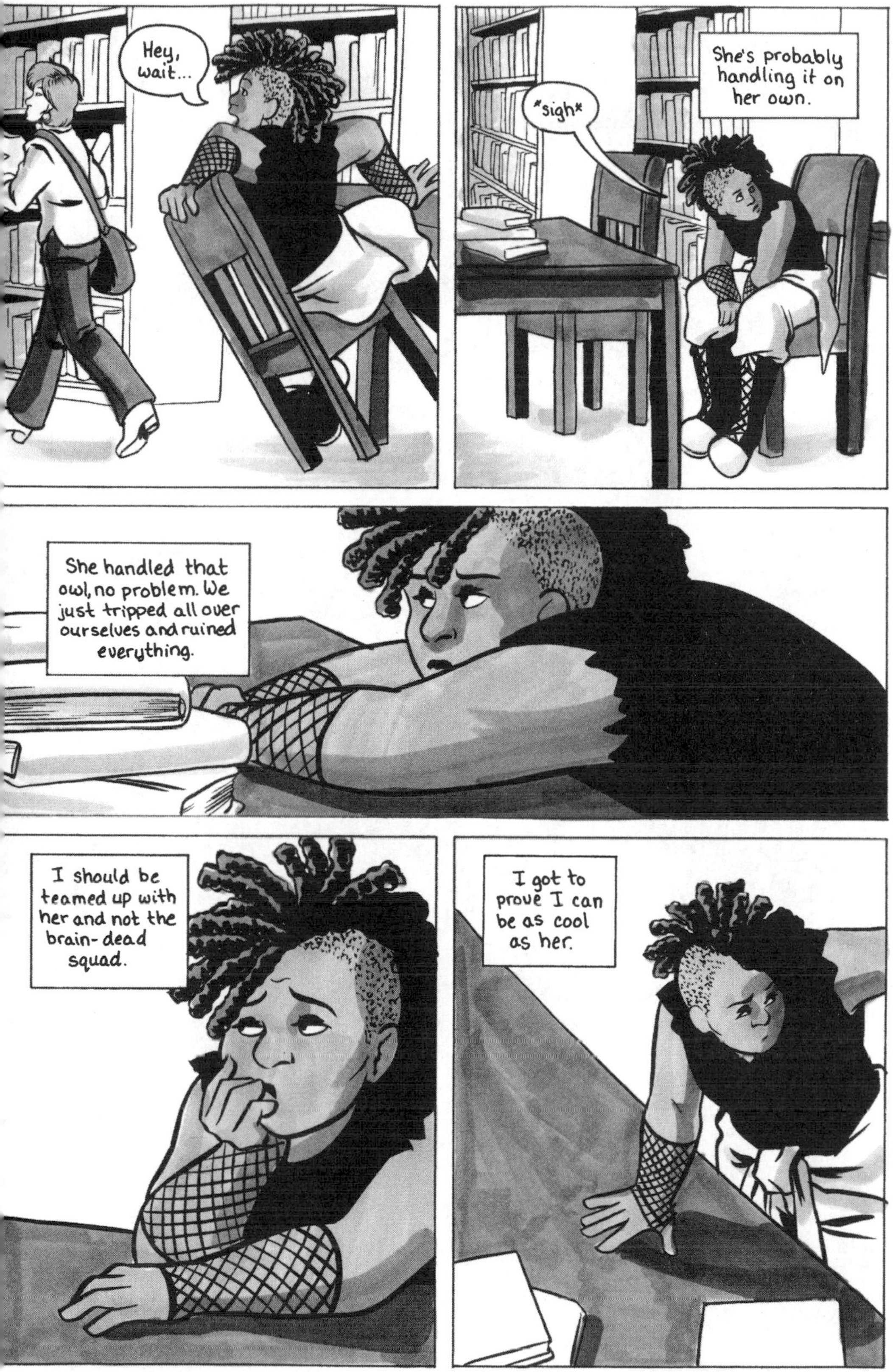
Hey, wait...
sigh
She's probably handling it on her own.
She handled that owl, no problem. We just tripped all over ourselves and ruined everything.
I should be teamed up with her and not the brain-dead squad.
I got to prove I can be as cool as her.

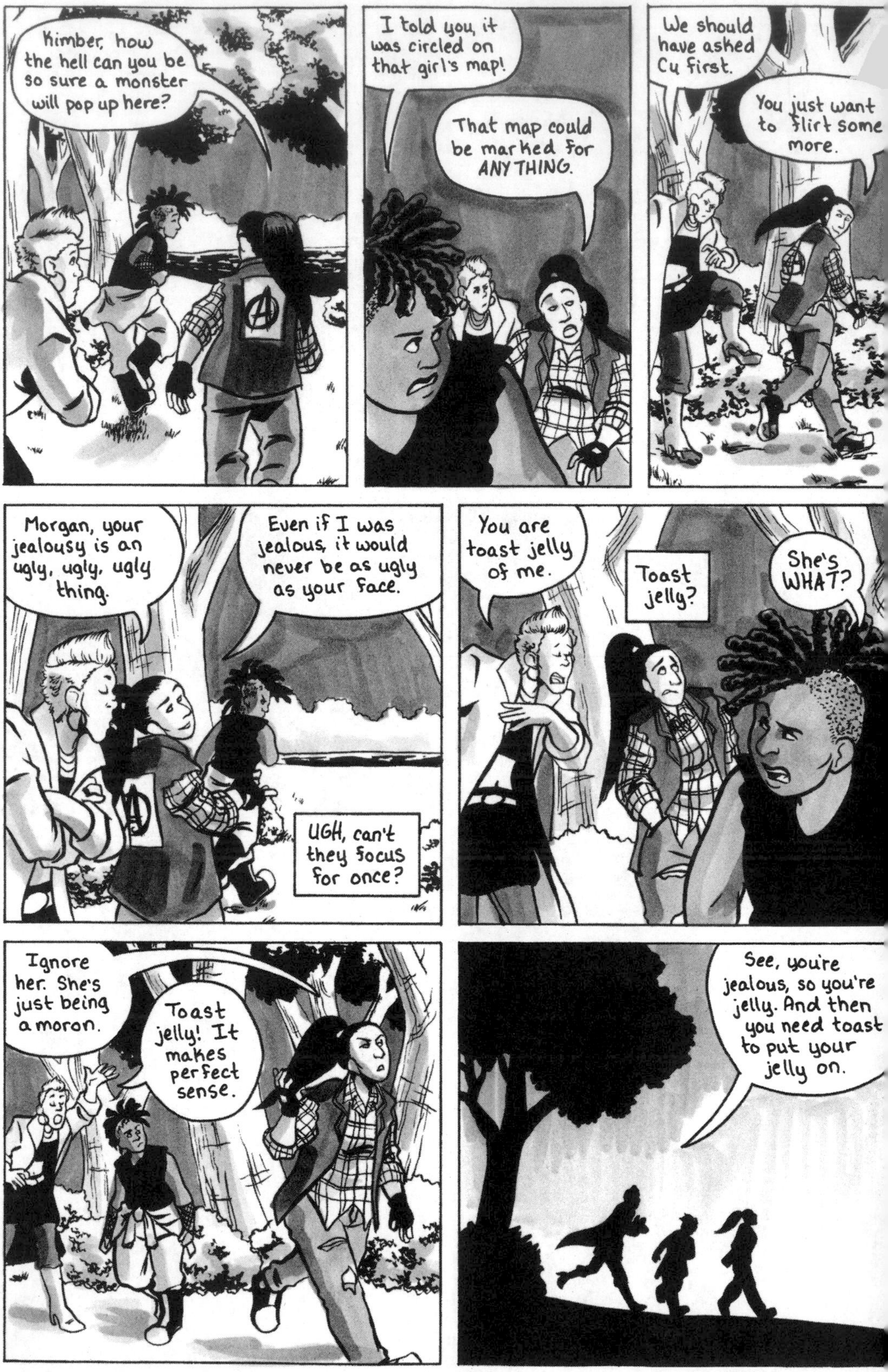
Kimber, how the hell can you be so sure a monster will pop up here?
I told you, it was circled on that girl's map!
That map could be marked for ANYTHING.
We should have asked Cu first.
You just want to flirt some more.
Morgan, your jealousy is an ugly, ugly, ugly thing.
Even if I was jealous, it would never be as ugly as your face.
UGH, can't they focus for once?
You are toast jelly of me.
Toast jelly?
She's WHAT?
Ignore her. She's just being a moron.
Toast jelly! It makes perfect sense.
See, you're jealous, so you're jelly. And then you need toast to put your jelly on.

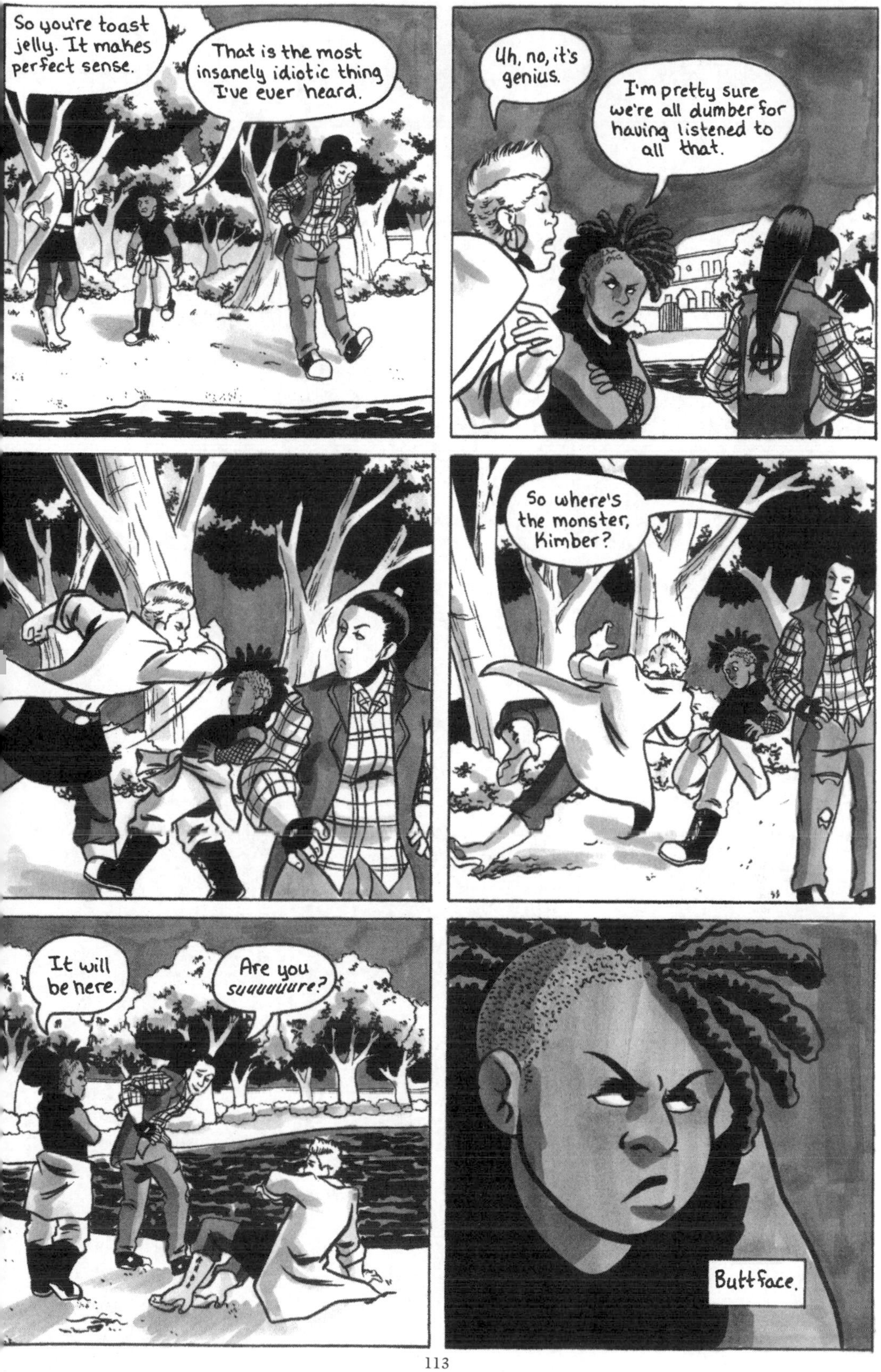
So you're toast jelly. It makes perfect sense.
That is the most insanely idiotic thing I've ever heard.
Uh, no, it's genius.
I'm pretty sure we're all dumber for having listened to all that.
So where's the monster, Kimber?
It will be here.
Are you *suuuuuure*?
Buttface.

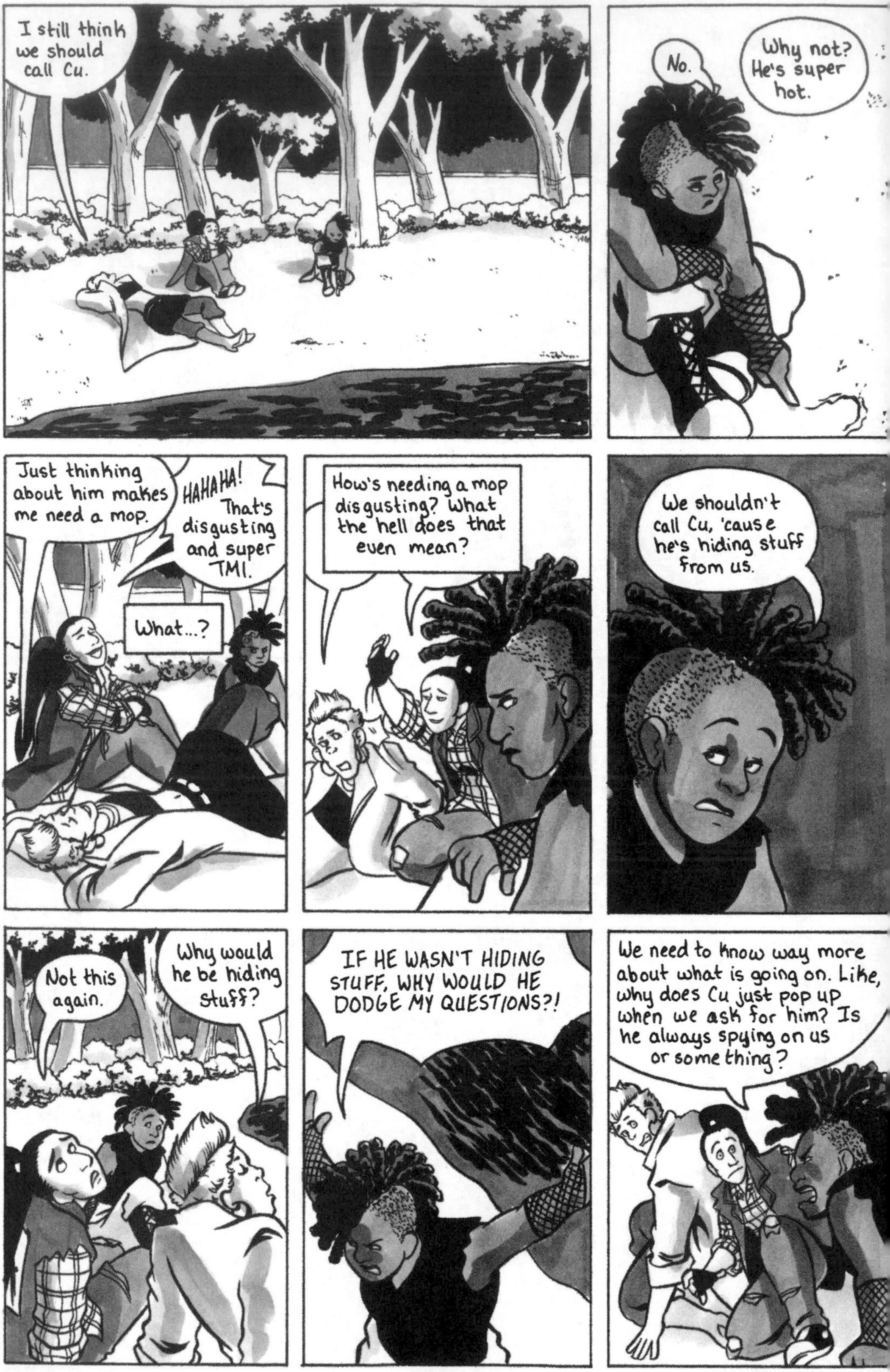

I still think we should call Cu.
No.
Why not? He's super hot.
Just thinking about him makes me need a mop.
HAHAHA! That's disgusting and super TMI.
What...?
How's needing a mop disgusting? What the hell does that even mean?
We shouldn't call Cu, 'cause he's hiding stuff from us.
Not this again.
Why would he be hiding stuff?
IF HE WASN'T HIDING STUFF, WHY WOULD HE DODGE MY QUESTIONS?!
We need to know way more about what is going on. Like, why does Cu just pop up when we ask for him? Is he always spying on us or something?

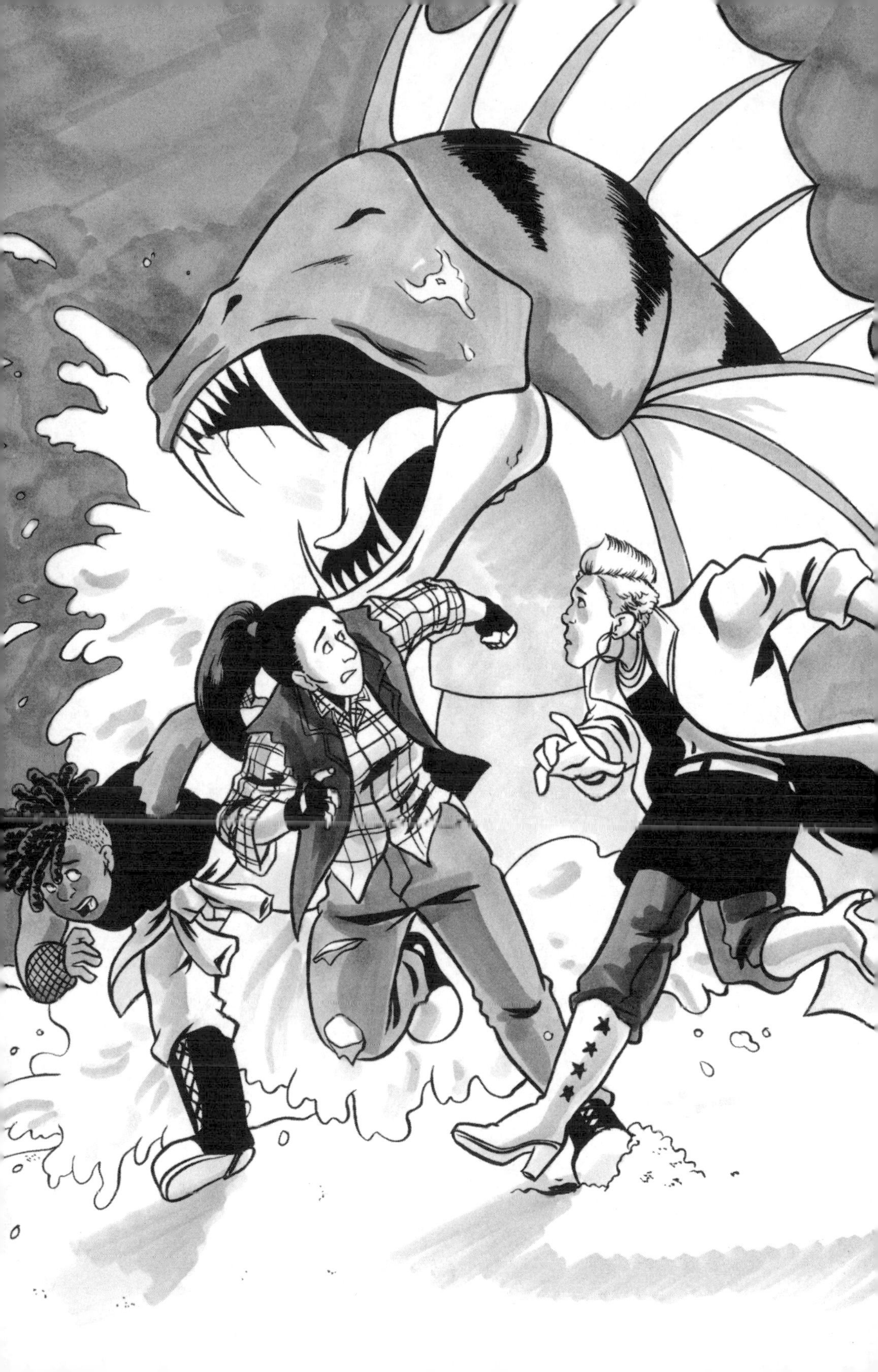

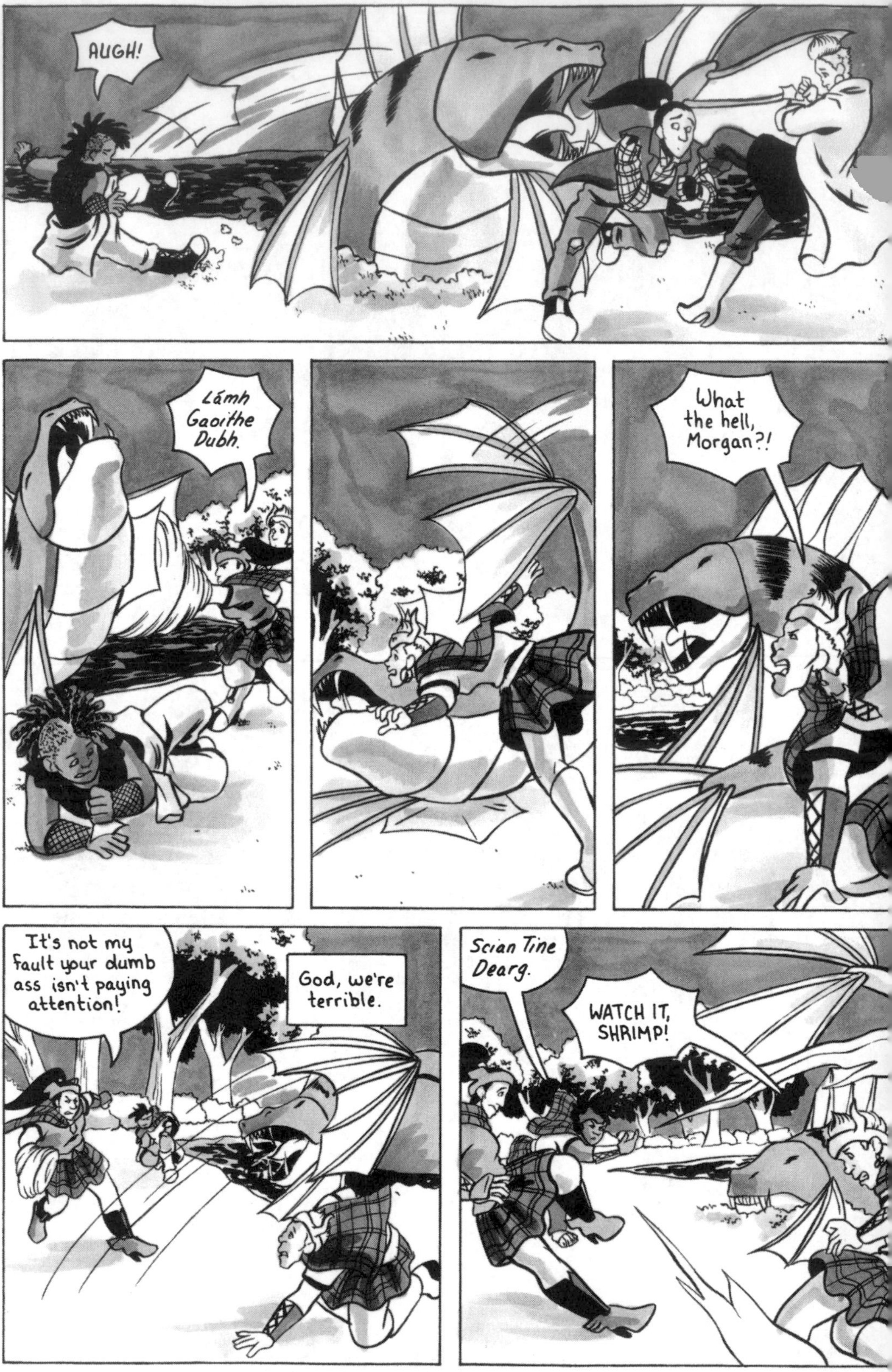
AUGH!
Lámh Gaoithe Dubh.
What the hell, Morgan?!
It's not my fault your dumb ass isn't paying attention!
God, we're terrible.
Scian Tine Dearg.
WATCH IT, SHRIMP!

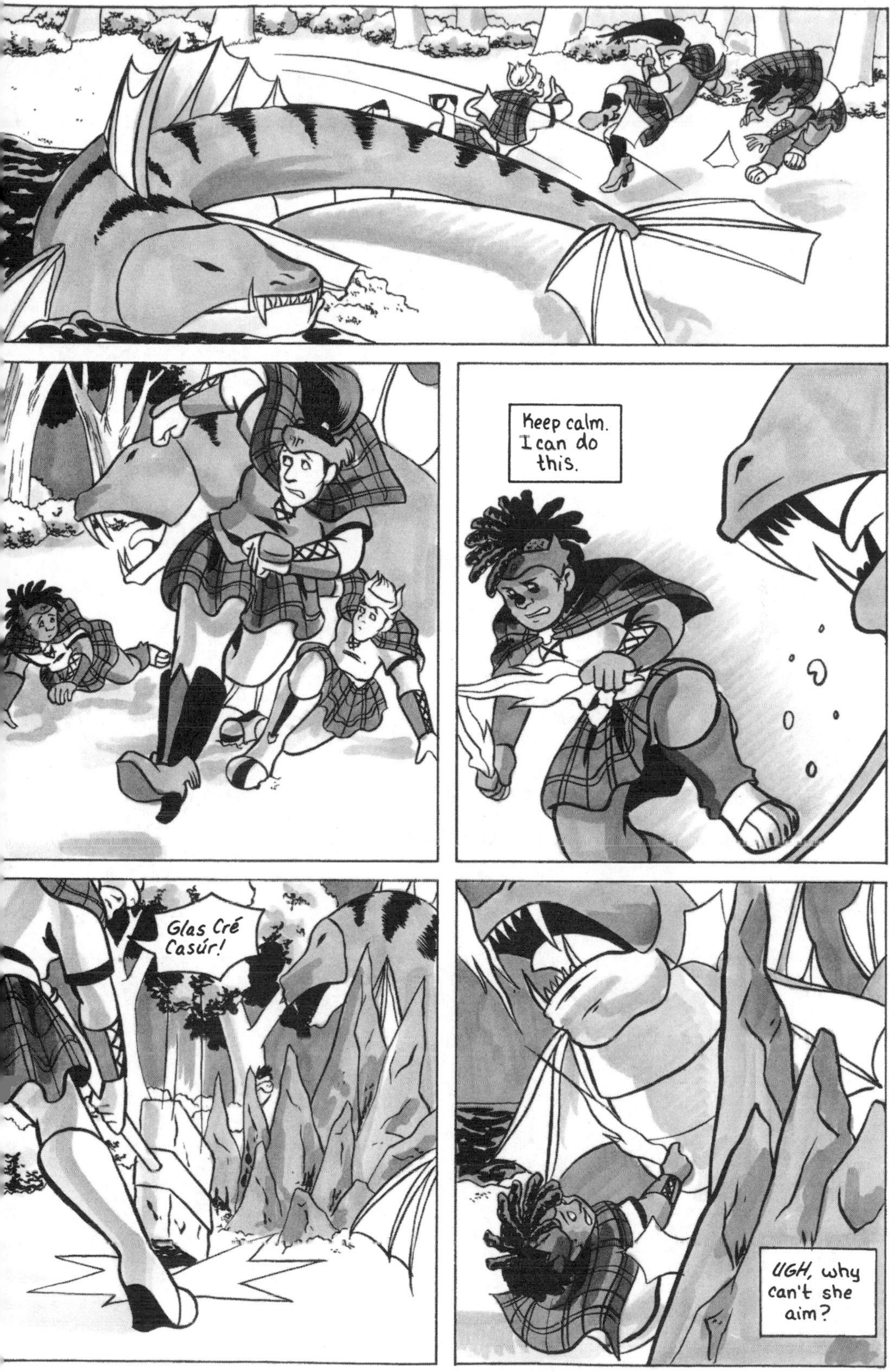
Keep calm. I can do this.
Glas Cré Casúr!
UGH, why can't she aim?

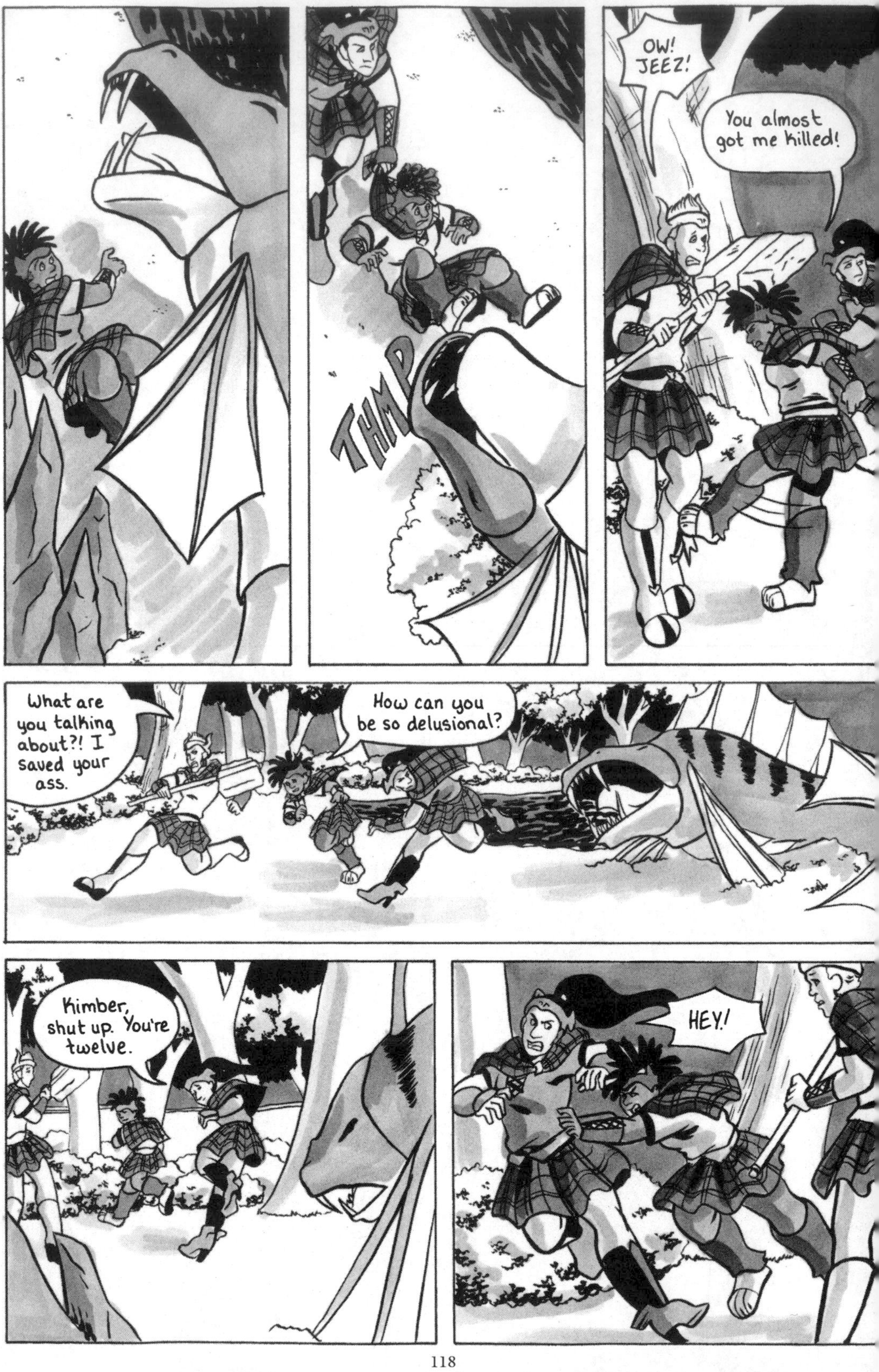
THMP
OW! JEEZ!
You almost got me killed!
What are you talking about?! I saved your ass.
How can you be so delusional?
Kimber, shut up. You're twelve.
HEY!

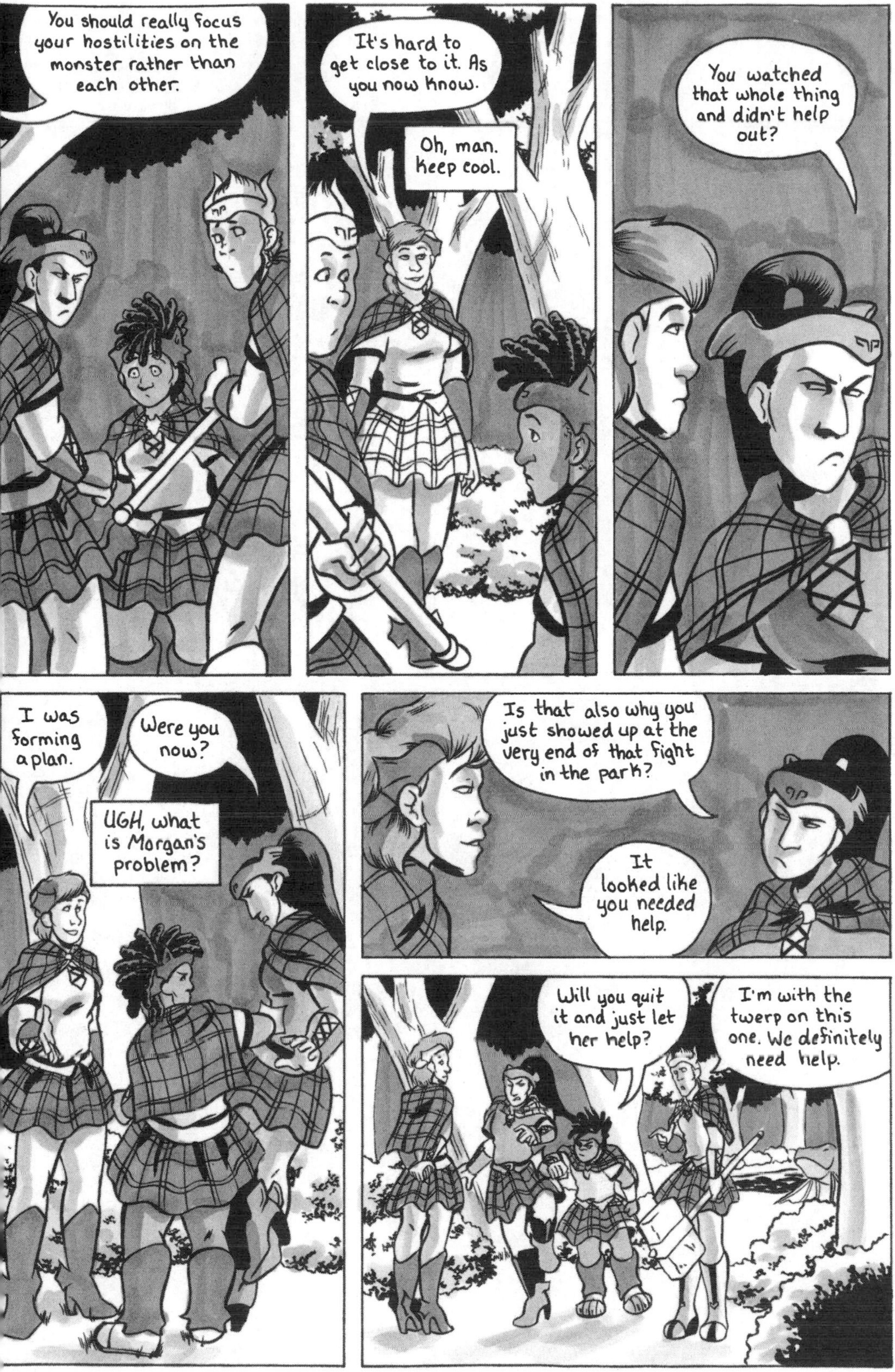

You should really focus your hostilities on the monster rather than each other.
It's hard to get close to it. As you now know.
Oh, man. Keep cool.
You watched that whole thing and didn't help out?
I was forming a plan.
Were you now?
UGH, what is Morgan's problem?
Is that also why you just showed up at the very end of that fight in the park?
It looked like you needed help.
Will you quit it and just let her help?
I'm with the twerp on this one. We definitely need help.

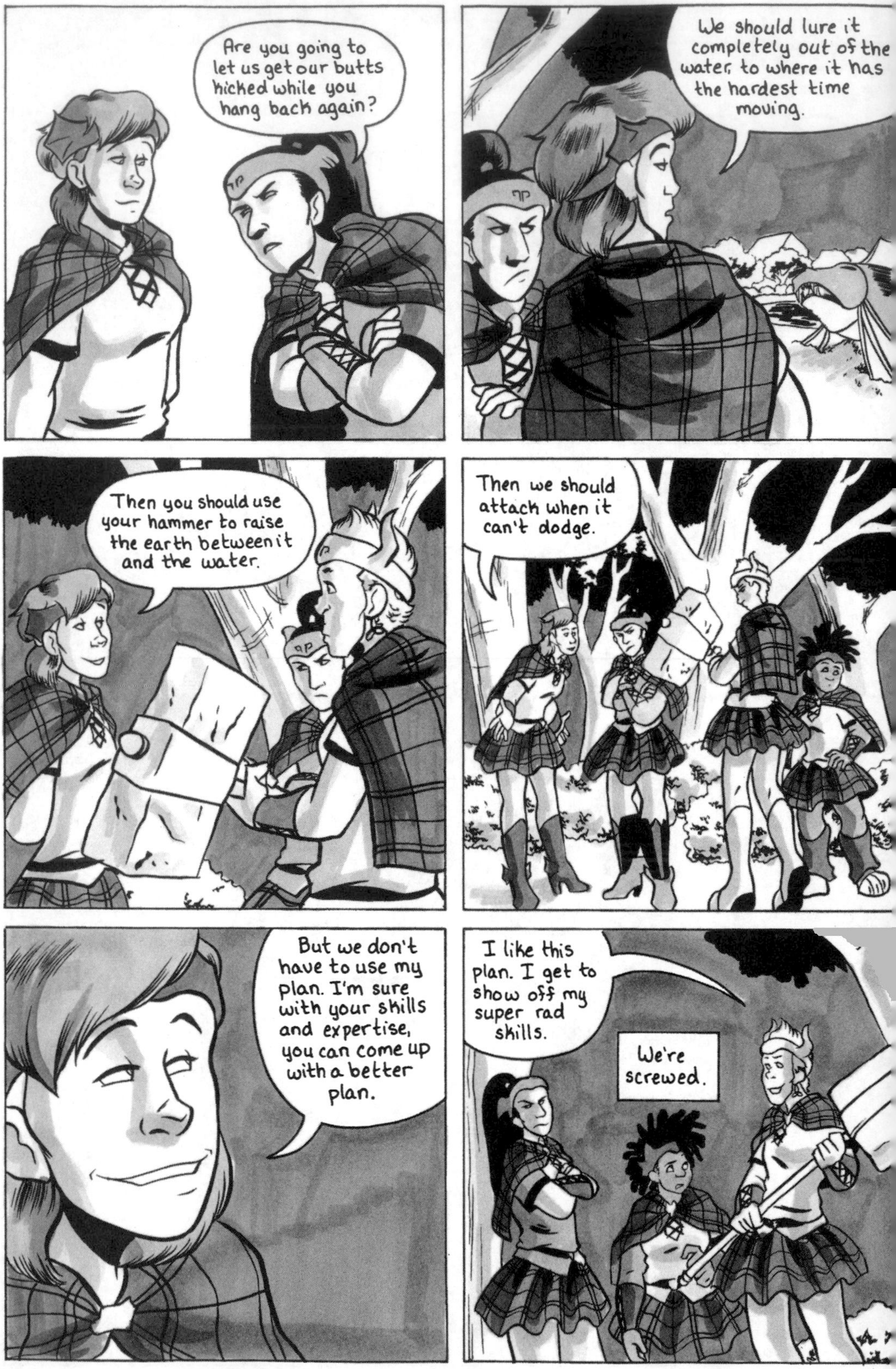
Are you going to let us get our butts kicked while you hang back again?
We should lure it completely out of the water, to where it has the hardest time moving.
Then you should use your hammer to raise the earth between it and the water.
Then we should attack when it can't dodge.
But we don't have to use my plan. I'm sure with your skills and expertise, you can come up with a better plan.
I like this plan. I get to show off my super rad skills.
We're screwed.

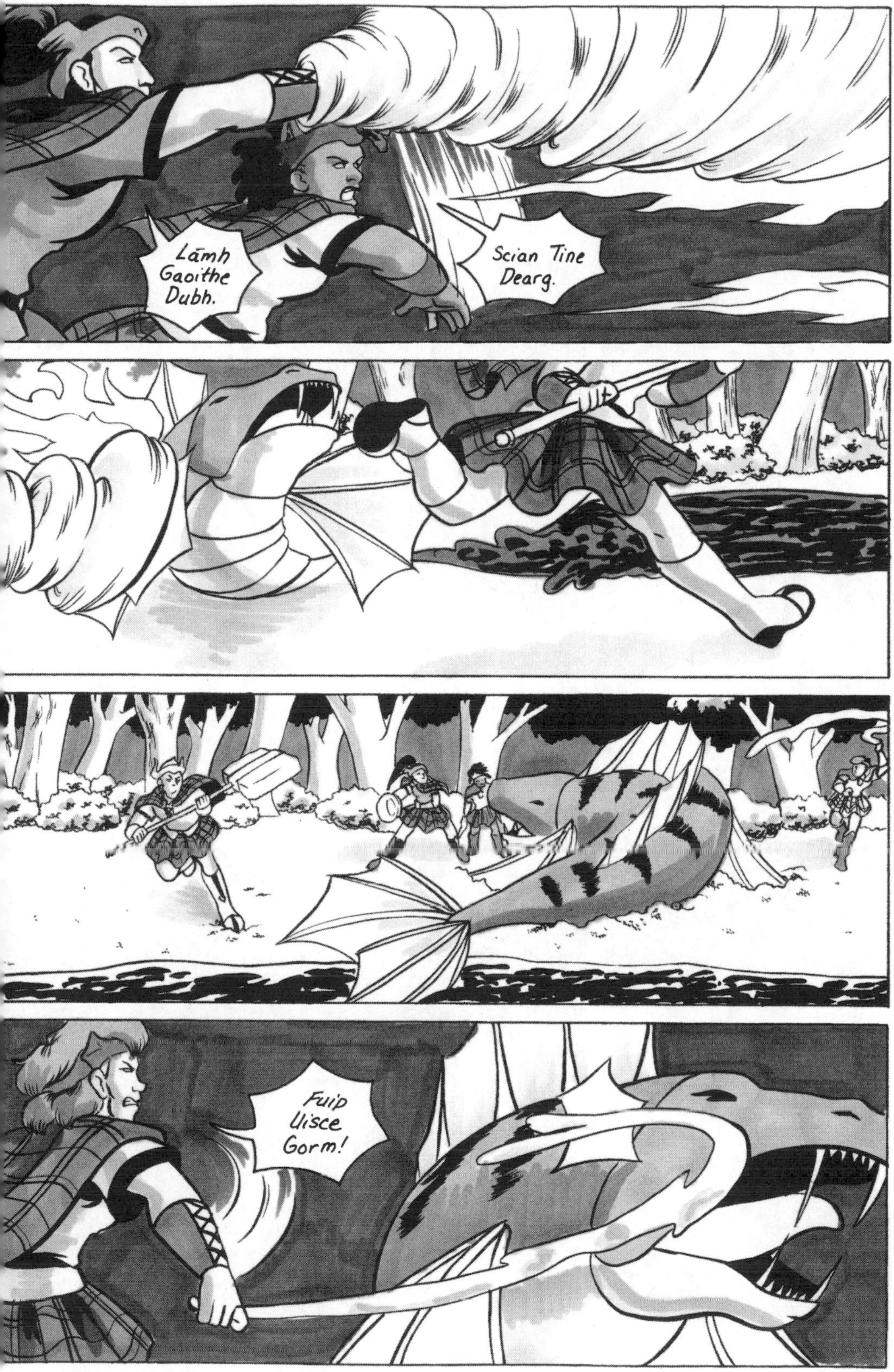
Lāmh Gaoithe Dubh.
Scian Tine Dearg.
Fuip Uisce Gorm!

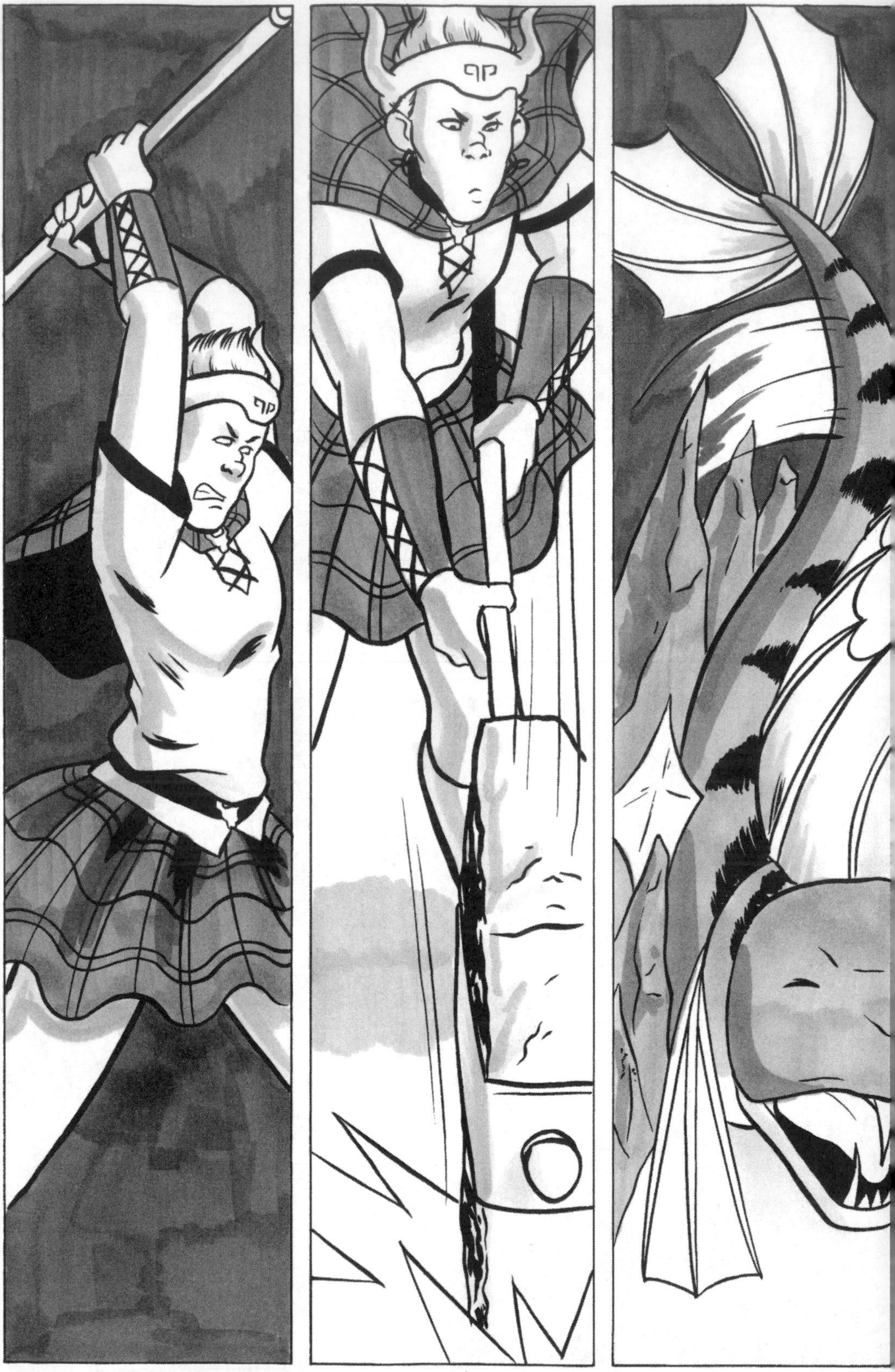

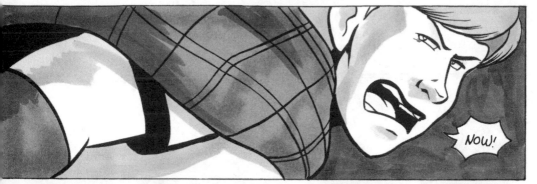

NOW!

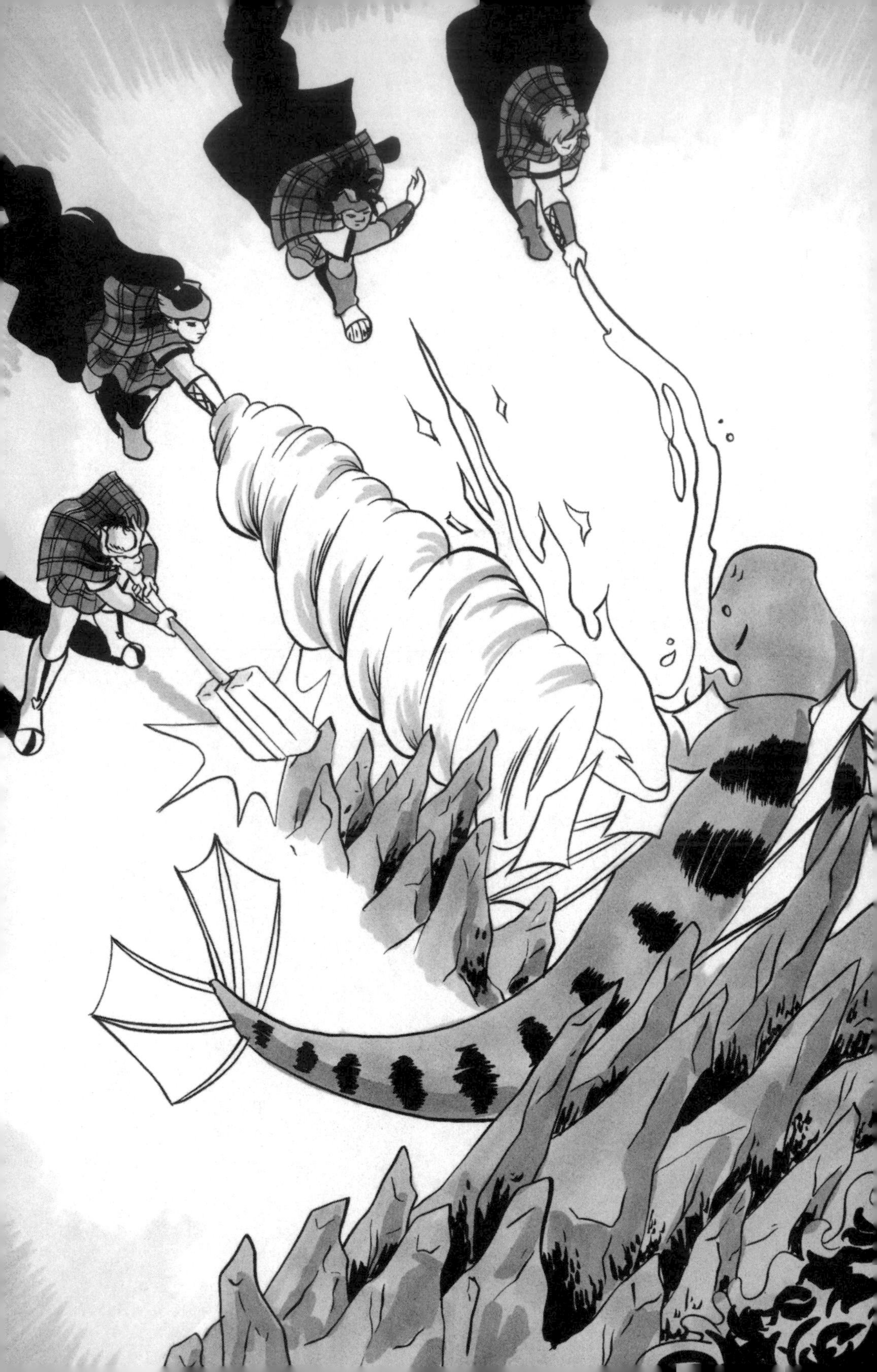

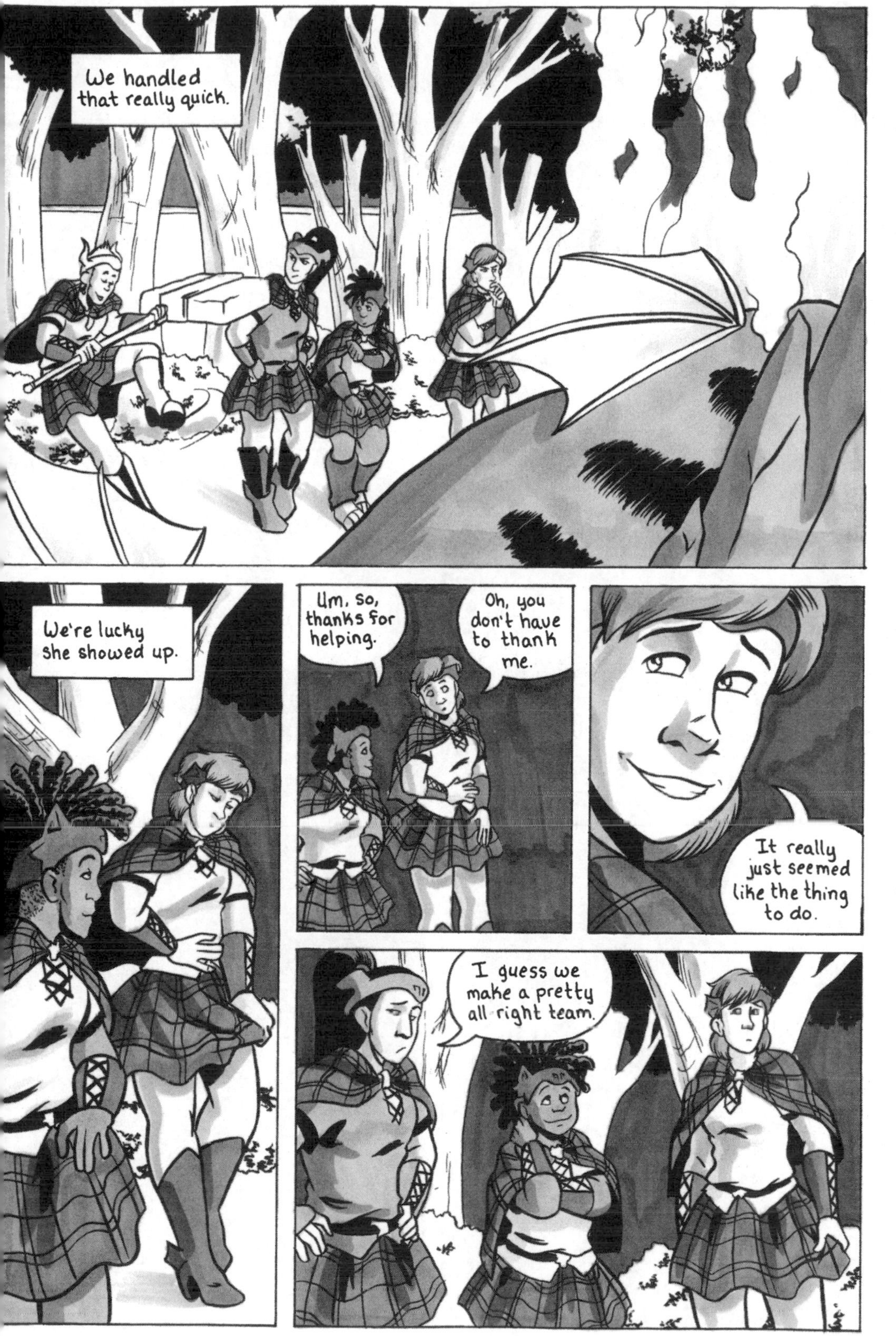
We handled that really quick.
We're lucky she showed up.
Um, so, thanks for helping.
Oh, you don't have to thank me.
It really just seemed like the thing to do.
I guess we make a pretty all right team.

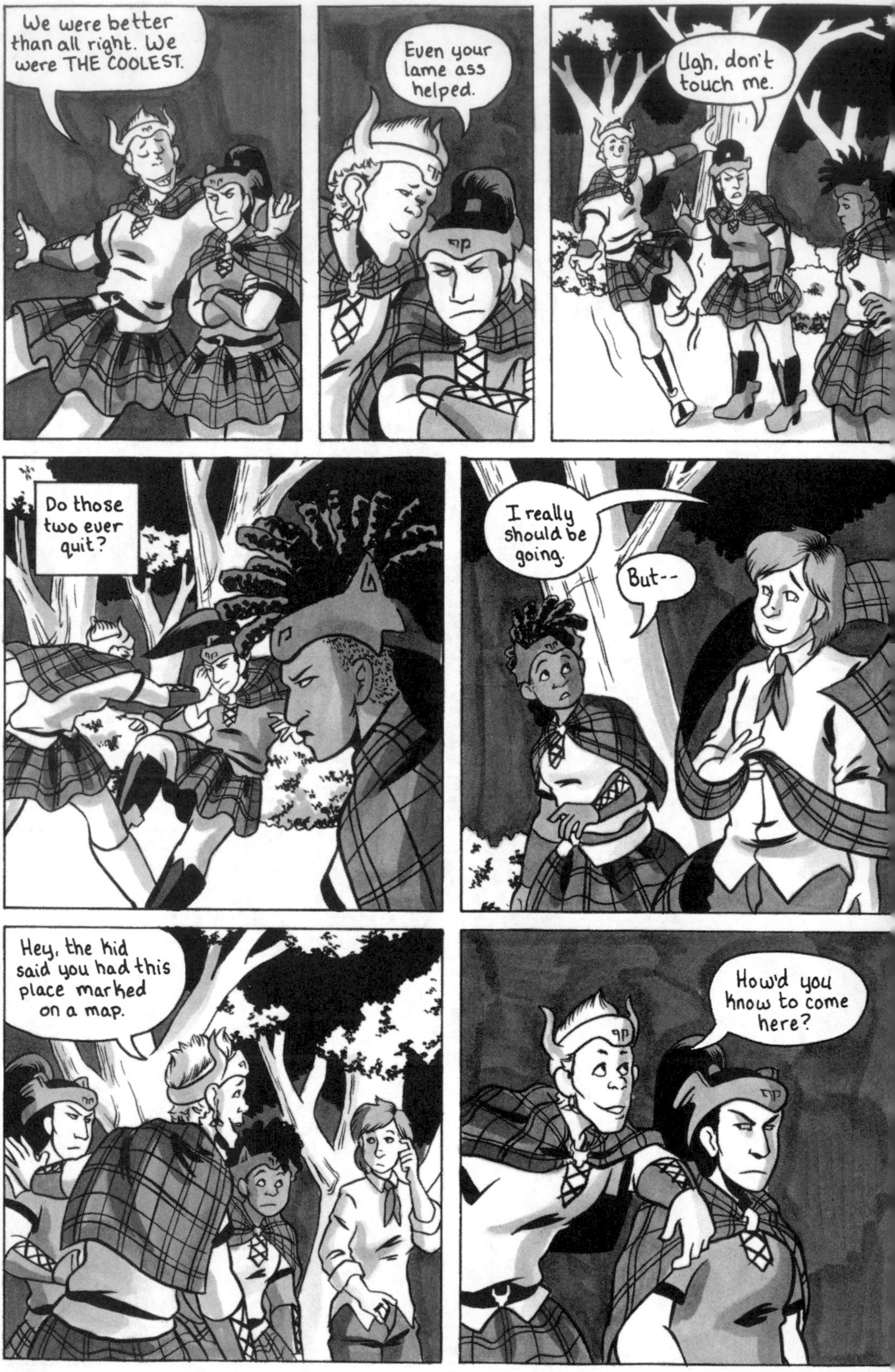

We were better than all right. We were THE COOLEST.
Even your lame ass helped.
Ugh, don't touch me.
Do those two ever quit?
I really should be going.
But--
Hey, the kid said you had this place marked on a map.
How'd you know to come here?

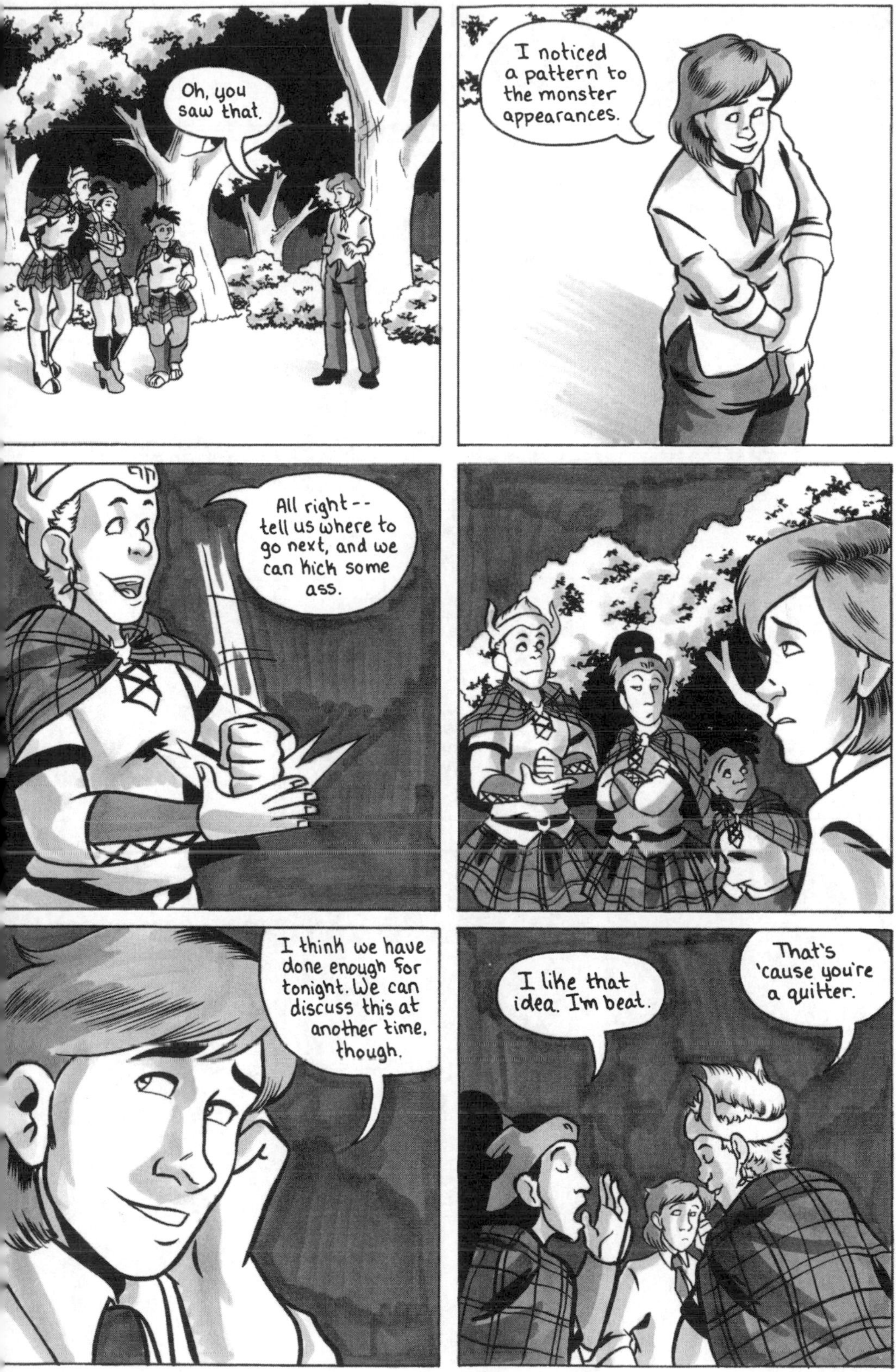
Oh, you saw that.
I noticed a pattern to the monster appearances.
All right -- tell us where to go next, and we can kick some ass.
I think we have done enough for tonight. We can discuss this at another time, though.
I like that idea. I'm beat.
That's 'cause you're a quitter.

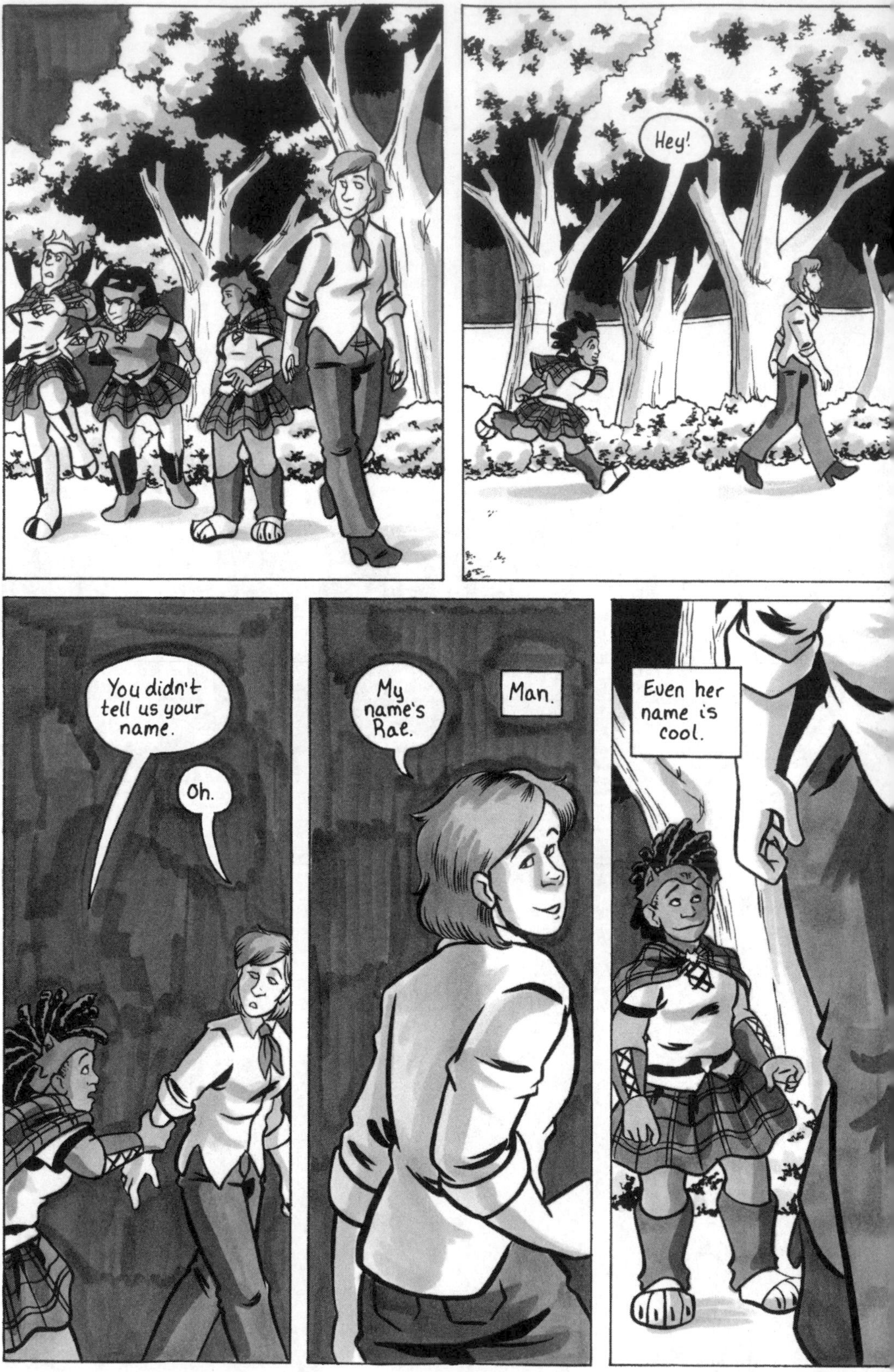

Hey!
You didn't tell us your name.
Oh.
My name's Rae.
Man.
Even her name is cool.

CHAPTER 4:
Rae the Water Eel

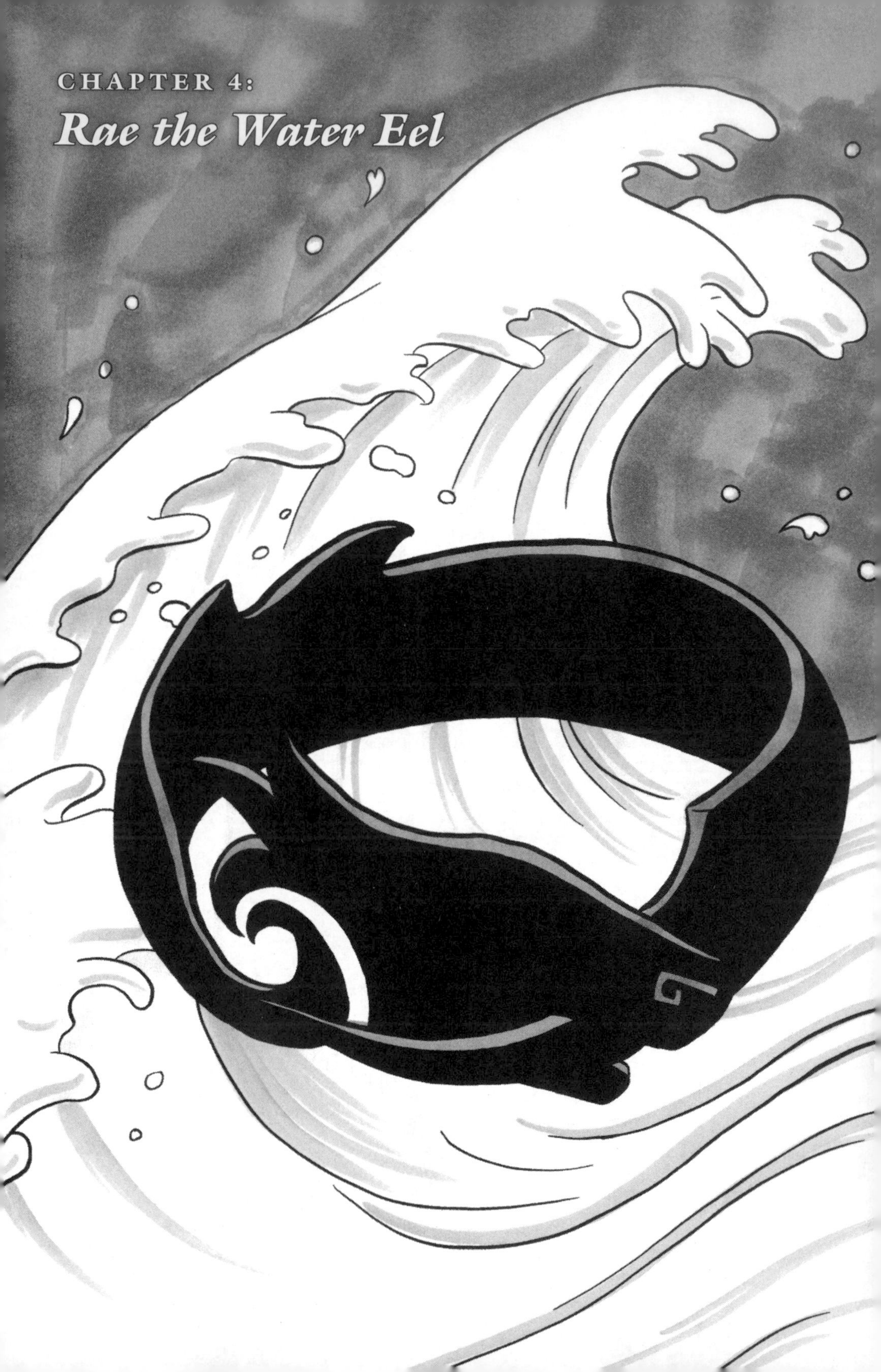

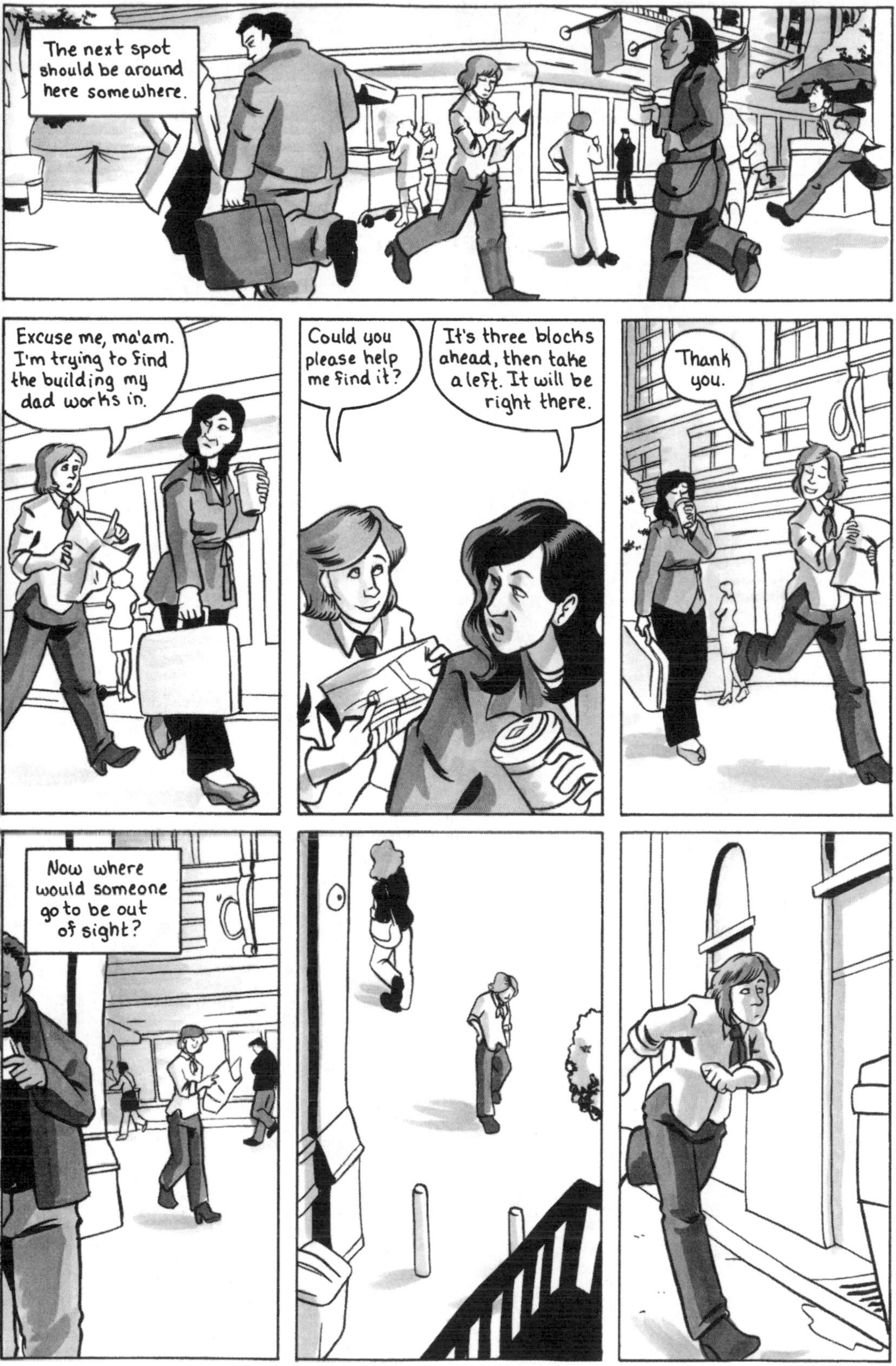

The next spot should be around here somewhere.
Excuse me, ma'am. I'm trying to find the building my dad works in.
Could you please help me find it?
It's three blocks ahead, then take a left. It will be right there.
Thank you.
Now where would someone go to be out of sight?

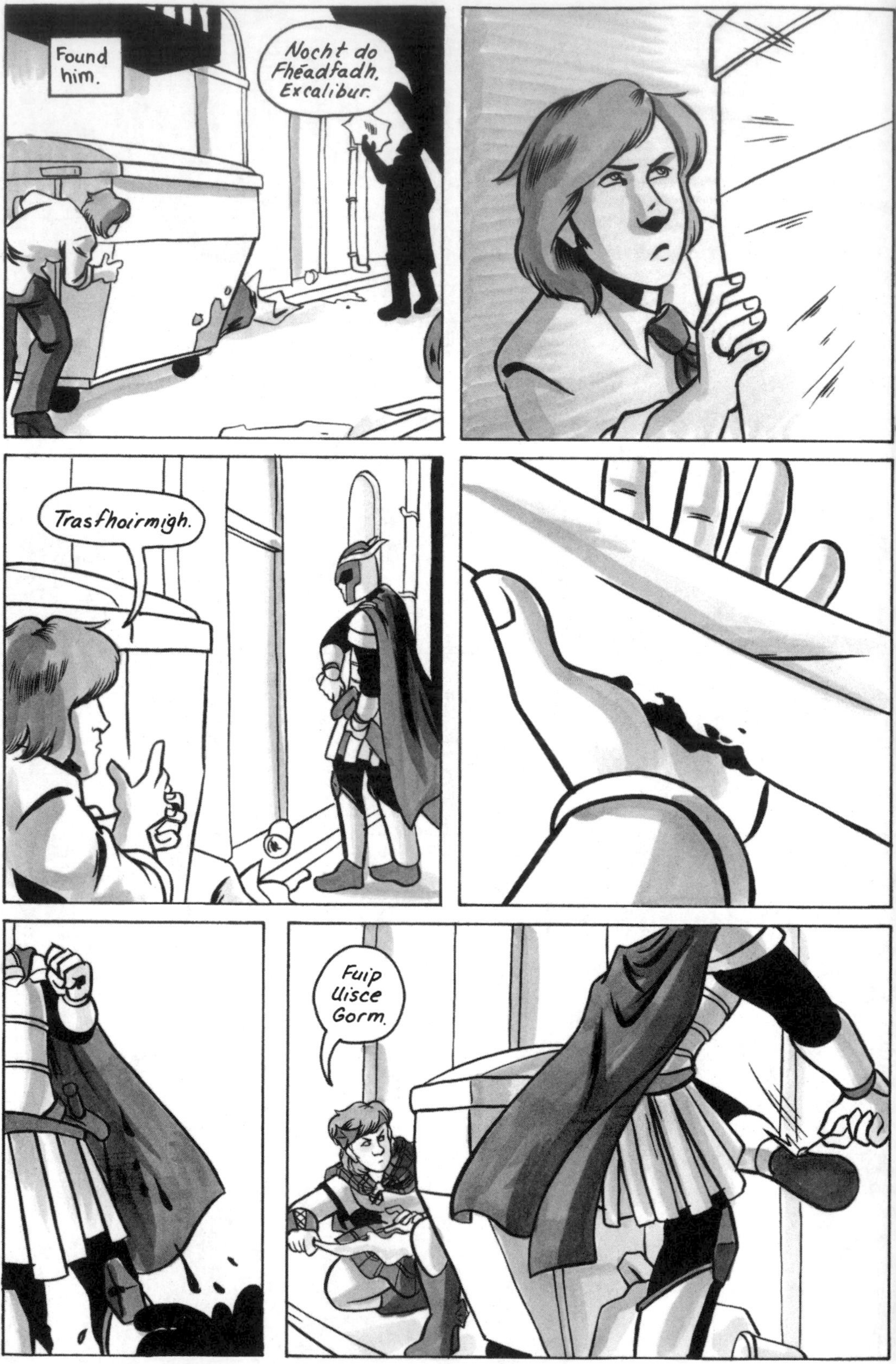
Found him.
Nocht do Fheadfadh. Excalibur.
Trasfhoirmigh.
Fuip Uisce Gorm.

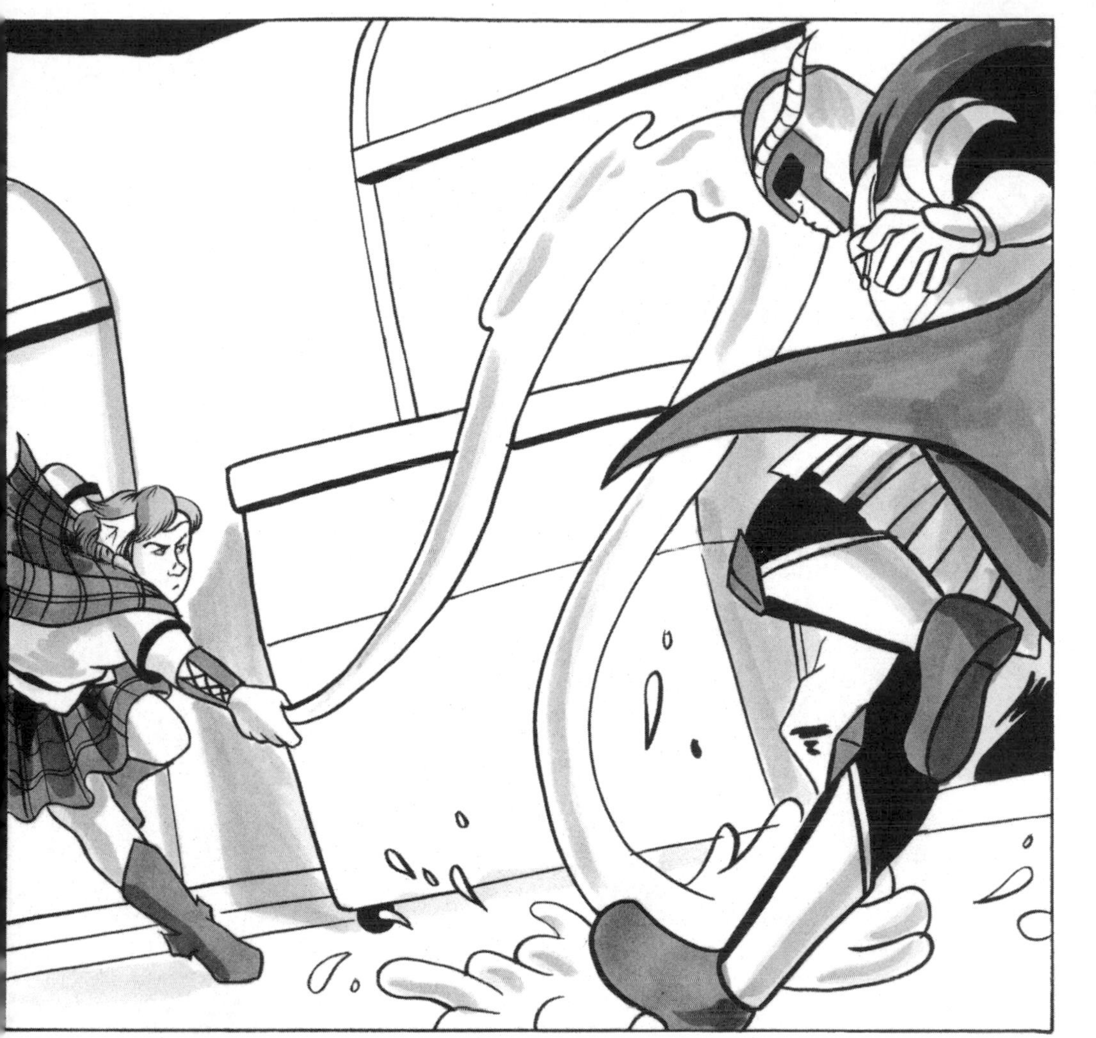

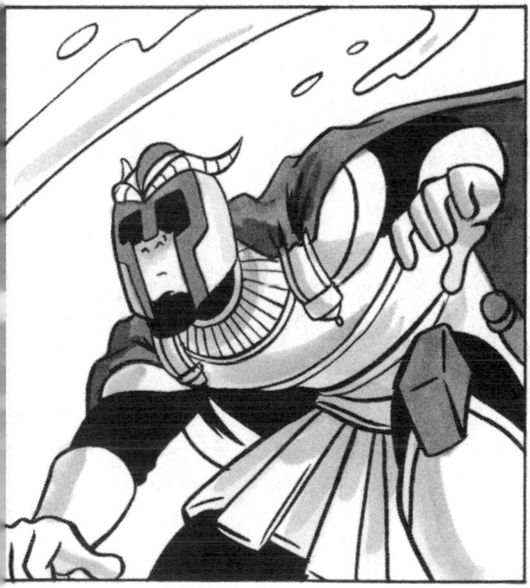

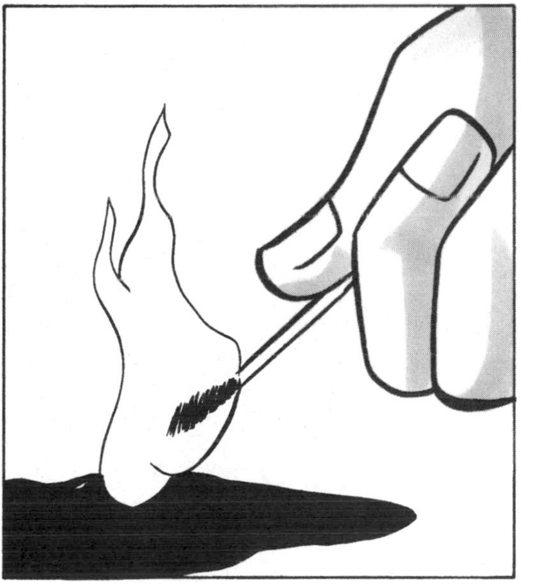

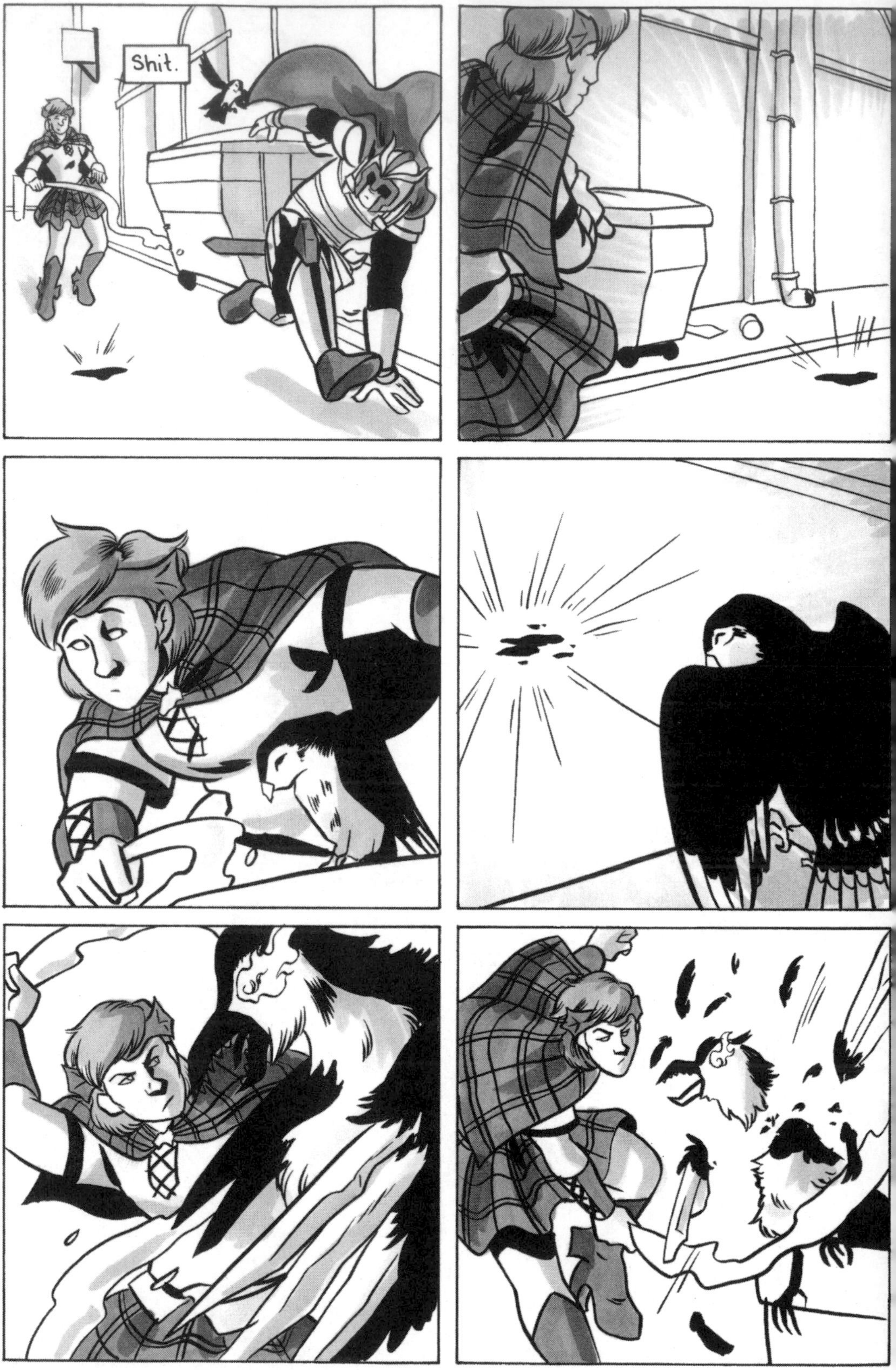
Shit.

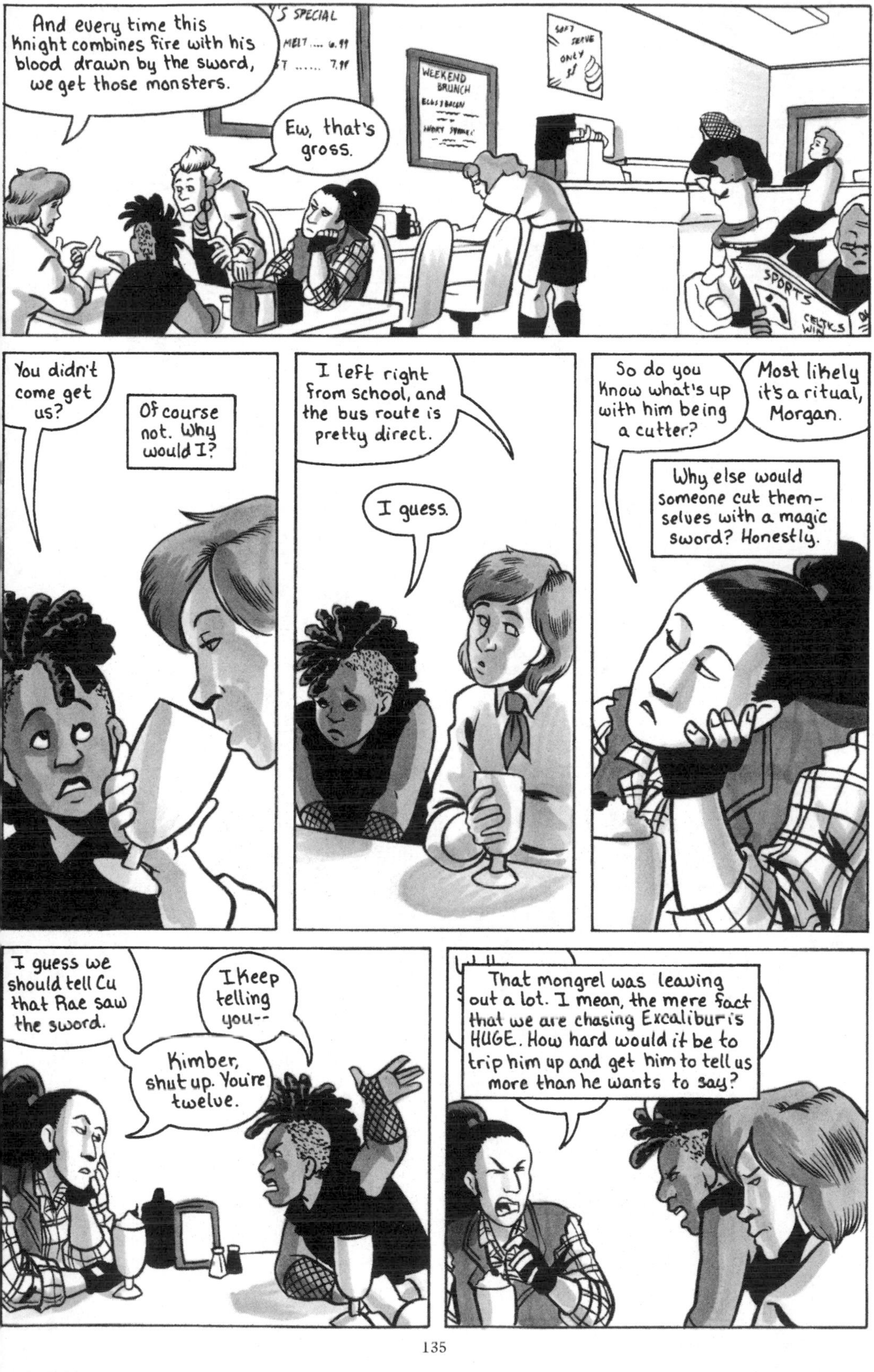
And every time this Knight combines fire with his blood drawn by the sword, we get those monsters.
Ew, that's gross.
WEEKEND BRUNCH
SOFT SERVE ONLY
SPORTS
CELTICS WIN
You didn't come get us?
Of course not. Why would I?
I left right from school, and the bus route is pretty direct.
I guess.
So do you know what's up with him being a cutter?
Most likely it's a ritual, Morgan.
Why else would someone cut them-selves with a magic sword? Honestly.
I guess we should tell Cu that Rae saw the sword.
I keep telling you--
Kimber, shut up. You're twelve.
That mongrel was leaving out a lot. I mean, the mere fact that we are chasing Excalibur is HUGE. How hard would it be to trip him up and get him to tell us more than he wants to say?

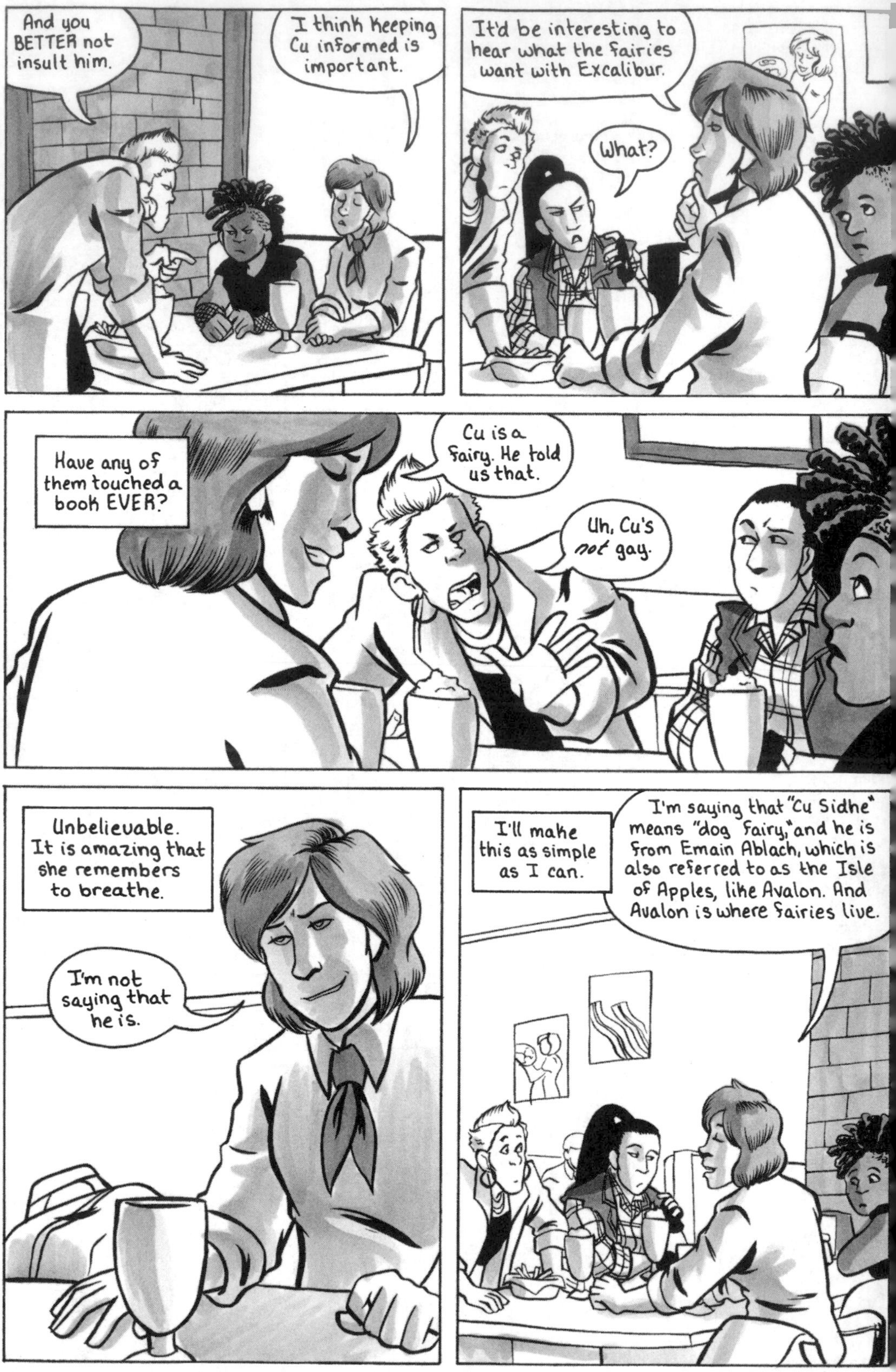
And you BETTER not insult him.
I think keeping Cu informed is important.
It'd be interesting to hear what the fairies want with Excalibur.
What?
Have any of them touched a book EVER?
Cu is a fairy. He told us that.
Uh, Cu's not gay.
Unbelievable. It is amazing that she remembers to breathe.
I'm not saying that he is.
I'll make this as simple as I can.
I'm saying that "Cu Sidhe" means "dog fairy," and he is from Emain Ablach, which is also referred to as the Isle of Apples, like Avalon. And Avalon is where fairies live.

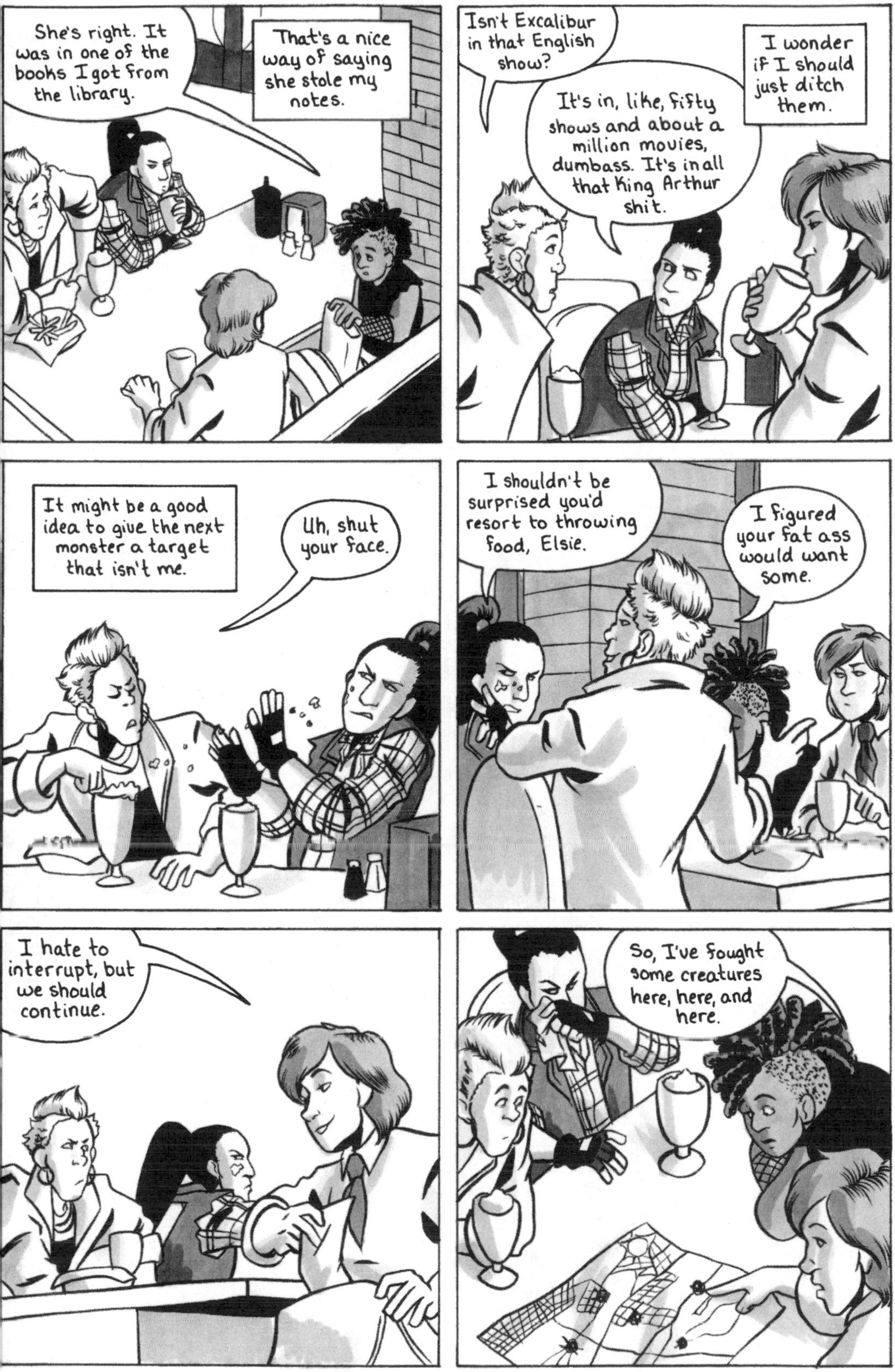
She's right. It was in one of the books I got from the library.
That's a nice way of saying she stole my notes.
Isn't Excalibur in that English show?
It's in, like, fifty shows and about a million movies, dumbass. It's in all that King Arthur shit.
I wonder if I should just ditch them.
It might be a good idea to give the next monster a target that isn't me.
Uh, shut your face.
I shouldn't be surprised you'd resort to throwing food, Elsie.
I figured your fat ass would want some.
I hate to interrupt, but we should continue.
So, I've fought some creatures here, here, and here.

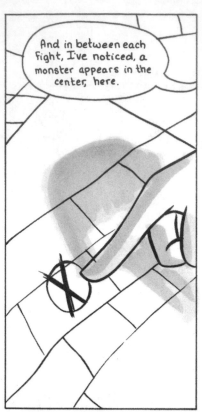

And in between each fight, I've noticed, a monster appears in the center, here.

So this would be next?

Yes.

So tonight we should--

WHERE THE HELL HAVE YOU BEEN?!

Sorry, Ma.

You're a half-hour late! Customers are dying of starvation!

They seem to be feeding themselves just fine.

DON'T BACK TALK ME!

AND CLEAN THAT UP! IT LOOKS LIKE SOMEBODY DIED IN HERE!

Okay, Ma.

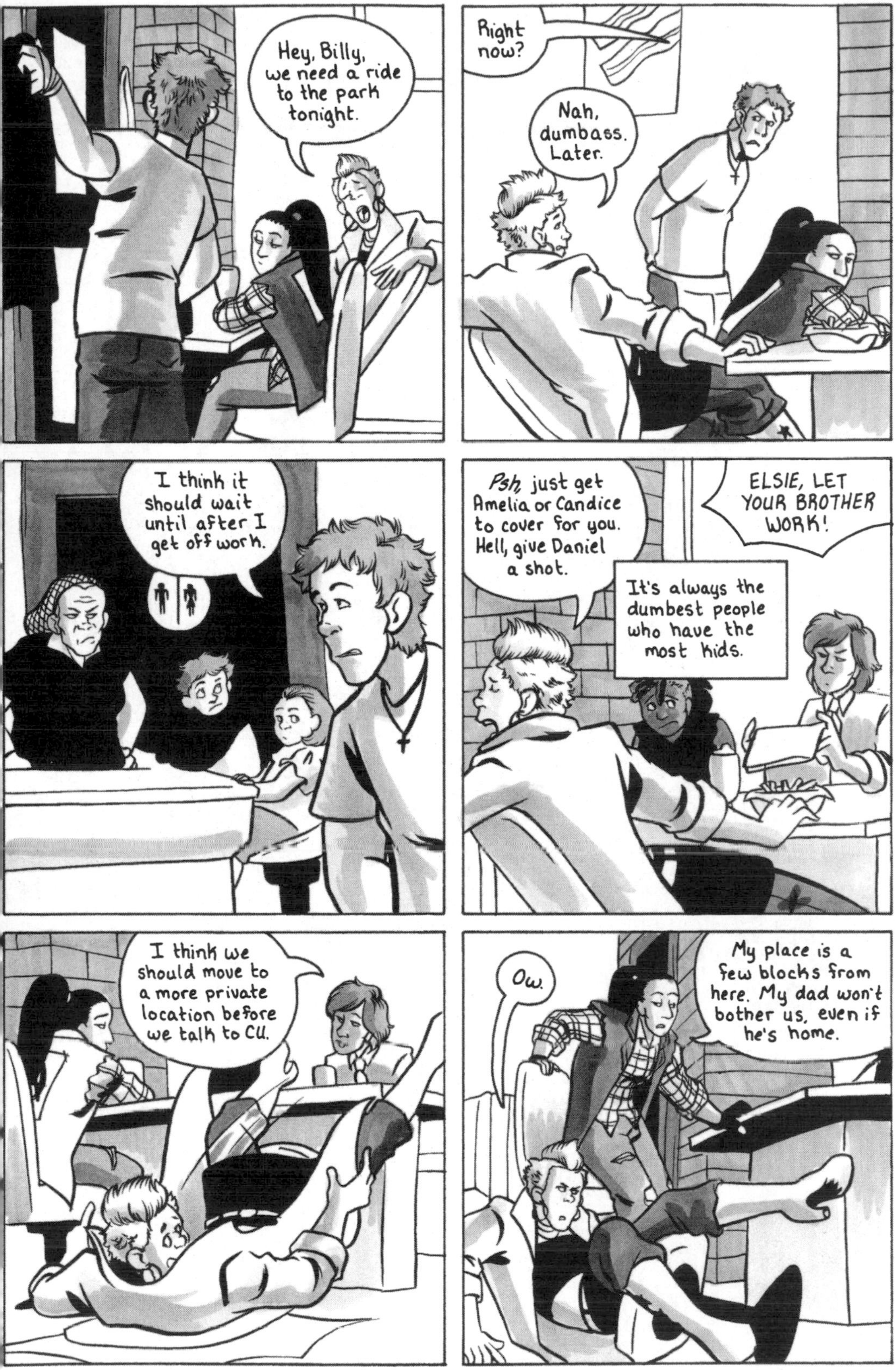
Hey, Billy, we need a ride to the park tonight.
Right now?
Nah, dumbass. Later.
I think it should wait until after I get off work.
Psh, just get Amelia or Candice to cover for you. Hell, give Daniel a shot.
ELSIE, LET YOUR BROTHER WORK!
It's always the dumbest people who have the most kids.
I think we should move to a more private location before we talk to CU.
Ow.
My place is a few blocks from here. My dad won't bother us, even if he's home.

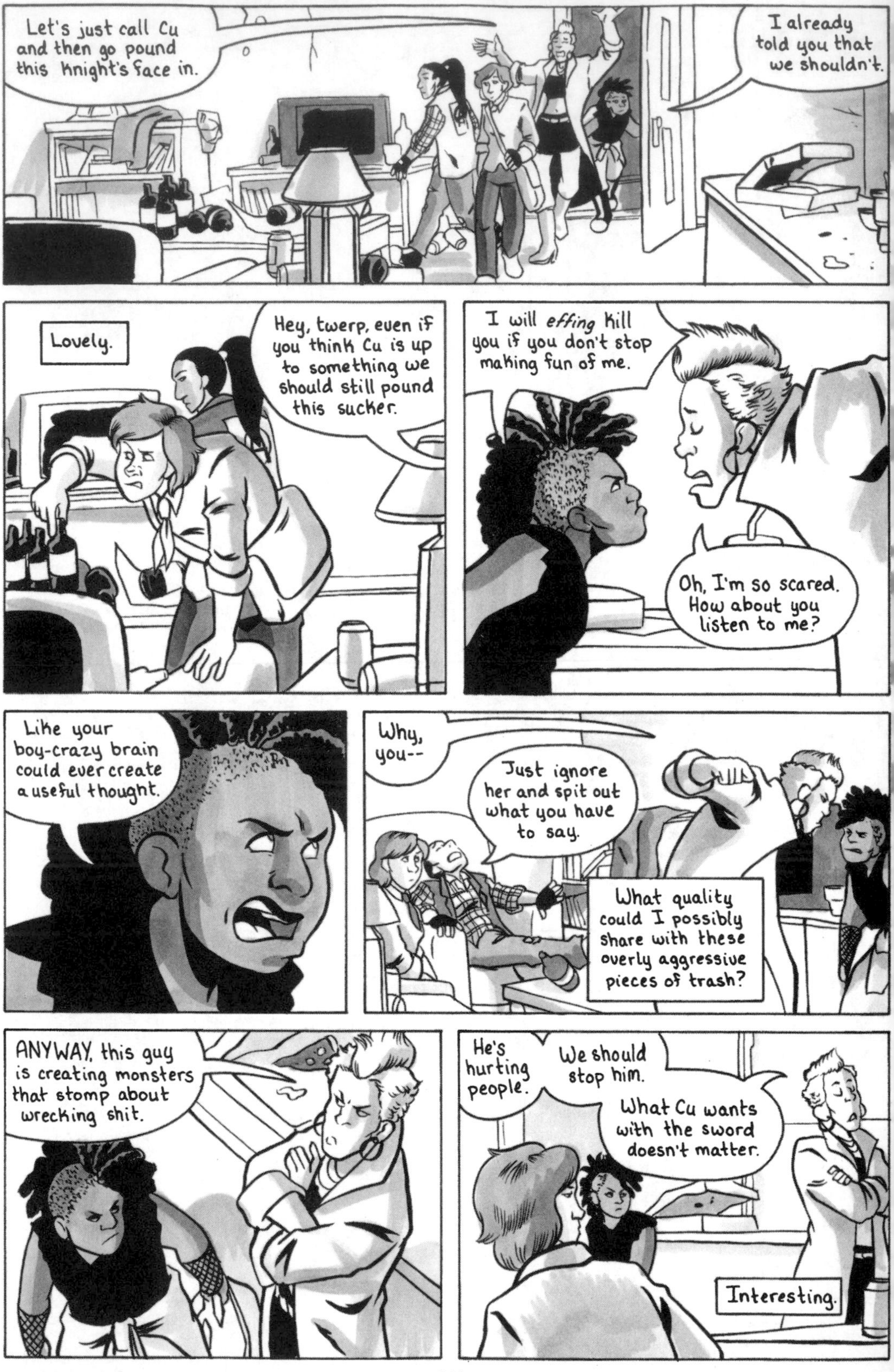

Let's just call Cu and then go pound this knight's face in.
I already told you that we shouldn't.
Lovely.
Hey, twerp, even if you think Cu is up to something we should still pound this sucker.
I will *effing* kill you if you don't stop making fun of me.
Oh, I'm so scared. How about you listen to me?
Like your boy-crazy brain could ever create a useful thought.
Why, you--
Just ignore her and spit out what you have to say.
What quality could I possibly share with these overly aggressive pieces of trash?
ANYWAY, this guy is creating monsters that stomp about wrecking shit.
He's hurting people.
We should stop him.
What Cu wants with the sword doesn't matter.
Interesting.

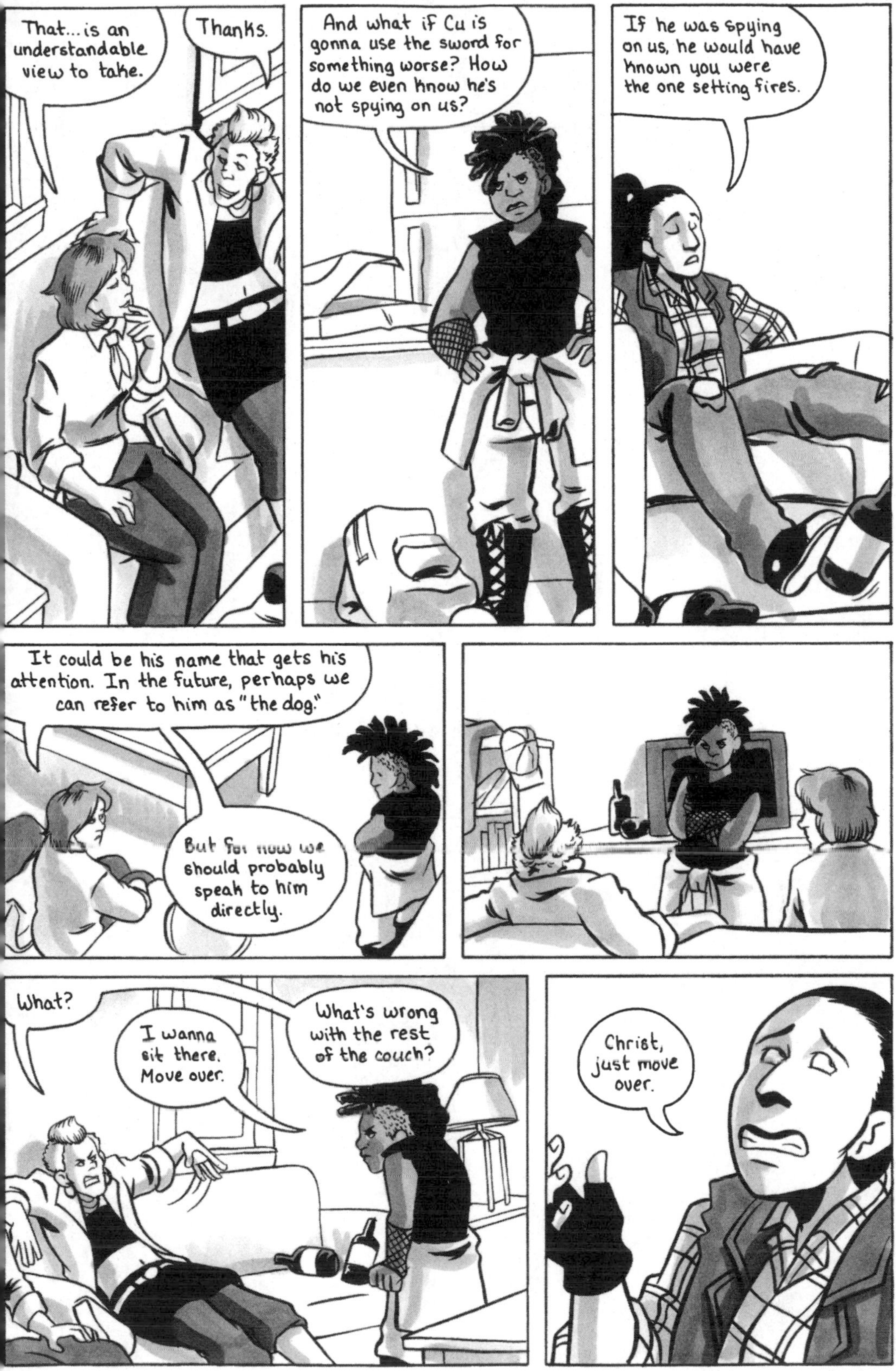

That... is an understandable view to take.
Thanks.
And what if Cu is gonna use the sword for something worse? How do we even know he's not spying on us?
If he was spying on us, he would have known you were the one setting fires.
It could be his name that gets his attention. In the future, perhaps we can refer to him as "the dog."
But for now we should probably speak to him directly.
What?
I wanna sit there. Move over.
What's wrong with the rest of the couch?
Christ, just move over.

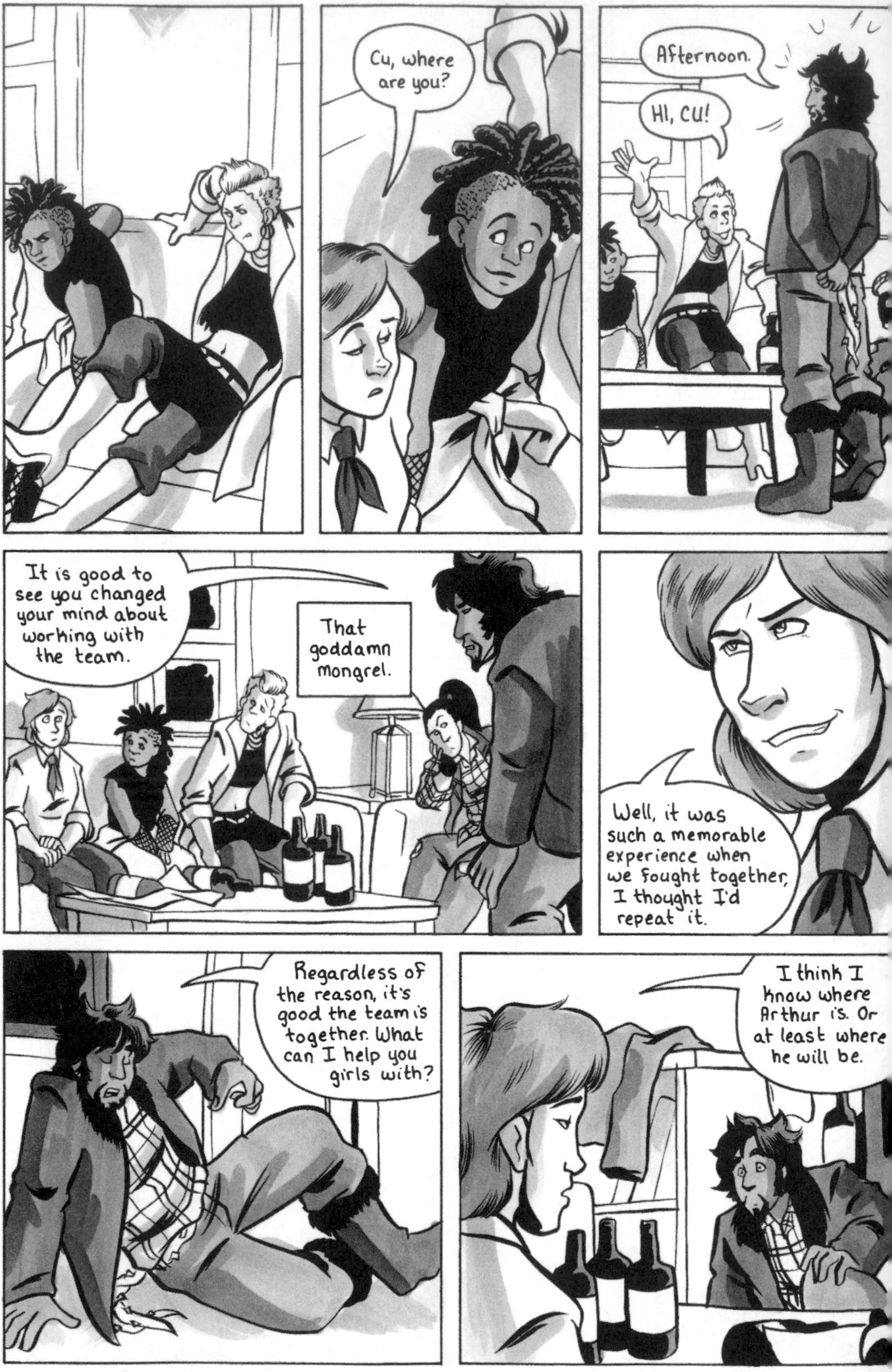
Cu, where are you?
Afternoon.
HI, CU!
It is good to see you changed your mind about working with the team.
That goddamn mongrel.
Well, it was such a memorable experience when we fought together, I thought I'd repeat it.
Regardless of the reason, it's good the team is together. What can I help you girls with?
I think I know where Arthur is. Or at least where he will be.

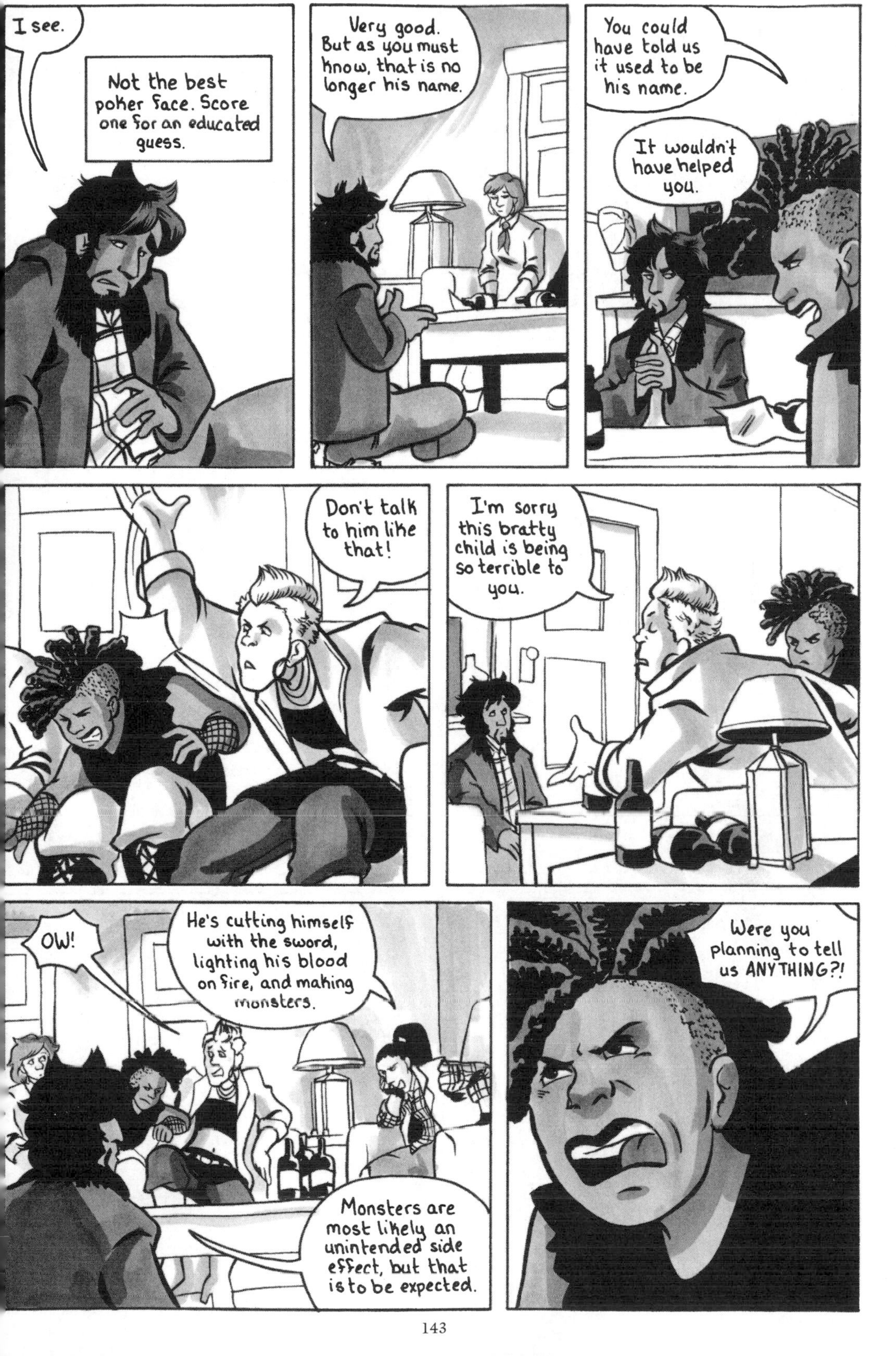
I see.
Not the best poker face. Score one for an educated guess.
Very good. But as you must know, that is no longer his name.
You could have told us it used to be his name.
It wouldn't have helped you.
Don't talk to him like that!
I'm sorry this bratty child is being so terrible to you.
OW!
He's cutting himself with the sword, lighting his blood on fire, and making monsters.
Monsters are most likely an unintended side effect, but that is to be expected.
Were you planning to tell us ANYTHING?!

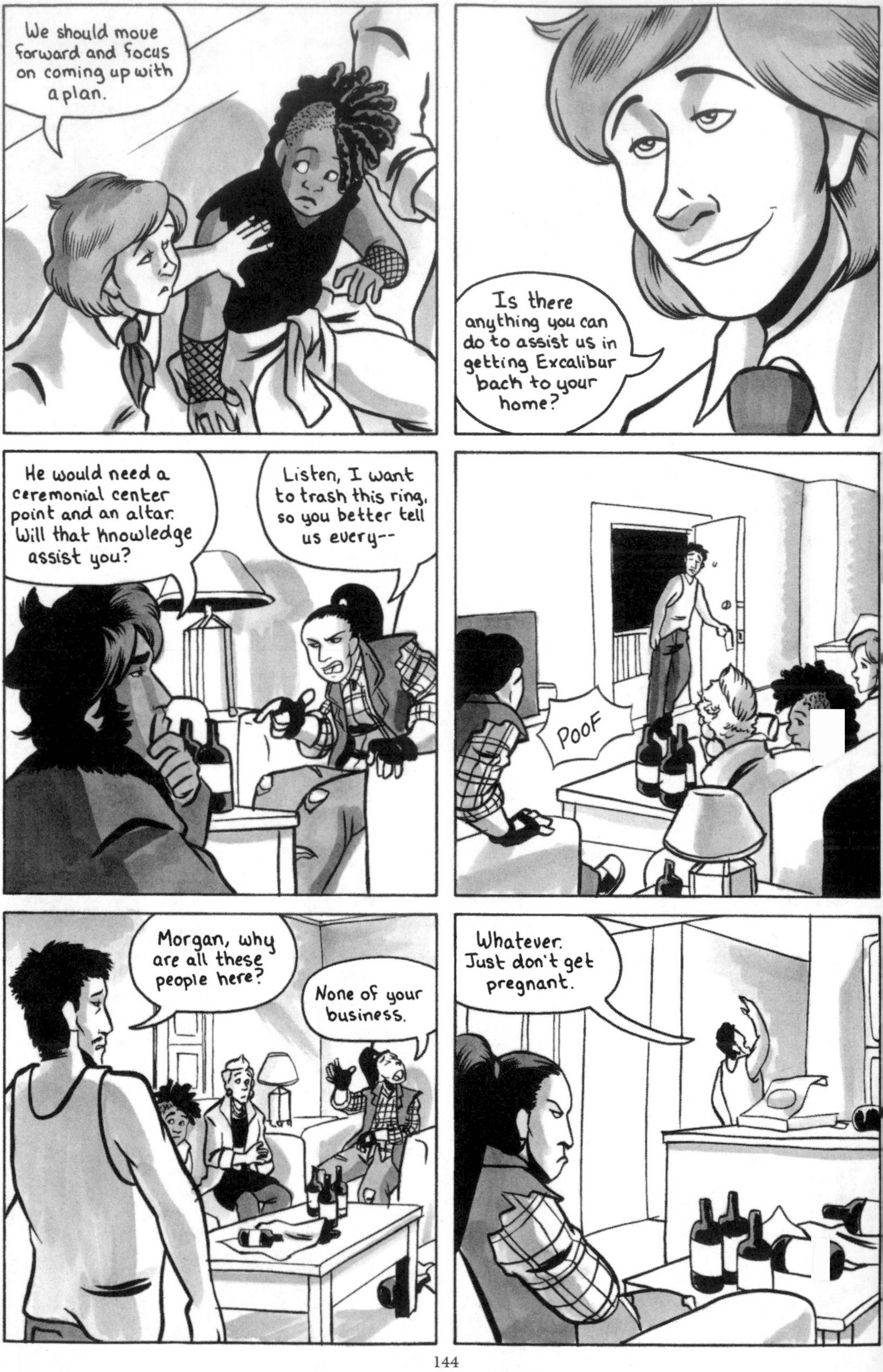
We should move forward and focus on coming up with a plan.
Is there anything you can do to assist us in getting Excalibur back to your home?
He would need a ceremonial center point and an altar. Will that knowledge assist you?
Listen, I want to trash this ring, so you better tell us every--
POOF
Morgan, why are all these people here?
None of your business.
Whatever. Just don't get pregnant.

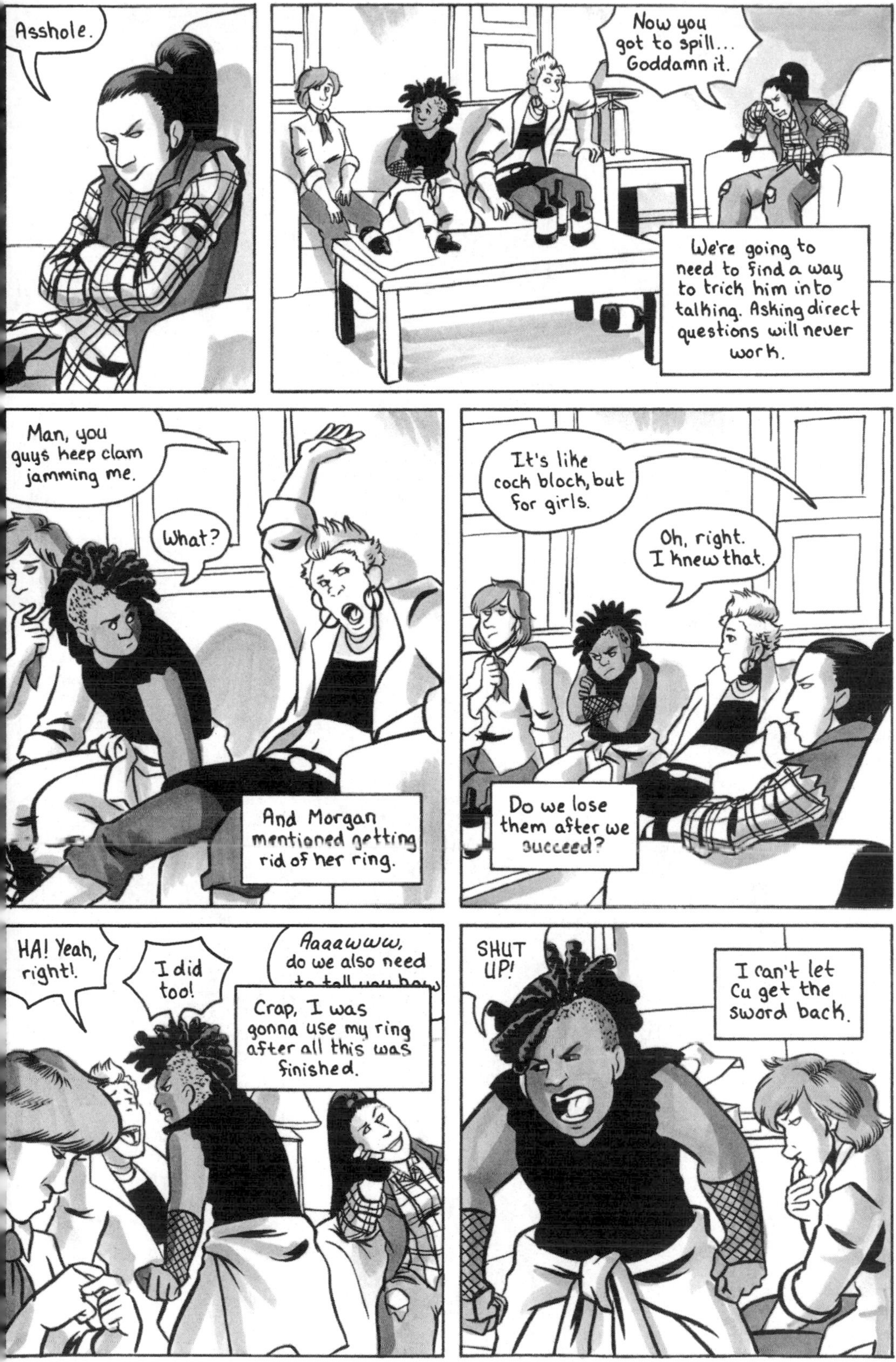
Asshole.
Now you got to spill... Goddamn it.
We're going to need to find a way to trick him into talking. Asking direct questions will never work.
Man, you guys keep clam jamming me.
What?
And Morgan mentioned getting rid of her ring.
It's like cock block, but for girls.
Oh, right. I knew that.
Do we lose them after we succeed?
HA! Yeah, right!
I did too!
Aaaawww, do we also need
Crap, I was gonna use my ring after all this was finished.
SHUT UP!
I can't let Cu get the sword back.

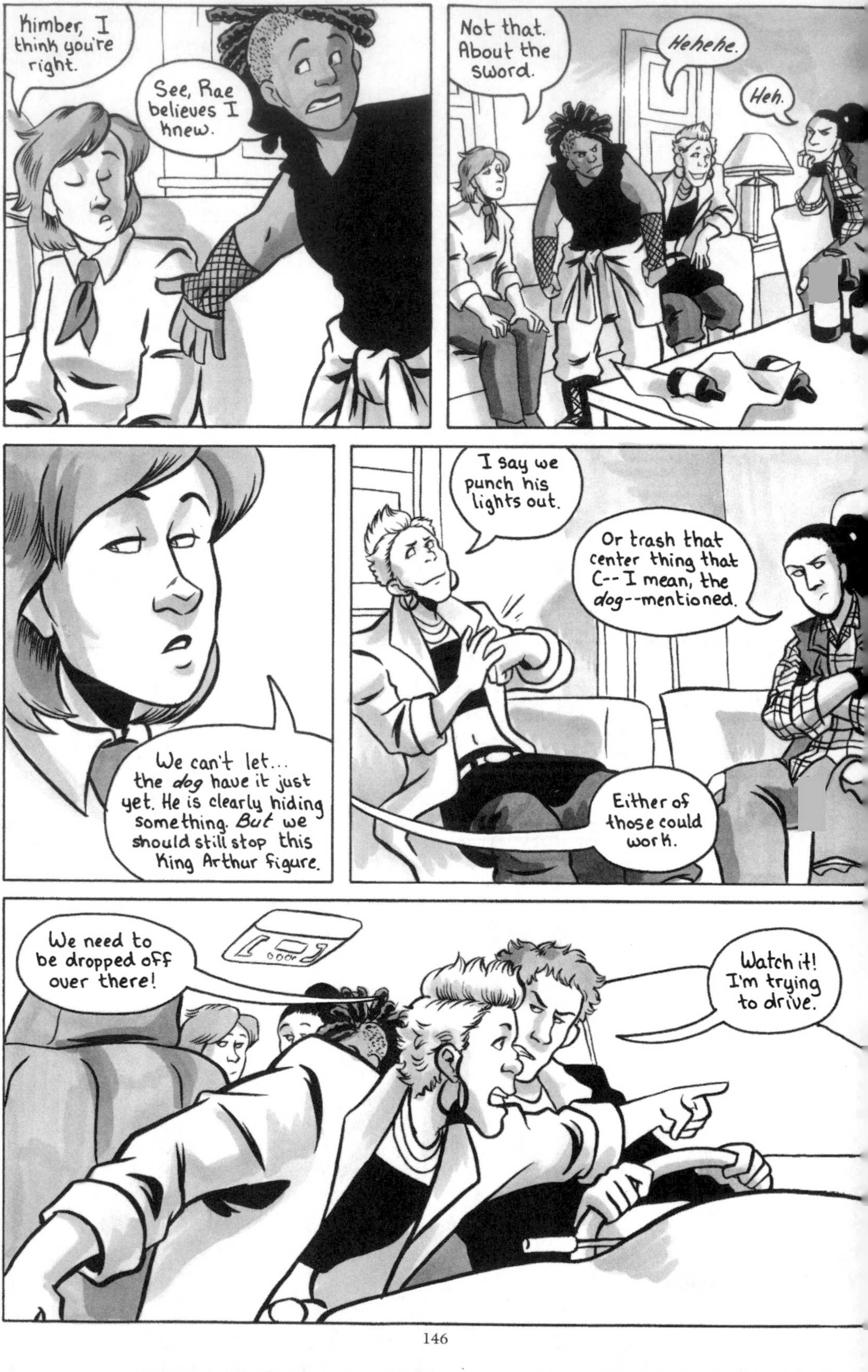
Kimber, I think you're right.
See, Rae believes I knew.
Not that. About the sword.
Hehehe.
Heh.
We can't let... the *dog* have it just yet. He is clearly hiding something. *But* we should still stop this King Arthur figure.
I say we punch his lights out.
Or trash that center thing that C-- I mean, the *dog*--mentioned.
Either of those could work.
We need to be dropped off over there!
Watch it! I'm trying to drive.

Thank you for the ride.

Oh...uh, you're welcome.

You gonna wait for us or we got to call you later?

I've gotta take care of some stuff nearby.

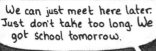

We can just meet here later. Just don't take too long. We got school tomorrow.

Some *stuff*? Are you buying drugs?

Goodbye, Elsie.

What kind? Pot? Shrooms? E? Tell me!

THMK

He's *totally* buying drugs.

He probably thinks that about us.

I mean, what else do people do in the park at night?

Sacrifice animals in satanic rituals?

You're a weird kid, Kimber.

Thanks. But I'm *not* a kid.

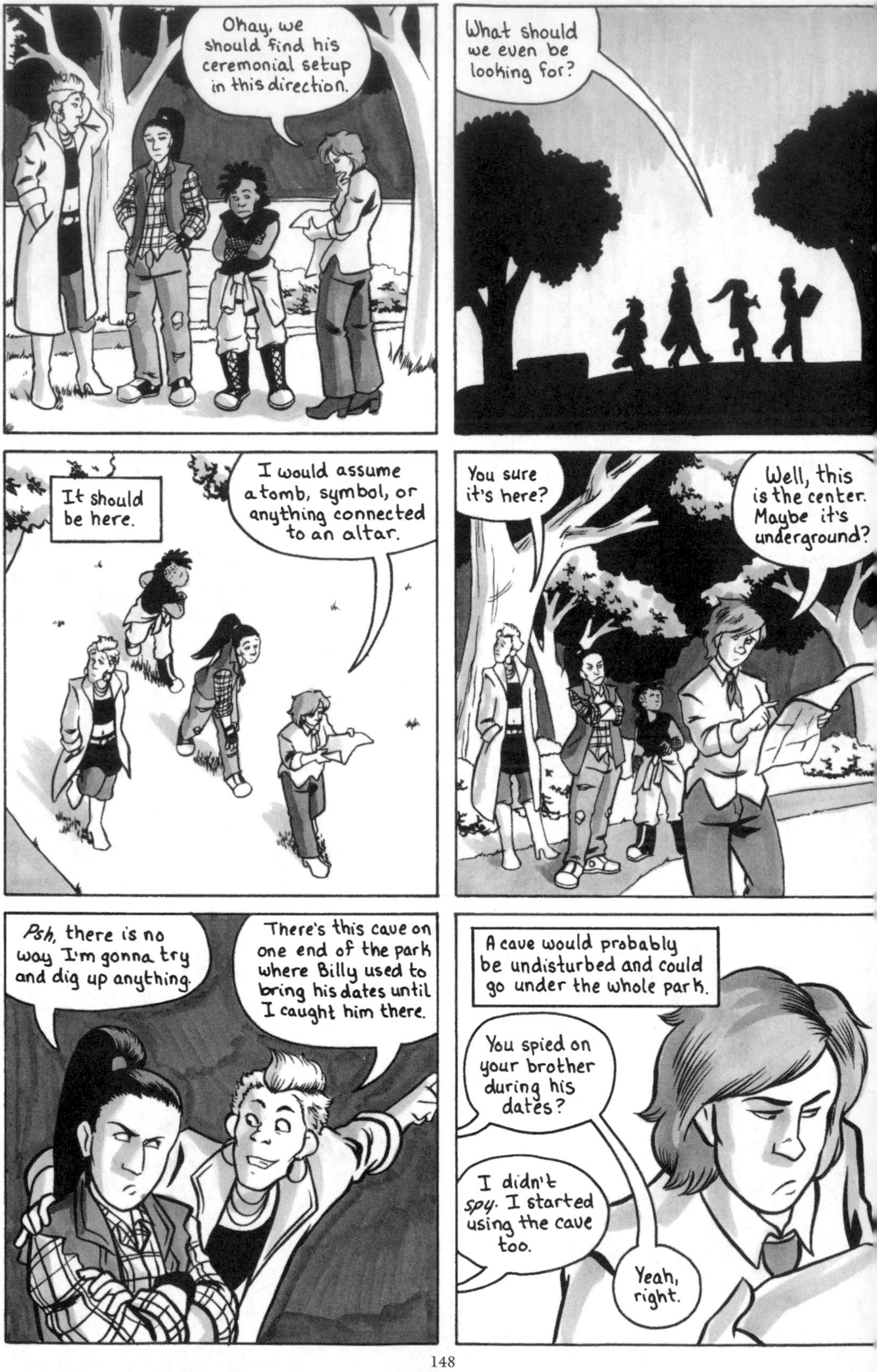
Okay, we should find his ceremonial setup in this direction.
What should we even be looking for?
It should be here.
I would assume a tomb, symbol, or anything connected to an altar.
You sure it's here?
Well, this is the center. Maybe it's underground?
Psh, there is no way I'm gonna try and dig up anything.
There's this cave on one end of the park where Billy used to bring his dates until I caught him there.
A cave would probably be undisturbed and could go under the whole park.
You spied on your brother during his dates?
I didn't spy. I started using the cave too.
Yeah, right.

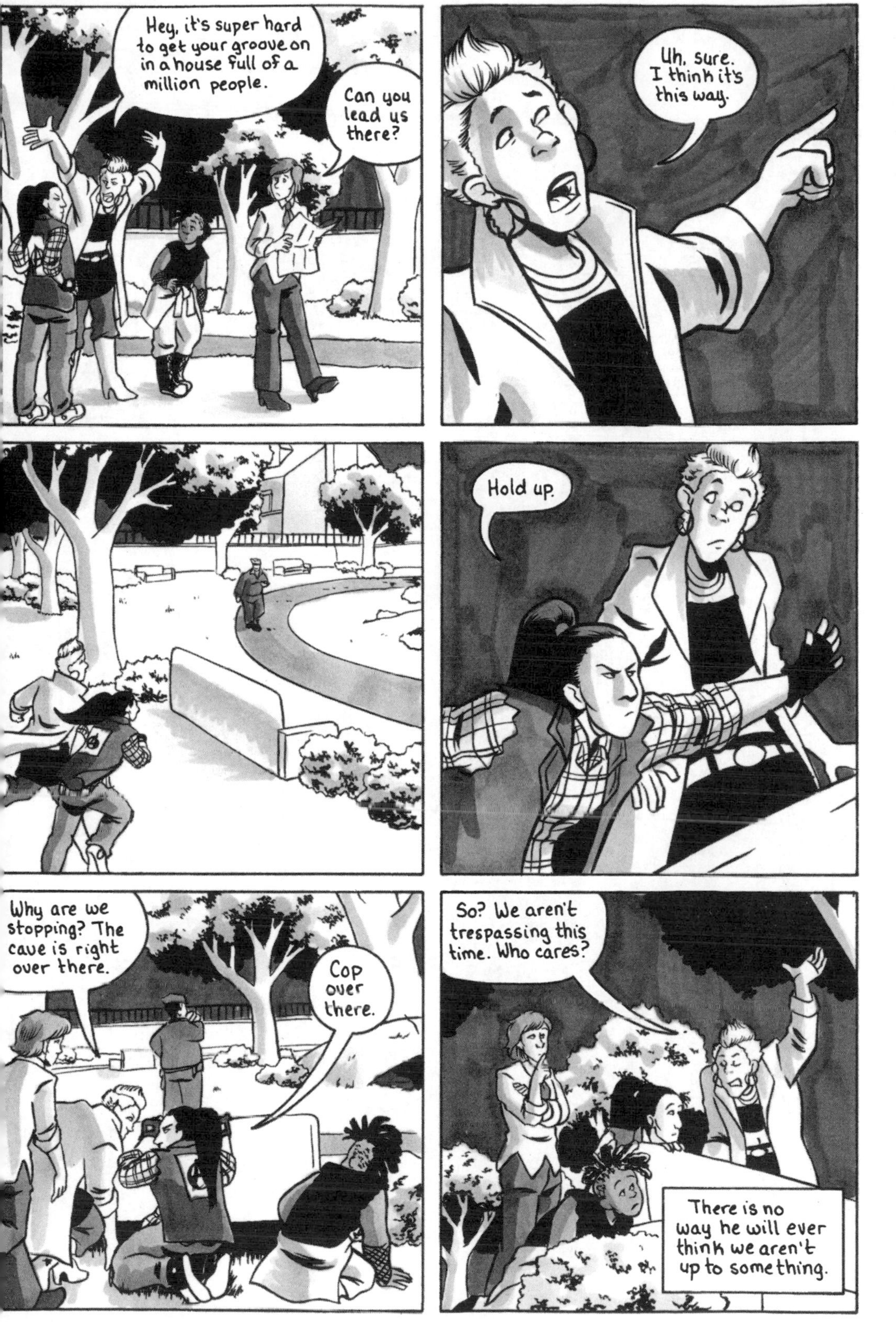
Hey, it's super hard to get your groove on in a house full of a million people.
Can you lead us there?
Uh, sure. I think it's this way.
Hold up.
Why are we stopping? The cave is right over there.
Cop over there.
So? We aren't trespassing this time. Who cares?
There is no way he will ever think we aren't up to something.

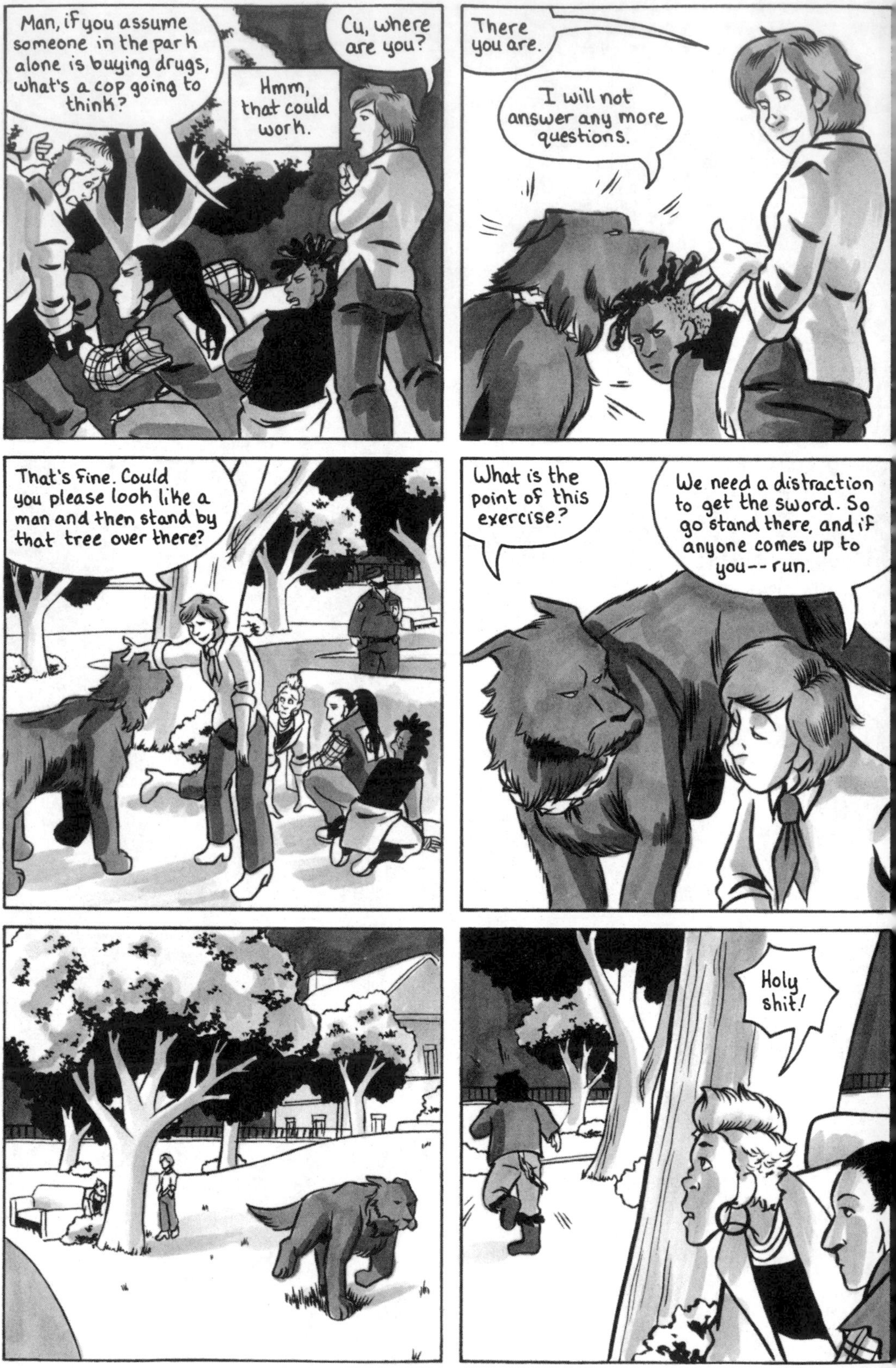
Man, if you assume someone in the park alone is buying drugs, what's a cop going to think?
Hmm, that could work.
Cu, where are you?
There you are.
I will not answer any more questions.
That's fine. Could you please look like a man and then stand by that tree over there?
What is the point of this exercise?
We need a distraction to get the sword. So go stand there, and if anyone comes up to you-- run.
Holy shit!

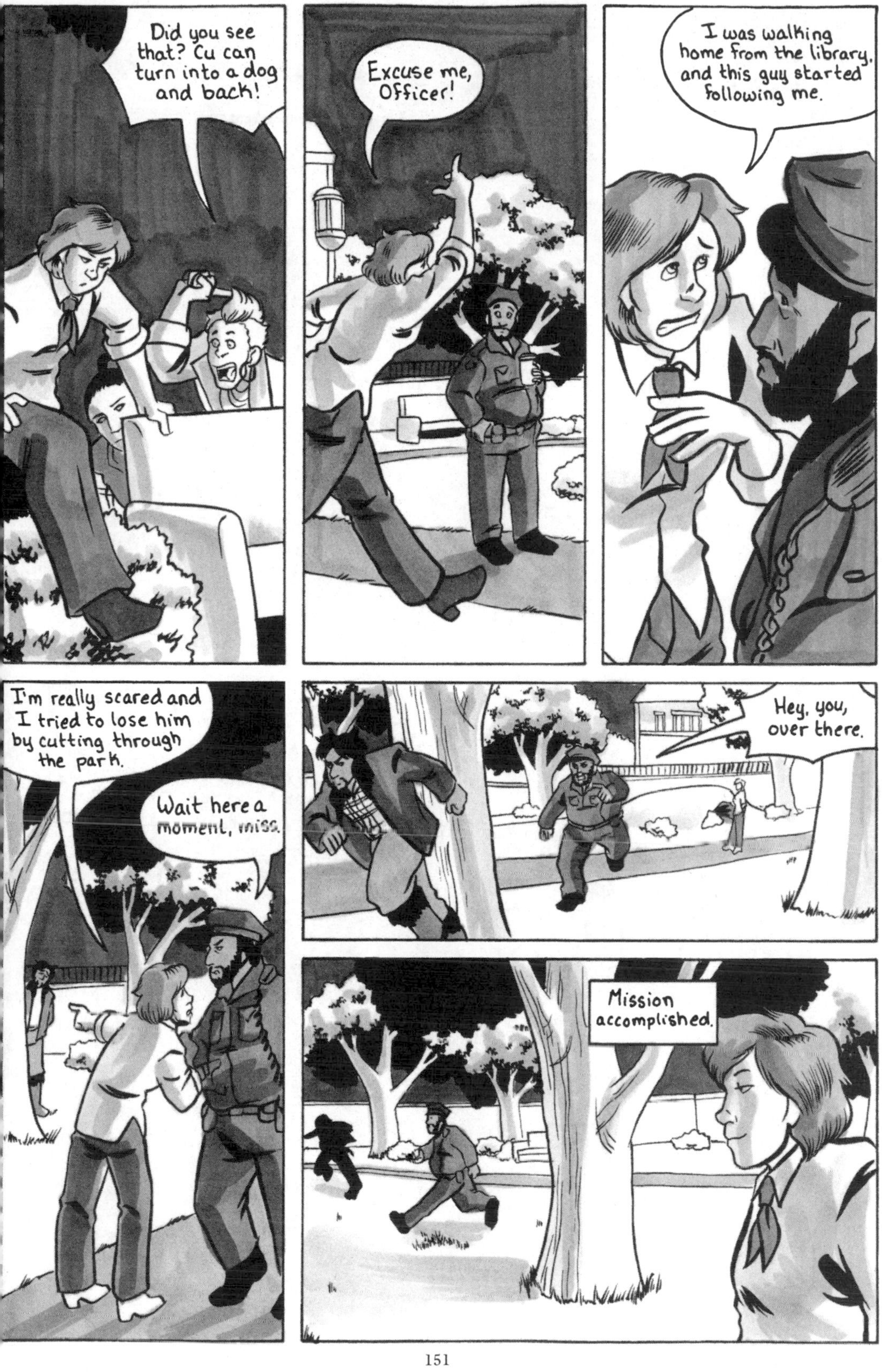
Did you see that? Cu can turn into a dog and back!
Excuse me, Officer!
I was walking home from the library, and this guy started following me.
I'm really scared and I tried to lose him by cutting through the park.
Wait here a moment, miss.
Hey, you, over there.
Mission accomplished.

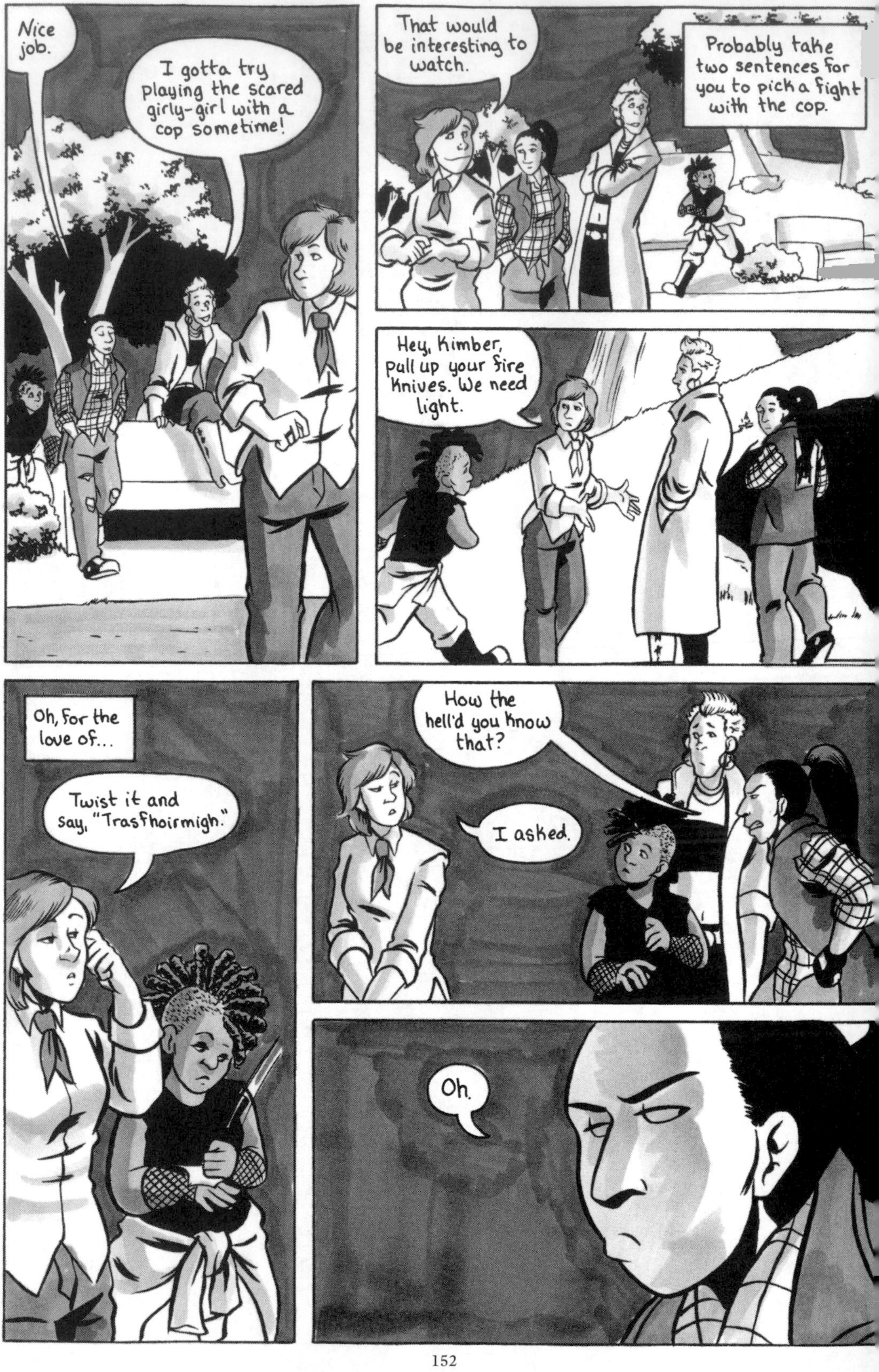
Nice job.
I gotta try playing the scared girly-girl with a cop sometime!
That would be interesting to watch.
Probably take two sentences for you to pick a fight with the cop.
Hey, Kimber, pull up your fire knives. We need light.
Oh, for the love of...
Twist it and say, "Trasfhoirmigh."
How the hell'd you know that?
I asked.
Oh.

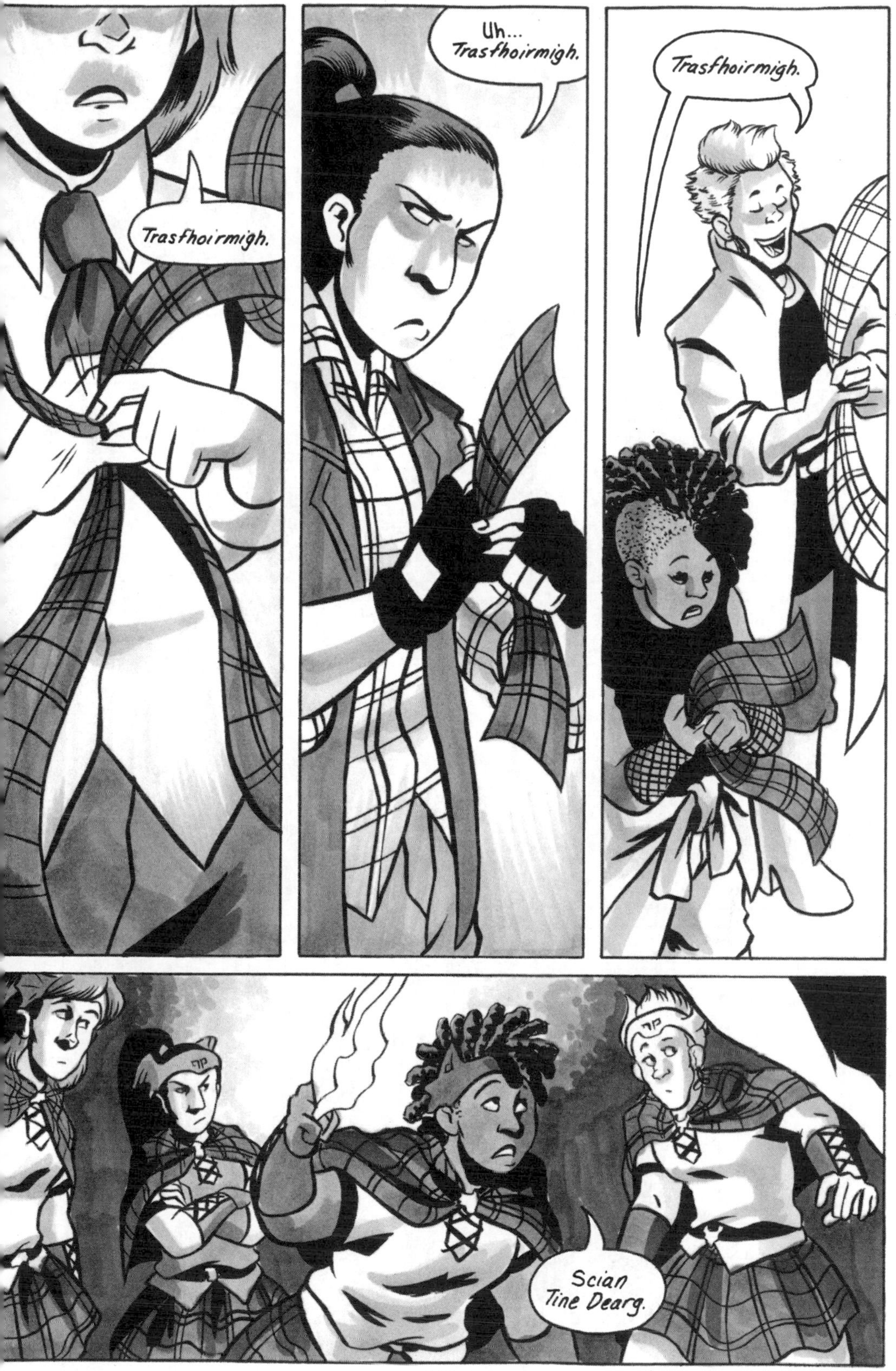
Trasfhoirmigh.
Uh... Trasfhoirmigh.
Trasfhoirmigh.
Scian Tine Dearg.

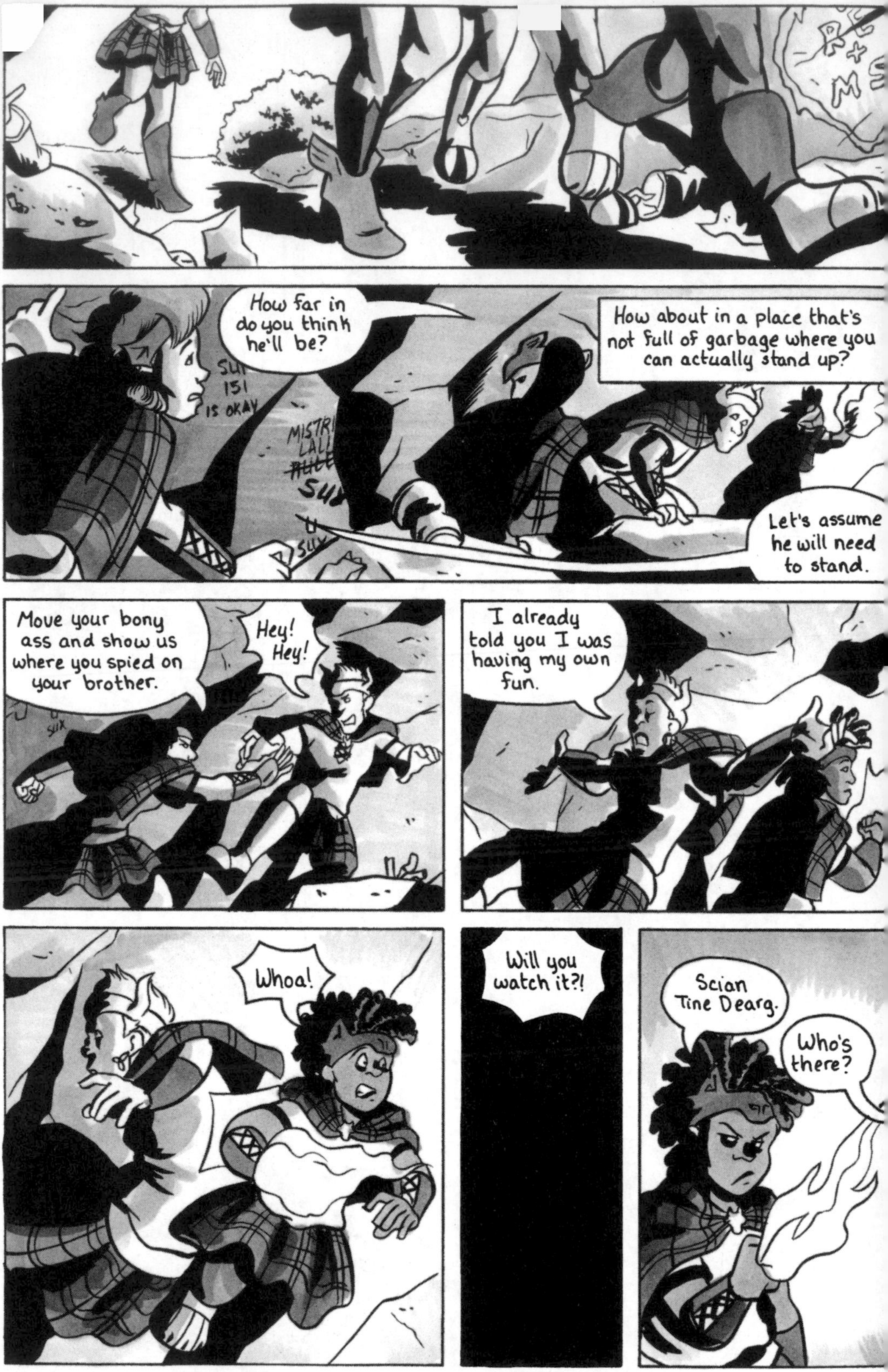

How far in do you think he'll be?
How about in a place that's not full of garbage where you can actually stand up?
Let's assume he will need to stand.
Move your bony ass and show us where you spied on your brother.
Hey! Hey!
I already told you I was having my own fun.
Whoa!
Will you watch it?!
Scian Tine Dearg.
Who's there?

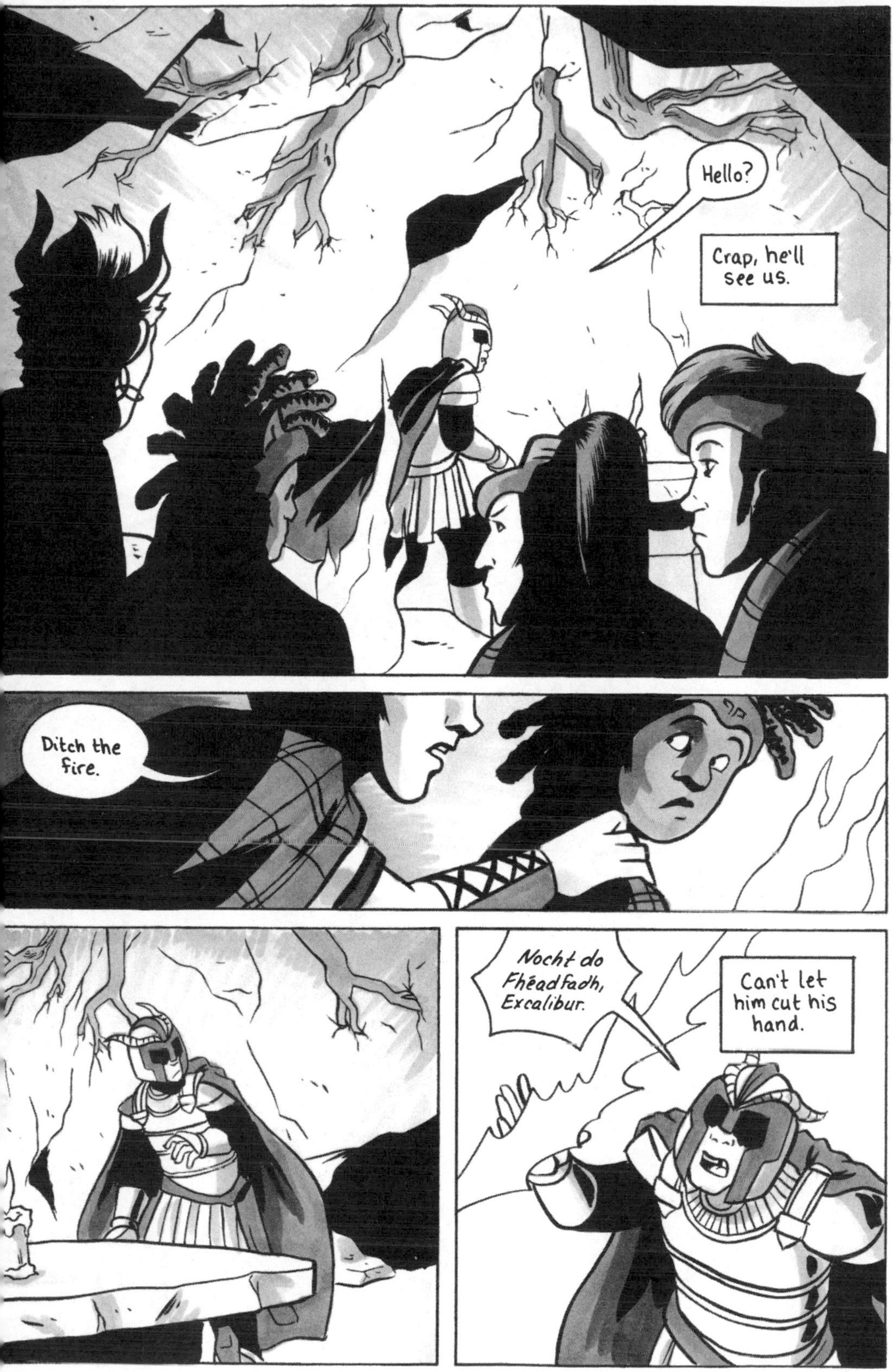
Hello?
Crap, he'll see us.
Ditch the fire.
Nocht do Fhéadfadh, Excalibur.
Can't let him cut his hand.

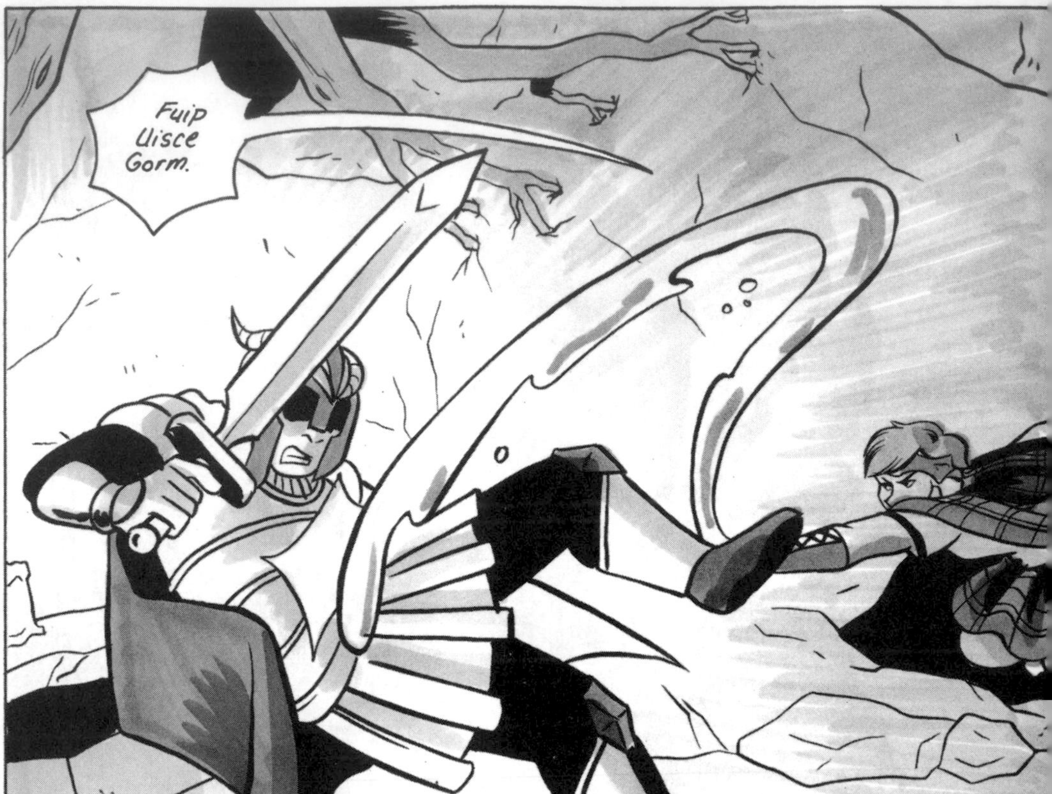
Fuip Uisce Gorm.

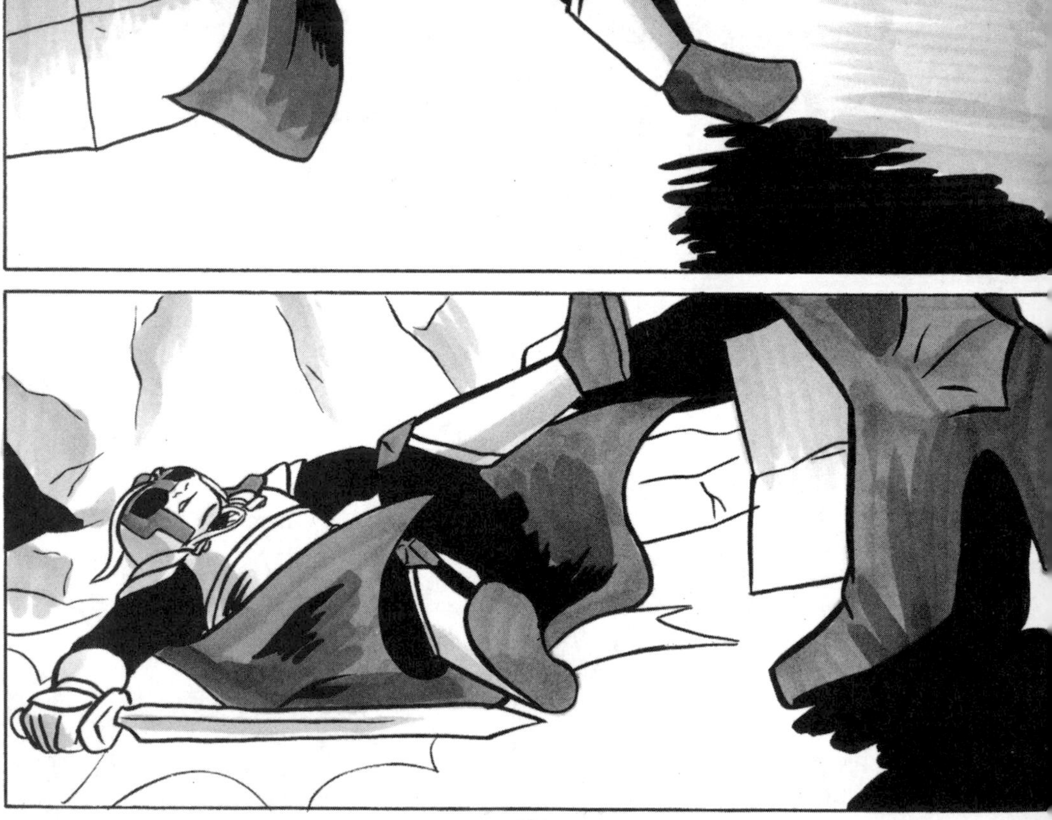

Sciatháin Pendragon!

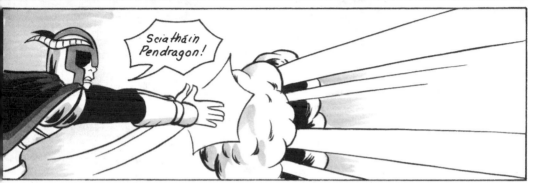

TAMB

Don't move.

I don't think he's cut himself yet.

What are those dolts waiting for?

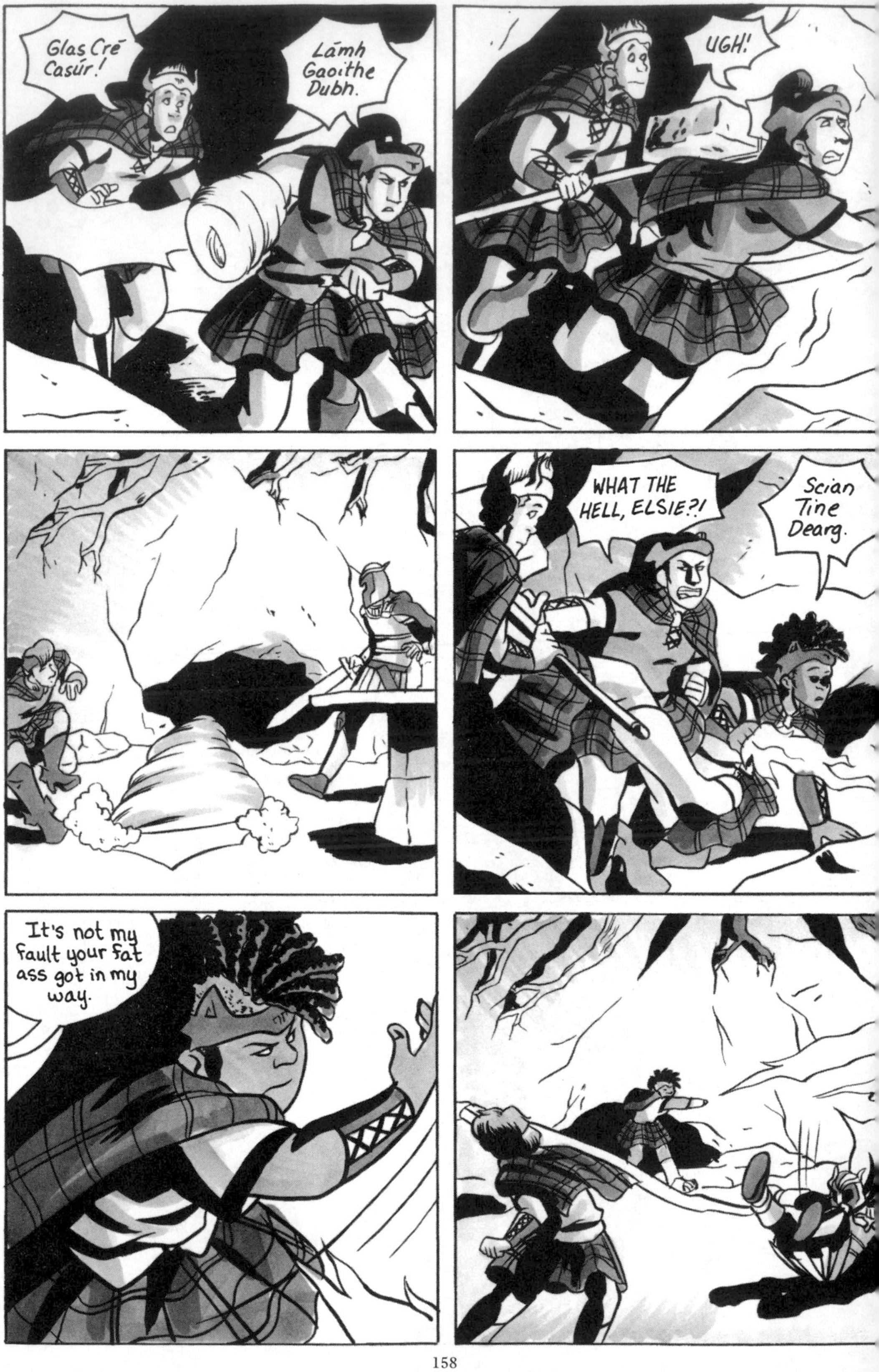
Glas Cré Casúr!
Lámh Gaoithe Dubh.
UGH!
WHAT THE HELL, ELSIE?!
Scian Tine Dearg.
It's not my fault your fat ass got in my way.

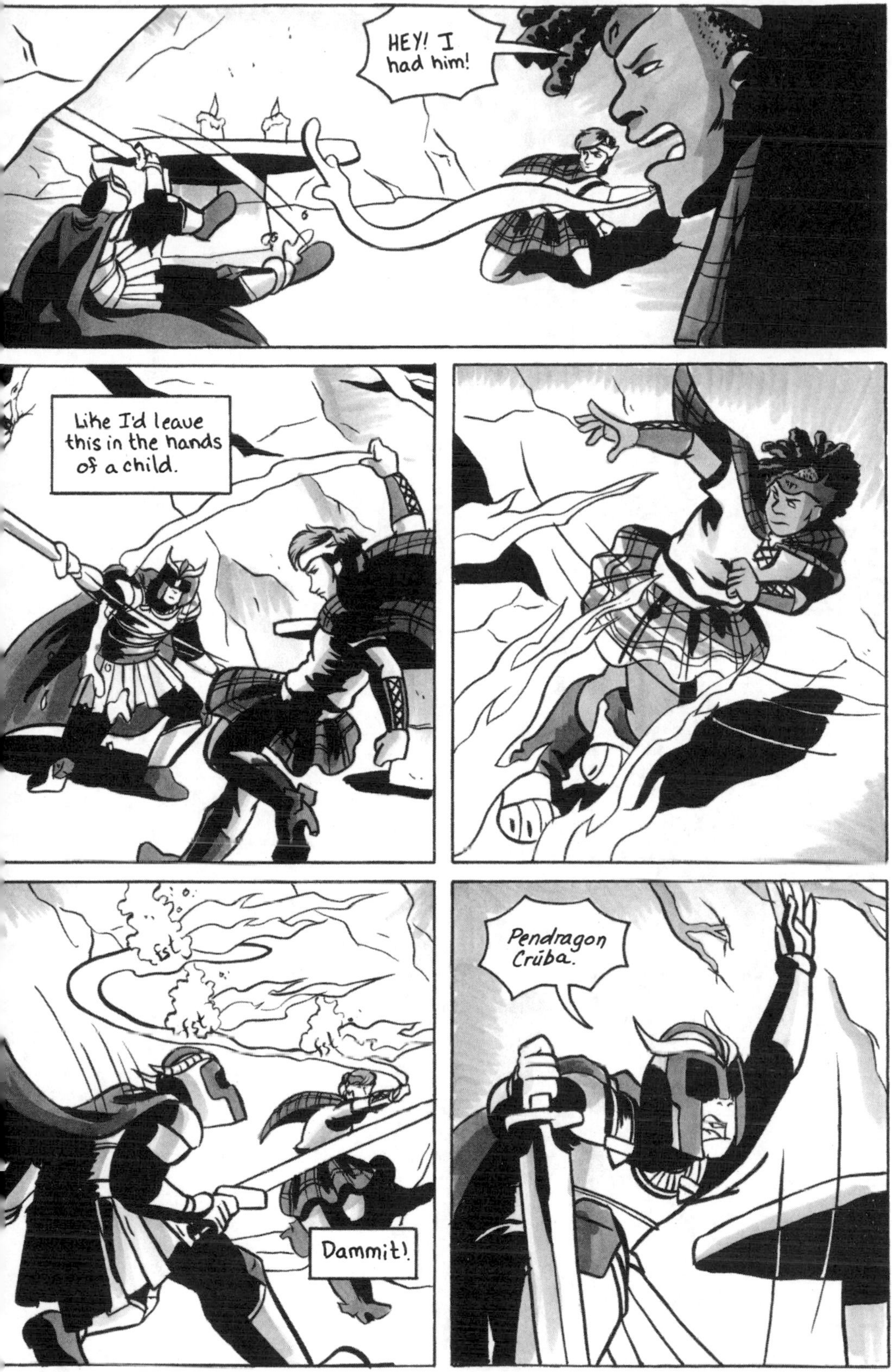
HEY! I had him!
Like I'd leave this in the hands of a child.
fst
fst
fst
Dammit!
Pendragon Crúba.

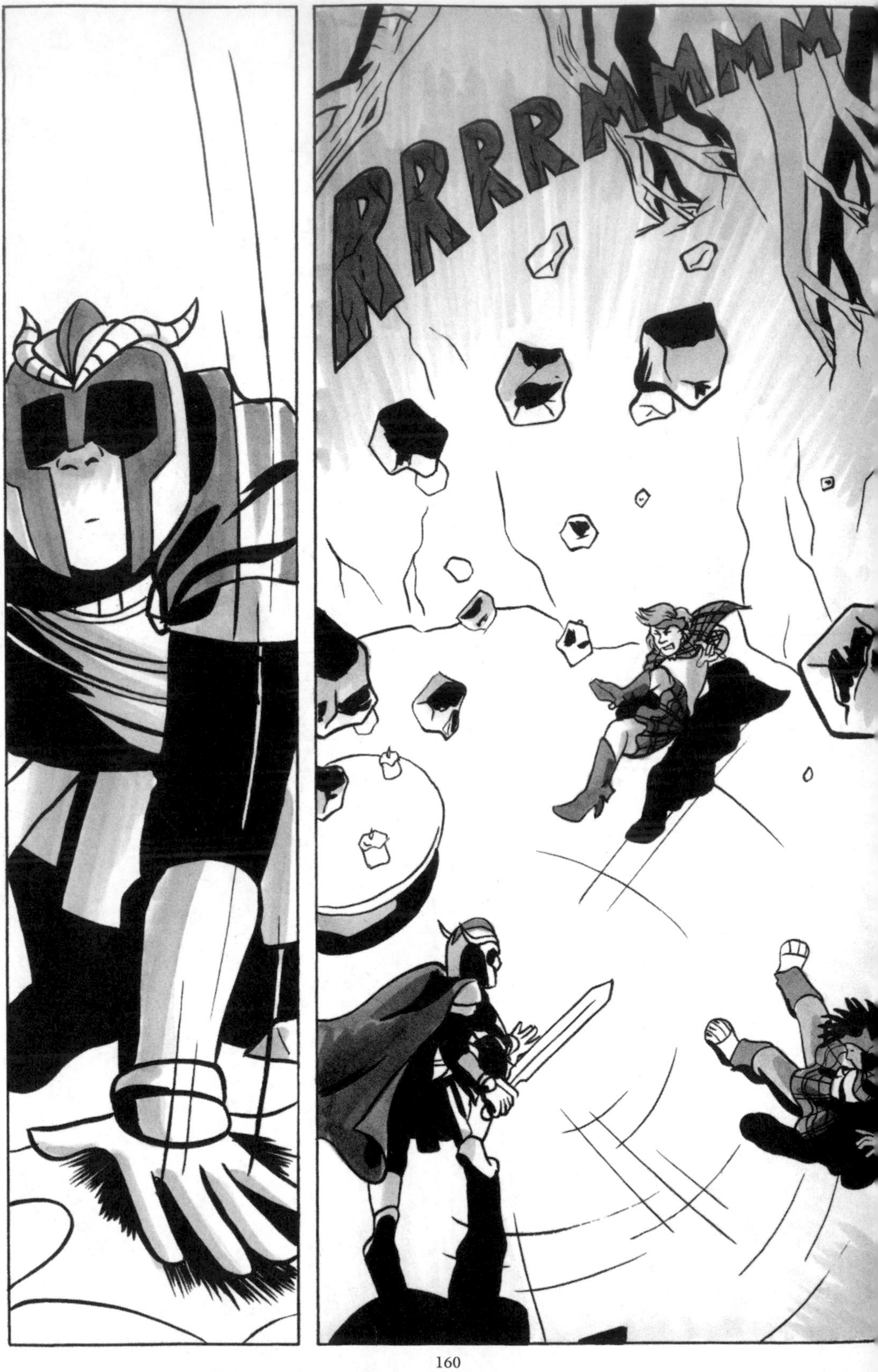
RRRRMMMMM

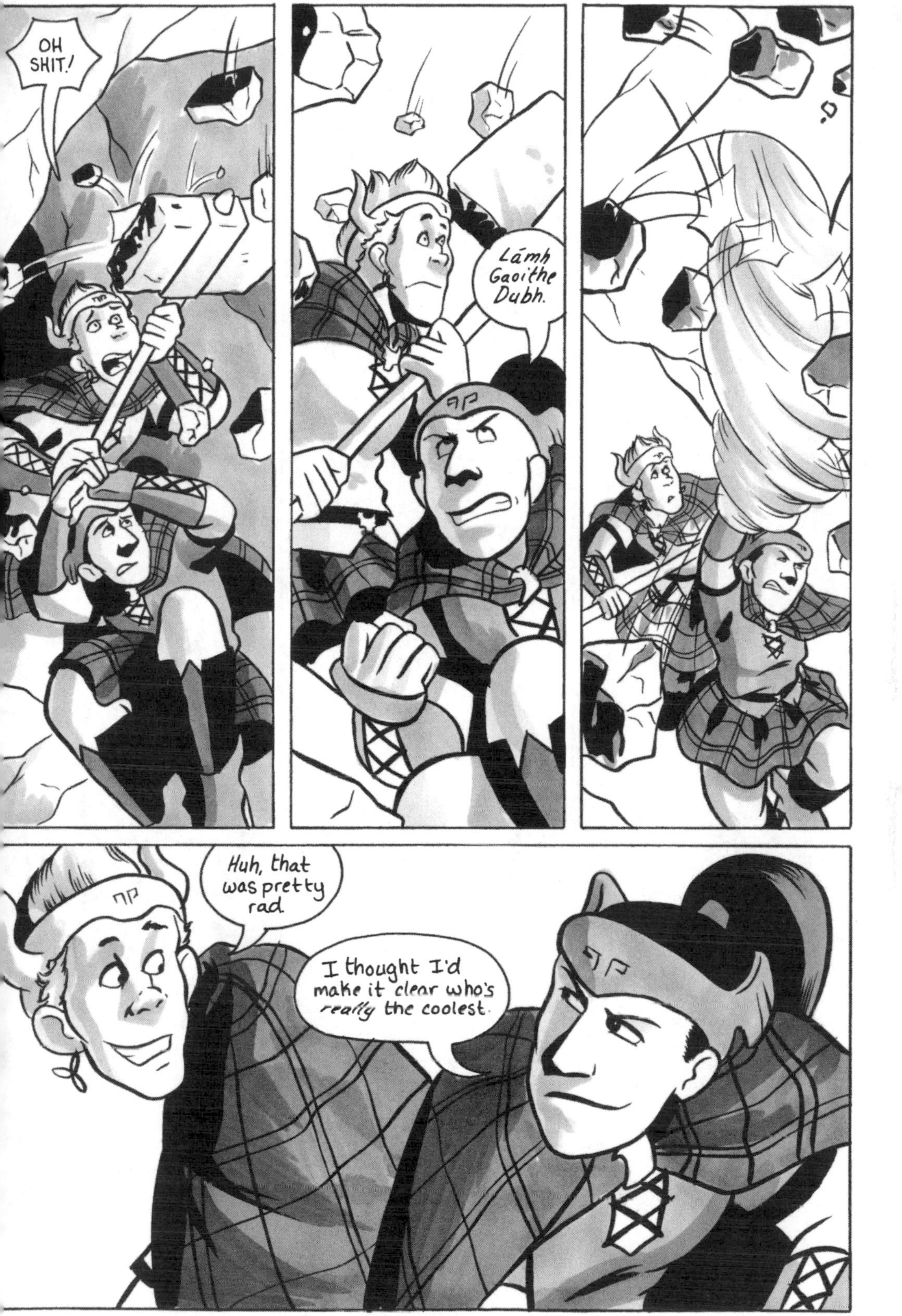
OH SHIT!
Lámh Gaoithe Dubh.
Huh, that was pretty rad.
I thought I'd make it clear who's *really* the coolest.

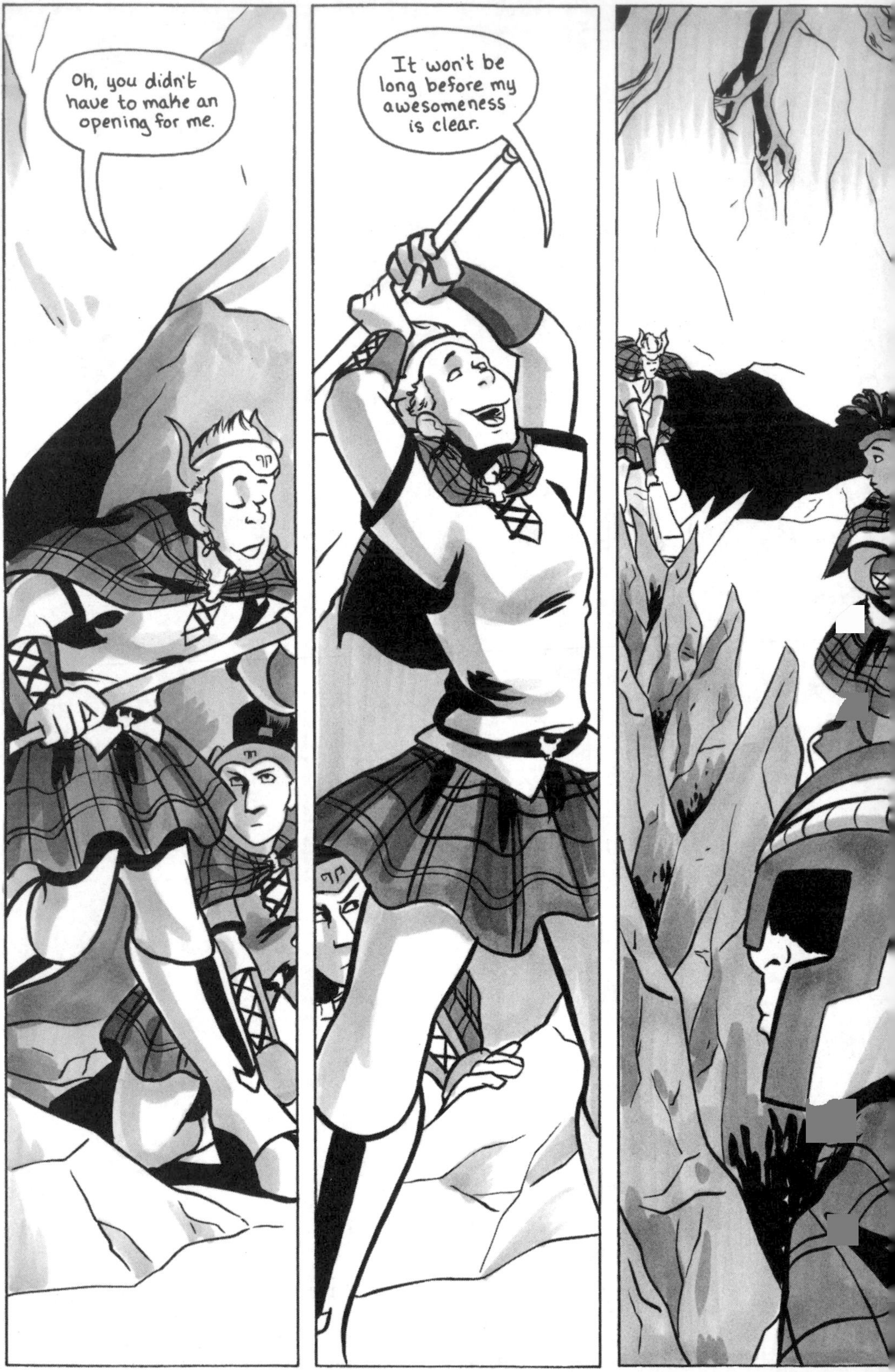
Oh, you didn't have to make an opening for me.
It won't be long before my awesomeness is clear.

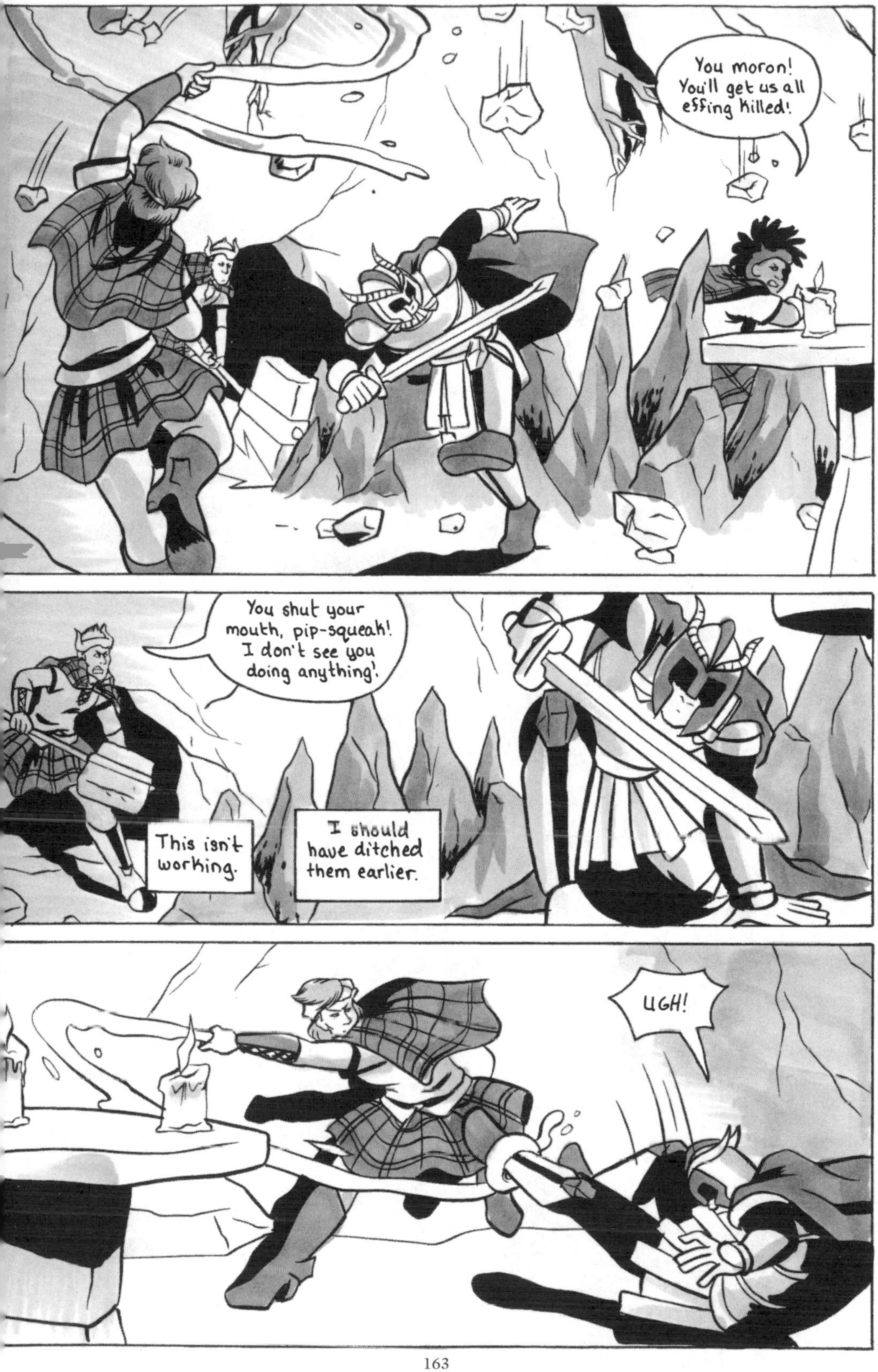
You moron! You'll get us all effing killed!
You shut your mouth, pip-squeak! I don't see you doing anything!
This isn't working.
I should have ditched them earlier.
UGH!

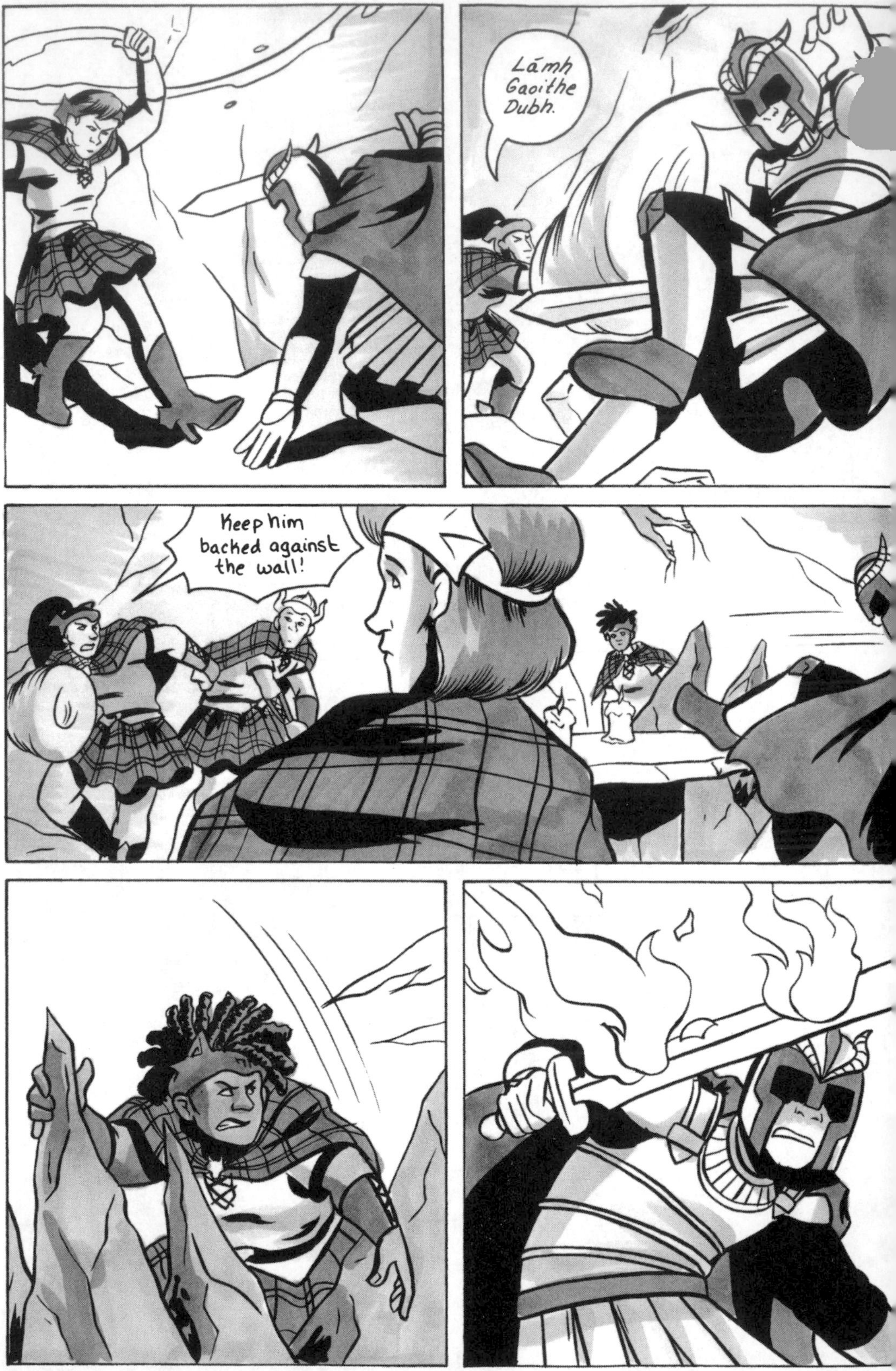
Lámh Gaoithe Dubh.
Keep him backed against the wall!

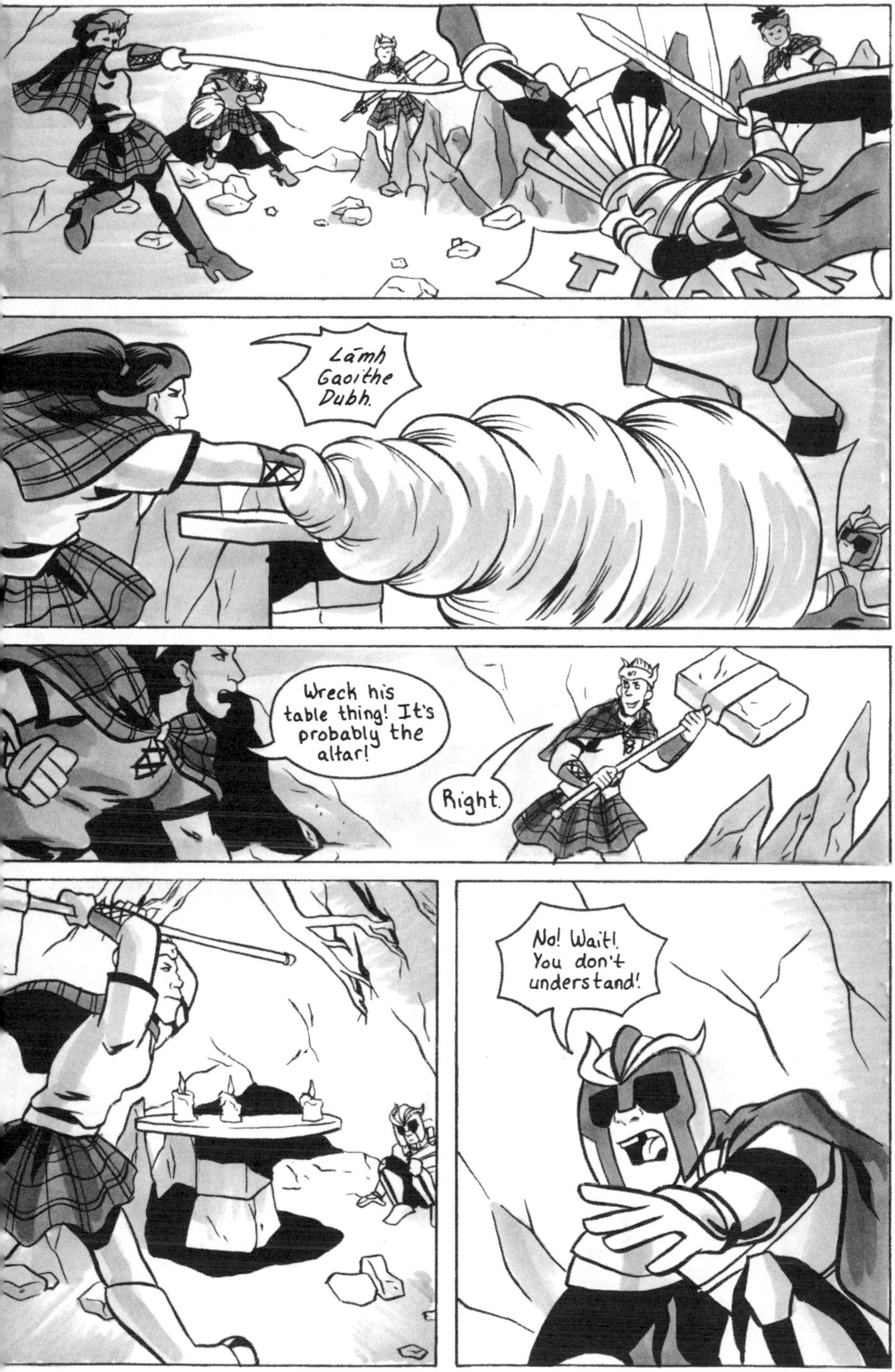
Lámh Gaoithe Dubh.
Wreck his table thing! It's probably the altar!
Right.
No! Wait! You don't understand!

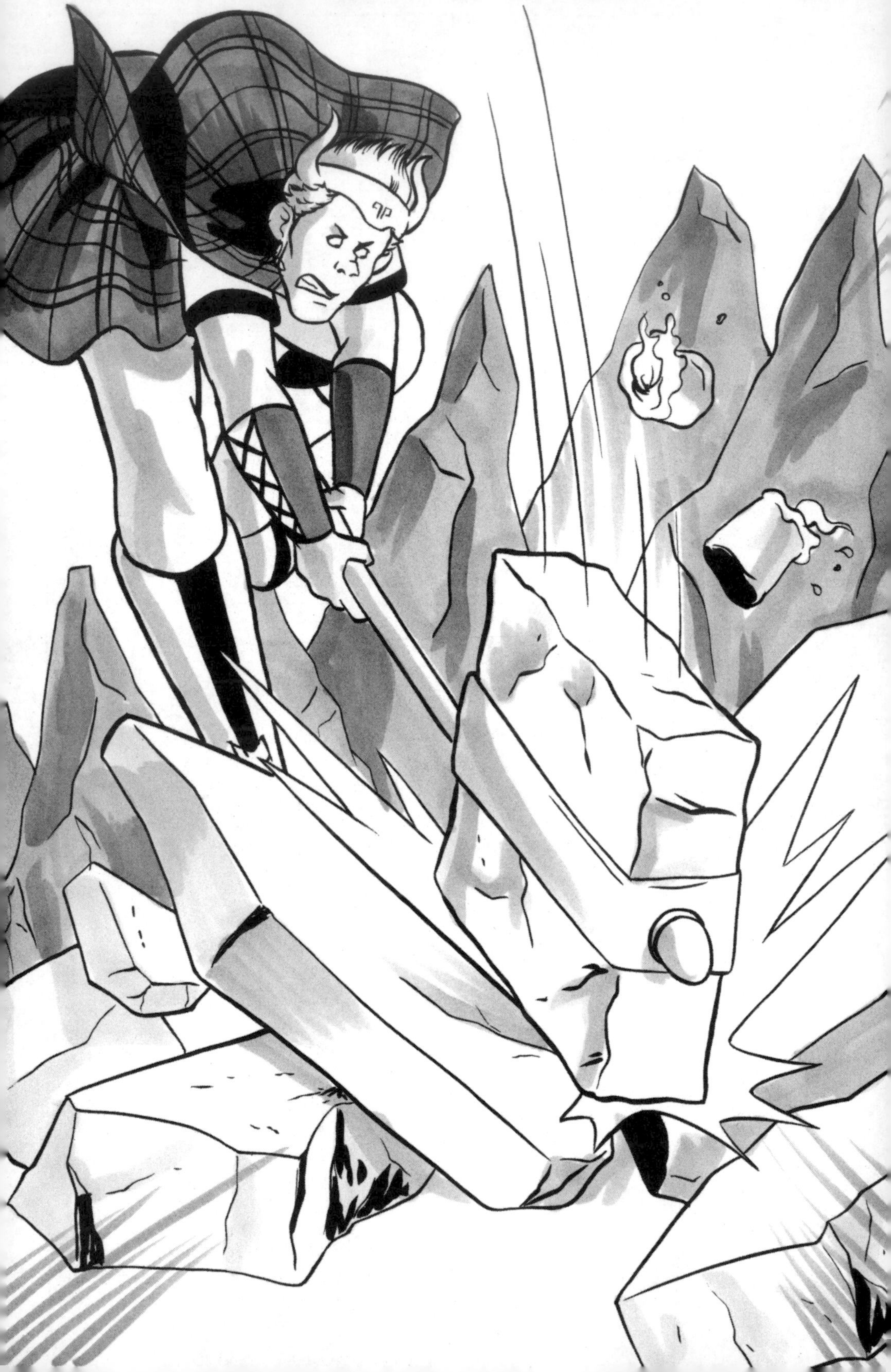

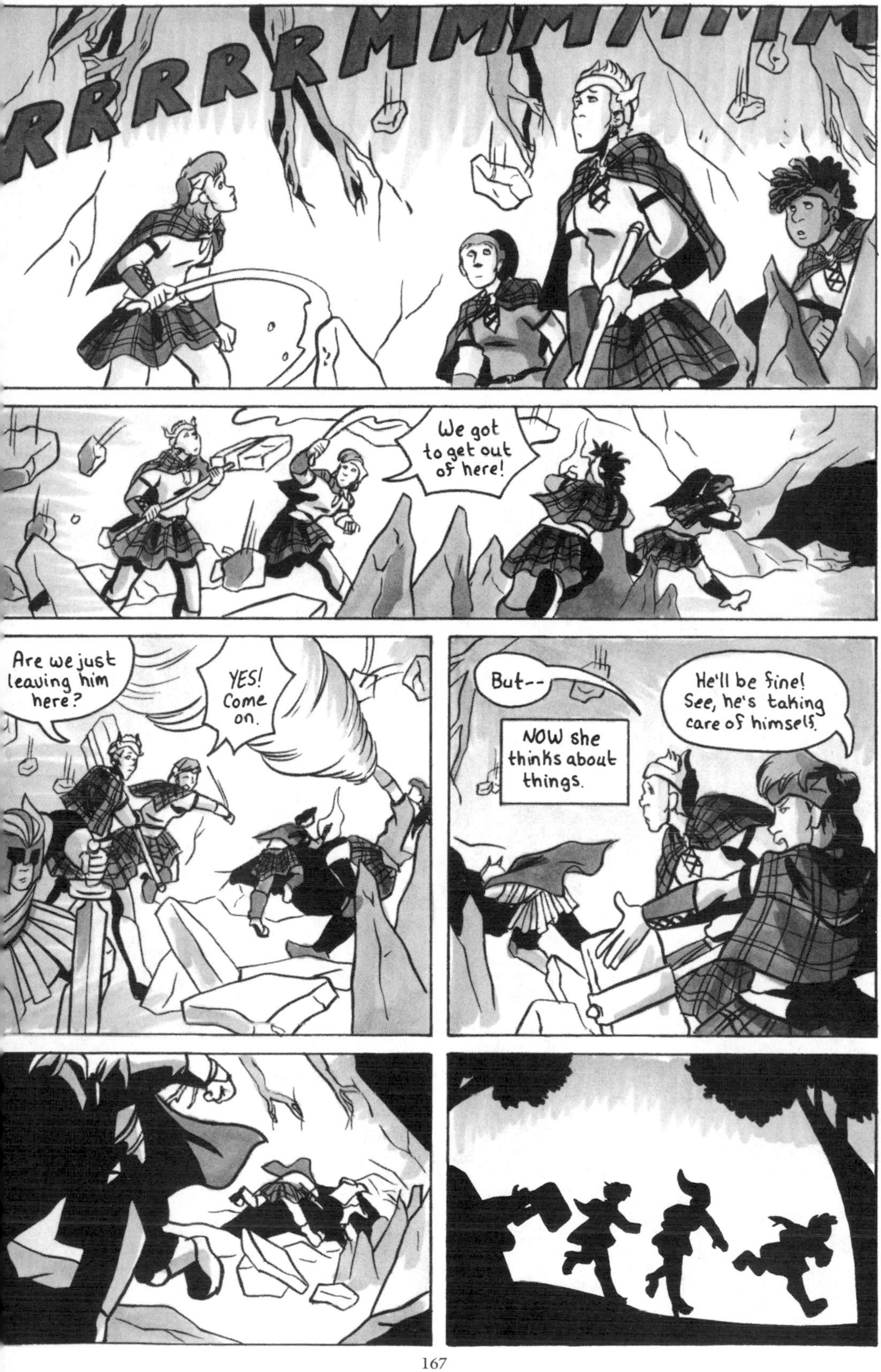
RRRRRRMMMMMM
We got to get out of here!
Are we just leaving him here?
YES! Come on.
But--
He'll be fine! See, he's taking care of himself.
NOW she thinks about things.

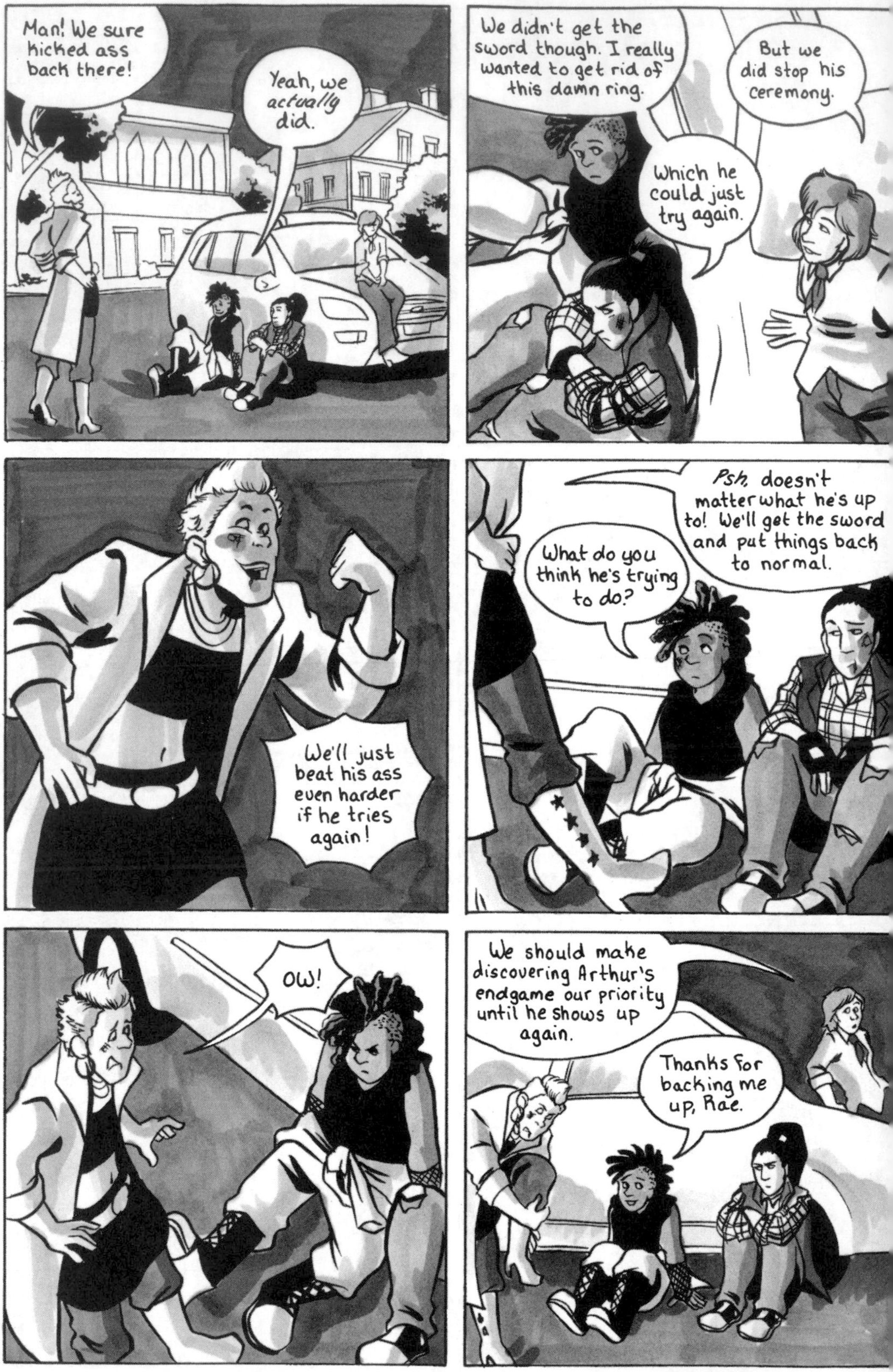
Man! We sure kicked ass back there!
Yeah, we actually did.
We didn't get the sword though. I really wanted to get rid of this damn ring.
But we did stop his ceremony.
Which he could just try again.
We'll just beat his ass even harder if he tries again!
Psh, doesn't matter what he's up to! We'll get the sword and put things back to normal.
What do you think he's trying to do?
OW!
We should make discovering Arthur's endgame our priority until he shows up again.
Thanks for backing me up, Rae.

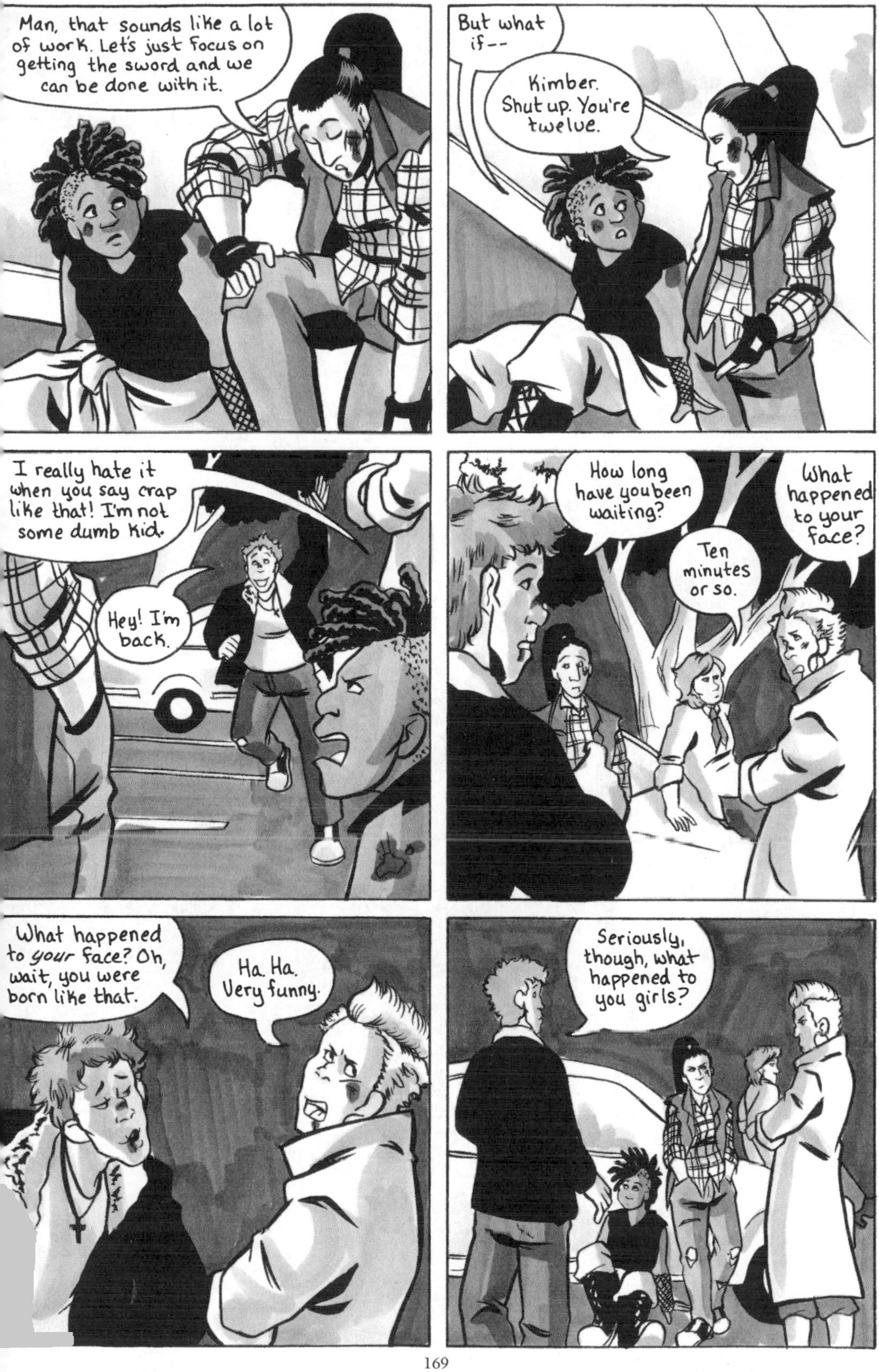

Man, that sounds like a lot of work. Let's just focus on getting the sword and we can be done with it.
But what if--
Kimber. Shut up. You're twelve.
I really hate it when you say crap like that! I'm not some dumb kid.
Hey! I'm back.
How long have you been waiting?
Ten minutes or so.
What happened to your face?
What happened to *your* face? Oh, wait, you were born like that.
Ha. Ha. Very funny.
Seriously, though, what happened to you girls?

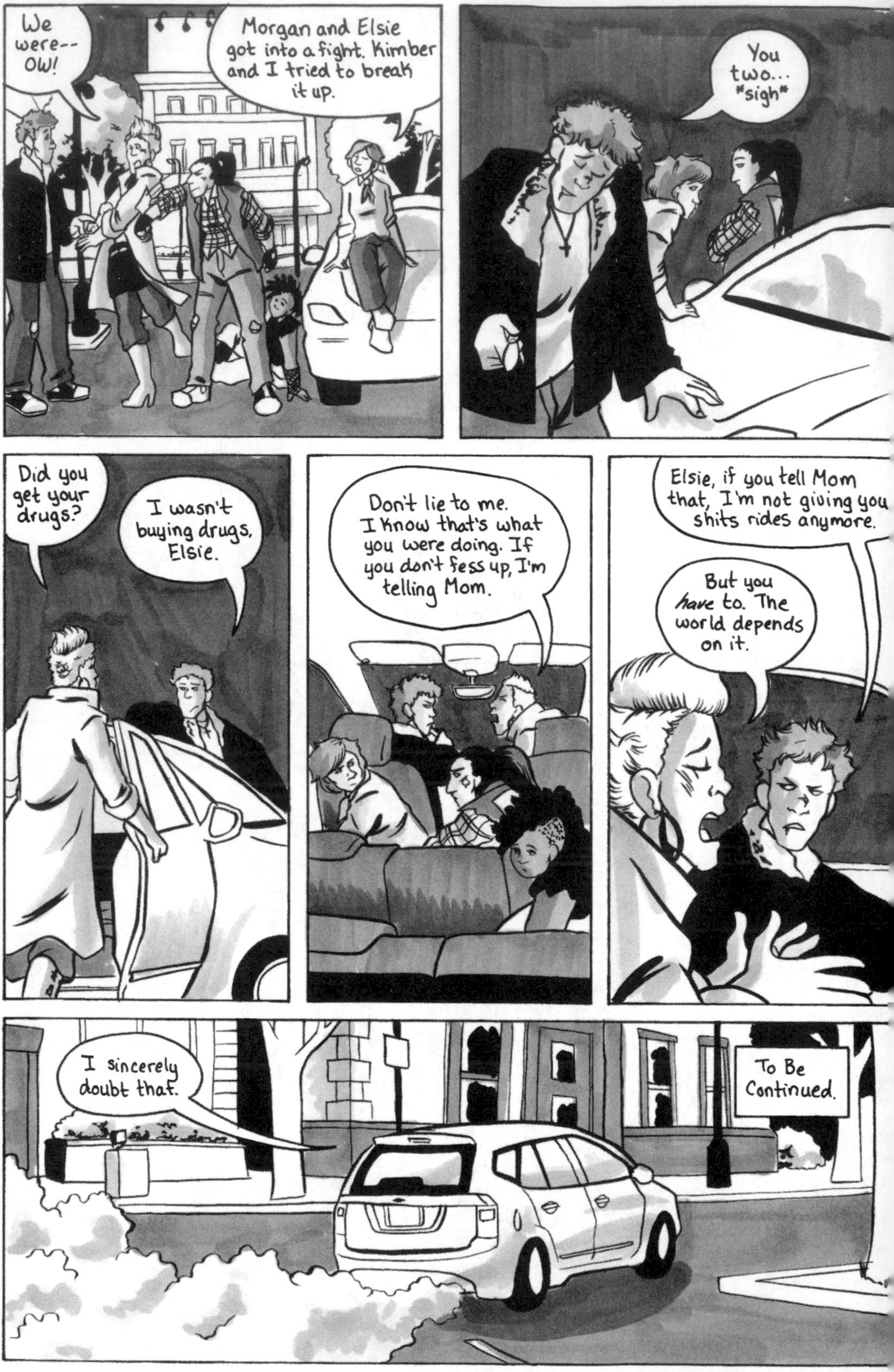
We were-- OW!
Morgan and Elsie got into a fight. Kimber and I tried to break it up.
You two... *sigh*
Did you get your drugs?
I wasn't buying drugs, Elsie.
Don't lie to me. I know that's what you were doing. If you don't fess up, I'm telling Mom.
Elsie, if you tell Mom that, I'm not giving you shits rides anymore.
But you *have* to. The world depends on it.
I sincerely doubt that.
To Be Continued.

Kel McDonald has been working in comics for the past nine years; she spent most of that time on her online comic *Sorcery 101*. More recently, she organized the *Cautionary Fables and Fairytales* anthology series, while contributing to other anthologies, such as *Dark Horse Presents*, *Smut Peddler*, and *The Sleep of Reason*. She is currently working on the next volumes of the series *Misfits of Avalon* for Dark Horse Comics.

DISCOVER THE ADVENTURE!

Explore these beloved books for the entire family.

KAWAII!

Dark Horse brings you the
best in magical-girl manga!

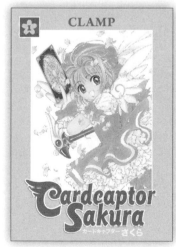